The
ABCs of LDAP

How to Install, Run, and Administer LDAP Services

OTHER AUERBACH PUBLICATIONS

The
ABCs of LDAP

How to Install, Run, and Administer LDAP Services

REINHARD E. VOGLMAIER

CRC Press
Taylor & Francis Group
Boca Raton London New York

CRC Press is an imprint of the
Taylor & Francis Group, an **informa** business

AN AUERBACH BOOK

CRC Press
Taylor & Francis Group
6000 Broken Sound Parkway NW, Suite 300
Boca Raton, FL 33487-2742

© 2004 by Taylor & Francis Group, LLC
CRC Press is an imprint of Taylor & Francis Group, an Informa business

No claim to original U.S. Government works

ISBN 13: 978-0-8493-1346-2 (pbk)
ISBN 13: 978-1-138-45363-0 (hbk)

**Visit the Taylor & Francis Web site at
http://www.taylorandfrancis.com**

**and the CRC Press Web site at
http://www.crcpress.com**

Library of Congress Cataloging-in-Publication Data

Voglmaier, Reinhard E.
    The ABCs of LDAP : how to install, run, and administer LDAP services / Reinhard E. Voglmaier.
        p. cm.
    Includes bibliographical references and index.
    ISBN 0-8493-1346-5 (alk. paper)
    1. LDAP (Computer network protocol) I. Title.

TK5105.5725.V64 2003
004.6′2--dc22   2003057821

Library of Congress Card Number 2003057821

Preface

With the enormous expansion of the World Wide Web over the past decade, internetworking has become widely diffused. Nearly all business enterprises have access to and a presence on the Internet. Beyond that, the number of intranets, private networks, and extranets has also grown exponentially. "Getting connected" has become as routine as having a telephone. Where we once exchanged telephone numbers and mailing addresses with friends and associates, we now routinely include an e-mail address too. Even children in elementary school are now communicating via e-mail and getting information about their favorite toys from the Internet.

As this distributed computing environment continues to grow, so does the storehouse of information, which makes locating the required information an increasingly challenging task. Sophisticated search engines have been created as a tool to help in locating information. Some of these search engines are specialized to provide information on particular topics. To locate persons on the Internet or intranet in a fast and easy way, a particular tool is being used that is very similar to a telephone directory, commonly referred to as "white pages" or "yellow pages." This tool is called a directory server.

If you want to get the news from CNN, you simply connect your Web browser to CNN's Web server by typing in the address (http://www.cnn.com) using the Hypertext Transfer Protocol (HTTP). Likewise, if you want to send e-mail, you use your mail client to transfer the mail to a mail server using the Simple Mail Transfer Protocol (SMTP). Similarly, if you want to look up information stored in a directory server, you would use a directory client that speaks with the directory server using the Lightweight Directory Access Protocol (LDAP), which is the subject of this book. These three protocols — HTTP, SMTP, and LDAP — have something in common. All are standard protocols running over the widely used Transmission Control Protocol/Internet Protocol (TCP/IP) stack.

This preface to the book will briefly review what you can do with LDAP. First we will learn what type of information you can store on a directory server. Then we will see some of the advantages that directory servers have over similar data stores such as, for example, relational databases.

Typical Usage of Directories

The concept of a directory server is much the same as the concept of a telephone directory, but it can also be used in a variety of other useful applications:

- Directories are frequently used to store information about persons. This could be for the company phone book, or it could be used to store information about the company organization. It could also hold information about customers and the enterprises for whom the customers work.
- Directory servers can handle security-related information, such as the public keys of your users of certificates.
- Directory services can be used to provide naming services, so you can store all your DNS (domain name system) maps in a directory. DNS resolves the human-readable computer names (such as www.cnn.com) into the sequence of dotted numbers that computers use to locate each other. You can also use directory services to resolve the names of databases to computer names.
- Directory servers can hold information about users and groups of your computer network and work as an NIS (network information system) server. NIS was created by Sun Microsystems to store information about users, such as their home directory, group memberships, and other important information.
- Directory servers can hold information such as e-mail addresses and further e-mail related information. This information can be shared by many e-mail clients or servers. An e-mail server can share such information as e-mail aliases, forwarding rules, and other mail-delivery information that the server needs to work properly.
- Directory servers can hold information for software packages distributed over the intranet or Internet. The configuration procedures can use this data that is centrally maintained by the directory server.

It is clear that directories can hold many types of information. Let us now briefly review the advantages provided by directory servers.

Advantages of Directories

You have seen a number of cases where it is advantageous to use directories. In each of these cases, however, there are other technologies that perform the same function. You may wonder why you should use a new technology instead of continuing to work with a technology that you know very well. You would not consider making such a change unless directory services offered some significant advantages over the technology you are already using. The following is a list of advantages:

- *Growing diffusion*: Because LDAP is a standard protocol, more and more software suppliers are adopting it in their products. For example, Microsoft uses LDAP to maintain configuration information in Win2000; Sun uses it to hold NIS maps in its Solaris 9 operating system; and Oracle uses it to resolve database names.
- *Low cost of ownership*: Because LDAP is a standard protocol, you can write your own clients to connect to directory servers. If you use a proprietary solution, you have to pay license fees every time you install a new client on your network.
- *Low training costs*: Because most LDAP servers are easy to install, configure, and maintain, the cost of training LDAP administrators is low.
- *Distributed solution*: Because LDAP is a protocol, it is natively network-enabled. Moreover, the LDAP protocol is natively enabled for a distributed architecture, allowing you to distribute information across the entire network for use in all applications. You can even replicate a part of your directory in the intranet and push it out to a server on the Internet.
- *Platform independence*: Because LDAP is a standard protocol, there is a wide choice of implementations of LDAP servers, ranging from important suppliers such as "Star Alliance" (SUN + Netscape) to open-source solutions such as the OpenLDAP implementation of the University of Michigan. From this large choice of vendors, you will find the one that best fits the platform you are using. Furthermore, client and server can run on completely different operating systems.
- *Easy client implementation*: The large number of LDAP application programming interfaces (API) — for nearly every programming language you can imagine — allows you to easily add LDAP support to a great many applications. Consequently, a large number of commercial applications have already been LDAP-enabled or will become LDAP-enabled in the near future. Home-grown applications are also easily LDAP-enabled.
- *Built-in security in the repository*: The access information is stored in the repository itself and can be very fine grained. Some products also give you the ability to control access rights to external factors, such as the IP number the client is connecting from, the time that

a connection is requested, the type of data that is requested, and so on. Because these controls are executed centrally by the server, they are easy to maintain. Clients therefore do not have to worry about these details.

Directory Server Implementations

At the time of this writing, there are a number of directory server implementations. Please note that the following list is not exhaustive and that there may well be implementations I am not aware of. The fact that I am ignorant of a particular implementation does not imply anything about its quality. Note also that this section does not contain any comments. Many products have been developed during the writing of this book, and the list is constantly changing.

- *Star Alliance*: This is a collaboration between Sun Microsystems and Netscape Corporation. The product offered is the Sun One server. The previous products were called i-Planet directory server and Netscape directory server.
- *IBM*: IBM directory server
- *Novell*: eDirectory available for Win2000/NT, Linux, Solaris, AIX, and Novell Netware (more information is available from the Web site of Novell)
- *Oracle*: Oracle Internet directory
- *Critical Path*: Directory server
- *Computer Associates*: eTrust, the former OpenDirectory
- *Microsoft Corporation*: Support of LDAP in active directory service
- *Lotus*: Directory server for use with the Lotus name and address book
- *University of Michigan*: The OpenLDAP project has replaced the Umich server, which is now obsolete.

Why This Book?

If you want to learn more about LDAP, you can buy a book or search the Internet. Before writing this volume, I searched in bookstores and online using Amazon for a book explaining LDAP without being product specific. However, the ones I found were all product specific. If you search the Internet for information about LDAP, you will find a lot of general documentation, but you will get too much information. It would take a lot of time to put all of this very useful information together. In the end, I concluded that no one had yet written a book offering a comprehensive view of LDAP. This volume combines all of the relevant information available on the Internet along with a number of arguments treated in the various books that are available.

This volume is intended for readers who want to start using LDAP. It provides a theoretical background so that the reader has a general understanding of how LDAP servers work. It avoids speaking about one particular implementation.

This book provides many examples of LDAP code. Most of these examples will work with any LDAP server implementing the LDAP standard. It is impossible to discuss the installation of an LDAP server without using a concrete implementation. For this purpose, I chose a commercial product (SUN/Netscape server) and an open-source project (OpenLDAP server). Both are available for a number of operating systems. Furthermore, the Sun/Netscape server is available for evaluation purposes for free, so if you want to try it out, you can download it.

Now that I have said what this book is, I will also mention what it is not. It is not an in-depth treatise on the nuts and bolts of LDAP, so the level of detail is not sufficient to enable you to write your own directory server. If you want to do so, please have a look at the Web site where you can also download OpenLDAP, i.e., http://www.openldap.org. This book also cannot serve as a substitute for the documentation that is normally shipped with servers, such as users guide, administrators guide, and so on. If you use a particular LDAP server, please read the documentation shipped with the product.

A Little Road Map

This section provides an overview of the book so that you can, if you wish, go directly to the chapter of your major interest. I have tried to isolate each chapter as a stand-alone discussion of a particular topic. However, there is inevitably some overlap. For example, if you would like to understand the LDAP API, it is good to have some knowledge of the operations that the LDAP protocol knows about and how the LDAP protocol itself behaves when executing these operations on the server. Wherever possible, I briefly repeat the important information from the relevant chapter. However, this cannot substitute for a deeper discussion of the argument, and in many cases the reader will be referred to another section of the book.

Chapter 1, The LDAP Protocol

This chapter introduces the concept of a directory and a directory server. Because LDAP is a communication protocol, the chapter also provides a brief introduction to protocols, focusing on the TCP/IP protocol stack and how the LDAP protocol fits in the picture. Finally, the chapter explains the LDAP protocol itself.

Chapter 2, LDAP Basics

Here we begin to "play around" using the LDAP command line tools. To try out the examples in this chapter, you need a working LDAP implementation. You can download and use the Sun One LDAP server or the open-source OpenLDAP server, both available for Win32 and UNIX. A good workbench would be Linux with OpenLDAP. Most Linux implementations arrive with a ready-to-use LDAP implementation. In any case, this chapter gives you a number of examples so that you can become somewhat fluent with LDAP.

Chapter 3, LDAP Models

Theory. This chapter gives you the basics to better understand LDAP. LDAP can be described better with the help of four models: the information model, the naming model, the functional model, and the security model. The information model describes how LDAP holds the information. The naming model shows how LDAP organizes this information using a naming convention. The functional model defines the operations the LDAP protocol knows about. And the security model shows how to control access to the information held in the directory.

Chapter 4, LDAP: Some Practical Details

The previous chapter described the underlying theory and standards of LDAP. This chapter addresses the practical details of implementation. It helps you explore by yourself the points previously shown. It goes into details of the search process in a directory, explaining what a search filter is and what it should look like. It speaks in greater detail about the schema of the directory, how to explore it, and how to extend the standard schemas. It also shows how to speed up your directory server with indices and shows more details about the import/export format of LDAP directories.

Chapter 5, Distributed Architectures

This chapter addresses the issues of replication and partitioning. Replication mirrors all or one part of the directory on another directory server. Partitioning allows you to distribute your directory over several servers. Both methods can be combined to facilitate load balancing while ensuring the availability of directory services.

Chapter 6, LDAP APIs

This is another chapter focusing on practical issues. We speak about APIs. For nearly every programming language, there is an API implementing the operations defined by the LDAP protocol. In this chapter, we have a look at the most prominent APIs. We speak in this context also about the command-line tools as an LDAP client distributed with nearly every LDAP implementation. You can write your own. Because the OpenLDAP implementation is shipped with the command-line tools in source code, you can have a look at how these are implemented and change them to fit your personal taste and needs.

Chapter 7, LDAP Directory-Server Administration

This chapter discusses the fundamentals of LDAP administration. Here you will see the activities involved in maintaining an LDAP implementation.

Chapter 8, LDAP and Web Services

Here we see how LDAP fits into your existing environment. It shows you how to integrate it into your UNIX environment, i.e., how you can define users, groups, and other system information in LDAP instead of traditional UNIX files. It also shows you how the Microsoft world can be integrated and how you can Web-enable your LDAP server.

Chapter 9, The Design of Directory Services

The concluding chapter briefly reviews how to design a directory. This chapter provides only an introduction into the design of a directory, which is a very complex activity and requires a certain level of experience. The design hints suggested here should reduce the probability of making a catastrophic design error. A project can recover from smaller design errors, which happen even to experienced specialists.

The Author

Reinhard Voglmaier studied physics at the University of Munich in Germany (TUM) and graduated from the Max Planck Institute for Astrophysics and Extraterrestrial Physics in Munich. After working in the Information Technology (IT) Department at the German University of the Army in the field of computer architecture, he was hired as a hardware specialist for automation by Honeywell. He then moved on to Siemens Nixdorf, where he worked for several years as a UNIX systems specialist for performance questions in database/network installations. For the past six years, he has worked at Glaxo Smith Kline in the field of Web and LDAP services. He is currently a member of an international team developing a companywide LDAP implementation for Glaxo Smith Kline.

Contents

Chapter 1

The LDAP Protocol

This chapter has two goals. The first goal is to introduce the basic concepts of the Lightweight Directory Access Protocol (LDAP). To do this, we will have to answer four questions:

1. What is a directory?
2. What is a protocol?
3. What is a Directory Access Protocol (DAP)?
4. Why is LDAP called a "lightweight" Directory Access Protocol?

The second goal of this first chapter is to introduce some of the terminology you will need to know to work with LDAP. This is important because these terms are used repeatedly throughout this book, and they are part of the everyday vocabulary for someone working in LDAP production. After reading this chapter, you will have a basic understanding of what a Directory Access Protocol is and what it is used for.

The remaining chapters should help you in exploring the details and enable you to begin working with LDAP. After finishing this book you will understand the basics of LDAP and be ready to explore the subject further on your own. Further research will be necessary because LDAP is a work in progress, and at the time of this writing, some aspects of the protocol have not yet been clearly defined. One of these points is replication between directories. We will hear more about replication in Chapter 5, which explains the use of distributed directories. For now, it is enough to know that LDAP is not yet a fully defined protocol. Other aspects of the protocol are still in development, and yet others are not even at the planning stage. For example, the question of transaction management is still open. A transaction is a number of actions that, together, build a single atomic operation.

("Atomic" means that a number of physical operations can be logically considered as one single operation. Or that all single physical operations are completed or none at all.) Transaction management guarantees that the system executes all these steps together or does nothing at all (more about this at the end of this chapter). A banking application example makes this clear. The transfer of money from account A to account B consists of subtracting an amount from account A and adding the same amount to account B. This should be an atomic operation. If one of these actions fails, the other one should not be performed. At the moment, the issue of transaction management is not even on the table, although there are user requirements. A future version of LDAP will likely include transaction management. The Lightweight Directory Access Protocol is a very interesting and dynamic topic, so you will have to stay tuned to keep up with the latest developments.

In this chapter, we first look at what LDAP can do for you. This section introduces the concepts of a "directory" and a "directory server," and it explains the function of each.

In the next section, we begin to develop a more technical understanding of LDAP, which involves a discussion of protocols. We learn what a protocol is and are introduced to protocols relevant to LDAP. As we will see, these protocols and, most importantly, LDAP itself are protocols in the networking environment. We learn how the concepts of networking and internetworking have evolved over time and how LDAP fits into this picture. We then encounter the TCP/IP (Transmission Control Protocol/Internet Protocol) and OSI (Open Systems Interconnection) protocol stacks, which are the foundation for all modern network implementations. The most commonly used directory access protocols are laid on top of one of these two protocol stacks, depending on the operating system. After reading this section, you will understand how a protocol stack works, where a Directory Access Protocol is located, and how the network protocols interact with the DAP. If you are not very interested in these concepts, you can skip this section about protocols entirely and continue at the point where we discuss the LDAP protocol. These protocols are presented here only as background to help you better understand the networking aspects of the LDAP protocol.

Another concept closely linked to LDAP is the "request for comments" (RFC). RFCs are used as a tool for proposing, discussing, and defining standards in the Internet community. Many readers may never have to deal with documents defining the LDAP standards, and they can safely ignore the RFCs and still work with LDAP. However, a basic knowledge of RFCs is useful for those readers who need to dig more deeply into the details than this book will do.

After this, we finally address the main topic of this book: the Directory Access Protocol. First we look at X.500, also called DAP, which was developed together with the OSI protocol stack. The lightweight counterpart of DAP (LDAP) is a subset of DAP that was developed for use with TCP/IP. Again, it is helpful to understand the basics of OSI and TCP/IP because the concepts of DAP and LDAP are tightly connected to these two protocols. You will see that DAP requires the OSI protocol and that the lightweight version of DAP (LDAP) runs happily atop TCP/IP. The fact that a given protocol stack is required to run DAP or LDAP has a number of implications. A discussion of these will help you understand the need for the lightweight version of DAP.

In the next section we learn what kind of data travels over the network and see what a typical LDAP conversation between client and server looks like.

In the final section, we learn where the data is kept. Up to this point, the discussion has focused on protocols, i.e., how the communication between client and server occurs. Using the LDAP protocol, clients ask a server to perform certain actions. As you will see, the LDAP server performs its actions on data — data maintenance, data administration, and data delivery to the clients. This data clearly has to be stored somewhere, and this "somewhere" is a repository or database. At this point, you might wonder whether it might be better to use a database instead of implementing yet another new technology. The chapter concludes with a brief discussion about the differences between a relational database management system (RDBMS) and a directory accessed via the LDAP protocol.

Directories and Directory Server

Everyone working in information technology (IT) knows what a directory is, and even people who only occasionally use a computer encounter a directory sooner or later. To be more precise, they do not encounter a directory, but what they see is a directory listing similar to that shown in Exhibit 1. Note that the exact layout of a directory listing depends on the computer's operating system and the type of view configured for the directory listing.

Exhibit 1 shows a listing of a directory. This kind of directory may be helpful as a first approach, but in the context of our particular needs, this view is somewhat specialized and we would like to have a broader view. For our purpose, it is more instructive to use the definition of "directory" as we find it in a general dictionary, i.e., one that is not specialized on information technologies. For example, the Oxford Dictionary defines a directory as a "book containing a list of telephone subscribers, inhabitants of a district, members of a profession." This gives exactly the concept of directory that we will use throughout this book.

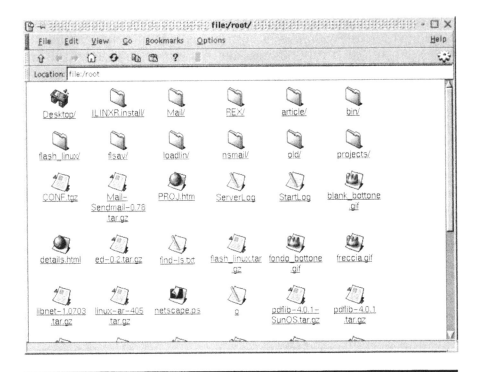

Exhibit 1. A Typical Directory Listing

For our purposes, a directory is an ordered list of objects. For example, the "white pages" of a telephone book is an ordered list of persons arranged in alphabetic order by surname and given name or initials. Using the white pages, one can find the phone number, street, and district of anyone listed in the book. In contrast, the "yellow pages" provides an ordered list of professions where one can look up, for example, a nearby barbershop. A further example from an IT environment might be a list of printers ordered by printer name. Using this directory, one could find the printer's location, the printer model, or the server to which the printer is attached. You could also search for a postscript-enabled printer near your office or base a search on some other criterion. Even whole network information systems can be stored in a directory.

As an ordered list of objects, a directory is an information storehouse that can be searched swiftly and easily. There are many potential applications for directories. Consider a domain name system (DNS) that correlates the human-friendly name of a computer (e.g., Google.com) with that computer's Internet Protocol (IP) number. NIS+ allows us to get information about users and groups. NIS+ is an improvement over NIS, the Network Information Service invented by Sun Microsystems. It allows the central administration of hostnames, users, and user home directories. If you want to find out more about NIS/NIS+, go on to Sun's Website. Gerald Carter dedicates a chapter of his book, *LDAP System Administration,*[1] to replacing NIS/NIS+ with LDAP. Both of these applications can be implemented as a directory, allowing the user to query the directory for information. The last two examples point out a further strength of LDAP. LDAP offers centralized information services across a whole network. Because LDAP is running over TCP/IP, all computers using the TCP/IP protocol can access the services offered by LDAP.

Exhibit 2 illustrates the hierachical structure of a directory where information is stored in a treelike structure that uses the DNS name space. As you can see, a hierarchical structure can accelerate searches by limiting the scope of the search to a branch of the tree. A further example of how to organize a hierarchy of different levels is shown by the number of names stored in the white pages. You can put the address where the person lives at the base level. The next higher level would be the district where that person lives. If you know the district, this knowledge will accelerate the performance of the query. The district furthermore is located in a city, the city in the country, and the country in a continent. The underlying hierarchy accelerates the search process, since you don't search for John Smith in the whole world, but you will first limit the search to Europe, then to the United Kingdom, then to London, and at the end to Bayswater. This hierarchical structure speeds the search process while keeping the results set low. You will find many more people named "John Smith" in the United Kingdom than in the district Bayswater. A smaller results set reduces network traffic and requires less work to elaborate the results.

The hierarchical structure depicted in Exhibit 2 also suggests the possibility of storing other attributes about the computer beyond its name and the IP number. For example, we might also want to record the disk space available, the memory available, the installed software, and similar relevant information. The directory stores all of this information in an object called an "entry." Thus the directory is an object-

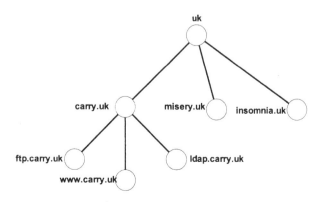

Exhibit 2. Hierarchical Structure of DNS

oriented repository. Note, however, that the LDAP standard does not specify how the information is stored in the repository. We will return to this subject later in this chapter. Note also that directories are stored on hard disks on computers. The precise method of storage is discussed at the end of this chapter. For now, we will simply assume that information is held "somewhere."

Imagine several people trying to look up the information stored on a system. If the information is to be accessed swiftly and easily, then there is a clear need for an efficient agent that serves as an intermediary between the user and the information. This mediator should shield the user from the complexity of the information-retrieval process and simply provide the requested information. Note that a "user" could be a person or a client application acting upon a user request.

Again, the example of the white pages is useful. If you do not have a copy of the local telephone directory (or are too busy to look up the number yourself), or if you need the phone number of a person or enterprise in another country or continent, you can dial an operator who will search for the number for you. This operator has access to specialized search tools that can isolate the requested phone number. Similarly, a specialized server can access a computer directory and isolate the information requested by the user. A server that looks up directory information for a client is called a "directory server." This approach has the advantage of masking the information-retrieval process. The user simply makes a request and gets a fast answer without worrying about the mechanics of the information system (how the information is maintained, stored, or organized to provide fast access).

In a client–server environment, the user needs a directory client that can access a directory server. This approach allows each side to do its specialized job. The client can concentrate on requesting information from the server and then presenting the information obtained, while the server can focus on system issues such as the efficiency of information retrieval. The directory server uses a protocol to communicate with the client; therefore, both the server and the client have to implement a common protocol. This book explores the use of LDAP as an efficient protocol.

At this point, let us observe another important point. The objective of a directory server is swift information retrieval. The speed of updating the information in the directory is not an issue. For example, consider the white pages that you use at home. The time it takes to compile the information and print the book is not a relevant issue to the user. Finding a person's phone number takes only a few seconds. For this type of application, the only important consideration is the time you spend to get the desired information, not the time it takes to update the white pages. We will come back to this point later in this chapter when we discuss the differences between databases and directories.

In this section, we learned two key definitions that will help in understanding LDAP:

- A directory server is a highly specialized server designed to facilitate fast information retrieval from directories.
- A directory is an indexed list of things or persons that is maintained in a hierarchical, object-oriented repository.

Network Protocols

A deeper understanding of LDAP requires some concept of network protocols. This section provides only a brief overview. Readers seeking greater detail can consult either *Internetworking with TCP/IP* by D.E. Comer[2] or *TCP/IP Illustrated* by R.W. Stevens.[3]

Protocols are formal rules dictating the format of messages so that they can be understood by the sending and receiving partners (the computers). Note that protocols are only rules. Protocols are not software or a piece of software; they simply specify how the software should behave. Thus it is the job of the programmer to write the software so that it can implement the protocol.

Why do we need protocols? In a middle-sized enterprise, you normally have several hundred computers running different operating systems on different platforms. (Consider the number of UNIX dialects or the different versions of Microsoft systems.) These differences prevent us from simply plugging these computers on the same line and letting them talk to each other. What is needed is a common way of communicating at a higher level. This higher level of communication is provided by the internetworking protocol.

At the time of this writing, the most important internetworking protocol is the Transmission Control Protocol/Internet Protocol (TCP/IP). The TCP/IP protocol is an open standard, i.e., the specifications of the TCP/IP standard are available to everyone. Consequently, every vendor can develop its products to obey these internetworking standards and thus be able to communicate with any machine operating the same protocol. This is very important because it allows different computers from different suppliers using different operating systems to be connected so that they can "speak" with each other. It also allows software developers to use any number of application programming interfaces (APIs) and still be able to communicate with each other without caring about the underlying hardware or operating system.

The story of networking began in the late 1960s. At that time, networking and network design were at the cutting edge of modern technology. Within the next few years, there was a substantial increase in the number of projects, with a consequential increase in the number of network protocols, nearly all of them different from each other.

These early protocols spanned the range from very complex and highly specialized protocols to simple protocols designed for high-speed networks with no error checking. This was a very innovative and productive time, but soon technicians and research people recognized that the diversity of protocols was a big problem. With the various network systems using different protocols, there was no way to exchange information between the systems. The enormity of the problem becomes clear when you consider today's computing environment, where electronic mail, file transfers, and Web services are routine activities made possible by the development of robust interoperating protocols. For example, people exchange e-mail through intermediate systems without worrying about compatibility issues between different operating systems and different types of e-mail software.

Universities and research institutes were not the only organizations interested in connecting different computer systems. Government agencies as well as business enterprises were also hobbled by the lack of interconnectivity. Efforts to solve this problem led DARPA (Defense Advanced Research Projects Agency) to fund an important research project in the mid 1970s that resulted in the development of the ARPANet. Once it was completed in 1983, the ARPANet took a new turn in development. DCA (Defense Communication Agency), the owner of the project, split the project in two. One part, called MILNet, was destined to focus on the military application of the project. DARPA, on the other hand, made the ARPANet available for further development by universities. This led to the development of the Internet Protocol, known today as TCP/IP.

The TCP/IP Protocol Stack

The Transmission Control Protocol/Internet Protocol (TCP/IP) is organized in several layers. Each layer has a well-defined functionality (as shown in Exhibit 3) and clearly defined interfaces to the layers situated above and below. This makes it possible to develop each layer separately or to exchange for particular applications one of the layers without affecting the other ones. Thus one can develop a layer without knowledge of the inner working of the other layers. This is particularly helpful if one wants to develop a high-level protocol because there is no need to touch the lower levels. The programmer simply uses the interfaces offered by the lower levels. Programmers commonly use the socket interface because it offers them the convenience of accessing network services with a comfortable library of system calls.

TCP/IP is organized in a stack of four layers, as seen in Exhibit 3. Data moving on the Internet travels in packets called "datagrams." On the sending end, each layer takes the datagram from the layer above and adds information to this datagram in the form of a header.

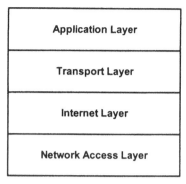

Exhibit 3. The TCP/IP Protocol Stack

It then hands the new datagram over to the next lower level. The act of adding a header to the datagram received from the higher level is called "data encapsulation." On the receiving end, the sequence is reversed. Each layer takes the datagram from the layer below, extracts the header to understand what to do with the datagram, and then hands it over to the layer above. In this way, information arrives from one layer at the sending end to the corresponding layer at the receiving end.

The four layers in the TCP/IP stack are as follows, starting at the bottom layer:

- *Network interface layer.* This lowest layer is responsible for accessing the underlying hardware. The network interface layer is constantly revised as new hardware is developed. TCP/IP does not prescribe any specific interface for the actual hardware. You can find Ethernet, token–ring, X.25, ATM, or other systems. This layer also maps IP addresses into physical addresses and transforms the data into frames before transmission.
- *Internet layer.* This next higher level is the heart of the TCP/IP protocol. The IP (Internet Protocol), described in RFC 791 (RFCs are discussed later in this chapter), is the most important protocol of this layer. IP facilitates fast delivery of packets by ignoring the details of datagram delivery. It does not care whether the datagrams arrive in the correct order, whether they arrive more than once, or whether they arrive at all. The IP level can afford to be unreliable because it depends on other levels to align the packets in the correct order.
- *Transport layer.* This is the layer just above the internet layer, which facilitates the datagram delivery from one computer to another. The transport layer delivers the data to the correct application, providing end-to-end communication between applications. There are two substantially different protocols that can do this:

- User Datagram Protocol (UDP), an unreliable, connectionless protocol
- Transmission Control Protocol (TCP), which provides a reliable stream of delivery. TCP guarantees that the packets are delivered in the correct order and ensures the retransmission of any packets that do not arrive from the underlying IP layer. This guarantee comes at the cost of a certain overhead. For short messages sent across the network, this overhead is too high, and UDP is used instead. UDP avoids these time-consuming controls. If necessary, the application layer can provide these controls.

- *Application layer*: The application layer can be one or several of a series of well-known protocols, including:
  - FTP: the File Transfer Protocol that facilitates file transfer from one computer to another
  - SMTP: the Simple Mail Transfer Protocol that makes e-mail possible
  - Telnet: a remote terminal protocol
  - HTTP: the Hypertext Transfer Protocol used by Web servers and browsers
  - LDAP: the Lightweight Directory Access Protocol, which is the subject of this book

There are many, many other application-layer protocols. For a complete list, refer to a book about networking, such as the one by Comer.[1] By now it should be clear that TCP/IP is a combination of the two most important protocols — TCP and IP.

The OSI Protocol Stack

Parallel to these efforts to develop TCP/IP, two other institutions — the ISO (International Standardization Organization) and the CCITT (Consultative Committee in International Telephony and Telegraphy) — began work on internetworking standards. The work of these institutions resulted in the Open Systems Interconnection (OSI) model.

The OSI protocol stack has seven layers, as seen in Exhibit 4. It is similar to the architecture of TCP/IP. To facilitate communication, every protocol layer offers a set of functions to the layer above and uses the functions provided by the layer below. The OSI protocol stack is as follows, starting at the bottom layer:

- *Physical layer*: As in the TCP/IP protocol stack, the lowest level is the level accessing the hardware.
- *Data link layer*: The next higher level, this layer is responsible for putting the data into datagrams and error checking.
- *Network layer*: Sometimes called "communication layer," this layer is responsible for the packet delivery. It isolates the upper levels

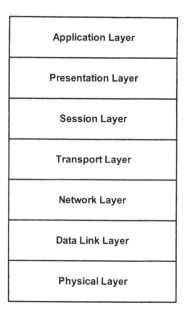

Exhibit 4. The OSI Protocol Stack

from network details, such as routing, and provides just at this level reliable transfer of information.

- *Transport layer.* This next layer has functions corresponding to the TCP protocol providing end-to-end reliability. This is a second check for reliability at a higher level. For details, see Comer.[1]
- *Session layer.* As the name suggests, this layer is responsible for the management of sessions, i.e., the setup, the maintenance, and the correct closing of sessions. This can be, for example, remote terminal access.
- *Presentation layer.* This layer handles such issues as data decription and encryption, text or graphics compression, conversion, and formatting.
- *Application layer.* In this top layer, we encounter old friends like telnet or file transfer applications.

TCP/IP and OSI can be considered as two different approaches to the internetworking problem. OSI defines a standard in a formal taskforce approach without requiring practical implementations. The TCP/IP approach is instead based on practical implementations. The OSI model is a complete protocol stack offering the services needed in a large, distributed computing environment. These services include security services, distributed file services, global directory services, time services, and many others. Since OSI offers the complete spectrum of services, including even seldom-used facilities, it is much heavier and much more resource consuming than TCP/IP. This was a big problem for small clients such as PCs. At the time TCP/IP became important, limitations in disk space and main memory were real issues, so it is no wonder why the tinier TCP/IP became the industry standard.

The OSI stack is included in this discussion because it is a full implementation of the protocol stack and serves as a reference implementation of a network protocol stack. As such, it addresses issues important in large distributed systems. One of these issues addressed by OSI is the global directory service standard, also known as the X.500 standard. As we will see throughout this book, LDAP inherited its fundamental concepts from the X.500 standard.

In this section, we learned that computers use communication protocols to communicate with each other. The OSI and TCP/IP protocols have been evolving since the late 1960s. TCP/IP became the industry standard because it is easier to implement. Nevertheless, OSI provides some very interesting features, such as the X.500 global directory service standard. LDAP is a direct descendent of X.500.

Internet Standards: RFCs

We have introduced several open standards, including TCP/IP, LDAP, DAP, and X.500. You may be wondering where you can get more information about them. Where exactly do we find the standards, and how are they produced and maintained?

The Internet Engineering Task Force (IETF) maintains the complete list of Internet standards on its Web site at http://www.ietf.org.

A mechanism known as "requests for comment" (RFC) is used to facilitate collaboration and sharing of open standards. Since you will frequently encounter the word "RFCs" when working with LDAP, it is a good idea to know what it is all about.

When a researcher implements a new protocol, she proposes it as a standard to the IETF. This proposal is published first as a draft on the RFC list. There is one RFC (RFC 2223) that defines the rules RFC authors must obey and outlines the procedure to submit an RFC to the IETF. Once the RFC is published, it can be updated or revised. This process produces a new RFC that substitutes or "obsoletes" (in RFC parlance) the previous one. Every RFC has a status describing its validity. The proposal of an RFC author has the status "draft," and the final status is "standard." The six categories of status are:

- *Draft*: the first stage of an RFC, i.e., proposed for discussion
- *Proposed*: a protocol existing for future use by IETF where a revision is very likely
- *Standard*: the final status of an accepted RFC
- *Experimental*: a specification used by the developer of a project
- *Informational*: a specification published for general information of the Internet community only

■ *Historic*: a specification that has been substituted by a more recent one

Because all standards are defined in the RFCs, the method of defining these RFC standards is itself the subject of an RFC or, rather, of several RFCs. The most important of these for the standardization process is RFC 2026, "The Internet Standards Process v.3." Anyone interested in contributing to the RFC forum should review RFC 2223, "Instructions to RFC Authors."

In this section, we learned that standard protocols are defined in the RFCs (request for comments) maintained by the Internet Engineering Task Force.

DAP: X.500 Standard

As previously noted, the OSI protocol stack was developed mainly for large distributed systems, which typically consist of a great number of computers manufactured by different suppliers and running different operating systems. This distributed computing environment (DCE) can be located in one building, or it might be distributed among several buildings in different countries. As the number of computers in a companywide network increases, so too does the amount of administrative data.

Examples of such administrative data are the IP numbers of all computers attached to the company network and the corresponding host names. Another example would be the accounts of all employees and consultants with authorization to access the different computers. Moreover, the user accounts are organized in user groups, each of them having access rights to different resources. All of this information is maintained by NIS+, for example.

A system must fulfill several requirements if it is to handle this amount of data:

■ *Centralized database*: There must be one place that holds all of the data for the whole company.
■ *Systemwide access to data*: The data must be available across the entire network. The user's ID would have to be unique across the whole enterprise. A user ID in an international company must be known not only in one country, but all over the world.
■ *Data reliability*: The data must be correct.
■ *Controlled access to data*: Not all data should be available to everyone. For example, some private information about a user should be available only to the human resources department. At the same time, only the human resources department would have the access rights to insert new data or update existing information in its files.

The OSI protocol stack provides the DAP protocol, also known as X.500 standard or ISO 9594, to fulfill these requirements. However, the standard also has a couple of disadvantages. For one thing, to use X.500, you need to implement the whole OSI protocol stack, which is very heavy and resource consuming. As such, it is difficult to implement OSI on clients at the scale of a personal computer.

Finally ... LDAP

The Lightweight Directory Access Protocol (LDAP) was developed as an alternative to the heavyweight DAP. LDAP simplifies the conversation between the server and the client while leaving out the seldom-used and rather esoteric features of DAP. The most significant advantage of LDAP is that it runs on top of the TCP/IP protocol stack.

The first LDAP applications used a gateway between the client and the directory server, as seen in Exhibit 5. The gateway is called the "LDAP server." For communication between the LDAP server and the client, the less-resource-consuming LDAP protocol is used. Communication between the LDAP server and the directory server continues to rely on DAP, thus freeing the client from the burden of supporting the OSI stack and placing it on the LDAP server instead. The server now has to know to communicate using both TCP/IP-enabled LDAP to communicate with the client and OSI-enabled DAP to access the directory.

The problem of the gateway solution was that it was not possible to use the LDAP protocol in an environment that did not support the OSI protocol. There were also a number of companies that simply did not wish to install an X.500 server on their networks just to be able

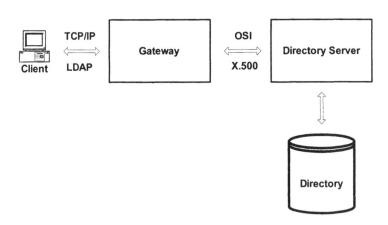

Exhibit 5. Gateway to Access an X.500 Server

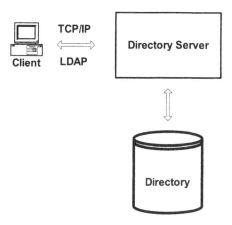

Exhibit 6. LDAP Server in a Pure TCP/IP Environment

to use LDAP. To solve this problem, an LDAP server was developed that worked in a pure TXP/IP environment and instead of acting as a gateway, used LDAP on its front end and accessed the directory on its back end, as seen in Exhibit 6.

Most of the LDAP work was coordinated at the University of Michigan. The first protocols are defined in RFC 1202, "Directory Assistance Service," and RFC 1249, "DIXIE Protocol Specification." These are not proposed standards but, rather, only informational RFCs. The first LDAP specification was RFC 1487, "X.500 Lightweight Access," which was later replaced by the final version RFC 1777, "Lightweight Directory Access Protocol." This RFC version, also referenced as LDAP (v2), has been qualified as a draft standard by IETF. The exact details about this protocol and its extensions can be found in following RFCs:

- RFC 1777, "Lightweight Directory Access Protocol"
- RFC 1778, "The String Representation of Standard Attribute Syntaxes"
- RFC 1779, "A String Representation of Distinguished Names"
- RFC 1959, "An LDAP URL Format"
- RFC 1960, "A String Representation of LDAP Search Filters"

As the popularity of LDAP grew, more and more applications began to use LDAP services. An improved version has been defined in RFC 2251, "LDAP (v3) Protocol." Instead of being a "draft standard," like the LDAP (v2) protocol in RFC 1777, the LDAP (v3) protocol defined in RCF 2251 has been assigned the "proposed standard" status. If you want to consult the official protocol definitions of LDAP (v3), refer to the following RFCs:

- RFC 2251, "Lightweight Directory Access Protocol (v3)"
- RFC 2252, "Lightweight Directory Access Protocol (v3): Attribute Syntax Definitions"
- RFC 2253, "Lightweight Directory Access Protocol (v3): UTF-8 String Representation of Distinguished Names"
- RFC 2254, "The String Representation of LDAP Search Filters"
- RFC 2255, "The LDAP URL Format"
- RFC 2256, "A Summary of the X.500(96) User Schema for use with LDAP (v3)"
- RFC 2829, "Authentication Methods for LDAP"
- RFC 2830, "Lightweight Directory Access Protocol (v3):Extension for Transport Layer Security"
- RFC 3377, "Lightweight Directory Access Protocol (v3): Technical Specification"

Version 3 has a number of improvements over Version 2. These improvements are listed here and discussed in greater detail in later chapters, such as in Chapter 3, where we discuss the theory behind the LDAP models. This information is taken from RFC 2251. Interested readers should consult this RFC.

- Most protocol data elements can be encoded as ordinary strings.
- Referrals can be returned. This means that a directory server not containing the requested data can ask another directory server for that information and turn it back to the client.
- SASL (simple authentication and security layer) mechanisms can be used with LDAP to provide associated security services.
- Attribute values and distinguished names have been internationalized through the use of the ISO character set (10,646 characters).
- The protocol can be extended to support new operations, and controls can be used to extend existing operations.
- The schema describing the data structures found in the directory is published in the directory for use by clients.

In this section, we learned that the Directory Access Protocol (DAP) is useful for accessing directories. However, DAP proved to be too heavy for implementation on client machines. Furthermore, not all environments had X.500 (DAP) servers available or had the ability to implement the required OSI protocol on the network. The TCP/IP-compatible lightweight alternative became the Lightweight Directory Access Protocol (LWDAP), available at the time of this writing as LDAP Version 3.

LDAP: How It Works

This section is intended to provide a "physical understanding" of what the LDAP protocol actually does as information travels over your network. Some of these concepts appear later in the book, so impatient readers can skip this section without losing the continuity of the discussion of LDAP.

The Lightweight Directory Access Protocol is nothing more than a communication protocol. As we have seen, the LDAP standard mediates communication between client and server and does nothing else. Note that LDAP is a standard and is not a program or software you can buy. What you will install on your computer is the implementation of this protocol. This is an important detail. The question of how to store the data is left to the vendor implementing the final standard. The LDAP protocol specification does not even contain the LDAP C API used to access the LDAP server from an application. This API is defined in RFC 1823 instead. Chapter 5 presents more information about APIs for the most important programming languages.

In contrast to TCP, LDAP is a message-oriented protocol. What does this mean? In a conversation on your network, you always have one sending computer and one receiving computer. For a message-oriented protocol, such as LDAP, the logical unit transferred is a message, i.e., as soon as a complete message arrives, the "receive" operation is finished. TCP instead is a stream-oriented protocol, which means that the "receive" operation stops only when a specified number of bytes have arrived. One consequence of this behavior is that LDAP does not need a type of "\r\n" delimiter to specify the end of a request.

As mentioned previously, the basic unit of information transmitted is a message contained in the message envelope. The message envelope has a well-defined format. All messages sent back and forth between server and client are sent in this format, including requests the client sends to the server, results the server sends back to the client, and the result codes. The LDAP message envelope is also called a "protocol data unit" (PDU). The PDU message envelope must contain two pieces of information:

- The message identifier identifying the message
- The operation

The message identifier is very important because the LDAP model does not require the requests and responses to be made synchronously. The message identifier allows the client and the server to assign a corresponding response to every request. The operation can be the request the client made to the server or the response sent back from the server to the client. Exhibit 7 shows the possible protocol operations.

Let us now have a closer look at the LDAP message model. The LDAP client sends a request to the LDAP server. The server executes one or more operations as specified in the request. In the case of a successful transmission, the server sends the results; in the case of an

Exhibit 7.   Protocol Operations

Operation	Description
bindRequest	bind request
bindResponse	bind response
unbindRequest	unbind request
searchRequest	search request
searchResEntry	search result entry
searchResDone	search result done
searchResRef	search result reference
modifyRequest	modify request
modifyResponse	modify response
addRequest	add request
addResponse	add response
delRequest	delete request
delResponse	delete response
modDNRequest	modify DN request
modDNResponse	modify DN response
abandonRequest	abandon request
extendedReq	extended request
extendedResponse	extended response

error, the corresponding error code is sent back to the client. Every LDAP message — both requests and responses — contains the message ID, an operation code, and data. The message ID is needed to identify the response on behalf of a request.

There is no need to explain these protocol operations in detail here, as they will become clear later on when we speak about the single models laying behind LDAP in Chapter 3. Additional information on this topic is also presented in Chapter 4. For now, it is enough to know that, for nearly all operations, there is a request operation and a response operation. The exceptions include the unbind request and the abandon request, which do not require any response. The search request can have one of three results: the data the search has resulted in, a message indicating the execution of the query, or a reference indicating where the requested data could be found. Chapter 3 provides additional information.

To illustrate this process, consider the following example of searching for an entry in a directory. Exhibit 8 provides an overview of what happens. At the beginning, the client opens a connection to the computer where the directory server is installed. Then the client "binds" to the LDAP server. The process of binding qualifies the client using a valid user ID and password. If the user ID and password are omitted, the server assumes the client wishes a connection as an "anonymous user," a user with the lowest access rights (if any). The server answers with a result code to show if the bind has been successful. Then the client constructs the query and sends it to the server. Again, the server executes the request and sends back the result data, if any, and also sends the result code of the operation in a separate message. If the server finds more than one results set, it sends them back in a number of LDAP messages. At the end of the conversation, the client sends the "unbind" request, upon which the server closes the connection. In Exhibit 8, the ID should show you the message identifier sent with each message.

One client can send multiple requests to an LDAP server, but there is no guarantee that the server will answer the requests in the order they are posted. As mentioned before, every message sent to the server by the client has a unique message identifier. The server sends this message identifier back with the answer to let the client know which request corresponds to the answer. Exhibit 9 shows this situation.

The data being sent back and forth between client and server is encoded. Data has to be encoded because the data stored in the directory contains every data type, ranging from names in ASCII (American Standard Code for Information Interchange) strings to binary data for images. LDAP uses a lightweight version of the ASN.1 (Abstract Syntax Notation One) basic encoding rules, also called "lightweight basic encoding rules" (LBER). This encoding is needed to transmit all

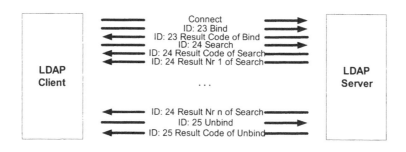

Exhibit 8. Conversation between LDAP Client and Server

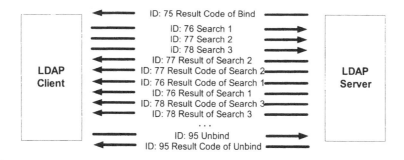

Exhibit 9. Multiple Responses to One Client Request

of the data structures LDAP knows about, including binary data and encoded passwords, in an operating-system-independent way. This distinguishes LDAP from other application protocols, such as HTTP. Using HTTP, you can open a telnet session to the server using the port it is listening to and type commands (such as a GET of an HTML page). This is not possible using LDAP because the conversation does not consist of simple strings. What you could do instead is to use LDAP URLs in your browser (more about this in Chapter 2).

Here is a sample URL:

ldap://my.ldap.server.com:389/e=ldap_abc.de?phone?(sn=Voglmaier)

and here is the URL with the syntax:

ldap://<hostname:port>/<base DN>?<attributes>?<scope>?<search filter>

where

- *Hostname* is the name of the host where your LDAP server is installed.
- *Port* is the number of the port your LDAP server is listening on (the standard port is 389).
- *Base_DN* is the base distinguished name, i.e., the distinguished name where the query has to be started (more about this in Chapter 2).
- *Attributes* are the fields to be returned by the query.
- *Scope* specifies how deep the query should enter in the directory tree (again, see Chapter 2).
- *Search filter* indicates the conditions the entries should meet in order to be returned.

Note, however, that the LDAP URL syntax allows only the search command; other operations are not supported. For additional information about LDAP URLs, see Chapter 4, which provides more details about LDAP, or Chapter 7, which examines LDAP and the Web.

In this section, we learned about the different messages that LDAP understands:

- *Bind, unbind, abandon*: These messages are needed to connect and authenticate (bind), disconnect (unbind), or abort (abandon) a connection to the server.
- *Search, compare*: These messages are sent to query information from the directory.
- *Add, delete, modify*: These messages are needed to manipulate data contained in the directory.

These operations are discussed in greater detail in Chapter 3, which examines various LDAP models.

Under the Hood: The Database Holding Information

After a whole chapter speaking about protocols, communication standards, servers, and clients, you might be wondering where the data is finally held.

As stated previously, LDAP is a standard for communication protocols between server and client. As such, it does not define how or where the data should be held. Indeed, the choice of where the data goes is independent of the implementation. In any case, some kind of repository working as a back end is needed to store the data. The repository can be implemented in any number of ways, but we will limit our brief discussion to two examples: Netscape and OpenLDAP. Both Netscape and OpenLDAP are based on the University of Michigan implementation. Netscape uses a lightweight database management (LDBM) system. LDBM is a so-called embedded database. This means that you have a subset of data storage and access methods that are available with a full fledged RDBMS. Like LDAP, an embedded database avoids all unneeded resource-consuming activities. OpenLDAP is very interesting inasmuch as it offers a big choice of back ends. This includes, first of all, various embedded databases (LDBM, for example, like Netscape). It also allows you to write your own back end. OpenLDAP has a Perl back end that lets you write the real back end using the Perl programming language and a shell back end that lets you write the back end using the standard UNIX shell. But this is not all. You can also use a back end that accesses another LDAP server; in other words, you have an LDAP proxy server. Last but not least, OpenLDAP also has an SQL back end. This back end allows you to use an RDBMS such as the one from Oracle. So you combine LDAP with a RDBMS. Messaging Direct offers an interesting white paper[4] that discusses this. At this point, you might reasonably ask: What is the difference between LDAP and an RDBMS? An RDBMS and a directory server address two different purposes. The following list itemizes the differences:

- The directory server does not know about transactions. A transaction is an all-or-nothing process. The purpose of a transaction is to guarantee data consistency. For example, if you transfer money from one bank account to another, you must be sure not to add the money to the receiving account and forget to delete this amount from the paying account. An RDBMS offers transactional support. LDAP does not guarantee such data integrity.
- The directory server does not readily support complicated joins between different tables.
- The directory server does not know about report-building utilities.
- The directory server — in contrast to an RDBMS — does provide a complicated replication mechanism. It also supports a multimaster model in addition to the master–slave replication model. (The

replication mechanism is not yet a standard at the time of this writing. Efforts are under way to create a standard.)

- Directories are optimized for reading, not for updates. An application updating hundreds of tables per minute would not be a good candidate for directories. A better choice would be an application making thousands of queries per minute.
- Directories are organized in an object-oriented, hierarchical way. This information-storage method helps to mirror exact replicates of objects into the directory.
- Directories are delivered with ready-to-use schemas, many of which are even standardized. An RDBMS schema must be defined before use.
- Directories rely on open standards, which guarantees the interoperation of different applications on different platforms.
- Since directories are a network protocol, they are natively network-enabled. This means that the user has access to functions such as data distribution and data replication implemented inside the software.
- Directories offer a lightweight method of connecting to a repository, grabbing the data, and closing the connection. An RDBMS takes much more time to establish a connection. Once opened, however, the RDBMS system offers a wider array of services. As always, system administrators must balance the cost of a higher overhead with the required services.

Conclusion

We have seen that a directory is a hierarchical repository of objects. A specialized agent, the directory server provides access to the directory. The objects in the directory are organized to optimize fast access.

Directory access protocols are used to provide directory services in a networked environment. The first commonly used directory access protocol (DAP) was the X.500 standard, a very powerful and complete protocol based on the OSI protocol stack. This DAP protocol offered many advantages and a very rich set of features. However, this feature-rich protocol is too heavy for use on personal computers, and it requires the resource-consuming OSI protocol stack. Consequently, a new protocol was developed to run over the TCP/IP protocol stack. Because this protocol leaves out the less commonly used features of DAP, it is called Lightweight Directory Access Protocol (LDAP). The less-resource-consuming LDAP protocol has had much greater acceptance than X.500. At the time of this writing, it is still a work in progress, although it is used in a production environment.

This chapter introduced the concept of LDAP and examined rudimentary applications. Chapter 2 extends the discussion, focusing on how to use an LDAP installation, how to get data in, how to define queries, how to make updates, and how to delete data. You will see the command-line utilities as well as the import and export possibilities LDAP offers. You will also learn about the LDIF (LDAP data interchange format) format that is produced by the export utilities.

References

1. Carter, G., LDAP System Administration, O'Reilly, Sebastopol, CA, 2003.
2. Comer, D.E., *Internetworking with TCP/IP*, 3 vols., Prentice Hall.
3. Stevens, R.W., *TCP/IP Illustrated*, 3 vols., Addison-Wesley.
4. MessagingDirect Limited, Combining Directories, and Relational Databases in the Enterprise, white paper, Document IC-6055-V2.0, Edmonton, Canada, 2000; available online at http://www.messagingdirect.com.

Chapter 2

LDAP Basics

This chapter is a guided tour through a mini-application using LDAP. It is intended to give you a basic impression of what you can do with LDAP. Experience has shown that the best way to understand a new tool is simply to use and play around with it. That is what we will do in this chapter. As mentioned previously, we will use OpenLDAP for the examples. OpenLDAP is available for UNIX and Win32 platforms. Because LDAP is an open standard, users of Netscape or other non-standard products are not excluded from trying out the examples presented in this book. Note that the exact syntax might be different between the various implementations. The syntax of the command-line tools in Netscape is almost identical. In any case, take a look at the documentation delivered with whatever product you are using.

First, we learn about the data structures that we will be using throughout the rest of this chapter. This example is far from complete. Indeed, it is not really an example of directory design. Rather, the example is intended to give the reader a feeling of how to use a directory server. It shows you a basic configuration so that you can begin working with LDAP. Next, we install a few entries by hand using the command-line tools. Once these entries are installed, we will try to make the usual operations on data in a repository: We will search for the entries we stored in the directory; we will update the data; and then we will delete some entries. Then we will learn how to insert bulk data, and at the end we will use the import/export utilities. We will also learn about the LDIF (LDAP data interchange format) file format, which is the format that LDAP uses to import and export files. Finally, we will learn to use the URL form of an LDAP query to find entries in the directory. This form was briefly introduced in Chapter 1. In this chapter, you can see it at work and play around with it.

This chapter provides only a rough overview of what you can do with LDAP and does not get into the details. This will be done in later chapters, mostly in Chapter 6 (LDAP APIs) but also in Chapter 4, where we will see some of the details of LDAP, and in Chapter 7, where we will see how the World Wide Web and LDAP can be used together.

Example: An Enterprise with a Few Departments

First of all, let us look at the problem at hand. We will use a classic example to illustrate an LDAP application: a directory of employees. Note that this is a widely used LDAP application, but it is not the only one. We will see other applications later in this book.

Let us assume that we have an enterprise named ldap_abc. To simplify, let this enterprise work in only one country. The enterprise ldap_abc has a number of departments, and a certain number of people work in each department. Our goal is to find the phone number of a certain employee, knowing surname and given name. For now, we will not concentrate much on the overall design. This aspect will be treated in Chapter 9. This chapter is only intended to give a quick overview of what you can do with LDAP. Nor will we care about performance or more sophisticated queries, such as finding a Mr. Smith working in Australia whose given name begins with A and who does not have a fax. Be patient, we will address these and other arguments later.

The first job on our to-do list is to reproduce the hierarchical structure of our enterprise in the tree structure in LDAP. The root of this treelike data structure defines the "namespace" within which we will work. Now you may well ask, "What is our tree made of?" The answer is that the tree is made of objects. Exhibit 1 shows a small part of the tree.

Looking at Exhibit 1, you may wonder what o=1dap_abc.de and the other abbreviations mean. We will discuss this in Chapter 3 when we look at the theory behind LDAP. For now it is enough to know that o stands for organization, ou for organizational unit and cn for common name, i.e., surname. All these abbreviations must be declared in the schema defining the data structures the directory can hold.

Now let us have a look at the individual objects: The root of the tree is the enterprise itself, ldap_abc. The root branches out into individual departments. To simplify the discussion, we will limit ourselves to four: Marketing, Sales, Research, and IT. Note that every department is one object, as is the root element. What is missing now are the employees. Every employee is an object under the corresponding department.

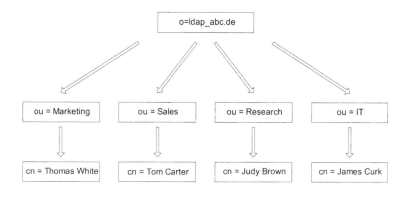

Exhibit 1. Example Directory Tree

In developing our design, we learned that the LDAP database is organized in a tree structure of objects. This tree spans the namespace we are moving in. Now that we have completed our design, we can proceed to implement the single objects.

Objects in LDAP: Object Classes, Attributes, and Schema

Before you can enter any objects into a directory, you must first define what kind of objects the directory will accept. This is much like the design of an object-oriented database. We begin the process by declaring the object classes the directory should accept. In our example we will have an object class called "organization" corresponding to the whole enterprise, a number of objects called "organizational unit," and objects of the object class "person." (Forgive me for calling a person an object, but let us agree to accept this point of view in the context of this discussion.)

You do not have to invent these object classes by yourself. There are a number of predefined standard object classes from which you can choose. The names of these object classes are standardized too, most of them being derived from the original X.500 protocol. You will learn more about this in Chapter 3, which discusses the models standing behind LDAP.

The directory will also contain a number of entries, with each of the entries corresponding to an object in the real world. Each class is characterized by a number of "attributes." For example, a person has a name, surname, phone number, and so on. The attributes are made up of an attribute name and one or more attribute values. The attribute names, like the class names, are standard, most of them being inherited from the X.500 protocol.

To refer unambiguously to an object, a special attribute called a "distinguished name" is used. There are no particular rules of how to build this distinguished name; the only important thing is that this name be unique within the namespace. Chapter 3 discusses the distinguished name in detail.

To define the data structures for the directory, you must first define a schema. A schema comprises object classes accepted by the implementation and governs how these object classes should interact. Chapter 3 discusses this issue in greater depth. For now, it is sufficient to know that the directory server has a number of schema files that contain the description of the object classes the directory can contain. This description is nothing but a list of attributes the entries can contain, together with a specification of the type and properties of these attributes. The schema also contains a specification for making comparisons between the values of these attributes. For example, the name or surname is not case sensitive, so if you are searching for King, KING, or king, you will find the entry. Similarly, consider the attribute "telephone number." There are several ways to write a phone number. The directory should ensure that you find the number:

> 0-100-203-440

even if you typed in:

> 0 100 203 440

This behavior is important not only for queries, but also for the ordering of values. Again, we will learn more about this in Chapter 3.

Every LDAP implementation is shipped with ready-to-use schema files. Both object classes and attributes are fixed in standards distributed in the form of requests for comments (RFCs), but you can extend these standards to fit your particular requirements. That is enough theory for now. Let us move on to the praxis.

Server Configuration

The first thing you have to do is configure your directory server. You do this by setting up the root of your directory tree and then including the schemas you are going to use.

The root of our directory tree is "o = ldap_abc.de," where "o" stands for "organization." Chapter 3 provides more details about selecting the directory root. Most commercial products have only a few predefined schemas. They also have a graphical user interface to browse through the object classes and attributes that are known by the directory server. The vendor documentation provides specific details. The OpenLDAP software that we are using has one simple configuration file where you can set up the root DN and select the schema files you wish to use.

Next, you will need to set up the distinguished name (DN) and the password of the LDAP administrator. For our example, we will choose:

```
DN: uid=Administrator, o=ldap_abc.de
Password: pass1
```

Using the i-planet directory server, you have to set up DN and password, the administrator password, and the server's port number during software installation. Other commercial products behave similarly.

As mentioned previously, when using OpenLDAP, you have to include the schema files you are going to use. For this example, you need the object class "inetOrgPerson," so make sure you include the schema file where the inetOrgPerson class is defined. To complete the examples that follow, you must include the following schemas:

- *core.schema* for the basic classes and attributes
- *cosine.schema* for some useful extensions as defined by RFC 1274, such as userID, mail, etc.
- *inetorgperson.schema* for some further extensions needed for additional attributes as specified in RFC 2798

First Steps with LDAP

Now that the server is set up correctly and running, we are ready to take our first steps in the land of LDAP. LDAP organizes the information it holds in a treelike namespace called a "directory information tree" (DIT). In our case, the root of the tree is the enterprise called ldap_abc.

The command to add an entry with the command-line tool is:

```
ldapmodify —a
```

Exhibit 2 illustrates the command you have to use. From this command we can note other useful things.

The first line of the actual data begins with

```
dn: o=ldap_abc.de
```

where dn means distinguished name. The distinguished name is just a key to access this particular entry. Therefore, it must be unique across the whole directory, as explained previously.

The following lines also appear in Exhibit 2:

```
objectclass: top
objectclass: organization
```

Note that ldap_abc.de is an object of the class "organization," and "organization" is a subclass of "top." Both top and organization are declared in the configuration files. If you look at the configuration files of your LDAP implementation, you will see that the only element that top requires is the attribute "objectClass." So the function of the

---

Exhibit 2. Adding the "organization" Entry with ldapmodify

```
# ldapmodify —a —D "uid=admin, o=ldap_abc.de" —w pass1
dn: o=ldap_abc.de
objectclass: top
objectclass: organization
o: ldap_abc.de
l: Munich

adding new entry "o=ldap_abc.de"
```

---

object class "top" is also to ensure that all object classes will have the objectClass property.

The organization ldap_abc.de has two other properties: "o" (organization) and "l" (location), both of them defined in the schema. As noted previously, these are historical names derived from the original X.500 protocol. Reading your configuration files, you will note that some properties are required, and others are optional. A number of attributes can also be multivalued. Chapter 3 will address these issues.

The last line:

```
adding new entry "o=ldap_abc.de"
```

is the output the command line echoes to confirm that the command has been executed successfully. Otherwise, you will get an error message. If you get

```
ldap_bind: Invalid credentials (49)
```

you mistyped DN or password.

Be sure to enclose the distinguished name in quotation marks. Otherwise, the shell will interpret the command incorrectly, and the command-line utility will complain about the syntax. If you hit the "enter" key after the first line, the command-line utility waits for you to type the data in. Press "enter" only once to finish each line. If you press it twice, the utility assumes the entry you are typing is complete and parses the entry. It complains if required attributes are missing and quits. For example, if you push "enter" twice after the first line, as in:

```
# ldapmodify —a —D "uid=admin, o=ldap_abc.de" —w pass1
dn: o=ldap_abc.de
```

the utility answers:

```
ldapmodify: no attributes to change or add (entry="o=ldap_abc.de")
```

After that, the program waits for further input. You can continue to add further entries. When you are finished, you can exit from the program with Control-C.

Once we have added the root of the directory, we can proceed to add the various departments, called "organizationalUnit" in LDAP. Exhibit 3 shows how to proceed. In this case, we add an entry of the type "organizationalUnit." Obviously the dn attribute is now different. It is built up from the previous one "o = ldap_abc.de" plus an additional string "ou = Information Technologies." The additional string is called a "relative distinguished name" (RDN). The relative distinguished name has to be unique inside its scope. This means that, at the tree below o = ldap_abc.de, there can be no further "ou = IT" entry. Exhibit 4 shows the syntax for adding three additional organizational units.

Exhibit 3. Adding the "organizationUnit" Entry with ldapmodify

```
# ldapmodify —a —D "uid = admin, o=ldap_abc.de" —w pass1
dn: ou=IT, o=ldap_abc.de
objectclass: top
objectclass: organizationalUnit
ou: IT
description: Information Technologies

adding new entry "ou=IT, o=ldap_abc.de"
```

Exhibit 4. Adding Three Other "organizationUnit" Entries with ldapmodify

```
# ldapmodify —a —D "cn=admin, o=ldap_abc.de" —w password1
dn: ou=HR, o=ldap_abc.de
objectclass: top
objectclass: organizationalUnit
ou: IT
description: Human Resources

adding new entry "ou=HR, o=ldap_abc.de"

dn: ou=R&D, o=ldap_abc.de
objectclass: top
objectclass: organizationalUnit
ou: IT
description: Research and Development

adding new entry "ou=R&D, o=ldap_abc.de"

dn: ou=Mkt, o=ldap_abc.de
objectclass: top
objectclass: organizationalUnit
ou: IT
description: Marketing

adding new entry "ou=Mkt, o=ldap_abc.de"
```

Now that we have added so many entries, we will look in the directory to verify that the data in the directory matches what we typed in. The tool we use is called "ldapsearch." Exhibit 5 shows it in action, and the result shows that the output is exactly what we put in.

Let us take a closer look at the ldapsearch command.

```
ldapsearch —b "o=ldap_abc.de" "(objectclass=*)"
```

Exhibit 5. Searching the Directory

```
ldapsearch —b "o=ldap_abc.de" "(objectclass=*)"
# extended LDIF
#
# LDAPv3
# filter: (objectclass=*)
# requesting: ALL
#
# ldap_abc.de

dn: o=ldap_abc.de
objectclass: top
objectclass: organization
o: ldap_abc.de
l: Munich

# IT, ldap_abc.de
dn: ou=IT, o=ldap_abc.de
objectclass: top
objectclass: organizationalUnit
ou: IT
description: Information Technologies

# HR, ldap_abc.de
dn: ou=HR, o=ldap_abc.de
objectclass: top
objectclass: organizationalUnit
ou: IT
description: Human Resources

# R&D, ldap_abc.de
dn: ou=R&D, o=ldap_abc.de
objectclass: top
objectclass: organizationalUnit
ou: IT
description: Research and Development

# Mkt, ldap_abc.de
dn: ou=Mkt, o=ldap_abc.de
objectclass: top
objectclass: organizationalUnit
ou: IT
description: Marketing

# search result
search: 2
result: 0 Success

# numResponses: 6
# numEntries: 5
```

The switch "-b" specifies the base from which we want to see all entries, here the root of the directory. The term "(objectclass = *)" specifies that we are interested in seeing all object classes in the directory, not just a particular one. Again, leave the quotation marks where there are. The parentheses in this case are optional, but for more complicated queries, it is a good practice to use parentheses.

If you are not working on the same machine the directory server is running on, you should specify the switch "-h servername" to indicate the machine where the directory server is running. For example, if your server was installed on www.directoryserver.de, your search would look like this:

```
ldapsearch –h www.directoryserver.de –b o=ldap_abc.de "objectclass
= *"
```

Later in this chapter we will examine the search operation in greater detail.

Now let us finally add an entry for a person. Exhibit 6 shows the command line. This time there are more object-class attributes. The object we want to insert is an inetOrgPerson. It should contain a user ID (uid), a password (userPassword), and an e-mail address (mail).

At this point, if you get an error message complaining about "object class violation" specifying an "unrecognized objectClass: 'inetOrgPerson'," you may have forgotten to include the schema file containing the definition of the object class inetOrgPerson into your configuration file. Put the schema in, stop the server, and restart it again. If the server does not start, complaining instead of a missing attribute type, then you forgot to include another schema file the server needs. In this case, it is the file containing the definition of the attribute type "audio," provided by the file cosine.schema. At startup the directory server loads the schema files and checks to see if all attributes mentioned in the object classes have been defined.

Now that we have provided definitions for all object classes and attribute types, you will get a message confirming that the person has been successfully added. (See last line in Exhibit 6.)

The object class in LDAP offering these entries is inetOrgPerson. We notice that inetOrgPerson derives from organizationalPerson, which in turn derives from person. As stated before, person finally derives from the top, which enforces the presence of the object-class attributes.

If you look at the point where the object classes are defined, you will see that "person" defines a number of attributes, such as "sn," the surname, and "cn," the common name, with the full name being composed of surname + given name. Optionally, the "person" entry can contain a userPassword, a telephoneNumber, a seeAlso reference, and a description. Look at the definition of organizationalPerson. Because this object class inherits from person, the above-listed

---

Exhibit 6. Adding the "inetOrgPerson" Entry with ldapmodify

```
# ldapmodify —a —D "uid=admin, o=ldap_abc.de" —w pass1
dn: uid=RVoglmaier, ou=IT, o=ldap_abc.de
objectclass: top
objectclass: person
objectclass: organizationalPerson
objectclass: inetOrgPerson
cn: Reinhard E. Voglmaier
cn: Reinhard Erich Voglmaier
cn: Reinhard Voglmaier
sn: Voglmaier
givenName: Reinhard Erich
ou: IT
uid: RVoglmaier
mail: Reinhard.Voglmaier@ldap_abc.de

adding new entry "uid=RVoglmaier, ou=IT, o=ldap_abc.de"
```

---

attributes are not listed anymore. Instead, only the new attributes extending the person class are listed.

Let us do another search, but this time we are interested in the object classes of type "organizationalUnit." Exhibit 7 shows the syntax.

If we want to see the entries for all persons, we must make a query like that shown in Exhibit 8.

At this point, you know enough to start playing around with the software. Add some entries, try to find different object classes, and see what happens. You could also add an "inetOrgPerson" object and an "organizationalPerson" object. Then try to search for "organizationalPerson" or "inetOrgPerson" and see the different results. The more you play, the more you will learn.

Updating a Directory with a Batch Process

We have been typing commands using the command-line tool. This has two drawbacks: the risk of typos and the lack of documentation showing what you typed in. Fortunately, the ldapmodify command also accepts a file as input. Exhibit 9 shows what this file looks like. You will recognize the same input as you gave at the command line. Exhibit 10 shows the messages confirming execution of the file in Exhibit 9.

Until now, we have used ldapmodify only in an interactive mode. Now that we know how to insert the data and instructions from a file, there is no need to use a command line to communicate with ldapmodify. Use Control-C to stop reading input from the prompt.

So far, we have learned that the directory is made up of a hierarchical tree of objects. We have seen that the position of a single object

Exhibit 7. Searching for All Classes of Type "organizationalUnit"

```
ldapsearch —b "ldap_abc.de" "(objectclass=organizationalUnit)"
# extended LDIF
#
# LDAPv3
# filter: (objectclass=organizationalUnit)
# requesting: ALL
#

# IT, ldap_abc.de
dn: ou=IT, o=ldap_abc.de
objectClass: top
objectClass: organizationalUnit
ou: IT
description: Information Technologies

# HR, ldap_abc.de
dn: ou=HR, o=ldap_abc.de
objectClass: top
objectClass: organizationalUnit
ou: HR
description: Human Resources

# R&D, ldap_abc.de
dn: ou=R&D, o=ldap_abc.de
objectClass: top
objectClass: organizationalUnit
ou: R&D
description: Research and Development

# Mkt, ldap_abc.de
dn: ou=HR, o=ldap_abc.de
objectClass: top
objectClass: organizationalUnit
ou: Mkt
description: Marketing

# search result
search: 2
result: 0 Success

# numResponses: 5
# numEntries: 4
```

is given by its distinguished name (DN), which must be unique inside the directory. We have also seen that the distinguished name is constructed from the distinguished name of its ancestor plus its own relative distinguished name (RDN). Further, we have learned how to add entries and how to search in the directory. Finally, we have seen that instead of manually typing command-line entries, we can instruct ldapmodify to take its input from a file instead of from the command line. In the next section, we will see that ldapmodify has other functions beyond adding entries.

Exhibit 8. Searching for All Classes of Type "person"

```
ldapsearch —b "ldap_abc.de" "(objectclass=person)"
# extended LDIF
#
# LDAPv3
# filter: objectclass=person
# requesting: ALL
#

# RVoglmaier, IT, ldap_abc.de
dn: uid=RVoglmaier, ou=IT, o=ldap_abc.de
objectClass: top
objectClass: person
objectClass: organizationalPerson
objectClass: inetOrgPerson
cn: Reinhard E. Voglmaier
cn: Reinhard Erich Voglmaier
cn: Reinhard Voglmaier
givenname: Reinhard Erich
sn: Voglmaier
ou: IT
uid: RVoglmaier
mail: RVoglmaier@ldap_abc.de
mobile: 149 170 36273 3747 3747

# search result
search: 2
result: 0 Success

# numResponses: 2
# numEntries: 1
```

The LDIF Standard

Let us make a small change in our command file. After the first line (i.e., the line specifying the distinguished name), add the following line:

```
changetype: add
```

Now you can execute the ldapmodify command without the "-a" switch. You might not consider this to be an elegant solution, but look at Exhibit 11, where we execute ldapmodify without using the -a switch and give it some new instructions. Exhibit 12 shows the command together with the program's output.

Let us look more closely at the instruction file in Exhibit 11. The first line of each instruction contains, as always, the distinguished name we wish to operate on. The rest is self-explanatory: Next to the distinguished name, we specify the operation we want. First we add an entry, a command we have already seen in action. We specify with "changetype," which allows us to add, modify, or delete an entry. In this case, we want to modify some entries. Specifically, we want to replace the value for the mail attribute "RVoglmaier@ldap_abc.de,"

Exhibit 9. Input File for ldapmodify

```
# cat Persons.ldif

dn: uid=TKlein, ou=Mkt, o=ldap_abc.de
objectClass: top
objectClass: person
objectClass: organizationalPerson
objectClass: inetOrgPerson
cn: Thomas Klein
sn: Klein
givenName: Thomas
ou: Mkt
uid: TKlein
mail: ThomasKlein@ldap_abc.de

dn: uid=PSmith, ou=Mkt, o=ldap_abc.de
objectClass: top
objectClass: person
objectClass: organizationalPerson
objectClass: inetOrgPerson
cn: Peter Smith
sn: Smith
givenName: Peter
ou: Mkt
uid: PSmith
mail: PeterSmith@ldap_abc.de
```

Exhibit 10. Execution of ldapmodify with Input from a File

```
ldapmodify -a -D "uid=admin, o=ldap_abc.de" -w "pass1" -f
Persons.ldif
adding new entry "uid=TKlein, ou=Mkt, o=ldap_abc.de"
adding new entry "uid=PSmith, ou=Mkt, o=ldap_abc.de"
```

---

which we entered in Exhibit 8, into the correct name "ReinhardVogl-maier@ldap_abc.de." After the instruction "changetype: modify," we insert a line instructing ldapmodify that we want to replace the value of the mail attribute. In the next line, we simply specify the new value.

Next, we add a new attribute — the mobile phone number — for the qualified entry. Again, we specify what we intend to do: We want to modify an entry, adding a new attribute.

Finally, we instruct ldapmodify to delete an entry. Again, the syntax is straightforward: Identify the distinguished name and carry out the associated action, "delete."

All of these commands are executed with the familiar ldapmodify command, but without the -a switch.

Now you can really play around with your LDAP installation. You can add, delete, and modify entries, and you can see what you have in your directory.

Exhibit 11. More Instructions for ldapmodify

```
# cat modify.ldif
dn: uid=SParker, ou=HR, o=ldap_abc.de
changetype: add
objectClass: top
objectClass: person
objectClass: organizationalPerson
objectClass: inetOrgPerson
cn: Sarah Parker
sn: Parker
givenName: Sarah
ou: HR
uid: SParker
mail: SarahParker@ldap_abc.de

dn: uid=RVoglmaier, ou=IT, o=ldap_abc.de
changetype: modify
replace: mail
mail: ReinhardVoglmaier@ldap_abc.de

dn: uid=RVoglmaier, ou=IT, o=ldap_abc.de
changetype: modify
add: mobile
mobile: (0049) 89 671 293

dn: uid=TKlein, ou=Mkt, o=ldap_abc.de
changetype: modify
delete: mail

dn: uid=PSmith, ou=HR, o=ldap_abc.de
changetype: delete
```

Exhibit 12. Execution of ldapmodify Using the Instructions from the File in Exhibit 11 in the ldapmodify Command

```
# ldapmodify -D "uid=admin, o=ldap_abc.de" -w "pass1" -f
Persons.ldif

adding new entry "uid=SParker, ou=HR, o=ldap_abc.de"

modifying entry "uid=RVoglmaier, ou=IT, o=ldap_abc.de"

modifying entry "uid=RVoglmaier, ou=IT, o=ldap_abc.de"

modifying entry "uid=TKlein, ou=Mkt, o=ldap_abc.de"

deleting entry "uid=PSmith, ou=HR, o=ldap_abc.de"
```

The format of the input file is standardized and is defined in the RFCs, as explained in Chapter 1. The RFC for this standard LDIF format is RFC 2849, "The LDAP Data Interchange Format (LDIF) — Technical Specification."

An LDIF file is an ASCII file containing all instructions to modify the directory. Using a pure ASCII file is enormously helpful. First of all it is easy for you to read and understand. This makes it possible for you to control without great effort the contents of this file. An ASCII file is furthermore very easy to produce using home grown scripts, and debugging is facilitated. Finally, it is self-explaining. The LDIF file has further advantages as a tool for directory migration. You can export your entire directory as an LDIF file and import it to another directory implementation, even if both directories are incompatible with each other. You can also use LDIF to save your directory on a storage medium such as tape or CD. And because the format is standardized, you can produce LDIF files in your preferred programming language. If you want to modify the structure of your directory, you can do it easily using a scripting language such as the powerful Perl language. First you export the directory as an LDIF file, make the conversion, and then delete the obsolete directory and import the new LDIF files.

Rewriting and then destroying the old directory might seem to be an overly aggressive management style. Why destroy the whole directory if you only have to make a few changes? Consider what should be a trivial operation: changing the distinguished name of a single organizational unit. If you wanted to change the distinguished name for "human resources," giving it a more self-explanatory name, you might proceed as follows. The previous name was:

```
dn: ou=HR, o=ldap_abc.de
```

Now we would like to rename it as:

```
dn: ou=Human Resources, o=ldap_abc.de
```

The directory server will refuse the name change because the "HR" entry has subentries. The "HR" organizational unit has sibling entries of the objectClass "person." The logical approach would be to change the "person" entries, but this does not solve the problem because the "person" entries would no longer have an ancestor. Using this "logical" approach, the only solution is to create a new entry of the objectClass "organizational unit," move all relevant persons to the new name, and then delete the obsolete organizational unit. A simpler solution is the "aggressive" approach mentioned above: Export the directory in a file, clear the directory, modify the exported file, and re-import it.

Consider this common real-world example. Two companies have merged. Every entry in the LDAP directory has to be changed.

- In the object "organization," you have to change the attributes "distinguished name" and "organization."
- In the object "organizationalUnit," you have to change the attribute "distinguished name."
- In the object "inetOrgPerson," you have to change the attributes "distinguished name" and "mail."

Exhibit 13. Simple Perl Script to Modify the Enterprise Name

```
#!/usr/bin/perl -w

# Name:          convert.pl
# Version:       1.0
# Author:        Reinhard E. Voglmaier
# Description:   Conversion Utility per LDAP repository
# Date:          10.09.2002

$in_ldif = "Directory_In.ldif" ;
$out_ldif = "Directory_Out.ldif" ;

# open the original file
open(IN,">$in_ldif") || die "could not open input file:
$in_ldif" ;

#open the output file
open(OUT,"> $out_ldif") || die "could not open output file:
$out_ldif" ;

# Conversion:
while (<IN>) {
  # we simply substitute the enterprise name
  s/ldap_abc.de/LdapAbc.org/g ;
  # here we could change other things, too
  s/Mkt/Marketing/g ;
  s/HR/Human Resources/g;
  print OUT ;
}

# close INPUT and OUTPUT files

close(IN);
close(OUT);
```

Exhibit 13 shows a Perl script that automates this process. The script may be simplistic, but it effectively illustrates how easy it is to make changes in a running directory while maintaining consistency.

Ldapsearch Revisited: Search Filter

The output of our previous search was not particularly sophisticated, nor was the query we made to our directory. Had we been searching a directory with millions of entries (like a phone book), we would have produced a simple dump of all entries.

Let us concentrate first on refining the output. You can easily specify relevant fields for an ldapsearch, such as the full name (common name called "cn" and surname called "sn") and the e-mail address (called "mail"), for example. Exhibit 14 shows how this is done.

Remember that we had some entries with more than one value for the attribute "common name." Suppose we want to pull the data for someone and we only know the surname. The query string in LDAP parlance is called "filter." Here, the filter is rather simple: We wish to get all persons whose name is "Parker." The filter would therefore simply be:

```
sn=Parker
```

Look at Exhibit 15 to get the correct syntax. An exact description of this syntax is found in Chapter 5, where we will not only look at the command-line tools, but also at other, more-sophisticated APIs, such as Perl or Java.

The query produced two entries with the sn Parker. To further refine the query, we could search for all people named Parker and working in the Research department. The additional condition is:

```
(ou=Research)
```

Exhibit 14. Limited Output with ldapsearch

```
ldapsearch —b "LdapAbc.org" "(objectclass=person)" cn mail

# extended LDIF
#
# LDAPv3
# filter: (objectclass=person)
# requesting: cn mail
#

# RVoglmaier, IT, LdapAbc.org
dn: uid=RVoglmaier, ou=IT, o=LdapAbc.org

cn: Reinhard E. Voglmaier
cn: Reinhard Erich Voglmaier
cn: Reinhard Voglmaier
givenname: Reinhard Erich
mail: RVoglmaier@LdapAbc.org

# TKlein, Mkt, LdapAbc.org
dn: uid=TKlein, ou=Mkt, o=LdapAbc.org
cn: Thomas Klein
# PSmith, Mkt, LdapAbc.org
dn: uid=PSmith, ou=Mkt, o=LdapAbc.org
cn: Peter Smith
mail: PeterSmith@LdapAbc.org

# SParker, HR, LdapAbc.org
dn: uid=SParker, ou=HR, o=LdapAbc.org
cn: Sarah Parker
mail: SarahParker@LdapAbc.org

# search result
search: 2
result: 0 Success

# numResponses: 5
# numEntries: 4
```

Exhibit 15. A Simple Query Filter

```
ldapsearch -b "LdapAbc.org" "(sn=Parker)"
# extended LDIF
#
# LDAPv3
#
# filter: (sn=Parker)
# requesting: ALL
#

# JParker, Human Resources, LdapAbc.org
dn: uid=JParker, ou=Human Resources, o=LdapAbc.org
objectClass: top
objectClass: person
objectClass: organizationalPerson
objectClass: inetOrgPerson
cn: James Parker
sn: Parker
givenName: James
ou: Human Resources
uid: JParker
mail: JParker@LdapAbc.org

# TParker, Research, LdapAbc.org
dn: uid=JParker, ou=Human Resources, o=LdapAbc.org
objectClass: top
objectClass: person
objectClass: organizationalPerson
objectClass: inetOrgPerson
cn: Tina Parker
sn: Parker
givenName: Tina
ou: Human Resources
uid: TParker
mail: TParker@LdapAbc.org
# search result
search: 2
result: 0 Success

# numResponses: 3
# numEntries: 2
```

However, the two filters have to be joined by a logical AND operator. LDAP uses a particular notation known as Polish notation, or prefix notation, where the two operands to be connected are prefixed by the operator.* The AND condition reads:

```
(& (sn=Parker) (ou=Research))
```

Exhibit 16 shows the result.

The Polish notation was published by the Polish philosopher and mathematician Jan Lucasiewicz (1878–1956). Reverse Polish notation (RPN), which postfixes the operands with the operator, was used in the first Hewlett-Packard electronic calculators.

Exhibit 16. A Somewhat More Complicated Query

```
ldapsearch —b "LdapAbc.org" "(&(sn=Parker)(ou=Research))"
# extended LDIF
#
# LDAPv3
# filter: (&(sn=Parker)(ou=Research))
# requesting: ALL
#

# TParker, Research, LdapAbc.org
dn: uid=JParker, ou=Human Resources, o=LdapAbc.org
objectClass: top
objectClass: person
objectClass: organizationalPerson
objectClass: inetOrgPerson
cn: Tina Parker
sn: Parker

givenName: Tina
ou: Human Resources
uid: TParker
mail: TParker@LdapAbc.org

# search result
search: 2
result: 0 Success

# numResponses: 2
# numEntries: 1
```

The attribute values can also contain white spaces as well as special characters. However, a number of special characters that have a specific meaning for the LDAP protocol cannot be used directly as attribute values. They have to be encoded. Chapter 4 provides more information on this topic. LDAP also recognizes other logical operators such as OR and NOT. For example, you could search for a person named Parker working in the IT department or in Marketing. The filter would look like this:

```
(& (sn=Parker) (| (ou=Information Technologies)(ou=Marketing)))
```

If you were searching for Parker but NOT in the Human Resources department, the filter would be as follows:

```
(& (sn=Parker) (!(ou=Human Resources)))
```

The example search in Exhibit 17 simply shows all entries having a certain attribute, in this case a mobile phone number.

The final example of a query filter is presented in Exhibit 19, which illustrates the use of wild cards in a filter. In this case, the ldapsearch tool is instructed to print only the common name, the surname, and the e-mail address. The ldapsearch tool suppresses any additional information, printing only the explicitly requested information. Here we search for all entries with sn beginning with "Vogl," so it finds sn = Vogl and sn = Voglmaier.

Exhibit 17. Search with Query Filter

```
ldapsearch —b "LdapAbc.org" "(mobile=*)"

# extended LDIF
#
# LDAPv3
#
# filter: (mobile=*)
# requesting: ALL
#

# RVoglmaier, IT, LdapAbc.org
dn: uid=RVoglmaier, ou=IT, o=LdapAbc.org
objectClass: top
objectClass: person
objectClass: organizationalPerson
objectClass: inetOrgPerson
cn: Reinhard E. Voglmaier
cn: Reinhard Erich Voglmaier
cn: Reinhard Voglmaier
givenname: Reinhard Erich
sn: Voglmaier
ou: IT
uid: RVoglmaier
mail: RVoglmaier@LdapAbc.org
mobile: +49 170 36273 3747 3747

# search result
search: 2
result: 0 Success

# numResponses: 2
# numEntries: 1
```

Exhibit 18. A More Complete Example of Search

```
ldapsearch —LLL —b "LdapAbc.org" "(sn=Vogl*)" cn sn mail
dn: uid=RVoglmaier, ou=IT, o=LdapAbc.org
cn: Reinhard E. Voglmaier
cn: Reinhard Erich Voglmaier
cn: Reinhard Voglmaier
givenname: Reinhard Erich
sn: Voglmaier
mail: RVoglmaier@LdapAbc.org

dn: uid=KVogl, ou=Research, o=LdapAbc.org
cn: Kurt Vogl
sn: Vogl
mail: KVogl@LdapAbc.org
```

That will be the last example of a filter application for now. Nevertheless, you will see the filter again in Chapter 3, when we speak about the theory of LDAP, and again in Chapter 6, which covers the other LDAP APIs.

As you have seen, the filter mechanism is robust and LDAP can execute powerful queries using Polish notation. LDAP, however, does not offer joins between different objects as does a relational database management system (RDBMS). Having seen the examples presented in this section, you should play with the command-line language to become more familiar with the directory server. Again, the syntax of the ldapsearch utility could be slightly different on your server implementation. However, the logic should be the same. Refer to the documentation delivered with the product you are using.

LDAP: Is This a Protocol?

In Chapter 1, we learned that LDAP is the abbreviation for Lightweight Directory Access Protocol. Until now, however, it did not matter that it is a network protocol. You should not need to pay attention to that fact unless you are using a directory server installed on a remote machine. If you are using a directory server such as this, you will need to jump from the beginning of this chapter to here. I will explain to you how you have to proceed in order to try out the examples. You have to specify on which computer the directory server is running. You do so using the –h <computername> switch. Exhibit 19 shows you how to do this. In this example, you need to assume that the directory server is running on a computer named "1dap2.co.uk." With this knowledge, you can execute all exercises that we have had up until now as if they were running on the local computer. Now let us discuss the LDAP protocol.

The LDAP protocol runs over TCP/IP (Transmission Control Protocol/Internet Protocol), and the command-line tools are no more than small client applications. Of course, the client application has to be installed on your system, and it is the client application that imposes the syntax of the commands entered by the user. The client application then speaks with the directory server using the standard LDAP protocol.

To speak with a directory server located on the remote machine http://ldap2.co.uk, you simply have to specify the host in the command-line tool. On my implementation (OpenLDAP), the -h switch specifies the host where LDAP is running. Exhibit 19 shows the transaction.

In this example, I have also specified the port number for the directory server. This is not necessary unless the server runs on a nonstandard port, such as might occur if you have an administration server and a data server. The administration server might run on a

---

Exhibit 19. A Search against a Remote Directory Server

```
ldapsearch —h ldap2.co.uk —p 389 —LLL —b "LdapAbc.org"
"(sn=Vogl*)" cn sn mail
dn: uid=RVoglmaier, ou=IT, o=LdapAbc.org
cn: Reinhard E. Voglmaier
cn: Reinhard Erich Voglmaier
cn: Reinhard Voglmaier
givenname: Reinhard Erich
sn: Voglmaier
mail: RVoglmaier@LdapAbc.org

dn: uid=KVogl, ou=Research, o=LdapAbc.org
cn: Kurt Vogl
sn: Vogl
mail: KVogl@LdapAbc.org
```

---

different port than the data server, improving the performance of the data server by freeing it from administration traffic. The administration server also could be shut down when not in use and restarted only when it had work to do.

Your Favorite Browser Speaks LDAP

The following example demonstrates that your browser speaks LDAP. For this exercise, you need

1. A directory server running on a machine (call it "ldap.mycompany.uk")
2. A Web browser installed on your machine

That is all you need. Open your favorite browser and type in the following:

```
ldap://ldap.mycompany.uk/o=LdapAbc.de
```

I assume that the directory is named that way, but if you use a different baseDN, change it according to your installation. Exhibit 20 shows what I see on my machine (SuSE Linux with the Konqueror browser). It also works with Netscape or IE.

Now that you have located the directory, you can navigate the whole tree. In the Konqueror browser, one simply clicks on the icons and the correct LDAP URL opens. On other browsers, you have to do the typing yourself. Either way, the information you get is the same. Exhibit 21 shows the view after opening the Human Resources object. Exhibit 22 shows the view for one of the inetOrg-Person entries in the Human Resources object. Note that it is possible to specify selected values for an entry, such as the cn, sn, and mail attributes.

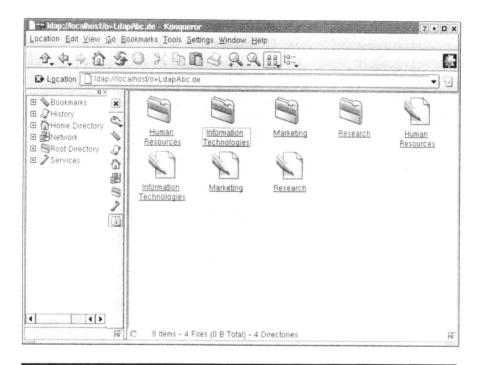

Exhibit 20.   Base URL via Web Browser

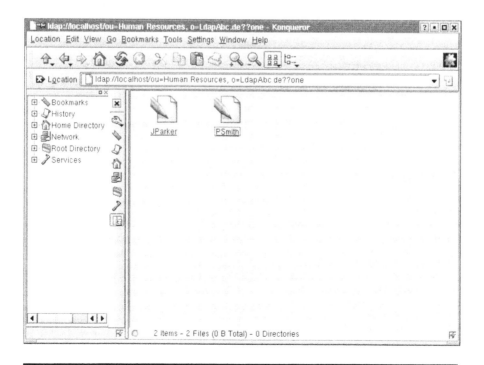

Exhibit 21.   Human Resources DN via Web Browser

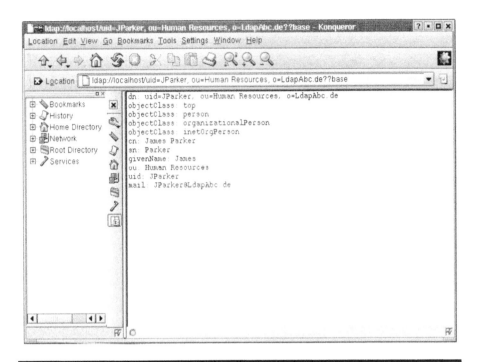

Exhibit 22.   InetOrgPerson Entry via Web Browser

The LDAP URL format is standardized and defined in RFC 2255, "The LDAP URL Format." It is treated in Chapter 4 of this book when we discuss the details of LDAP. For now, we will, just for completeness, show the syntax of the command:

```
"ldap://"[hostname [":" portNumber] ] "/" baseDN [ query ]
```

where the query is:

```
["?" attributeList ["?" scope "?" filter ["?" extensions ] ] ]
```

Conclusion

This chapter covered many aspects of LDAP without going into the details. The scope was simply to introduce some key concepts and present examples of LDAP at work so that the reader could begin using basic LDAP commands. The best way to learn how to use new software is to install it and then play around with it. Armed with the basic concepts presented here in Chapter 2, we are ready to delve further into the details covered in Chapter 3, a chapter of pure theory explaining how LDAP works.

Chapter 3

Chapter 3

LDAP Models

Chapter 1 provided a rough overview of LDAP. This chapter provides some theoretical background that will give you an impression of the concepts underlying LDAP. Most of these concepts are covered in the requests for comments (RFCs). The standardization of LDAP is still a work in progress, so please refer to RFCs on the IETF Web site (www.ietf.org) if you want stay up to date. Recall from Chapter 1 that LDAP is the lightweight counterpart of the original X.500 Directory Access Protocol. Consequently, most of the concepts in LDAP are inherited from X.500. As a lightweight protocol, LDAP lacks several seldom-used features included in the X.500 protocol. However, some of these features are now being added to the protocol. As we said, LDAP is a work in progress.

Introduction

LDAP can be viewed as an implementation of four models. This is a useful approach because it allows us to view the LDAP protocol from four different points of view. The four models are:

1. Information model
2. Naming model
3. Functional model
4. Security model

The *information model* describes the basic units that LDAP uses to store information. Recall from the previous chapter that these basic units are called "entries," which map real-world objects to data structures in the directory. Every entry has a unique name and a unique

object identifier (OID) to be identified among all LDAP implementations. The information model describes what these entries look like.
You will see that the entries consist of entities called "attributes" and
that every one of these attributes is built from two pieces of information: an attribute name and one or more attribute values. The attribute
name, like the entry name, has to be unique and also has an object
identifier. It is also a good idea to register the OIDs with the Internet
Assigned Numbers Authority (IANA), which will guarantee compatibility with other implementations, for example, if you integrate a vendor-
supplied directory in your application. Furthermore, the information
model describes how searches execute comparisons between
attributes. This is needed to define matches during a search, to ascertain
whether an attribute is already present, and to sort attribute values.
The information model finds its implementation in the directory
schema, which consists of several configuration files that are loaded
at the start of the server process.

The *naming model* describes the structure of the directory. The
entries are accessed via an index called "distinguished name" (DN).
This distinguished name is constructed using a particular syntax that
we will discuss in this section. This particular syntax is used to construct
a treelike structure. Note that this method is not just used to be
syntactically "elegant," but has important performance implications. As
we have seen in Chapter 1, the entries are finally stored in a database.
Thus, the distinguished name is actually used to construct a tree. In
most implementations, the database uses the distinguished name to
construct index files that speed up information retrieval. Both the
indexing mechanism and the hierarchical tree increase the speed of
retrieving information in the directory.

The *functional model* defines the functions that LDAP offers to help
in accessing, maintaining, and managing the directory. There are
functions that make it possible to search, compare, add, modify, and
delete entries in the directory. Strictly speaking, LDAP does not offer
functions. Because LDAP is a message-oriented protocol, what LDAP
actually provides is a means of sending a server requests to search,
compare, add, modify, and delete entries in the directory on behalf
of a client. However, it is easier to refer to these as functions, so that
is what we will do. These requests, sent from the client to the server,
provide the basis for implementing functions or methods of accessing
LDAP directories using your preferred programming language. Nearly
every programming language has one or more "collections" of function
calls or methods. Chapter 6 provides more detail about the most
prominent application programming interfaces (API) available to the
programmer.

The *security model* describes two processes: authentication and
authorization. Authentication verifies the identity of the user before
granting access to the system. Authorization, also called "access control"

in LDAP literature, makes it possible to define the level of access for each user, thus controlling "who can do what with which data." Access control is normally stored in the form of access control lists (ACL), and the information that the ACLs provide for the server is called "access control information" (ACI). Authentication is defined in two RFCs (RFC 2829, "Authentication Methods for LDAP," and RFC 2830, "Lightweight Directory Access Protocol (v3): Extension for Transport Layer Security"). Access control is less standardized. At the time of this writing, the standards expressed in the RFCs offer only a recommendation describing what functionality the implementation should offer, but they do not describe any standards for implementing this functionality. The RFCs also do not define how and where the ACLs should be stored. However, this lack of standards does not mean that access control is not implemented. Any implementation has the means of providing the server with the ACI it needs to decide whether to allow or deny the client to perform the requested action. The downside is that every vendor uses its own mechanism to implement access control in its directory server. Thus access control information is stored in different ways in these different implementations, and there is no way to exchange information about access control between the different implementations.

With knowledge of these four models — combined with the protocol aspects of LDAP learned in Chapters 1 and 2 — we are finally ready to see how LDAP works. This is one of the longest chapters in this book. When you have finished it, you will have learned the most important information needed to understand LDAP.

Information Model

LDAP, the lightweight counterpart of the X.500 DAP, was first used as a front-end process to access X.500 via a gateway. Thus it is not surprising to learn that LDAP inherits one of the cornerstones of its architecture, the information model, from X.500. The information model contains many new concepts. Let us briefly review what you will encounter in this chapter.

You will learn that the information model is all about entries. These entries are made up of attributes, each attribute having an attribute type and one or more attribute values. The attribute type defines exactly the kind of values an attribute can hold, i.e., numbers, case-sensitive letters, case-insensitive letters, phone numbers, etc. This is achieved by the use of "syntax definitions." The attribute type also defines how the single attribute values are to be compared in the case of queries. This is achieved by the use of "matching rules."

Once we have a basic understanding, we can look at the details. It is possible to begin working with LDAP without a deep knowledge of the details, so if you are in a hurry to get to work, you can skip the details and come back later if you want to learn more. On the other hand, it is helpful to have a certain understanding of what is really going on. LDAP is defined in a number of RFCs. Unfortunately, the various implementations of this standard make their own extensions of these standards. Moreover, they often use their own syntax in configuration files or in the documentation delivered with the product. It is helpful to distinguish between what the standard requires and what the standard allows. Confronted with your particular implementation, you will find differences in the syntaxes used in the configuration file. This chapter will give you some help to understand the underlying concepts. Once you know what is going on "under the hood," you are less likely to be confused by the appearance of "strange names and numbers" in the configuration files of your LDAP product.

The following introductory section provides an overview of the whole picture to give you a rough understanding of the information model. In the later sections, we will look into the details. I hope that this approach keeps you from getting lost in details without understanding how the single pieces fit together.

Introduction

This introductory section gives a brief overview of the information model. The basic unit of information is the entry. We will see that the object class defines how an entry should look. Entries are made up of attributes, and just as entries are defined by object classes, so attributes are defined by the "attribute types." Everything is held together by the schema of the directory. Therefore we will now have a look at entries, objects, and object classes and see how these concepts are related. To make things easier, we will begin with an example.

The information model is centered on entries. To understand that better, let us have a look at a typical directory. Exhibit 1 shows you the content of a directory exported into an ASCII file. We use the directory that we created in Chapter 2, so you will be somewhat familiar with its content. Note that Exhibit 1 shows only a small part of the directory. The format of the ASCII file used here is called LDIF (LDAP data interchange format) and is standardized in RFC 2849, "The LDAP Data Interchange Format (LDIF) — Technical Specification." We have just seen the LDIF format in Chapter 2, and Chapter 4 examines LDIF in greater depth.

The excerpt of the directory shown in the exhibit can be broken down into smaller data structures. These data structures are the "entries" or objects that we will explore in this chapter. Exhibit 1 shows three different types of entries. The first type of entry describes the whole

---

Exhibit 1. Example of Entries

```
dn: o=ldap_abc.de
objectclass: top
objectclass: organization
o: ldap_abc.de
l: Munich

dn: ou=IT, o=ldap_abc.de
objectclass: top
objectclass: organizationalUnit
ou: IT
description: Information Technologies

dn: ou=HR, o=ldap_abc.de
objectclass: top
objectclass: organizationalUnit
ou: HR
description: Human Resources

dn: uid=RVoglmaier, ou=IT, o=ldap_abc.de
objectclass: top
objectclass: person
objectclass: organizationalPerson
objectclass: inetOrgPerson
ou: IT
cn: Reinhard Erich Voglmaier
cn: Reinhard E. Voglmaier
cn: Reinhard Voglmaier
sn: Voglmaier
givenName: Reinhard Erich
uid: RVoglmaier
mail: ReinhardVoglmaier@ldap_abc.de
mobile: (0049) 89 671 293

dn: uid=SParker, ou=HR, o=ldap_abc.de
objectclass: top
objectclass: person
objectclass: organizationalPerson
objectclass: inetOrgPerson
ou: HR
cn: Sarah Parker
sn: Parker
givenName: Sarah
uid: SParker
mail: SarahParker@ldap_abc.de
```

---

organization, the second a single organizational unit, and the third a single person.

Note that each of these entries begins with a field labeled "dn," an abbreviation of "distinguished name." This field identifies the entry unambiguously and has to be unique within the entire directory. Notice furthermore that each entry also contains information describing what it is or, more precisely, to which object class it belongs. This information is called "objectClass."

To summarize, we have three different types of objects, each representing a different object class:

1. The whole organization is identified by an "o":

```
o=ldap_abc.de
```

2. The individual departments, called "organizationalUnit," are abbreviated with "ou":

```
ou=IT,  o=ldap_abc.de
ou=HR,  o=ldap_abc.de
```

3. The entry for a single person, called "inetOrgPerson," is identified as follows:

```
uid=RVoglmaier, ou=IT, o=ldap_abc.de
uid=SParker,  ou=HR, o=ldap_abc.de
```

Each entry corresponds directly to an object in the real world, i.e., a person, a printer, a computer, an organization, etc.

Looking at Exhibit 1 again, note that each entry consists of several lines, with each line corresponding to one attribute. In other words, an entry is a collection of attributes. One of these attributes, the distinguished name (DN), we have already seen before. The distinguished name uniquely identifies the entry within the directory. We have also seen the attribute "objectClass." Note that the attribute "objectClass" is one of the attributes that can have more than one value.

Every attribute is made up of two pieces of information: the attribute name and one or more attribute values. Exhibit 2 shows how entries and attributes are related. Note that LDAP knows what entries can be inserted into the directory from its configuration files, which contain a number of class definitions and attribute-type definitions. The entries in the directory are instances of the classes defined in the configuration files, and the attributes building the entries are defined by the attribute types, such as the classes, fixed in the configuration files. Consider an object of the type "person." The entry for "person" contains such attributes as name, surname, phone number, etc. For example, there is an attribute with the name "surname" and the value "Voglmaier." For now, it is enough to understand that the directory contains a number of entries, each of them mapping real-world objects and consisting of a number of attributes.

If LDAP is to function as a well-behaved repository, it must have rules specifying how information is to be stored. The collection of these rules is called a "schema," and the schema information is kept in the configuration files. Using version 3 of the LDAP protocol, the client can explore the schema that the server is using. You may be familiar with the concept of a schema if you have experience working with a

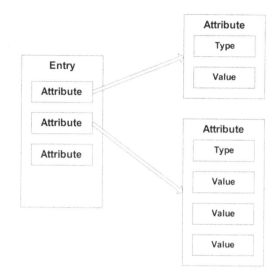

Exhibit 2. Relationship between Entries and Attributes

relational database management system (RDBMS). The schemas used by both systems are similar, but there are some important differences:

- LDAP software ships with a number of working schemas. The user selects a schema and begins filling in the data. With RDBMS software, the first thing the user has to do is define the schema. Until the schema is defined, the RDBMS software is useless.
- The LDAP schema is simpler and does not know anything about complicated structures such as "joins," nor are there any triggers, i.e., procedures to be executed when the data is inserted, deleted, or updated.

The schema in LDAP is defined in RFC 2252, "Lightweight Directory Access Protocol (v3): Attribute Syntax Definitions":

> The Schema is a collection of object class definitions and attribute type definitions and other information which a server uses to determine how to match a filter or attribute value assertion (in a "compare" operation) against the attributes of an entry, and whether to permit "add" and "modify" operations.

The schema therefore contains:

- Object-class definitions describing the different types of entries in the directory
- Attribute-type definitions describing the different attributes of the objects
- Syntax definitions to describe how the attribute values are to be compared during queries

At this point, you have an overview of the important aspects of the information model. You understand the concepts of entry and attribute, and you know that both of them are defined in configuration files in the form of object classes and attribute types. You know what a schema is and that a client can explore the contents of the schema. Now we will revisit all these preceding points in greater detail. We begin our journey through the information model with a section dedicated to the object classes.

Object Classes

A directory typically holds a large number of objects. The objects stored in the directory are called "entries." These entries in the directory correspond then to "real objects" in "the real world." Every entry in the directory is made up of a number of attributes, and each entry must have at least one attribute of the attribute type "objectClass."

If you write an application using an object-oriented language, the first thing you do is define classes. After that, you can define objects to implement the previously defined classes. The same thing holds in LDAP. Every directory is configured to recognize a number of classes, called "object classes." The objects in the directory (called "entries" in LDAP parlance) are implementations of these classes. In other words, the object class defines the nature of the entries in the directory. Every directory server implementation therefore needs a number of object-class definitions specifying the type of entries the directory can hold.

Let us revisit the previous example and look at Exhibit 1, which contains five entries. (Each entry begins with "dn:".) These five entries implement a total of three different object classes: the object class "organization," the object class "organizationalUnit," and the object class "inetOrgPerson." Therefore, we have:

■ One object or entry implementing the object class "organization":

```
o=ldap_abc.de
```

■ Two objects (entries) implementing the class "organizationalUnit":

```
ou=IT, o=ldap_abc.de
ou=HR, o=ldap_abc.de
```

■ Two objects (entries) implementing the class "inetOrgPerson":

```
uid=RVoglmaier, ou=IT, o=ldap_abc.de
uid=SParker, ou=HR, o=ldap_abc.de
```

You may be wondering why some entries (objects) have more than one value for the attribute "objectClass." New object classes can be constructed hierarchically by inheriting characteristics from an existing object class. For instance, the object class "organization" is derived from the "root" object class by inheritance. The root of all object classes, i.e., the object class from which all other object classes are inheriting, is the object class "top." Thus the object class "inetOrgPerson" derives from the previous object class "organizationalPerson," which inherits from the previous object class "person," which in turn inherits from the root object class "top." Given this hierarchical system of inheritance, we can see why most entries "belong" to more than one object class: Each entry belongs to a specific object class as well as the ladder of increasingly broader classes from which it was derived. The attribute "objectClass" describes all of the object classes to which the entry belongs.

The fact that an entry can belong to several object classes caused us to do some extra typing in Chapter 2, when we had to key in all of the object classes to which the object "person" belongs. In reality, these lines were just a shortcut for the list of characteristics of the single classes. In other words, instead of writing the characteristics of each object class, write only the object class. We will learn more about object-class inheritance later on. For the moment, it is enough to understand why the attribute "objectClass" has more than one value.

Some attributes in an entry are required, while other attributes are optional. Attributes that are neither required nor optional are not allowed at all. Thus every objectClass declaration contains a list of optional attributes and a list of required attributes for that specific object. Again, the reason for the multivalued attribute "objectClass" becomes clear. If an entry has more than one objectClass value, the entry must contain the union of all required attributes and may contain the union of all optional attributes of the object classes it implements.

The root object class "top" is the ancestor of all object classes and contains the required attribute "objectClass." Since all entries inherit directly or indirectly from the root "top," every object class MUST contain the attribute "objectClass." However, as we will learn later, the root object class cannot be used directly.

An example makes this clear. The object with the distinguished name "o = ldap_abc.de" implements the object class organization. Exhibit 1 shows that the attribute "objectClass" of this entry has the two values: "top" and "organization." Now look at Exhibit 3, which contains the object class definitions of "top" and "organization." The definition shows which attribute are required (MUST) and which attributes are optional (MAY). We see that "top" must only contain the attribute "objectClass." "Organization," on the other hand, inherits all attributes from top and must also contain o (organization). This means that the entry must contain the attributes "objectClass" and o (organization). We further note that "top" does not have any optional attributes. In contrast, "organization" has many optional attributes: userPassword,

---

Exhibit 3. Object-Class Definition for top and organizationalUnit

Objectclass top:

```
(2.5.6.0
 NAME 'top'
 ABSTRACT
 MUST (
 objectClass
 )
)
```

Objectclass organization:

```
(2.5.6.4
 NAME 'organization'
 SUP top
 STRUCTURAL
 MUST (
 o
 MAY (
 userPassword
 searchGuide
 seeAlso
 businessCategory
 x121Address
 registeredAddress
 destinationIndicator
 preferredDeliveryMethod
 telexNumber
 teletexTerminalIdentifier
 telephoneNumber
 internationaliSDNNumber
 facsimileTelephoneNumber
 street
 postOfficeBox
 postalCode
 postalAddress
 physicalDeliveryOfficeName
 st
 l
 description
 )
)
```

---

searchGuide, seeAlso, businessCategory, x121Address, registeredAddress, destinationIndicator, preferredDeliveryMethod, telexNumber, teletexTerminalIdentifier, telephoneNumber, internationaliSDNNumber, facsimileTelephoneNumber, street, postOfficeBox, postalCode, postalAddress, physicalDeliveryOfficeName, st, l, and description.

In this section we have learned what an object class looks like and that new object classes can be obtained from existing ones through inheritance.

Formal Definition of Object Classes

Before looking at further examples, let us see how object classes can be defined formally. This is not the only way you will find object classes defined, but this is the form you will find in most RFCs. Once you have seen this type of object-class definition, you will understand other syntaxes as well.

Exhibit 4 shows such an object-class description drawn from RFC 2252, "LADP (v3) Attributes." The syntax used in this RFC is Backus Naur form (BNF), used also in the construction of compilers, where it provides the formal description of the syntax of the language understood by the compiler. Following are some lines explaining the example cited in Exhibit 4.

- *whsp*: White space
- *numericoid*: Numeric object identifier (OID)
- *oid*: Either a numericoid or a human-readable description
- *qdescr*: A quoted description
- *qdstring*: A quoted-string UTF8-encoded string
- Strings included in round parentheses "()" are to be typed as they are. For example, "(" means that an object-class definition begins with a parenthesis.
- Strings surrounded with square brackets are optional. For example, the line ["NAME" qdescrs] means: NAME "inetOrgPerson."
- A semicolon ";" indicates that the line is a comment.

With this information at hand, let us look at the previous syntax of an object-class definition. It tells us that every description of an object class must contain first the numeric object identification of this object class. We will return to this object identification after a few examples of object-class descriptions. The remaining data — included in square brackets — is optional. Each of these lines is in the form of

---

Exhibit 4. Object-Class Description from RFC 2252

```
ObjectClassDescription = "(" whsp
 numericoid whsp ; ObjectClass identifier
 [ "NAME" qdescrs ]
 [ "DESC" qdstring ]
 [ "OBSOLETE" whsp ]
 [ "SUP" oids ] ; Superior ObjectClasses
 [ ("ABSTRACT"/"STRUCTURAL"/"AUXILIARY") whsp ]
 ; default structural
 [ "MUST" oids ] ; AttributeTypes
 [ "MAY" oids ] ; AttributeTypes
 whsp ")"
```

a keyword in capitals enclosed within quotation marks and an optional value. The allowed keywords are defined as follows:

- "NAME" is simply the name of the object.
- "DESC" is a human-readable description of the object.
- "OBSOLETE" does not need a value. It indicates that this object should not be used any more and exists only for compatibility with older implementations.
- "SUP" contains the OID of the object superclass. Here we see the reason for the existence of both "oid" and "numericoid." "Numericoid" is an OID consisting of only numbers, but the OID can also contain the description defined with the keyword "DESC," thus making it understandable to a human reader.
- "ABSTRACT"/"STRUCTURAL"/"AUXILIARY" are the three possible values used to specify the type of the object class. Every object can be one of these three types. In BNF the "/" means "or," so in this case it means one of these three keywords. You will learn more about these object types later, after the examples.
- "MUST" defines one or more attributes that an object of this class is required to contain.
- "MAY" defines the attributes that an object of this class may contain.

Some Words about Object-Class Inheritance

Before we get to the examples, we have a few more words about object classes and inheritance. As the object-oriented paradigm states, you do not have to reinvent the wheel every time you define a new object type. Instead, you can inherit from an existing object. In LDAP, this is achieved by inheriting from object classes.

As we have seen earlier, the fact that one object class inherits from another is expressed in LDIF format using the "objectClass" attribute. You see it furthermore for the attribute objectClass using the command-line tools when you have to type in several lines when you add new entries into the directory. However, the knowledge of inheritance should simply be defined in the directory schema or, better yet, in the standard definition of the object classes. Indeed, looking back to the previous section, you will notice the keyword "SUP" in the object-class definition.

The keyword "SUP" indicates the superclass from which the actual class is inheriting. This new class inherits all of its attributes from its ancestor. Therefore, the new class must contain all of the required attributes of the superclass plus the additional required attributes that define the new class. In addition, it may also contain all the optional attributes from its superclass along with any optional attributes defined in the new class. Attributes that are not defined in the superclass or in the actual class are not allowed at all.

All object classes have one common origin, the object class "top." It is also possible to subclass again an object class that is derived from another object class. A good example is the object class "inetOrgPerson," which is derived from the object class "organizationalPerson," which in turn is derived from "person," which, at last, has the parent "top."

Some Examples of Object-Class Definitions

To gain a better understanding of the concept of inheritance with object classes, take a look at Exhibit 5 through Exhibit 8, which show examples of object-class definitions for the object class "inetOrgPerson" that we encountered in Exhibit 1. This also illustrates the concept of multiple inheritance.

The object class "top" in Exhibit 5 is one of the simplest object classes. As mentioned previously, all object classes derive from the object class "top." The only purpose for the object class "top" is to ensure that every object contains the "objectClass" attribute, since it is the only required attribute in the object class "top." It exists only to be subclassed, as indicated by "ABSTRACT" in Exhibit 5. An object class not intended to be instantiated is called an "abstract object class." This means that you will not find an entry for object class "top" in the directory. The object class "top" holds only one (the only and required) attribute, the attribute "objectClass." Because every object class inherits from "top," every object class must contain the attribute "objectClass."

Exhibit 6 shows the objectClass "person," which derives from "top." Besides the attribute "objectClass" inherited from "top," every "person" entry also must have the attributes "sn" and "cn." The line with "SUP top" expresses that the object class "top" is its ancestor. We also could use the numeric OID here, so we could say as well:

```
SUP '2.5.6.0'
```

Exhibit 5. Example of Object-Class Definition, objectClass Top

```
(2.5.6.0
  NAME 'top'
  ABSTRACT
  MUST (
   objectClass
  )
)
```

Exhibit 6. Example of Object-Class Definition, objectClass Person

```
(2.5.6.6
  NAME 'person'
  SUP top
  STRUCTURAL
  MUST (
   sn $ cn
  )
  MAY (
    userPassword $ telephonNumber $ seeAlso $ description
  )
)
```

The only difference is that an alphabetic OID is more easily understood by a human user. Note that the attributes "userPassword," "telephone-Number," "seeAlso," and "description" are optional.

Exhibit 7 shows the object class "organizationalPerson," which is derived from, and is a specialization of, the object class "person." The organizationalPerson object class has a number of attributes useful for implementing an employee object, such as fax number, organizational unit, and so on. This means that, in addition to the optional attributes "userPassword," "telephoneNumber," "seeAlso," and "description" defined in the object class "person," the organizationalPerson object can also contain a title or any of the added properties indicated by the keyword "MAY." Note that no new required attributes are added, although the organizationalPerson still needs to contain the inherited required attributes "objectClass," "sn," and "cn."

The last item in the inheritance chain is the "inetOrgPerson" object class (see Exhibit 8), important enough to be defined in a separate RFC (RFC 2798, "Definition of the inetOrgPerson LDAP Object Class"). This class was intended to accommodate information about a person in a typical Internet/Intranet environment. Indeed, attributes like mail, userSMIMECertificate, and jpegPhoto have been added, as were other useful attributes like businessCategory or roomNumber which were still missing from "organizationalPerson."

Object-Class Types

As mentioned previously, there are three types of object classes:

1. Abstract
2. Structural
3. Auxiliary

An object in LDAP is a representation of a real-world object in the directory. Real-world objects can be classified using a set of common properties. In LDAP parlance, you would say that the classification is

---

Exhibit 7. Example of Object-Class Definition, Object Class "organizationalPerson"

```
(2.5.6.7
 NAME 'organizationalPerson'
 SUP person
 STRUCTURAL
 MAY (
   title $ x121Address $ registeredAddress
$destination Indicator $
   preferredDeliveryMethod $ telexNumber $
teletexTerminal Identifier
$   telephoneNumber $ internationaliSDNNumber $
   facsimileTelephoneNumber $ street $ postOfficeBox $
   postalCode $
   postalAddress $ physicalDeliveryOfficeName $ ou $ st $ l
 )
)
```

Exhibit 8. Example of Object-Class Definition, objectClass InetOrgPerson

```
(2.16.840.1.113730.3.2.2
 NAME ' inetOrgPerson '
 SUP organizationalPerson
 STRUCTURAL
 MAY (
   audio $ businessCategory $ carLicense $ departmentNumber $
   displayName $ employeeNumber $ employeeType $ givenName $
   homePhone $ homePostalAddress $ initials $ jpegPhoto $
   labeledURI $ mail $ manager $ mobile $ o $ pager $
   photo $ roomNumber $ secretary $ uid $ userCertificate $
   x500uniqueIdentifier $ preferredLanguage $
   userSMIMECertificate $ userPKCS12
 )
)
```

---

based on a common set of attributes. Classification in LDAP leads, via subclassing, to a certain object hierarchy.

The upper level of this hierarchy is built by classes of the type "abstract." Classes from the object class "abstract" are not intended to be actually implemented. An example is the "top" class. There is no entry implementing the object class "top," but it is from this class that all other classes are derived. The "top" class exists to ensure that all classes derived from it contain the attribute "objectClass." Consequently, there is no need to use an object of this class.

Objects whose object class is of the type "structural" can be stored in the directory. Examples of this type are person, organizationalPerson, and inetOrgPerson. Some server implementations use structural classes to define where in the directory information tree a certain object can be stored.

We could just be happy with these two object types, so what is the third one for? This is for situations when you need a new object class extending from an existing one. Unfortunately, new data such as this does not fit very well in the object structure. To get around this problem, you can define all the data the new object needs to hold together in an auxiliary class. An object of type "auxiliary" can be attached anywhere in the directory information tree.

An example of an object of the type "auxiliary" is the extensible-Object that can hold any number of attributes defined in the schema. Another example is the subschema object, which holds the schema for the directory server, i.e., object-class definitions, attribute-type definitions, matching rules, etc.

A further example of an auxiliary object class is the "dcObject" class. The abbreviation stands for "domain component object." It is used to describe objects having DN being similar to DNS like domain names. The object class "dcObject" has the attribute "dc," which stands for "domain component." More about this in the section called "Directory Suffix," which appears later in the chapter. This dcObject class can be used to implement an organization object with the DN: dc=LdapAbc,dc=org.

You cannot use the object class "o," because this objectClass does not allow the attribute "dc." The object class "dcObject," on the other hand, does not allow the attribute "o" or "description." The solution is to mix the two; the auxiliary object class allows this mixing. You can, therefore, obtain the following entry:

```
DN: dc=LdapAbc,dc=org
objectclass: top
objectclass: dcObject
objectclass: o
dc: LdapAbc
dc: org
o: Abc's of LDAP
description: Organization promoting usage of LDAP
1: Munich
```

Object Identifiers

Object identifiers (OIDs) are not only used for object classes, but also for attribute types. The concept of OID is another important concept imported into LDAP from the X.500 standard. The OID standard is not limited only to object classes and attribute types. It can be used to identify uniquely any type of object. It is not only used for LDAP and X.500, but also for other protocols such as SNMP (Simple Network Management Protocol), just to mention one frequent "user."

An OID is syntactically a string of numbers divided by dots, such as the OID 2.5.6.6 for the object class "person" (see Exhibit 6) or 2.16.840.1.113730.3.2.2 for the object class "inetOrgPerson" (see Exhibit 8). The namespace of all OIDs implements an OID tree. A subtree in the OID tree is called an "arc." This concept greatly simplifies the administration of the OID tree, inasmuch as it allows one to delegate administration of the subtrees or arcs.

You can get your own OID subtree from IANA (Internet Assigned Numbers Authority). Their Web site (http://www.iana.org) provides further information. The particular syntax makes it possible to understand where a certain object comes from. All you have to do is trace the route from the object to the root of the tree to understand the object's origin. For example, all attributes and objects defined by the IETF begin with 2.5.4, e.g., 2.5.4.0 for the attribute "object-Class."

You will need an OID subtree whenever you need to extend the directory schema. You can, of course, invent your own OIDs. However, you will run into trouble if you have to exchange information with systems that have reserved this OID for another purpose. So if you extend your schema, it is wise to ask for an OID and to construct your own hierarchy based on this OID. Remember to keep a list for what OID is used for which object to avoid name collisions.

A good introduction and much more information can be obtained from the Web site of Harald Alvestrand at http://www.alvestrand.no/objectid. From this site, you can also navigate in the OID tree.

Attribute-Type Definitions

Just as there are standard object classes known by all LDAP servers, there are also standard attributes for the classes. Some of these attributes we have already seen, for example the attribute called "objectClass." Every entry in the directory has two or more attributes (one of these being the attribute "objectClass"). Every attribute has an attribute name and one or more attribute values. Now we will look somewhat closer at the attribute types.

The attribute types all LDAP servers should implement are described in RFC 2252, "Lightweight Directory Access Protocol: Attribute Syntax Definitions." Before proceeding any further, see Exhibit 9 — showing a couple of attributes — to get an idea of what an attribute definition looks like. As you might surmise, attribute types can also inherit from each other. That happens, for example, with sn and c, which both derive their definition from the attribute type "name."

Exhibit 9. Examples of Attribute Definitions from RFC 2256

```
(2.5.4.41 NAME 'name' EQUALITY caseIgnoreMatch
  SUBSTR caseIgnoreSubstringsMatch
  SYNTAX 1.3.6.1.4.1.1466.115.121.1.15{32768})

(2.5.4.4 NAME 'sn' SUP name)

(2.5.4.6 NAME 'c' SUP name SINGLE-VALUE)
```

Formal Definition of Attributes

Like object classes, attribute types also can be defined formally. Exhibit 10 gives the complete definition as found in RFC 2252. The syntax used in this RFC is Backus Naur form (BNF), used for the formal description of syntaxes. What we need to know is that values included in square brackets, like ["SUP" woid], are optional; values between quotation marks are to be typed literally, for example the keyword "SUP" or the parenthesis "(" after the assignment operator. The quote-enclosed slash "/" means "or" and indicates alternative possibilities.

The attribute-type description is nearly self-explanatory, but we will take a closer look at it to resolve any potential doubts. Like the object-class description, the attribute-type description comprises the numeric object identification (OID) of this attribute type. You can learn more about the OID in the section on object classes presented earlier in this chapter. The rest of the data is optional, as indicated by the square brackets. The data is in the form of (1) a keyword in capitals enclosed within quotation marks and (2) an optional value. The allowed keywords are as follows:

Exhibit 10. Attribute-Type Description from RFC 2252

```
AttributeTypeDescription="(" whsp
  numericoid whsp                      ; AttributeType identifier
  [ "NAME" qdescrs ]                   ; name used in AttributeType
  [ "DESC" qdstring ]                  ; description
  [ "OBSOLETE" whsp ]
  [ "SUP" woid ]                       ; derived from this other
                                       ; AttributeType
  [ "EQUALITY" woid ]                  ; Matching Rule name
  [ "ORDERING" woid ]                  ; Matching Rule name
  [ "SUBSTR" woid ]                    ; Matching Rule name
  [ "SYNTAX" whsp noidlen whsp ] ;     see section 4.3
  [ "SINGLE-VALUE" whsp ]              ; default multi-valued
  [ "COLLECTIVE" whsp ]                ; default not collective
  [ "NO-USER-MODIFICATION" whsp ] ;    default user modifiable
  [ "USAGE" whsp AttributeUsage ] ;    default userApplications
  whsp ")"
```

- "NAME" is simply the name of the object.
- "DESC" is a human-readable description of the attribute.
- "OBSOLETE" does not need a value. It indicates that this object should not be used anymore and exists only for compatibility with older implementations.
- "SUP" contains the OID of the attribute from which this attribute is derived. The term "woid" indicates an OID surrounded by two white spaces. Remember that an OID can be the numericoid or a human-readable description.
- "EQUALITY" defines a matching rule to test equality. A later section in this chapter provides more information about matching rules.
- "ORDERING" defines a matching rule for ordering purposes, i.e., fewer or more operators. Matching rules are discussed later in this chapter.
- "SUBSTR" specifies that a query evaluates as true only if it matches a given substring. The matching requirements follow as a parameter. Matching rules are discussed later in this chapter.
- "SYNTAX" explains what type of data you can put into this attribute. The "noidlen" term specifies the maximum length of the attribute. Syntax is discussed later in this chapter.
- "SINGLE-VALUE" is a flag indicating that this attribute can have only a single value.
- "COLLECTIVE" is a flag indicating that this is a collective attribute. Collective attributes are inherited from X.500 and are stored not directly in this entry, but in a special entry called "subentry." An example of a collective attribute could be a fax number common to an entire group of entries.
- "NO-USER-MODIFICATION" is a flag indicating that the user cannot modify the entry.
- "USAGE" defines the use of this attribute. Exhibit 11 lists the possible uses.˙ This is discussed at greater length in the following "Attribute Types" section.

Attribute Types

There are two substantially different types of attributes: user attributes and operational attributes.

1. User attributes are modifiable by the user if the server is configured to allows this action.
2. Operational attributes apply to the server and are not modifiable by the user. We will see later that there are three different types of operational attributes.

˙ The DSA in Exhibit 11 means "directory server agent." It is a synonym for the directory server process, another word inherited from the X.500 standard.

Examples of operational attributes are the attribute "modifyTimeStamp," indicating the time the entry was last modified, or the attribute "modifierName," which identifies the user who modified the entry. Examples of user attributes are "cn" for Common Name (full name of a person) and "sn" for Surname.

The attribute type is defined within the "usage" parameter. Per default, the attribute type is set to "User Attribute," as expressed by the line

```
"USAGE" userApplications
```

inside the attribute-type description. You will seldom see this statement, even though it is the default value.

As seen in Exhibit 11, there are four possible values for the usage parameter: one for user attribute and three operational attributes:

- *userApplications*: A user attribute
- *directoryOperations*: An operational attribute relative to directory entries
- *distributedOperations*: An operational attribute relative to other directories
- *dsAOperations*: An operational attribute relative to the DSA

The "normal" or default attributes are of the type "userApplications." Two examples are:

- *cn*: Common name or full name of a person
- *sn*: Surname of a person

The operational attribute "directoryOperations" is the first of the three operational-attribute types to be used to maintain a kind of metadata. Examples include:

- modifyTimeStamp
- modifiersName

Exhibit 12 shows examples of the operational attributes "distributedOperations" and "dsaOperations."

Exhibit 11. Attribute Usage from RFC 2252

```
AttributeUsage=
  "userApplications"      /
  "directoryOperation"    /
  "distributedOperation"  / ; DSA-shared
  "dSAOperation"            ; DSA-specific, value depends on server
```

Exhibit 12. Examples of Most Frequently Used Attributes of Type "distributedOperations" and "dsaOperations"

distributedOperations: These attributes are used to maintain information of data distribution among several servers. Examples are:

- *ref*: also known as "named referral," is an attribute of the object class "referral" that is used to point the server to an entry that contains the requested information
- *sharedRef*: general information that can be shared among several servers in the global LDAP naming domain

dsaOperations: These attributes contain DSA (directory service agent) information about the directory. DSA is a simple synonym for the process or processes used to maintain the directory. Examples are:

- *supportedLDAPVersion*: gives information about the LDAP versions supported by this server, only available in LDAP (v3).
- *namingContexts*: identifies partitions of the directory held in a server, only available in LDAP (v3).
- *createTimeStamp*: time the entry was added
- *modifyTimeStamp*: time the entry was modified
- *creatorsName*: dn of user who added the entry
- *modifiersName*: dn of user who modified the entry
- *subschemaSubentry*: dn of subschema entry for this entry. For a complete description, see RFC 2252, "Lightweight Directory Access Protocol (v3): Attribute Syntax Definitions."
- dITStructureRules
- dITContentRules
- matchingRules
- attributeTypes
- objectClasses
- nameForms
- matchingRuleUse

Matching Rules

The entries in a directory can have a large numer of attributes. These attributes can be written in different forms.

There are attributes where lowercase or uppercase letters do not matter. Examples are the Distinguished Name, the description, the street, etc. There are also particular attributes, such as telephone number, that you can write in completely different ways; for example +49 200 300 903 can also be written as (0049) 0200 300 903.

In case of queries, you need to make comparisons in order to find from all entries the one you are interested in. Comparisons are not only necessary in query operations, but also in "delete," "update," and "add" operations.

You should also tell your directory server how to make comparisons between atribute values. You do this in the form of so-called "matching rules."

As an example, look at the telephone number attribute mentioned above. The two versions of the same telephone number should be considered equal by the server and therefore the matching rule should specify the following:

- ignore extra white spaces
- ignore hyphens ("-")
- ignore opening and closing parenthesis

The matching rules are defined by standard and everyone has a name and an OID. The rule describing the matching of telephone nubmers for example is called "telephoneNumberMatch" and has the OID 2.5.13.20.

As defined in RFC 2252, "Lightweight Directory Access Protocol (v3): Attribute Syntax Definitions," you can define three different matching behaviors:

- "EQUALITY" defines the matching rule for equality filters.
- "ORDERING" describes actions such as "less than" or "greater than" on attributes.
- "SUBSTRING" defines the matching rules that decide when the matching of the substring is sufficient.

Matching rules are defined in RFC 2252, and every matching rule has its own OID, as do object classes and attribute types. The method of obtaining a new OID for a matching rule is exactly the same as for every type of object, such as object classes or attribute types, and is described in the previous section about OIDs. Exhibit 13 shows the most frequently used matching rules. With their OIDs and the syntax of the attributes, the matching rule works on. The syntax is listed in the form of its OID. More about syntaxes in the following section. For a complete description of matching rules and the complete list of OIDs, refer to RFC 2252. The names of the matching rules are self-descriptive.

In theory, you could define your own matching rules, but this option is interesting only if you are writing your own implementation of a directory server, since you have to develop the code executing the matching algorithms.

Exhibit 13. Examples of Most Frequently Used Attributes Matching Rules

OID	Name	Syntax
2.5.13.1	distinguishedNameMatch	1.3.6.1.4.1.1466.115.12 1.1.12
2.5.13.2	caseIgnoreMatch	1.3.6.1.4.1.1466.115.12 1.1.15
2.5.13.8	numericStringMatch	1.3.6.1.4.1.1466.115.12 1.1.36
2.5.13.11	caseIgnoreListMatch	1.3.6.1.4.1.1466.115.12 1.1.41
2.5.13.14	integerMatch	1.3.6.1.4.1.1466.115.12 1.1.27
2.5.13.16	bitStringMatch	1.3.6.1.4.1.1466.115.12 1.1.6
2.5.13.20	telephoneNumberMatch	1.3.6.1.4.1.1466.115.12 1.1.50
2.5.13.22	presentationAddressMatch	1.3.6.1.4.1.1466.115.12 1.1.43
2.5.13.23	uniqueMemberMatch	1.3.6.1.4.1.1466.115.12 1.1.34
2.5.13.24	protocolInformationMatch	1.3.6.1.4.1.1466.115.12 1.1.42
2.5.13.27	generalizedTimeMatch	1.3.6.1.4.1.1466.115.12 1.1.24
1.3.6.1.4.1.1466.109. 114.1	caseExactIA5Match	1.3.6.1.4.1.1466.115.12 1.1.26
1.3.6.1.4.1.1466.109. 114.2	caseIgnoreIA5Match	1.3.6.1.4.1.1466.115.12 1.1.26
2.5.13.28	generalizedTimeOrdering Match	1.3.6.1.4.1.1466.115.12 1.1.24
2.5.13.3	caseIgnoreOrderingMatch	1.3.6.1.4.1.1466.115.12 1.1.15

Syntaxes

The last point we have to address are the syntaxes, which are simply a formal description of what values an entry can hold. Like the matching rules, which were covered in the previous section, syntaxes can be extended to fit your particular needs. This means that you can define your own syntaxes. However, this also means that you have to rewrite pieces of the code of your directory server to define the new syntaxes. This topic is interesting, but it is beyond the scope of this book. You can learn more about this subject on the Web site of the open-source project OpenLDAP and the connected discussion groups at http://www.openldap.org.

Syntaxes are defined in RFC 2252. The concept is inherited from the original X.500 protocol. We have just seen that matching rules, object classes, and attribute types are identified by a unique OID. The same holds true for syntaxes. You will find many shorthand names for the syntax in various LDAP implementations and in the literature. Exhibit 14 shows the most frequently used syntaxes with their shorthand names and OIDs.

Exhibit 15 shows some of the syntax definitions as defined in RFC 2252. It shows the same syntaxes as Exhibit 14. In the first column, you see the syntax name; in the second, you see if the information of the corresponding attribute is "Human Readable"; and in the last column, you see its unique OID. Note that not all vendors of LDAP implementations or authors of LDAP documentation divide the concepts of syntax and matching rule as we did here. When we discuss

Exhibit 14. The Most Frequently Used Syntaxes with Their Shorthand Names

OID	Shorthand	Description
1.3.6.1.4.1.1466.115.121.1.5	bin	binary value
1.3.6.1.4.1.1466.115.121.1.12	dn	distinguished name
1.3.6.1.4.1.1466.115.121.1.15	cis	case insensitive string
1.3.6.1.4.1.1466.115.121.1.26	ces	case sensitive string
1.3.6.1.4.1.1466.115.121.1.27	int	integer
1.3.6.1.4.1.1466.115.121.1.50	tel	telephone number

Exhibit 15. Example of Syntaxes from RFC 2252

Value Being Represented	Human Readable	Syntax
ACI item	Y	1.3.6.1.4.1.1466.115.121.1.1
Access point	Y	1.3.6.1.4.1.1466.115.121.1.2
Attribute type description	Y	1.3.6.1.4.1.1466.115.121.1.3
Audio	N	1.3.6.1.4.1.1466.115.121.1.4
Binary	N	1.3.6.1.4.1.1466.115.121.1.5
Bit string	Y	1.3.6.1.4.1.1466.115.121.1.6
Boolean	Y	1.3.6.1.4.1.1466.115.121.1.7
Certificate	N	1.3.6.1.4.1.1466.115.121.1.8
Certificate list	N	1.3.6.1.4.1.1466.115.121.1.9
Certificate pair	N	1.3.6.1.4.1.1466.115.121.1.10
Country string	Y	1.3.6.1.4.1.1466.115.121.1.11
DN	Y	1.3.6.1.4.1.1466.115.121.1.12

syntax, we mean a description of the values the attributes can hold (syntax) plus a description of how comparisons have to be executed (matching rule).

Conclusion for Information Model

The information model is a cornerstone of the Lightweight Directory Access Protocol, much of it inherited from its predecessor, X.500. In contrast to X.500, LDAP tends to use short mnemonic names for object classes and attribute types.

The directory holds a great number of entries, and each entry consists of attributes. In turn, each attribute has an attribute type and an attribute value. Both object classes and attribute types are identified uniquely by a string of integers and dots called an "object identifier" (OID). The attribute types are defined by (1) a syntax describing the values that the attribute can hold and (2) the matching rules governing how comparisons in operations are made. Every directory server holds a schema containing all relevant object classes and attribute types.

A warning regarding the notations used for object classes and attribute types: In this chapter we used the same notation used in the RFCs. An LDAP implementation can use other notations. We will learn more about them in Chapter 4, where we will also speak about the naming model, which explains how to assemble the various entries into a directory information tree.

Naming Model

In the previous section, we learned that the information model provides the basic elements to construct the directory. The naming model describes how these basic elements fit together to build up the directory. As in the information model, the LDAP naming model comprises several concepts imported from the original X.500 standard.

The naming model

- Describes how the data structures are built using the basic elements, i.e., entries and object classes.
- Makes it possible to refer unambiguously to the single entries it holds.

The naming model consists of only a few concepts. One of these concepts is the directory information tree (DIT), a treelike structure defining the namespace where the entries reside. We will have a look at the different naming models that can be used to form the DIT.

Further, we will see that the distinguished name (DN) is used as an index to access the single entries in the directory. The distinguished name is not new to us. We were introduced to it in Chapter 2 when we played around with LDAP, and we encountered it again in the previous section when we discussed attributes. We will learn more about it here. We will see how to construct the DN from the relative distinguished name (RDN) and learn the relative rules. At the end we will have a brief look at the syntax used to build the distinguished name. But first we will have a closer look at the directory information tree.

The Directory Information Tree

The directory information tree (DIT) is the most important concept of the naming model.* The DIT is helpful in organizing your data and thus makes it easier to reference the data later on. It defines the structure of the directory that you build up from the single entries. Exhibit 16 shows an example of a DIT based on the example we used in our guided tour through LDAP in Chapter 2. The enterprise (o = ldap_abc.de) has a number of organizational units (ou) that hold a number of people, identified here by their user identifiers (uid). The two organizational units "Research" and "IT" have triangles under them simply to avoid repeating the "user" items of the first two organizational units. However, the triangles could also represent a further extension of the hierarchy beneath the organizational units, perhaps even located on another directory. We will learn more about this subject later, when we speak about referrals. This is only one example of a DIT; the tree could be much simpler than the one shown or much more complicated.

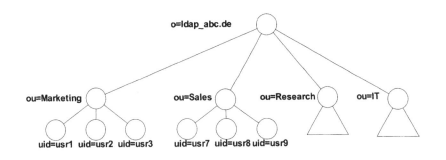

Exhibit 16. Example of a Directory Information Tree

---

* All the entries in the directory are organized in a tree-like structure. This structure is called DIT. The root of the DIT is also called "directory suffix." More about the directory suffix in a later section.

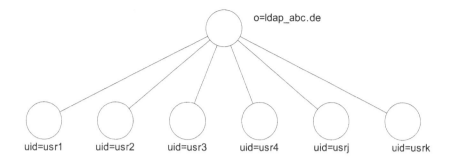

Exhibit 17. Example of a Flat Directory Information Tree

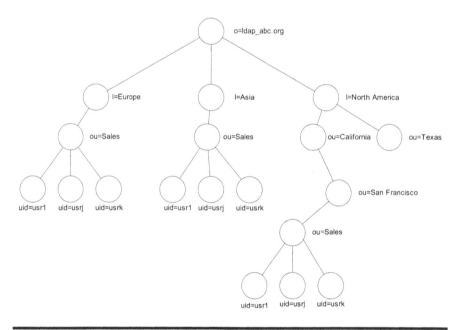

Exhibit 18. Example of a More-Complicated Directory Information Tree

Exhibit 17 shows an example of a much simpler, completely flat tree. Exhibit 18 shows part of a more complicated hierarchic tree. All of these examples are completely legitimate.

The layout of the directory information tree depends on a number of requirements and constraints. People normally use organizational or geographical criteria to build up the DIT, but administrative aspects could also determine the branching policy. We will learn more about this in Chapter 9, "Design of Directory Services."

LDAP provides a great deal of flexibility in the tree design, but that does not mean that everything is possible. The directory always has to be a treelike structure, i.e., every entry above the directory root has to have one ancestor. You cannot insert an entry that has no parent

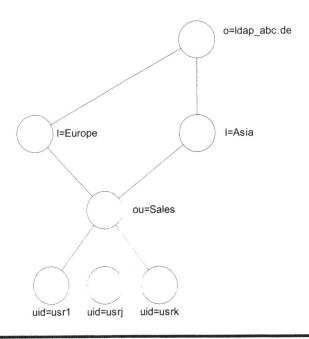

Exhibit 19. Example of a Not-Allowed Directory Structure

entry. It is not possible to construct a structure with one entry having two different ancestors as shown in Exhibit 19. This has consequences when you import a whole directory or if you add more entries. Assume you want to add a new department with new department members. Further, assume that you want to add the legal department, but instead of first adding the new department, you try to add the persons of the department first:

```
DN: uid=user312, ou=Legal Department, o=LdapAbc.de
```

The LDAP server would refuse to add this entry until you first add the parent entry:

```
DN: ou=Legal Department, o=LdapAbc.de
```

The same thing can happen when you move an entry inside the tree. Consider the example in Exhibit 18, where there is a sales department in San Francisco. Let us assume you want to have one sales department for North America instead of having one sales department in every town. As we will see later in this chapter when we discuss the functional model, there is a function renaming the relative distinguished name (RDN). Now let us assume you would like to rename the sales department in San Francisco

```
DN: ou=sales, ou=San Francisco, ou=California, l=North America
```

by assigning a new RDN:

```
RDN: ou=sales, l=North America
```

What happens? This would not be possible, since now all the children of the entry with the distinguished name — DN: ou = sales, ou = San Francisco, ou = California, ou = North America — would remain without a parent, which is not allowed.

Nor could you first rename the single children of the sales entry

```
RDN: uid=usrj, ou=sales, ou=San Francisco, ou=California, l=North
America
```

by assigning a new RDN:

```
RDN: uid=usrj, ou=sales, l=North America
```

Such situations are not infrequent, since reorganizations can occur in every organization for any number of reasons. The modification in the directory tree can also be much more complicated. For example, you might think it should be easy to rename the entire branch from

```
RDN: l=North America
```

to

```
RDN: l=US
```

Logically you may think that you are not really moving anything, only changing the name of one entry in the tree. However, you are actually moving the whole subtree, and every element has to be renamed from l = North America to l = US, i.e., from

```
RDN: uid=usrj, ou=sales, ou=San Francisco, ou=California, l=North
America
```

to

```
RDN: uid=usrj, ou=sales, ou=San Francisco, ou=California, l=US
```

What is missing now is a solution to this problem. There is, as usual, more than one way to do this. You could first create a new entry with RDN:

```
RDN: l=US
```

and then copy the entries under l = US, then copy the entries under those entries, and so on until you have copied the whole subtree without the leaves. At the end, you will rename the leaves. After you have created the whole subtree, you can cancel the old one.

Another solution would simply be to export the whole directory in LDIF, modify the RDN, i.e., modify every occurrence of l = North America to l = US, and reload the LDIF again. However, this requires the directory server to be stopped and restarted, since you have to delete the old directory before reloading the new LDIF file.

The third solution to this problem could be to avoid moving the entries around the directory by creating an alias instead. We will speak about aliases later on in this chapter. For now, it is enough to know that an alias is somewhat similar to a symbolic link in the UNIX operating system. The alias resides in the directory tree not as an entry but simply as a pointer to the location of the entry.

Distinguished Name

The concept of the distinguished name is the heart of the naming model. Each entry has an attribute called "distinguished name" (DN). This attribute is used to identify the entry unambiguously. From this, it is clear that the DN must be unique throughout the whole directory. The construction of the DN is used to construct the namespace and the directory information tree.

The distinguished name is a comma-separated list of subunits called "relative distinguished names." You obtain the distinguished name in postfixing the relative distinguished name (RDN) with the distinguished name of its ancestor.

Like the DN, the RDN has to be unique. However, the RDN has to be unique only in its scope. For example, if the parent is

```
DN: ou=sales, l=Europe, o=LdapAbc.org
```

under this subtree there can be only one RDN:

```
uid=usr1
```

resulting in the DN:

```
DN: uid=usr1, ou=sales, l=Europe, o=LdapAbc.org
```

This means that you can have an entry with an RDN of uid = usr1 under l = Asia, as shown in Exhibit 18, resulting in the unique DN:

```
DN: uid=usr1, ou=sales, l=Asia, o=LdapAbc.org
```

There is a certain analogy to a UNIX file system. Just as the complete pathname of a file in a file system contains the complete pathname of its ancestor, the distinguished name of an entry also contains the distinguished name of its ancestor. For example if you create a new file in the directory "/home/my_directory," you choose a name that does not yet exist in this directory, otherwise you will get an error message. The same holds for the directory information tree.

Examples of Distinguished Names

To gain a better understanding of DNs, let us see just a few more examples. If you want to create a new entry under an entry with the distinguished name

```
"DN: ou=IT, o=ldap_abc, c=de"
```

you have to choose a name that does not yet exist in this subtree, otherwise the directory server will refuse it with an error message. "c" in this example DN stands for "country." It is one of the attributes of the object class organization. Let us suppose you add the name "Bill Palmer." The new entry would look like this:

```
cn=Bill Palmer"
```

resulting in a distinguished name of:

```
"DN: cn=Bill Palmer, ou=IT, o=ldap_abc, c=de"
```

This new name, unique inside this subtree, is called a "relative distinguished name" (RDN). In our example, the RDN is:

```
"RDN: cn=Bill Palmer"
```

Until now, it seemed that, as in a UNIX file system, we could use anything we found appropriate to build up the RDN. In LDAP, you must use one of the attributes of the object class that the entry implements to construct the RDN, i.e., the RDN has the following form:

```
<Attribute Name>=<Attribute Value>
```

You cannot use an attribute that is not part of the object class in the DN. For example, it is not possible to give an entry of type organization (objectclass: "o") a DN that contains a "dc" attribute, because the dc attribute is not part of the object class organization. Until now we did not explain the concept of domain components. You will hear more about this concept in the section entitled "Directory Suffix." However, "dc" stands for domain component. The dc attribute is contained in the object dcObject standing for domain component object. The auxiliary class dcObject can be mixed with the object class "o" to obtain DN: dc=LdapAbc,dc=de for an organization entry. For a discussion about auxiliary object classes, look back at the section "Object Class Types" found earlier in this chapter.

Relative distinguished names can also be composed of multiple attributes. The attributes then have to be concatenated by the "+" sign. Spaces around the "+" sign are ignored. If one of the attributes should contain a "+" sign, it has to be "escaped." More about this in the section entitled "Distinguished-Name Syntax." For example

```
"cn=Bill Palmer + l=New York"
```

would produce the distinguished name

```
"cn=Bill Palmer + l=New York, ou=IT, o=ldap_abc, c=de"
```

This technique is not used very often. It is sometimes used to produce unique RDNs in situations of a homonym cn, i.e., if there is a Bill Palmer in Las Vegas and another one in New York. This notation would express clearly that you mean the New York one.

The bigger the enterprise, the higher is the probability that it employs two or more "John Smith" in New York. The best solution to this problem is to use an attribute that is guaranteed to be unique throughout the whole enterprise, for example, the e-mail address. (The e-mail address is unique within the organization; otherwise it would be difficult to direct the correct mail to the correct recipient.) The user identifier (uid) in most cases should do the job as well. Another similar attribute that is widely used in most enterprises is the employeeNumber, which should be unique throughout the enterprise.

By the way, the distinguished name can also contain spaces, as evidenced by the name "Bill Palmer." Additional spaces are ignored. For example, "cn = Bill Palmer" with one space and "cn = Bill Palmer" with two spaces are equivalent. Special characters are also allowed if preceded ("escaped") by the backslash character "\". We will address this issue in greater detail in the section entitled "Distinguished Name Syntax."

Directory Suffix

All entries in the directory have a common ancestor called the "directory suffix."* In the previous example, the directory suffix was

```
"o=ldap_abc, c=de"
```

How should you choose the suffix? Aside from the consideration of choosing a meaningful suffix for your directory implementation, there are three styles available for use. Unlike X.500, LDAP does not

---

* In the section entitled "Directory Information Tree," we learned that the DN of the root entry is called "uffix."

force you to use a specific style to construct the directory suffix. You can use any one of the three styles. As you might imagine, the traditional X.500 naming style is an option. The other two options are the domain name system (DNS) style and the domain-component style. All directory server implementations should support these styles, but add-on software may not. Look at the documentation for the directory server and for any add-on software to see if your implementation fully supports the style you choose.

1. The traditional X.500 naming style comprises the organization name followed by the country code, as in:

```
"o=ldapabc, c=de"
```

2. The DNS style reflects the DNS name of your company and is generally recommended, as it allows you to fit seamlessly within the existing DNS lookup mechanism, which helps your directory clients. The same entry now looks like:

```
"o=ldapabc.de"
```

3. The domain component style uses the dc attribute to split your domain name into dc components. The entry now looks like:

```
"dc=ldapabc, dc=de"
```

We previously mentioned the dcObject class, where dcObject stands for domain component Object. The dcObject class extends the top object class by adding one required attribute: the "dc" or domain component attribute. The dcObject class is used for entries with a DN of the domain component style. For an example of an object using the dcObject class, see the preceding section entitled "Object Class Types."

Aliases

When speaking about the directory information tree (DIT), we always referred to a "treelike" structure. Now the time has come to explain how the tree structure of the DIT could be somewhat scrambled. As we have seen, there are situations where it is advantageous to avoid inserting a real entry in the DIT, instead using a placeholder pointing to the actual entry. This "placeholder" is called an "alias." An alias can therefore be seen as a construction corresponding to the symbolic link in the UNIX operating system. Those working in the Win NT or Win2000 operating systems will recognize the same object under the name "shortcut." The underlying concept is the same.

A carelessly used alias can corrupt the design of the whole directory. Aliases can point wherever you want, even to a different directory server. Because an erroneous alias can spell disaster, not all directory implementations allow the use of aliases. If your implementation does not allow aliases, you can use referrals instead of an alias. To learn more about referrals, see the next subsection or turn to Chapter 5, which discusses partitioning in some detail.

Creating an alias is easy. The procedure is the same as that used to add a new entry. The alias has a distinguished name, as do all entries. The alias, obviously, is from the object-class type "alias" and has only one required attribute, the attribute "aliasedObjectName," indicating where the real entry resides.

Referrals

As mentioned in the previous section, not all directory servers allow aliases. A referral does the same job as an alias. Let us look at referrals and how they come into play.

As directories continue to increase in size, there may come a point where it is no longer useful to hold the whole directory tree on one server. For performance reasons, we might decide to put one part of the directory tree on another directory server. However, performance is not the only reason for placing one or more parts of the directory on other servers. Administrative considerations — allowing different policies for different parts of the directory tree — might also come into play. We are not yet ready to deal with the details of partitioning or discuss the reasons for partitioning a directory. These arguments will be treated in greater detail in Chapter 5, which also covers replication. For now, we will concentrate only on referrals.

Assume that our directory server does not hold the entire directory tree and that part of the tree is located on another server. Exhibit 20 shows a possible scenario for directory partitioning. In this example, the directory tree holding the information for North America has been moved to a separate server. At this point, a client searching an entry in the sales department located at San Francisco would not find anything, receiving instead an error message indicating that the required entry had not been found on the server. This is not what we wanted to achieve. We need an entry that points to the exact location where the entry can now be found. This special entry is called a "referral."

The referral is a special entry of the object class "referral." Like the alias, the referral has a distinguished name to locate it in the directory. The referral has one required attribute: the "ref" attribute. The ref attribute is an LDAP URL pointing to the location where the real entry can be found. Exhibit 21 shows the situation using a referral object.

Now, when a client connects to the server and asks for information about the sales department in San Francisco, the server understands that it does not hold the information but that Server 2 should know more about it. Server 1 reports to the client that it does not hold the requested information and directs the client to Server 2. Exhibit 22 shows what happens. The client then decides if it will follow the referral or not, depending on how the client has been programmed.

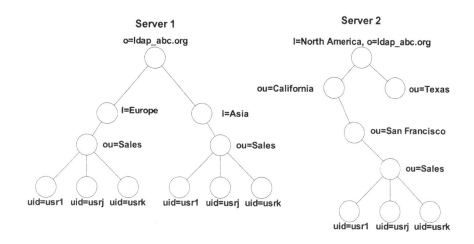

Exhibit 20. Example of Directory Distributed on Two Servers

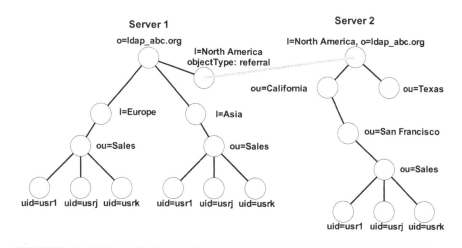

Exhibit 21. Example of Directory Distributed on Two Servers with a Referral from Server 1 to Server 2

The various APIs available offer the application programmer tools to handle the case of a referral correctly. Referrals do not exist yet in LDAP version 2; they appear in LDAP version 3 only.

Chapter 5 provides more details about how the server handles referrals, showing also a few examples from the API programmer's point of view. Chapter 6 provides more detail about APIs for the different programming languages.

Exhibit 23 shows another way to keep two directories together, called "chaining." However, the standards do not cover chaining; it is up to the vendor implementing the LDAP protocol to determine whether chaining is supported. As seen in Exhibit 23, the client asks the server for an entry it does not hold. This time, however, the server

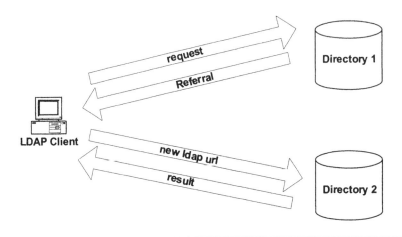

Exhibit 22. How the Client Sees a Referral

does not respond with an instant referral. Instead, it requests the information from the server holding the information on behalf of the client. Once the original server gets the desired information, it answers the client's request.

Distinguished-Name Syntax

As mentioned before, additional white spaces in the distinguished names are ignored. The same holds for leading or trailing white spaces in the RDN or DN. For example "cn = Bill Palmer" with a leading space and "cn = Bill Palmer" with a trailing space are equivalent. There could be situations where the leading space may be necessary. There are also other characters that have a special meaning, for example the comma character "," used to divide the single parts of the distinguished name. Let us look at an example of the entry for "LdapAbc, Ltd." in the United Kingdom. As mentioned before, special characters have to be preceded (escaped) by the backslash "\" character:

```
"o=LdapAbc\, Ltd., c=GB"
```

Exhibit 24 lists the special characters that must be "escaped" for inclusion in distinguished names.

Characters can also be represented in their hexadecimal value, prefixed with the octothorp character.

Exhibit 25 shows the exact syntax definition of a distinguished name in LDAP (v3) as defined in RTF 2253. This applies only to LDAP version 3, documented in RFC 2253. If you need more information about LDAP version 2 syntax, refer to RFC 1779. The syntax for LDAP (v2) is the same as that used for X.500 directory services. RFC 2253 is more strict than RFC 1779. The X.500 protocol and LDAP (v2) use abstract syntax

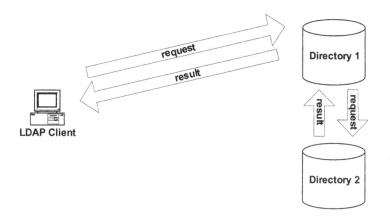

Exhibit 23. How the Client Sees a Referral (Same as Exhibit 22) Using Chaining

Exhibit 24. Prohibited Characters and Associated Escape Sequence for Use in Distinguished Names

Prohibited Characters	Escape Sequence
Leading or trailing white space (<space>)	\<space>
Leading or trailing octothorp character (#)	\#
Comma (,)	\,
Plus sign (+)	\+
Equal sign (=)	\ =
Double quote (")	\"
Backslash (\)	\\
Less than (<)	\>
Greater than (>)	\<
Semicolon (;)	\;

notation one (ASN.1) encoding, while LDAP (v3) has chosen a UTF-8 string representation, which is human readable.

Last but Not Least, Information about the Server

In LDAP version 3, the client can get information about the server, which provides a lot of information about itself inside the directory. This information can be queried just as normal entries are. Chapter 6 provides some practical examples of APIs, and Chapter 7 discusses the administration of a directory server. Here, we briefly review what information you can get from the server.

The server information is held in an entry called "root DSE." DSE stands for DSA Specific Entry. DSA is an abbreviation for the directory

---

**Exhibit 25. Distinguished-Name Syntax from RFC 2253,
"Lightweight Directory Access Protocol (v3): UTF-8 String
Representation of Distinguished Names"**

```
distinguishedName = [name] ; may be empty string

name = name-component *("," name-component)

name-component = attributeTypeAndValue *("+" attributeType
AndValue)

attributeTypeAndValue = attributeType "=" attributeValue

attributeType = (ALPHA 1*keychar)/oid
keychar = ALPHA/DIGIT/"-"

oid = 1*DIGIT *("." 1*DIGIT)

attributeValue = string

string      = *(stringchar/pair)
              /"#" hexstring
              /QUOTATION *(quotechar/pair) QUOTATION ; only from v2
quotechar   = <any character except "\" or QUOTATION >
special     = ","/"="/"+"/"<"/">"/"#"/";"
pair        = "\" (special/"\"/QUOTATION/hexpair)
stringchar  = <any character except one of special, "\" or QUOTATION >
hexstring   = 1*hexpair
hexpair     = hexchar hexchar
hexchar     = DIGIT/"A"/"B"/"C"/"D"/"E"/"F"
              /"a"/"b"/"c"/"d"/"e"/"f"
ALPHA       = <any ASCII alphabetic character>
                                    ; (decimal 65-90 and
97-122)
DIGIT       = <any ASCII decimal digit> ; (decimal 48-57)
QUOTATION   = <the ASCII double quotation mark character '"'
decimal 34>
```

---

server agent. However, the entry is special because it has a DN with length zero. Let us look at the information held in the root DSE.

- LDAP version supported by the server. The client can try to obtain the LDAP version that the server supports. If the client does not successfully retrieve this information, then the user can conclude that it is LDAP version 2, which does not support this feature.
- All object classes and attribute types recognized by the server.
- The suffixes stored on the directory server. Remember that some implementations can hold more than one suffix.
- The extended operations and controls supported by the directory server. We will learn more about the extended operations and controls in the next section about the "functional model."

- Information about the supported SASL mechanisms. We will learn more about the SASL mechanisms in the final section about the "security model."
- A list of LDAP servers to consult for information that the original server could not provide.

This is only a list of information the root DSE can provide. Chapter 6, "LDAP APIs," provides examples that show how users can get this information using different programming languages.

Conclusion for Naming Model

The naming model showed you how to build a directory information tree (DIT), how the distinguished name (DN) is built up from the RDN, how the DIT depends on the DN, and what problems can arise when moving an entry inside the directory. We have also seen two methods of modifying the logic standing behind the DIT — aliases and referrals — that dynamically change the static DIT. We also reviewed the exact syntax of the distinguished name, learned how to construct the directory root, and discussed naming conventions for the directory root. Finally, we learned that the directory holds information about itself (just as it holds other information) in the form of entries.

The next section addresses the functional model. It will show you what operations the server can execute on behalf of clients with the clearance to make such requests. The final section addresses the issue of security clearances.

Functional Model

The information model and the naming model describe the elements and the structure of the directory, respectively. The functional model describes the operations that can be performed on the directory.

At this point, it is useful to remember that LDAP is a protocol that mediates the messages sent between client and server. The client sends a message to the server requesting a certain action against the directory. The server then executes this action on behalf the client, sending a message back to the client containing the result code and the eventual results sets. Like every object class, attribute type, syntax, or matching rule, each of the operations requested in the messages also has a unique object identifier (OID). Thus the LDAP standard as defined in the RFC2251 describes the nature of the requests that the client can send to the server. Upon receipt of each request, the server then executes a response operation. How these operations are implemented in the server is not the subject of the LDAP standard. This decision is left to the vendor or to the organization implementing the directory server. Nevertheless, we will call these requests "functions" or "operations." This is the (lazy) terminology you will find in literature. Bear in mind that we are not really speaking of functions or methods in the sense of a programming language. It is the work of the programmers writing APIs to offer functions or methods etc. to the application programmer. With this in mind, you will understand the difference between the messages (alias "functions" and "operations") presented herein and the APIs treated in Chapter 6.

There are three groups of functions, plus one special group of the "extended operations." This group is new in version 3 of LDAP and has been defined in RFC 2251, "Lightweight Directory Access Protocol (v3)." The "extended operations" allow adding further functionality published in the form of RFCs or in private implementations. For example, the "StartTLS" (Transport Layer Security protocol) operation, not foreseen in RFC 2251, is an operation defined with an extended operation. The StartTLS operation is defined in RFC 2830, "Lightweight Directory Access Protocol (v3): Extension for Transport Layer Security." The StartTLS operation requests the server to begin the procedure for negotiating the security protocol to be used for securing the following LDAP session. We will learn more about this when we discuss the security model in the next section. You will also hear more about this in Chapter 7, "LDAP Directory Server Administration." The extended operations provide a high degree of flexibility for the LDAP protocol, which can be further extended in the future without changing the protocol definition as provided so far by the RFCs.

There is also another group of operations called "unsolicited notification." The unsolicited notification is a message sent from the server to the client in an extraordinary condition. At the time of this writing, there is only one of these unsolicited notifications, the "notice of disconnection." It occurs when, for some particular error condition, the LDAP server closes the connection.

But now let us get back to the three groups of operations. In this chapter we will learn what these operations are used for and then discuss each operation's functionality in greater detail. We will not examine the syntax of the various operations because this is implementation dependent, i.e., it depends of the directory client and the API you are using.

Overview of LDAP Operations

There are three types of operations:

1. Interrogation operations: search, compare
2. Update operations: add, delete, modify DN, modify
3. Authentication and control operations : bind, unbind, abandon

All of these operations are requests made by an LDAP client to an LDAP server. The server executes the requested operation and sends back to the client the result plus an error code.

Interrogation Operations

There are two interrogation operations: "search" and "compare."

"Search" looks up a part of the directory for entries matching a condition specified by a filter. It is possible to specify how deep the search should traverse the directory information tree (DIT), the point in the DIT where the server should start searching, and a time limit for the server's search through the entries. Furthermore you specify what attributes a query will return.

"Compare" does the same thing as "search" in that it searches the directory to find a match to an entry. However, in contrast to "search," it does not return any element, reporting only "true" if it found any entry and "false" if it did not. The "compare" operation remains from X.500 and could be managed by search also, except in one special case: when "search" is asked to return all entries matching a certain attribute and it comes back without a result. There can be two distinct reasons for this: The attribute in the entry does not match the one you searched, or the attribute has no value at all. In both cases, "search" returns the same result value, i.e., nothing. "Compare" instead returns a special value if the attribute does not exist at all.

Note that there is no read or iteration operation. These operations can be achieved by configuring the search filter appropriately.

Update Operations

The LDAP protocol has four update operations: "add," "delete," "modify DN," and "modify." The "add" operation simply adds a new entry to the directory. The "delete" operation deletes an entry. The "modify DN" operation modifies an entry. (In version 3, this includes modification of the distinguished name, which removes the entry from its old parent entry and inserts it into a new one. In version 2, it modifies only the relative distinguished name.) The "modify" operation modifies or deletes one or more attributes of an entry.

Authentication and Control Operations

LDAP has two authentication operations ("bind" and "unbind") and one control operation ("abandon"). The "bind" operation allows a user to connect to a directory server. This is an authentication operation because the user delivers userID and userPassword. The server controls the user credentials and gives access or returns an error code. "Unbind" finishes the connection. The "abandon" operation interrupts the connection between client and server.

LDAP Operations in Detail

Now that we know what operations the LDAP recognizes, we can review the previously mentioned operations in detail. It is important to understand them, since all software development kits rely on these operations. Once you have a clear understanding of what the directory server requests on behalf of these operations, you will have no problem in understanding the different APIs available.

One further note to these operations: All are atomic. This is important for some operations. "Atomic" means that an operation is executed as a whole or is aborted if an error occurs.

Consider an example: You want to update an entry changing more than one attribute. An atomic operation is either updated completely or it is aborted, with an error message sent to the user. If the update operation is completed, then all attributes of the entry you requested to be updated have been updated. You will not have some attributes updated and others not. This holds not only for the "update" operation, but also for the "add" and "delete" operations.

Interrogation Operations: Search

The most complicated operation is the search operation. It can have up to eight parameters: base, scope, derefAliases, sizeLimit, timeLimit, attrOnly, searchFilter, and attributeList:

1. *Base*: DN where the query should start
2. *Scope*: Extension of the query inside the directory information tree. The scope can have three different values:
   a. *baseObject*: Limits the search to the base object only. (See Exhibit 26.)
   b. *singleLevel*: Limits the search to the base objects and the immediate children. (See Exhibit 27.)
   c. *wholeSubtree*: Extends the search to the entire subtree from the base object. (See Exhibit 28.)
3. *derefAliases*: Indicates how alias dereferencing should be handled. Aliases are used as symbolic links in a file system. Instead of containing an entry, the corresponding leaf contains an object of a particular object class, the object class "alias," which points to the entry containing the data. Chapter 4 discusses aliases in greater detail. This parameter describes how the client should behave if it retrieves an alias, and it can have one of four values:
   a. *neverDerefAliases*: No dereferencing of aliases at all

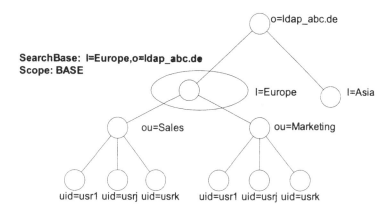

Exhibit 26. Search, scope = baseObject

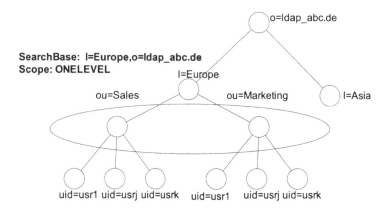

Exhibit 27.   Search, scope = singleLevel

    b. *derefInSearching*: Dereferences aliases in subordinates of the base object in searching, but not in locating the base object of the search

    c. *derefFindingBaseObj*: Dereferences aliases in locating the base object of the search, but not when searching subordinates of the base object

    d. *derefAlways*: Dereferences aliases both in searching and in locating the base object of the search

4. *sizeLimit*: Maximum number of entries a query will return. A number of "zero" means that there is no size limit. The server can impose a maximum number for this entry.

5. *timeLimit*: Maximum number of seconds a query can take. A number of "zero" means that the client does not impose any time limit.

6. *attrOnly*: A Boolean value. Set to "true," it indicates that only attribute types are returned; set to "false," it returns attribute types and attribute values.

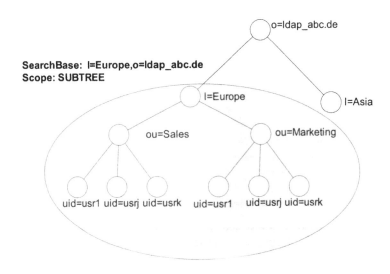

Exhibit 28.   Search, scope = wholeSubtree

7. *searchFilter*. Defines the conditions under which a search return is successful. The conditions can be combined with the Boolean "and," "or," and "not" operators. The filter evaluates to either "true," "false," or "undefined." If it evaluates to "true," the requested attributes of the entry are returned; if it evaluates to "false" or "undefined," the entry is ignored for the search. The search filter is treated in detail in the next chapter in the section entitled "Search Revisited."

8. *attributeList*. Attributes that should be returned if the searchFilter matches. Two values have a special meaning: an empty list with no attributes and an asterisk, "*". Both values instruct the server to return all attributes of the matching entries. The asterisk allows you to specify further operational attributes to be returned.

Interrogation Operations: Compare

The "compare" operation tests for the presence of a particular attribute in an entry with a given distinguished name. It returns "true" if the entry contains the attribute and "false" if the entry does not contain the attribute. You may wonder why you need a "compare" operation when there is already a "search" operation. One reason is a historical one, in that "compare" derives from X.500. The other reason is that the results of a "search" operation and a "compare" operation are not really identical. If you execute a "compare" on an attribute not contained in an entry, the "compare" operation returns a special value. Using the "search" operation, you cannot distinguish whether the attribute does not have this particular value or the attribute does not exist at all. Now look at the parameters for the "compare" operations:

- *entry*: Distinguished name of the entry you are searching for
- *ava*: Attribute name–value pair you want to verify is contained in the entry ("ava" means "attribute value assertion")

Update Operations: Add

The "add" operation is a relative easy one, as it contains only two parameters: entry and attributeList

- *entry*: Distinguished name of the new entry
- *attributeList*: A list of name–value pairs of the attributes contained in the entry

Update Operations: Delete

The "delete" operation is still easier than the "add" operation inasmuch as it takes one parameter only, the distinguished name of the entry to be deleted.

- *entry*: Distinguished name of the entry to be deleted

Update Operations: Modify

The "modify" operation is more complicated than the previous two. It takes three parameters: distinguished name, type of operation, and name–value pairs:

- *entry*: Distinguished name of the entry to be modified
- *operation*: Type of operation to be executed on this entry, with three possible values:
  - *add*: Adds a new attribute (name,value pair)
  - *delete*: Deletes an attribute
  - *modify*: Modifies an attribute
- *attributeList*: Produces a list of name–value pairs to be added/modified

Update Operations: ModifyDN

The modifyDN operation can be used for two purposes: to rename an entry or to move an entry within the directory. Exhibit 29 shows the first purpose. You modify only the leftmost, or least significant part, of the distinguished name. The parent remains the same, and only the RDN changes.

The other version of the modifyDN operation changes the hierarchy also, as shown in Exhibit 30.

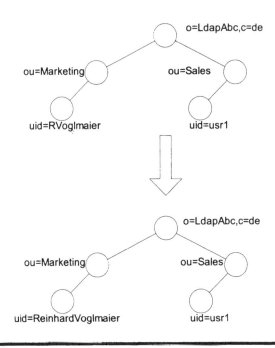

Exhibit 29. ModifyDN Name, the Hierarchy Remains the Same

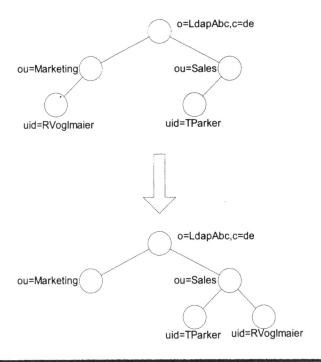

Exhibit 30. ModifyDN Name, the Hierarchy Is Modified

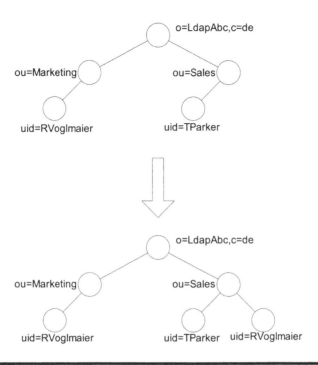

Exhibit 31. ModifyDN Name, as in Exhibit 30, but Keeping the Old RDN

You can also specify whether or not you wish to delete the old relative distinguished name. Keeping it would mean that the system copies the entry from its old location to a new one, as shown in Exhibit 31.

Exhibit 32 shows an example where there is a change in the hierarchy, i.e., the system moves the entry to a new location and changes its RDN.

The parameters that the modifyDN operation can take are as follows:

- *entry*: Distinguished name of the entry to be modified
- *newRDN*: New relative distinguished name
- *deleteOldRDN*: Boolean value indicating whether the old RDN should be kept in the directory
- *newSuperior*: Indicates a change in the hierarchy

Let us also look at what we must specify to initiate these actions. We begin by modifying only the RDN (see Exhibit 29):

```
Entry: uid=RVoglmaier, ou=Marketing, o=LdapAbc.org
newRDN: uid=ReinhardVoglmaier
deleteOldRDN: true
```

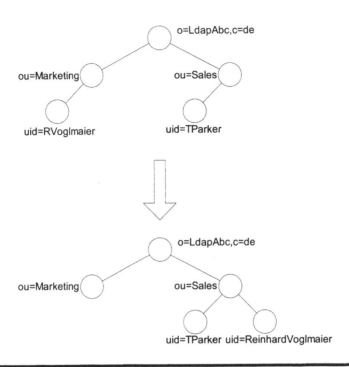

Exhibit 32. ModifyDN Name, Modify Hierarchy, and Change RDN

The next example changes the hierarchy while the RDN remains the same (see Exhibit 30):

```
Entry: uid=RVoglmaier, ou=Marketing, o=LdapAbc.org
newRDN: uid=RVoglmaier
deleteOldRDN: true
newSuperior: ou=Sales,o=LdapAbc.org
```

The following example is the same as the previous one, but this time we do not erase the old entry. The reason for doing this here is not yet clear, but this example is presented simply to show the syntax. A bit later, we will present an example where it makes sense (see Exhibit 31).

```
Entry: uid=RVoglmaier, ou=Marketing, o=LdapAbc.org
newRDN: uid=RVoglmaier
deleteOldRDN: false
newSuperior: ou=Sales,o=LdapAbc.org
```

Finally, we change nearly everything (see Exhibit 32):

```
Entry: uid=RVoglmaier, ou=Marketing, o=LdapAbc.org
newRDN: uid=ReinhardVoglmaier
deleteOldRDN: true
newSuperior: ou=Sales,o=LdapAbc.org
```

Note that modifying the distinguished name of an entry having children is somewhat more complicated. Look at the coding above to see what could happen. Let us assume we would like to change the name of the organizational unit from "HR" to the more user-friendly "Human Resources." After the modification, the entries under HR would be without a parent. This means that the namespace would be illegal. Most directory servers would refuse the modify operation. What you need to do is first create the new organizational unit, keeping the old entry. Then you rename all the children and delete the old organizational unit. If the children have further children, the situation can get even more complicated. Another possibility would be to export the whole directory, change all occurrences of the old name to the new name, and re-export the directory. We will learn more about this subject in Chapter 4, when we look at the details from a practical point of view.

Authentication Operations: Bind

The main purpose of the "bind" operation is to let the client authenticate itself against the directory server. The "bind" operation takes three parameters, version, name, and authentication:

- *version*: Version of LDAP the client wishes to use
- *name*: Name of the directory object the client wishes to bind to
- *authentication*: Authentication choice, which has two possible values:
    simple: Indicates that the password travels in clear text over the wire.
    sasl: Uses the SASL mechanism as described in RFC 2222, "Simple Authentication and Security Layer." (We will see more about SASL in the next section about the security model.)

Authentication Operations: Unbind

The operation "unbind" is very simple and does not take any parameters. The "unbind" operation does not return any value from the server. The client assumes that the connection to the server is now closed. The server releases any resources allocated for the client, discards any authentication information, and closes the TCP/IP connection with the client.

Control Operation: Abandon

Another simple operation, "abandon" takes only one parameter. The "abandon" operation is used to inform the server to stop a previously requested operation. The abandon operation typically is used by GUIs in the case of long-running operations on the server to inform the server that the client is no longer interested in the result of the operation. The operation takes only one parameter: the operationID.

■ *operationID*: ID of the operation to be abandoned

The server does not send any response to the "abandon" operation. The client does not expect any response, but it has to be prepared to continue to receive responses from the abandoned operation. This can happen when the "abandon" request from the server and the response from the operation to be abandoned cross each other on the wire.

Conclusion for Functional Model

In this section we have reviewed the operations embedded in the LDAP standards. These operations are then implemented in the various APIs provided by the different software development kits. Most of the LDAP implementations ship with a set of command-line tools. However, the command-line tools normally are nothing but a collection of compiled C programs. If you want, you could write your own code. However, I recommend that you get the OpenLDAP distribution, which already contains the source code written in C of the command-line tools, and change it to meet your personal taste and requirements. These C programs are also a very good example of how to use the C language to access a directory, since these programs are built from the ground up without relying on any API.

The most prominent API is the one for the C programming language. The LDAP C API for version 2 is documented in RFC 1823; the version 3 API is still proposed as draft and is available from IETF at http://www.ietf.org. Furthermore, there are APIs available for nearly every language, such as Java, Perl, Python, PHP, or Ruby. Chapter 5 shows some working examples in these languages.

In this section, you learned about the model defining the functions that can be performed on the directory. The two previous sections explained the data structures held by a directory. We are now ready to learn about the security structure proposed in the LDAP standard. As you will see, the standard does not cover all of the security requirements required by a stable LDAP implementation. However, this does not mean that LDAP implementations are, by definition, insecure. Every implementation covers security in a proprietary manner. Thus the problem remains the interoperability between LDAP implementations from different vendors.

Security Model

The previous three models provided us with many of the elements needed to construct a directory. The information model gave us the means to define the single elements to hold our data; the naming model helped us in building a hierarchical structure with these elements; and the functional model allowed us to access these data structures and manipulate them. What is still missing is a security model showing how to secure the data in the directory. There are two major arguments in place: authentication and authorization, also called "access control" in LDAP.

The security model is very important because LDAP is a connection-oriented protocol. In a typical conversation between client and server, the client opens a connection to the server. The client asks the server to perform an action upon this connection, and the server sends the results back. It is important that both server and client are always aware of the connection. After opening the connection with the server, the client can provide the server with user credentials (e.g., userID and userPassword) to prove its identity. If the server accepts these credentials, it associates or "binds" certain access rights to these user credentials. The client maintains these access rights bound to the user credentials until it unbinds or sends additional user information to obtain different access rights.

Note that not all protocols in the application layer are connection-oriented. An example of a protocol that does not know the concept of connection is the HTTP protocol. Every request the browser makes to the Web server has no connection with the previous one. The concept of connection in an HTTP conversation has to be implemented by server-side programs, i.e., the mechanism that maintains a session is implemented over the HTTP protocol. LDAP does not need such workarounds because the protocol itself maintains the connection.

Authentication and Authorization

Before a client can access data on an LDAP server, two processes must take place first: authorization and authentication. These two processes are quite different from each other. This section briefly reviews the different concepts behind these processes. The focus is on authentication, since authorization is not yet covered by standards.

Authentication takes place when the client identifies itself for the server as it tries to connect. The process depends very much on the authentication mechanism used. The easiest way is to connect to the server without the need to provide an identity. To such an anonymous connection, if allowed at all, the server grants the lowest access rights. There are authentication schemes ranging from simple authentication with user and password to authentication using certificates. These certificates give the assurance to the server that the client really is who it says it is. Certificates can also assure the client about the server's identity.

Once the client has been recognized by the server, the client will have certain access rights to the data. Authorization is the process by which the server grants the correct access rights to the previously authenticated client. This means that the user can read and write data with restrictions that depend on the level of access granted. To define what each client can do, the server must maintain an access control information (ACI) file.

More so than the other models, the security model is still a work in progress, especially regarding the authorization aspect. LDAP authentication is covered by a few RFC standard specifications, as we will see in the next section. Authorization, called "access control" in LDAP parlance, is not yet covered in LDAP standards. Meanwhile LDAP (v2) did not have any support for authorization methods. LDAP (v3) has a set of recommendations expressed in RFC 2820, "Access Control Requirements for LDAP." This RFC does not, however, express any standard; its recommendations are only informational. Nevertheless, this does not mean that LDAP implementations lack for authentication or access control. Instead, in the absence of a standard, every implementation has its own method for access control. Unfortunately, these methods are incompatible with each other. So once you have identified your needs, you have to check the vendor documentation to see whether the product contains the features you wish to use.

Authentication

The basic requirements for authentication in LDAP are defined in RFC 2829, "Authentication Methods for LDAP." The following is a brief list of the most important requirements:

- *Client authentication*: Client authenticates itself against the directory server using certificates, encryption, or clear text.
- *Client authorization*: By means of access-control mechanisms, the directory server controls what the client can request on the directory server based on the previous authentication (see next section).
- *Data integrity mechanisms*: Guarantee that what the client sent arrives at the server and vice versa.
- *Snooping protection*: Prevents a listener in the network from snooping using encrypted conversation.
- *Protection against monopolization*: Limits resources to prevent a user from monopolizing the system.
- *Server authentication*: Server authenticates itself against the client to guarantee to the client that the server is responding.

There are different levels of authentication. In the previous section (functional model), we saw the function "bind" used for the user authentication process. Binding to the server means authenticating the user against the server. There are various methods to authenticate the client.

- Anonymous access
- Basic authentication
- Authentication providing security via encryption
- Authentication using encryption and certificates

Anonymous Access

The first type of authentication is "no authentication at all," also called "anonymous bind" because the server has no idea of who actually is asking for a connection. Anonymous bind is used to access publicly available data, for example a public telephone book. The server configuration determines whether anonymous access is allowed and the level of access to data for the anonymous user.

Note that the server assumes anonymous access if the client does not provide user credentials to the server. Sometimes this may not be what you really wanted. If an application uses an LDAP server for authentication, it sends userID and userPassword to the LDAP server. If the LDAP does not report an error and opens a connection, the application assumes that the authentication was successful. Unfortunately, the LDAP server does not report an error if it does not receive any user information at all, and therefore connects the user as an anonymous user. Therefore the application has to control whether the user has supplied data for userID/userPassword and, if this information is missing, should refuse the connection.

Basic Authentication

After anonymous access, the simplest authentication is the basic authentication, which is also used in other protocols like HTTP. The client simply sends the user credentials across the wire. In the case of LDAP, this means the user's distinguished name and the userPassword. Both of them are sent over the network in plain view without encryption. This method may be okay in a trusted environment, but even in an intranet environment, sending around unencrypted passwords is not a good idea. Remember the false assumption that the bad guy is always "outside."

The server looks for an attribute named "userPassword" in the entry corresponding to the distinguished name. The value of this attribute is compared with the user input. If the password matches, the connection with the LDAP server is established. If there is no match, an error message is sent and the connection dropped. Again, this is not the safest of all methods, but it could be acceptable in an intranet environment.

Although the user credentials are sent in plain ASCII text, this does not mean that you can read or write them as easily as you can with other protocols such as HTTP. Recall from Chapter 1 that LDAP messages are encoded using BER encoding. By the way, LDAP (v2) also offered the ability to encode user credentials using base-64 encoding as defined in the MIME extensions in RFC 1521.

LDAP over SSL/TLS

The SSL (Secure Sockets Layer) protocol implements security mechanisms in the TCP/IP protocol stack right between the transport layer and the application layer, i.e., the layer below LDAP. SSL is based upon public-key cryptography and was developed by Netscape. The TLS 1 (Transport Layer Security) protocol was born from SSL version 3 and is documented in RFC 2246, "TLS Protocol version 1.0."

The standard requires providing TLS in the form of an extended request. From discussion of the functional model in the previous section, recall that the client — via the startTLS, an extended operation — requests the beginning of a TLS session. Recall also that a unique object identifier (OID) identifies each operation. For example, the "startTLS" operation is requested by its OID "1.3.6.1.4.1.1466.20037." The server confirms the TLS session if it supports TLS.

The TLS integration in LDAP is defined in RFC 2830, "Lightweight Directory Access Protocol (v3): Extension for Transport Layer Security." Meanwhile, RFC 2246 describes the TLS protocol, and RFC 2830 describes how the TLS protocol has to be established between client and server.

The goal of the TLS protocol is to provide both data integrity and privacy. This means that the TLS protocol guarantees that data sent between two partners arrives unmodified and that the conversation is encrypted, i.e., that a person sitting between client and server can not intercept the conversation. TLS requires a reliable protocol and is based upon TCP. TLS itself comprises two different protocols, the TLS Record protocol and the TLS Handshake protocol. The function of the TLS Record Protocol is only the encapsulation of the higher protocol, the TLS Handshake protocol. The TLS Handshake protocol instead provides the security mechanisms. It allows server and client to authenticate each other and negotiate encryption protocol and cryptographic keys. The TLS Handshake protocol supports the public key mechanism.

Kerberos

LDAP (v2) supports a bind mechanism based on Kerberos, but it is not directly supported in LDAP (v3). By "not directly supported," we mean that it can be used as a security mechanism upon an agreement established using the SASL protocol, which is discussed in the next section. Kerberos itself is a protocol that relies upon a third authority, the authentication server. Kerberos is defined in RFC 1510, "The Kerberos Network Authentication Service (v5)." Kerberos is a security mechanism planned for use in an extremely insecure environment such as the Internet. Kerberos does not make any assumption about the integrity of the messages sent between the two communicating partners. The communication is encrypted, and both partners can be confident about the identity of the other.

While TLS or SSL involve only the two communicating partners. Kerberos needs a dedicated authentication server, which means that a third partner is involved. The client asks the authentication server for credentials. With this request, it also specifies which server it intends to speak with. The Kerberos gives to the client these requested credentials in the form of two pieces: a ticket for the server the client wants to contact and a "session key." The session key is a temporary encryption key valid for this particular session. Now the client is ready to contact the server. The server encrypts the ticket and the session key with the server's key and sends it to the server. At this point, the server and the client both know the session key. Further into the conversation, this key is used to authenticate the client or the server. This key can be used to encrypt the conversation between client and server or to exchange a further subsession key to be used for the conversation. The ticket and the session key both cannot be recycled because they are temporary and can only be used from a certain client to contact a certain server.

This mechanism is also designed to work across organizational boundaries. The client can ask an authentication server to send credentials for a conversation with a server in another organization. The context within which the partners are located is called a "realm." In this case, the client asks the authentication server for credentials for a server in another realm. The realm the client is located in is part of the client's name. The server can furthermore decide to speak only with clients within a certain realm.

The Kerberos protocol is a very stable and reliable protocol covering a most of the requirements for securing the conversation in an insecure environment. It can be used from a great number of protocols and is platform independent.

SASL

The simple authentication and security layer (SASL) is a method of providing authentication services to a connection-oriented protocol such as LADP. The SASL standard is defined in RFC 2222, "Simple Authentication and Security Layer." This standard makes it possible for a client and server to agree upon a security layer for encryption. Once the server and client are connected, they agree upon a security mechanism for the ongoing conversation. One of these mechanisms is Kerberos. At the time of this writing, a number of mechanisms are supported by SASL, including:

- Anonymous, described by RFC 2245, "Anonymous SASL Mechanism"
- CRAM-MD5, described by RFC 2195, "IMAP/POP AUTHorize Extension for Simple Challenge/Response"
- Digest-MD5, described by RFC 2831, "Using Digest Authentication as a SASL Mechanism"
- External, described by RFC 2222, "Simple Authentication and Security Layer (SASL)"; updated by RFC2444, "The One-Time-Password SASL Mechanism"
- Kerberos (v4), described by RFC 2222 and RFC 2444
- Kerberos (v5), described by RFC 2222 and RFC 2444
- SecurID, described by RFC 2808, "The SecurID® SASL Mechanism"
- Secure Remote Password, described by draft-burdis-cat-srp-sasl-07.txt, "Secure Remote Password SASL Mechanism"
- S/Key, described by RFC 2222 and RFC 2444
- X.509, described by draft-ietf-ldapext-x509-sasl-03.txt, "X.509 Authentication SASL Mechanism"

Although TLS and SSL are simple layers between the application protocol (LDAP in our special case) and the TCP/IP protocol, the SASL protocol has particular requirements for an application protocol. It dictates that the client open the TLS connection. The server has to answer with success or an error message. Furthermore, it requires the application protocol to put at disposal a special message for the TLS request from the client and the TLS response from the server. This is why TLS is available only in version 3 of LDAP, which includes the extended startTLS operation. The exact requirements for implementation of SASL exceed the scope of this book and can be found in RFC 2222. The implementation of SASL in LDAP is covered in RFC 2830, "Lightweight Directory Access Protocol (v3): Extension for Transport Layer Security."

The TLS connection is established via the startTLS request. As the title of the RFC 2830 suggests, the standard defines TLS for version 3 of the LDAP protocol. The startTLS request is an example of an extended operation. Let us briefly review how the standard stipulates the establishment of a TLS session.

The client requests a secure connection via the extended operation startTLS. The server must answer with one of the following responses:

- *success*: Server is ready to negotiate TLS using the Handshake protocol of TLS.

- *operationsError*: Indicates an error in the sequence of the operation, e.g., TLS has just been established before the actual request. In other words, the server got the request for establishing TLS after TLS was already established.
- *protocolError*: Normally means that TLS is not supported by the server. This error is also produced if the client has sent a malformed protocol data unit (PDU).
- *referral*: If a server sends back a referral to another LDAP server, this means that the original server does not support TLS but knows an LDAP server that does.
- *unavailable*: Server is shutting down, or there is some problem with TLS on this server.

Once the server has sent the "success" response to the client, the negotiation of TLS can begin. The first thing both have to agree upon is the supported TLS version. The second thing is the security mechanism to use for the conversation. Both parties decide whether they accept the security level achieved. If the server or the client decides that the level is not high enough, it closes the TLS connection.

Concluding Authentication

Authentication gives the server the credentials needed to let the user access the server. It also allows both the server and the client to verify the other's identity. Once the connection is made, the client and server can exchange messages that arrive intact without modification or interception by any third party.

Until now, we have spoken only of clients and servers. This is just one of many scenarios requiring a high level of security. Replication is another scenario. The topic of replication is addressed at several points later in this book. For now, it is enough to know that replication allows you to mirror one part of the directory or the entire directory on another server. If you replicate the entries from one server to another, you can also replicate the security requirements protecting the information on both servers from unauthorized clients. However, to do so, the server-to-server authentication will have to be the same as that used to authenticate clients.

Another scenario is a mechanism known as chaining. If a server contacted by a client does not hold the required information, it might use an alias or a referral to direct the client to a server holding the relevant information. However, if the server supports chaining, it can access the relevant server and then deliver the requested information directly to the client. This is another case where the server-to-server security level must be the same as that between client and server.

Look at the documentation of your server implementation to see which authentication features it supports. It may be that your implementation does not support all of the features proposed by the standard, or it may have its own extensions that are different from the standard.

Authorization

Authorization — also called "access control" — is the process by which a server grants the correct access rights to a previously authenticated client. At the time of this writing, the standards do not say much about authorization. This does not mean that directory servers do not support authorization. Nearly every software vendor has a proprietary solution. The access control information (ACI) is held in an access control list (ACL). The bad news is that every server implementation has its own method of holding the ACI. At the time of this writing, OpenLDAP holds this information in the configuration files. Netscape keeps this information in the directory, which has a big advantage in that it can be inspected and updated using the LDAP protocol itself. Obviously only authenticated and authorized clients can view or update the access-control information.

Access-control information can contain the following specifications:

- *Data protection*: You can deny or allow access to the entire tree, a subtree, or a DN.
- *Data access*: You can define the clients who have access to the system:
  Anonymous: Every user, without authentication
  Authenticated users: Users that have been authenticated by the system
  Self: User associated with the target entry
  Distinguished name: User matching the expression in the distinguished name
- *Level of access*: You can define access rights for the user:
  No access
  Right to bind
  Right to execute or compare
  Right to execute search
  Right to read search results
  Right to modify entries
- *Further requirements*: You can further restrict the IP numbers or host names to be serviced, the time of day service would be granted or denied, etc.

It is important to remember that, at the time of this writing, access control information and access control lists are not covered by any standard. Vendors support them in any number of ways. Because each vendor provides a unique solution, there is no guarantee of interoperability between the solutions of different vendors. You should consult the documentation shipped with the product you are using to learn the exact functionality and the exact syntax.

Chapter 4

LDAP: Some Practical Details

Combining the knowledge gained from Chapters 2 and 3, we now have a fairly complete grasp of LDAP basics. Chapter 2 treated LDAP from the protocol point of view. Chapter 3 showed the four models that provide the basis of LDAP. We learned that the LDAP database contains a large number of objects stored in the form of entries. Each object is constructed of attributes. Each attribute has a name and one or more values. The objects are organized in the database in a hierarchical structure that builds a tree, much like a directory on a file system. LDAP offers a number of functions to facilitate access to these objects. There are also control structures to mediate who can access and manipulate the data.

In this chapter, we take a more practical approach. We revisit the search function and explain how to construct filters with the help of some examples. We then have a brief look at the directory schema and provide some practical examples. We also learn how the theoretical objectIDs and matching rules fit into the definitions that are in the configuration files. We learn more about the LDIF format and understand its importance for importing a directory. Finally, as promised in Chapter 2, we will have a closer look at LDAP URLs, further examine the differences between LDAPv2 and LDAPv3, and conclude with a short discussion of what is going on with the development of LDAP. I will also describe the workgroups active at the time of this writing.

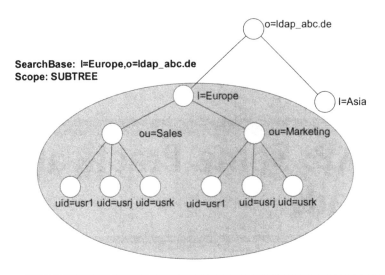

Exhibit 1. Example of Search, Scope Set to SUBTREE

Search Revisited

In the preceding chapters, we have seen the search function in action a number of times. Before initiating a search, you specify several parameters. Let us take a look at an example. Look at Exhibit 1. We want to know name of the users working in Europe. First, we define the search base, i.e., the location in the tree from which the search should begin.

```
BaseDN: l=Europe, ou=ldap_abc.de
```

Next, we have to specify how deeply we wish to search. This specifies the scope parameter, as explained in Chapter 3. The three possibilities are:

- *subtree*: Searches the whole subtree, including the search base, as shown in Exhibit 1
- *onelevel*: Searches one level below the search base, thus excluding the search base from the search scope
- *base*: Limits the search to the search base

In Exhibit 1, it is clear that "subtree" means the whole subtree, beginning at the search base. Exhibit 2 shows the "onelevel" search scope. Note that the search base itself is excluded from the search. You can verify this by searching with the filter:

```
objectclass=*
```

Note that the exact name of the constant used for the scope depends on the API you are using. In the C API, the constants are called:

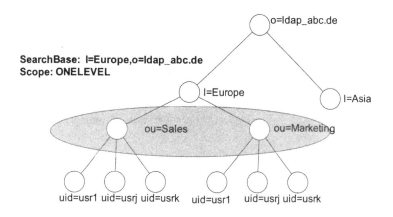

SearchBase: l=Europe,o=ldap_abc.de
Scope: ONELEVEL

Exhibit 2. Example of Search, Scope Set to ONELEVEL

- LDAP_SCOPE_SUBTREE
- LDAP_SCOPE_ONELEVEL
- LDAP_SCOPE_BASE

To complete the picture, see Exhibit 3, which shows an example of "search" with the scope set to "base," i.e., the search is executed only in the immediate search base.

The most important thing in the search is the filter. The filter defines what you want to know, perhaps which objects belong to a certain objectclass, the list of persons with surnames beginning with "A," and so on.

Query Filters

Now, finally, we will have a closer look at how to construct a query filter. If you would like more information about filters, you can look

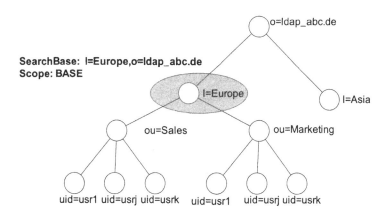

SearchBase: l=Europe,o=ldap_abc.de
Scope: BASE

Exhibit 3. Example of Search, Scope Set to BASE

at RFC 2254, "The String Representation of LDAP Search Filters." This RFC supersedes RFC 1960, "A String Representation of LDAP Search Filters" describing LDAP (v2) filters. The difference between the two RFCs is that LDAP (v3) adds the extended match filter. In LDAP (v2) you could not search in the distinguished name. The extensible match makes this possible and allows the user to define different behaviors in comparisons. We will discuss this aspect in greater detail later.

Exhibit 4 lists the filter definitions that can be used in an LDAP search. The following sections give a brief example of each filter listed in Exhibit 4.

equalityMatch

This is the simplest form of the filter. It tests for exact equality between the string searched and the attribute value.

```
(sn=Parker)
(mail=Mparker@ldap_abc.com)
```

Substring

Evaluates to "true" if the attribute value contains the query string:

- *(sn = Pa*)*: Matches every sn beginning with "Pa," e.g., Parker, Paul
- *(sn = *man)*: Matches every sn ending with "man," e.g., Woodman, Goldman
- *(sn = s*n)*: Matches every sn beginning with "s" and ending with "n," e.g., Simon
- *(sn = *str*)*: Matches every sn containing "str," e.g., Astrid

greaterOrEqual, lessOrEqual

The greaterOrEqual filter matches every attribute value that is greater than or equal to the query string, and the lessOrEqual filter matches every attribute value that is less than or equal to the query string. The ordering depends on the syntax of the attribute you are comparing. For example, integer attributes are ordered numerically. ASCII values are ordered lexicographically. Attributes with caseIgnoreString syntax and attributes with caseSensitiveSyntax are ordered in a different way. Attributes that cannot be ordered, such as binary data, cannot be searched with this operator.

Exhibit 4. LDAP Search Filters

Name	Operator
equalityMatch	=
substring	=
greaterOrEqual	>=
lessOrEqual	<=
present	=*
approxMatch	=~
Boolean Operators:	
and	&
or	|
not	!
LDAP (v3)	
extensibleMatch:	
NAME?	"attr [":dn"] [":" matchingrule] ": = " value
NAME?	[":dn"] ":" matchingrule ": = " value

Present

This is a simple filter type, testing only for the presence of the requested attribute. For example,

```
fax=*
```

reports entries that have a value for the attribute "fax."

approxMatch

The approxMatch filter is a question of implementation. It returns true if the attribute values "sounds like" the search string. This is clearly dependent on the language used. For example,

```
(sn=~ Parker)
```

returns true if the attribute value of sn "sounds like" Parker, the meaning of which depends on the particular implementation.

Boolean Operators: And, Or, Not

Finally, we have the Boolean operators. These operators are used in combination with all of the operators described in this section so far. The notation, however, is somewhat cumbersome and not recommended for the end user. The syntax used is called "prefix notation."

Those who recall the postfix notation of the first pocket calculators (namely Hewlett-Packard) will remember it. With prefix notation, the operator precedes the operands.

Examples

The following examples illustrate the use of the Boolean operators alone and in combination:

- (! (sn = A*)): Matches every entry with an sn that does not begin with A
- (& (sn = A*) (l = NewYork)): Matches every entry with an sn beginning with A and living in New York
- (| (l = New York) (l = Washington)): Matches every entry with location New York or location Washington
- (& (l = California) (! (l = San Francisco))): Matches every entry with location California, excluding San Francisco

Using these Boolean operators, it is possible to build whatever logical construction you want.

extensibleMatch

Do you remember that it was not possible to search in the distinguished name in LDAP (v2)? Now, in LDAP (v3) with this search filter you can. You express your wish to search in the distinguished name in this way:

```
(l:dn :=San Francisco)
```

With this command, the search would include all entries containing the distinct name "San Francisco" in the location field.

However, this filter can do much more. The user can also specify which matching rule the query should use. For example, suppose you wanted to use the caseExactString match to look up a common name. The common name (cn) normally uses caseIgnoreString, so Carter and carter and CARTER are all the same thing. You could specify

```
(sn:caseExactString:=Carter)
```

to distinguish "Carter" from the other possibilities.

In Backus Naur form (BNF) (see Chapter 3, Exhibit 4), the syntax definition for the extensible match statement would be as follows::

```
attr [":dn"] [":" matchingrule] ":=" value | [":dn"] ":" matching-
rule ":=" value
```

with the following:

- *attr*: Attribute name
- *matchingRule*: Matching rule to be applied. In this case, the object identifier (OID) is used. See "Information Model" in Chapter 3 for details. You could use the human-readable aliases as well, for example "caseExactString." You will find the values appropriate for your server in its configuration files.
- *value*: Value to be used for the query

The square brackets indicate that the enclosed expression is optional. The logical operator "|" means OR. If you omit the attribute name, you have to express the matching rule your query will use.

To finish this section, let us review several examples copied from RFC 2254, "The String Representation of LDAP Search Filters":

- (sn:dn:2.4.6.8.10: = Barney Rubble): Illustrates the use of the ":dn" notation to indicate that (1) matching rule "2.4.6.8.10" should be used when making comparisons and (2) the attributes of an entry's distinguished name should be considered part of the entry when evaluating the match.
- (o:dn: = Ace Industry): Denotes an equality match, except that DN components should be considered part of the entry when doing the match.
- (:dn:2.4.6.8.10: = Dino): A filter that should be applied to any attribute supporting the given matching rule (because the attribute has been left off). Attributes supporting the matching rule contained in the DN should also be considered in the search.

The filter mechanism itself uses a handful of characters for its own purpose. The "*" character is used in substring matches; left and right parentheses are used for grouping; the backslash character is used for "escaping" characters; and the NULL string is reserved. If you need to use these characters as part of the search value, they have to be "escaped" using their hexadecimal values. Exhibit 5 lists the values and shows the associated escape sequences.

The following are other useful examples from RFC 2254:

- First we try to use opening (\28) and closing parentheses in the "cn" attribute. The phrase "Parens R Us (for all your parenthetical needs)" would result in:

```
(o=Parens R Us \28for all your parenthetical needs\29)
```

- Next, we try to use the star character in cn, preventing it from being interpreted as a wild card. cn = * would result in:

```
(cn=*\2A*)
```

Exhibit 5. Characters with Their ASCII Values and Escape Sequences

Character	ASCII Value	Escape Sequence
*	$0 \times 2a$	\2A
(	0×28	\28
)	0×29	\29
\	$0 \times 5c$	\5C
NUL	0×00	\00

- The backslash used in a Win32 filename is encoded as \5c, therefore filename = C:\MyFile would be written as:

```
(filename=C:\5cMyFile)
```

- Now we want to write a four-byte word bin = hex value 0004 as follows:

```
(bin=\00\00\00\04)
```

- The last example shows how to assign to "sn" a numer of non-ASCII characters, such as:

```
(sn=Lu\c4\8di\c4\87)
```

Directory Schema Revisited

From a practical point of view, the directory schema is defined in the configuration files. The problem for the beginner, however, is that the naming conventions in the configuration files may differ from those used in the RFCs. To make things even more complicated, there are not two different ways of describing the schema, but three! The description depends on which implementation you are using and which of these dialects you have installed.

Schema Descriptions

ASN.1 Schema Format

Abstract syntax notation one (ASN.1) is a framework used to describe tree-structured data. ASN.1 consists of two parts. One part describes the syntax rules, the other part the encoding of the data. The interesting part for us is part one. You will find a detailed description in Recommendation X.208 from the Consultative Committee in International Telephony and Telegraphy (CCITT). This notation is used mainly in the X.500 documentation. In the LDAP RFCs, it is used to describe some protocol elements. Look at the definition to learn more about it. For compatibility with X.500 servers, some schema files also contain the ASN.1 version of their schema in the form of comments.

slapd.conf Schema Format

This is the format used by the University of Michigan "standalone LDAP server," commonly referred to as "slapd." The slapd.conf schema format derives its name from the configuration file called "slapd.conf." It is used by other implementations too, for example by Netscape Directory Server versions 3 and 4. Thanks to its simplicity, it is very popular. It contains the whole schema in two configuration files, one containing the attribute definitions and one containing the object definitions. The OpenLDAP (v2) implementation called these configuration files "slapd.at.conf" and "slapd.oc.conf," respectively. OpenLDAP is based on the University of Michigan implementation of LDAP. Exhibit 6 shows an example the file "slapd.at.conf" defining the attributes. Note the attribute syntax notation,

Exhibit 6. Attribute Definitions Using the slapd.conf Schema Format

attribute	photo	bin	
attribute	personalsignature	bin	
attribute	jpegphoto	bin	
attribute	audio	bin	
attribute	labeledurl	ces	
attribute	ref	ces	
attribute	userpassword	ces	
attribute	telephonenumber	tel	
attribute	facsimiletelephonenumber	fax	tel
attribute	pagertelephonenumber	pager	tel
attribute	homephone	tel	
attribute	mobiletelephonenumber	mobile	tel
attribute	aliasedObjectName	dn	
attribute	member	dn	
attribute	owner	dn	
attribute	seealso	dn	
attribute	manager	dn	
attribute	documentauthor	dn	
attribute	secretary	dn	
attribute	lastmodifiedby	dn	
attribute	associatedname	dn	
attribute	naminglink	dn	
attribute	reciprocalnaminglink	dn	
attribute	dn	dn	

Exhibit 7. Attribute Definitions Using slapd.conf Schema Format; Excerpt from OpenLDAP Manual Page

```
attribute <name> [<name2>] { bin | ces | cis | tel | dn }
```

Associate a syntax with an attribute name. By default, an attribute is assumed to have syntax **cis**. An optional alternate name can be given for an attribute. The possible syntaxes and their meanings are:

- **bin** binary
- **ces** case exact string
- **cis** case ignore string
- **tel** telephone number string
- **dn** distinguished name

which provides human-readable aliases. Exhibit 7 presents an exerpt of the manual page for slapd.conf from OpenLDAP, which shows the syntax of the attributes. Exhibit 8 shows some object definitions using the slapd.conf schema format. Exhibit 9 shows an attribute definition as drawn from a page in the OpenLDAP manual.

LDAP (v3) Schema Format

This new schema format has been introduced, as the name suggests, with version 3 of the LDAP protocol. The schema format is described in RFC 2252, "LDAP (v3) Attribute Syntax Definitions." New in this schema format is that it enables the directory server to publish its schema using LDAP. This allows clients to retrieve the schema information from the directory server itself. With this knowledge, the client can tailor its actions specifically for this server. The information is held in the attribute "subschemaSubentry," which is one of the operational attributes. See the section "Information Model" in Chapter 3 to learn more about operational attributes. Exhibit 10 shows some typical definitions of attributes. Exhibit 11 shows some examples of object-class definitions.

Checking the Directory Schema

We have learned that a schema defines what type of data the directory can hold. But how do you know that, in the end, only data complying with your schema will be inserted into the directory server? It is the directory server itself that verifies whether inserted or modified data on the directory is compliant with the schemas defined for the directory.

The process of checking entries takes some time. If you have to insert only a few objects or change only a few attributes, time is not a factor. Problems arise when you have to insert bulk data or modify a large number of entries. In such cases, you can simply switch off

Exhibit 8. A Few Object Definitions Using the slapd.conf Schema Format

```
objectclass person
  requires
    objectClass,
    sn,
    cn
  allows
    description,
    seeAlso,
    telephoneNumber,
    userPassword
objectclass organizationalPerson
  requires
    objectClass,
    sn,
    cn
  allows
    description,
    destinationIndicator,
    facsimileTelephoneNumber,
    internationaliSDNNumber,
    l,
    ou,
    physicalDeliveryOfficeName,
    postOfficeBox,
    postalAddress,
    postalCode,
    preferredDeliveryMethod,
    registeredAddress,
    seeAlso,
    st,
    streetAddress,
    telephoneNumber,
    teletexTerminalIdentifier,
    telexNumber,
    title,
    userPassword,
    x121Address
```

Exhibit 9. Attribute Definitions Using slapd.conf Schema Format; Excerpt from OpenLDAP Manual Page

```
objectclass <name>
  requires <attrs>
  allows <attrs>
```

Define the schema rules for the object class named <name>. These are used in conjunction with the schemacheck option.

schema checking and switch it back on after you have inserted the data. This will enormously speed up the updating process. However, if the objects inserted into your directory do not conform to the schema, you will run into trouble later on.

Exhibit 10. Typical Attribute-Type Definitions Using LDAP (v3) Schema Format

```
attributetype (2.5.4.6 NAME ('c' 'countryName')
 DESC 'RFC2256: ISO-3166 country 2-letter code'
 SUP name SINGLE-VALUE)

attributetype (2.5.4.7 NAME ('l' 'localityName')
 DESC 'RFC2256: locality which this object resides in'
 SUP name)

attributetype (2.5.4.8 NAME ('st' 'stateOrProvinceName')
 DESC 'RFC2256: state or province which this object resides in'
 SUP name
```

Exhibit 11. Typical Object-Class Definitions Using LDAP (v3) Schema Format

```
objectclass (2.5.6.3 NAME 'locality'
 DESC 'RFC2256: a locality'
 SUP top STRUCTURAL
 MAY (street $ seeAlso $ searchGuide $ st $ l $ description))

objectclass (2.5.6.4 NAME 'organization'
 DESC 'RFC2256: an organization'
 SUP top STRUCTURAL
 MUST o
 MAY (userPassword $ searchGuide $ seeAlso $ businessCategory $
   x121Address $ registeredAddress $ destinationIndicator $
preferredDeliveryMethod $ telexNumber $ teletexTerminalIden-
tifier $
 telephoneNumber $ internationaliSDNNumber $
facsimileTelephoneNumber $ street $ postOfficeBox $ postalCode
$postalAddress $ physicalDeliveryOfficeName $ st $ l $ descrip-
tion))
```

Exploring the Directory Schema

A practical look at the schema should help resolve any remaining questions. We will use the Perl LDAP API, available on most operating systems. Perl syntax is straightforward; indeed, it even looks like a kind of pseudocode. Guided by line-by-line comments, readers who are not familiar with Perl should have no problem understanding the following examples. Some readers may even find the language attractive and decide to use it in the future.

Exhibit 12 is an example of a simple dump of the schema used by the directory server. The first line simply calls the Perl interpreter. If you have installed the interpreter at a different location, this line will be different on your system. The next line informs the interpreter that you will use the Net::LDAP library, which we will learn more about in Chapter 6 when we speak about the LDAP APIs. The Net::LDAP library offers all the functionality necessary to implement an LDAP client. Line 4 configures the variable "Host" that is used in line 6 when you open a connection to the machine where the LDAP server is running. In this example we assume that LDAP is running on the local machine. If it runs on a remote machine, put the network address or the DNS name of the computer instead of the local host. Line 6 also creates an LDAP object. In line 7, you bind to the LDAP server using a method of the LDAP object. The interesting stuff happens beginning with line 8. The method "schema" delivers the schema of the LDAP server; it delivers an object of the type "schema." In this example, we use the method "dump" on behalf the object "schema." This will fill your screen with a lot of information, most of which we will encounter in the following examples. You will have a complete listing of the attribute types, the object classes, the syntaxes, and the matching rules used by the directory. This information can be very helpful for the client, who can explore the directory schema and adapt its behavior to comply with the specific configuration. Line 13 releases the resources using the "unbind" method call.

Exhibit 12. Perl Script Dumping out the Schema

```
01  #!/usr/bin/perl -w
02  use Net::LDAP ;
03
04  local $Host = "localhost" ;
05
06  $ldap = Net::LDAP->new($Host) or die "$@" ;
07  $ldap->bind();
08  my $schema = $ldap->schema();
09  if ($schema) {
10      printf("Dump of Schema\n");
11      $schema->dump();
12  }
13  $ldap->unbind();
```

Exhibit 13. Perl Script Printing the Object Classes

```
...
@ObjectClasses = $schema->objectclasses();
foreach my $ObjectClass (@ObjectClasses) {
   printf("%s:%s\n", $ObjectClass,
                    $schema->name2oid($ObjectClass));
}
...
```

Instead of dumping the whole schema, we could specify the particular information we need. For example, if we want a list of all object classes used in our directory, we would substitute line 13 ($schema->dump) in Exhibit 12 with the lines shown in Exhibit 13. These lines, besides dumping all object classes, instruct the server to print out another bit of interesting information, the OID of the object class. Even more interesting, using the piece of code displayed in Exhibit 14, we obtain the matching rules in the implementation of our LDAP server and the mapping between the numbers I mentioned in Chapter 3, when we discussed matching rules. Recall that every matching rule has a unique object identifier (OID) associated with it. The printout of matching rules will resemble the example depicted in Exhibit 15.

Finally, we present another piece of interesting information about the syntaxes recognized by the directory server. The code is shown in Exhibit 16, and a piece of the listing is shown in Exhibit 17. You can request this information for the whole directory or for single attributes or entries. The library, however, can do much more. For example, you can distinguish between which attributes an entry *must* have and which attributes it *may* have with the two methods calls:

Exhibit 14. Perl Script Printing the Matching Rules

```
@MatchingRules = $schema->matchingrules();
printf("MatchingRules\n");
foreach my $MatchingRule (@MatchingRules) {
        printf("%s: %s\n",$MatchingRule,
        $schema->name2oid($MatchingRule));
}
```

Exhibit 15. Example of Matching Rules

```
CERTIFICATEEXACTMATCH:              2.5.13.34
CASEEXACTIA5MATCH:                  1.3.6.1.4.1.1466.109.114.1
CASEIGNOREIA5MATCH:                 1.3.6.1.4.1.1466.109.114.2
CASEIGNOREIA5SUBSTRINGSMATCH:       1.3.6.1.4.1.1466.109.114.3
CASEEXACTIA5SUBSTRINGSMATCH:        1.3.6.1.4.1.4203.1.2.1
INTEGERBITANDMATCH:                 1.2.840.113556.1.4.803
INTEGERBITORMATCH:                  1.2.840.113556.1.4.804
```

Exhibit 16. Perl Script Printing the Syntaxes

```
@Syntaxes = $schema->syntaxes();
printf("Syntaxes\n");
foreach my $Syntax (@Syntaxes) {
    printf("%s:%s\n",$Syntax,
                $schema->name2oid($Syntax));
}
```

Exhibit 17. Example of Syntaxes

```
AUDIO:                1.3.6.1.4.1.1466.115.121.1.4
BINARY:               1.3.6.1.4.1.1466.115.121.1.5
BITSTRING:            1.3.6.1.4.1.1466.115.121.1.6
BOOLEAN:              1.3.6.1.4.1.1466.115.121.1.7
CERTIFICATE:          1.3.6.1.4.1.1466.115.121.1.8
CERTIFICATELIST:      1.3.6.1.4.1.1466.115.121.1.9
CERTIFICATEPAIR:      1.3.6.1.4.1.1466.115.121.1.10
COUNTRYSTRING:        1.3.6.1.4.1.1466.115.121.1.11
DISTINGUISHEDNAME:    1.3.6.1.4.1.1466.115.121.1.12
```

```
foreach my $Attr ($schema->must($Object)) {
  $Must .= sprintf("%s ",$Attr);
}
foreach my $Attr (@May=$schema->may($Object)) {
  $May .= sprintf("%s ",$Attr);
}
printf("Required Attributes:%s\n",$Must);
printf("Allowed Attributes:%s\n",$May);
```

This delivers the information for the object class "person":

```
Required Attributes: cn sn
Allowed Attributes: telephoneNumber description userPassword
seeAlso
```

A word of warning, however: This method works only if the LDAP server supports LDAP (v3). It does not work with LDAP (v2).

If you want to learn more about the possibilities of exploring the directory schema, refer to the documentation of the software development kit (SDK) you will use. Most languages offer a number of methods or function calls allowing your client software to recognize the features offered by the LDAP server.

Extending the Directory Schema

If you look at the configuration files of your directory server implementation, you will see that you are using more than one schema file. In OpenLDAP, you must include all of these schema files. In other LDAP implementations, things may be slightly different, but you have to always include in some way the schema(s) you intend to use. Recall the example presented in Chapter 2, where we explicitly included three schema files: core.schema, cosine.schema, and inetorgperson.schema. Each of these files contains a number of object classes and attribute definitions. Sometimes, however, you have to store data that does not fit into any of the schemas declared in your directory implementation. The reasons for storage are manifold: Schemas do not take into account particular local requirements, and the data set of employees is very different between single enterprises. An example should make this clear. Let us assume you need a directory that holds data from a physician and that the physician's data (i.e., attributes) is not yet contained in any person object class, for example, the medical association the physician has joined, the year he subscribed to the medical association, and the subscription number to this association. These three attributes are not present in any object class defining persons. In this case, you have to extend the schema to hold the physician's object class.

If your schema files do not fit your requirements, then you have to extend your schema. This is no great problem, although you do have to consider a few things to arrive at a consistent schema. We address these immediate considerations in this chapter. The global planning phase is addressed in Chapter 9, when we discuss the design of directory services.

There are several ways to extend the schema. The following approach is a reasonable way to proceed, but there may be other approaches that are equally viable.

- *Analyze your exact requirements and compare with actual schema*: Once you understand exactly your requirements, you can see if one of your objects would satisfy your needs. Because most directory server implementations are shipped with a large number of schemas — standard schemas, vendor extensions, and application-specific schemas — it may be that you already have the schema elements suitable for the job at hand.
- *Analyze existing schemas*: Check the Internet to see if there are available schema elements that fit your needs. It is quite probable that someone else had the same requirements and has defined and published a solution to the Internet.
- *Design new schema elements*: You can subclass existing object classes if you find an analogous class or create a new one. You can also construct a new entry using an auxiliary object class. This is a solution if two or more object classes contain just the attributes you are interested in. Then you can mix up the entry from two or more object classes. This solution can, however, lead to an unclear directory design.
- *Use naming conventions*: It is important to use names that are not used by someone else because the namespace of a directory is flat. One way to assure uniqueness of attribute and object-class names is to prefix them with the enterprise name.
- *Obtain OIDs*: Once you are sure that you have to extend the schema and have defined the elements you need, the next step is to obtain object identifiers for them. Recall from the previous chapter that each schema element object class and attribute type must have an OID assigned to it. The schema contains not only object classes and attribute types, but also matching rules. However, it is not very likely that you will add matching rules because that

would entail changing the source code of the directory server implementation. You can obtain OIDs from the Internet Assigned Numbers Authority (IANA).

- *Document your object classes and attribute-type definitions*: This documentation should be available in your intranet environment. You should also think of publishing them on the Internet to prevent future name conflicts.

This was only a brief technical discussion about the possibility of extending the directory schema. We will address this issue in greater detail in Chapter 9, when we speak about the design of directory services.

Indexes

In Chapter 1, we saw that the directory server is specialized for high performance in information retrieval. Indexes are a tool to facilitate high-speed information retrieval. Besides the database files containing the actual data, there are index files used to access this data more rapidly. Indexes are built on behalf of attributes. Depending on your implementation, a few of them are predefined. On most directory servers, you will find an index for the attribute "objectClass." This index helps to speed up subtree searches in the directory.

You can configure further indexes, depending on the requirements of the directory server. This means that you should know which attributes in your implementation are frequently used for searches. These could be, for example, the "sn" and "givenName" and "uid" attributes. Again, this depends strongly on the purpose of your particular implementation. In a company phone book, users often look up a phone number using the surname and name. The opposite approach — using a phone number to look up a surname and name — is used less frequently. You can configure a number of indexes and verify their usage later on with the help of the log files.

You can even fine-tune the indexes. However, to do so, you need a thorough knowledge of the exact needs of the applications requesting data from your directory server. There are a number of different index types. Most directory server implementations recognize the following types:

- *Presence*: This type of filter is useful if the directory server executes a lot of queries that only look to see whether an attribute is defined in a given entry. For example, the filter (mobile = *) could be used to identify everyone in the organization who has a mobile phone.
- *Equality*: This filter parses for simple equality, e.g., the query filter (sn = Parker).

- *Substring*: The substring increases search efficiency if you frequently use wildcards. For example, the query (sn = *ker) would find all words ending in "ker," such as Parker or Marker. This filter type is resource intensive and is the most expensive to maintain.
- *Approximate*: We discussed the concept of "approximate matching" earlier in this chapter. This index type is used to accelerate the "sounds like" search in the database you. Remember, however, that this feature is language dependent. Consult the documentation that ships with your software to find out more. It may be that your language is not even supported. A number of vendors support U.S. English only.

Depending on your implementation, you may find other useful types of filters.

You will find that indexes are quite handy, but they come at a cost, depending on the index type and the number of indexes you define. The costs come in three forms:

1. *Increased modify and insert time*: The more indexes you have defined, the longer it will take to update or create them all in a modification or insert request.
2. *Increased memory usage*: Indexes are held in memory to increase their efficiency. The more indexes you use, the greater is the memory occupied by your directory server process.
3. *Increased disk file usage*: Index files occupy additional disk space.

You should carefully evaluate the benefit of indexes against these drawbacks and only use the indexes that you truly need. Of course, the choice of indexes depends on the demands that applications make upon your directory.

LDIF

We were introduced to LDIF (LDAP data interchange format) in Chapter 2, when we played around with some of the LDAP command lines. We learned that LDIF is a way of representing the directory in a human-readable format. However, some questions remained open. For example, how do we use special characters required in some languages, such as the "umlaut" characters in German or binary data? In this section, we take a deeper look at the LDIF format.

The initial use of the LDIF format was for the University of Michigan Project, where LDIF was used to describe the entries held in the directory. Exhibit 18 shows a piece of our example directory dumped as an LDIF file. As you can see, it is the same format the command-line tool "ldapmodify -a" uses as input to load bulk data into the directory. The LDIF format is defined in RFC 2849, "The LDAP Data

---

Exhibit 18. A Piece of the Example Directory in LDIF Format

```
dn: o=LdapAbc.org
objectClass: top
objectClass: organization
o: LdapAbc.org

dn: ou=IT,o=LdapAbc.org
objectClass: top
objectClass: organizationalUnit
ou: IT

dn: ou=HR,o=LdapAbc.org
objectClass: top
objectClass: organizationalUnit
ou: HR

dn: ou=Marketing,o=LdapAbc.org
objectClass: top
objectClass: organizationalUnit
ou: Marketing

dn: ou=Research,o=LdapAbc.org
objectClass: top
objectClass: organizationalUnit
ou: Research

dn: uid=RVoglmaier,ou=IT,o=LdapAbc.org
objectClass: top
objectClass: person
objectClass: organizationalPerson
objectClass: inetOrgPerson
cn: Reinhard Erich Voglmaier
sn: Voglmaier
givenName: Reinhard Erich
ou: IT
uid: RVoglmaier
mail: RVoglmaier@LdapAbc.org
```

Interchange Format (LDIF) — Technical Specification." The file format now has two different purposes:

- Description of directory entries
- Update of directory entries

File Format

As the name suggests, LDIF is a data interchange format that provides a description of directory entries. Because LDIF is an ASCII format, the data can be exported easily from one directory and imported into another. With the data in ASCII format, the database can easily be transported over different architectures, e.g., from a directory running on Win2000 to UNIX. Furthermore, you can dump data from a legacy system or, indeed, from any repository, convert it into LDIF, and then import it into a directory.

The second purpose of LDIF is to describe the changes to be made to a directory. We used this capability in Chapter 2 when we applied the "ldapmodify" utility to change the directory. Exhibit 19 shows an example. Because there is a one-to-one relationship between the operations on the directory and the change-records defined in LDIF, you can use LDIF to describe the changes to be made to the directory.

It is clear that the formats for the "description" and "update description" differ slightly. In the following, we will examine both formats in greater detail.

Description of Directory Entries

The LDIF file contains a dump of a number of entries. Each entry consists of a number of records, and each record is listed separately on a new line. Every entry consists of three parts:

- The distinguished name that uniquely identifies the entry
- The object class or object classes the entry belongs to
- The attributes with their respective value or values

Exhibit 18 shows a real-life example of directory entries. Exhibit 20 is a formal representation of what an LDIF file describing directory entries should look like.

There are a few exceptions to the described format of an LDIF file. For example, even though each record is separated by a new line, an

---

Exhibit 19. Example of LDIF File with Change Description

```
dn: uid=JParker, ou=IT, o=LdapAbc.org
changetype: modify
replace: mail
mail: Jparker1@LdapAbc.org

dn: uid=MJohnson, ou=Marketing, o=LdapAbc.org
changetype: delete
```

Exhibit 20. Formal Definition of LDIF File: Description of Entries

```
dn: <Distinguished Name>
objectClass: <ObjectClass>
objectClass: <ObjectClass>
?..
<attribute name>: <attribute value>
??.
```

Exhibit 21. LDIF File with a Record Containing a Folded-Attribute Value (Example Copied from RFC 2849)

```
version: 1
dn:cn=Barbara Jensen, ou=Product Development, dc=airius, dc=com
objectclass:top
objectclass:person
objectclass:organizationalPerson
cn:Barbara Jensen
cn:Barbara J Jensen
cn:Babs Jensen
sn:Jensen
uid:bjensen
telephonenumber:+1 408 555 1212
description:Babs is a big sailing fan, and travels extensively
   in search of perfect sailing conditions.
title:Product Manager, Rod and Reel Division
```

attribute value could occupy more than one line. In this case, a white space at the beginning of a line indicates the continuation of the previous line. In LDAP parlance, this is called a "folded-attribute value." See Exhibit 21 for an entry containing a record with a folded-attribute value.

You also could have an entry containing binary data. Such data has to be encoded using base-64 encoding. There are libraries available for base-64 encoding for most programming and scripting languages. An entry containing a photo would look like the example in Exhibit 22. Instead of encoding the JPEG photo using base-64, you could also include an external file in the LDIF file. Exhibit 23 shows an example.

You can also use attributes with language-specific values. These attribute values then have to be UTF-8 encoded. UTF-8 (Unicode Transformation Format-8) is an encoding that produces human-readable strings. It is a standard encoding system defined by the Unicode Consortium. Users in the United States will seldom be bothered with data in different character sets. Luckily, the ASCII characters in UTF-8 are represented with the same 7-bit code as in ASCII. If you need more information, see RFC 2253, "Lightweight Directory Access Protocol (v3): UTF-8 String Representation of Distinguished Names." For more information about the LDIF syntax, refer to RFC 2849, "The LDAP Data Interchange Format (LDIF) — Technical Specification."

Update of Directory Entries

Now let us have a look at the update description, the second form of an LDIF file. This second form describes the modification applied or to be applied to a directory. It reflects the actions upon the directory described by the functional model (see the functional model in Chapter 3 for additional details). The syntax of this LDIF format is quite similar

Exhibit 22. LDIF File with a Record Containing a Base-64-Encoded Attribute Value

```
dn: uid=JMiller,ou=IT,o=LdapAbc.org
objectClass: top
objectClass: person
objectClass: organizationalPerson
objectClass: inetOrgPerson
cn: Johann Miller
sn: Miller
givenName: Johann
ou: IT
jpegPhoto::V2hhdCBhIGNhcmVmdWwgcmVhZGVyIHlvdSBhcmUhICBUa
 GlzIGlzIGJhc2UtNjQtZW5jb2RlZCBiZWNhdXN1IGl0IGhhcyBhIGNvbnRl
 VyIGluIGl0IChhIENSKS4NICBCeSB0aGUgd2F5LCB5b3Ugc2hvdWxkIH
 JlYWxseSBnZXQgyb2wgY2hhcmFjdGVyV2OIG1vcmUu
uid: JMiller
mail: JMiller@LdapAbc.org
```

Exhibit 23. LDIF File with a Record Including a File Containing the Attribute Value

```
dn: uid=JMiller,ou=IT,o=LdapAbc.org
objectClass: top
objectClass: person
objectClass: organizationalPerson
objectClass: inetOrgPerson
cn: Johann Miller
sn: Miller
givenName: Johann
ou: IT
jpegPhoto: < file:///opt/directory/photos/jmiller.jpg
uid: JMiller
mail: JMiller@LdapAbc.org
```

to the one previously described. The encoding rules are the same, so they will not be repeated here.

Recall that the functional model knows three types of functions:

1. Interrogation operations: search, compare
2. Update operations: add, delete, modify DN, modify
3. Authentication and control operations: bind, unbind, abandon

The functions used by the LDIF format are the update operations, i.e.,

- The add function
- The delete function
- The modifyDN function
- The modify function

The general syntax of these operations is:

```
dn: <Distinguished Name>
changetype: <Type of Operation>
<attribute name>: <attribute value> <attribute value>...
...
```

Let us see one example for each of these operations to get a better idea of what they look like. Here we use "Barbara Jensen" as an example, also called "Babs," which is also used for examples in the RFCs and in the LDAP literature.

The Add Function

The changeType "add" indicates that a new entry is to be added to the directory.

Syntax —

```
dn: <Distinguished Name>
changetype: add
<attribute name>: <attribute value> <attribute value>...
...
```

Example —

```
dn: uid=BJensen, ou=IT,o=LdapAbc.org
changetype: add
objectClass: top
objectClass: person
objectClass: organizationalPerson
objectClass: inetOrgPerson
cn: Barbara Jensen
cn: Babs Jensen
sn: Jensen
givenName: Barbara
ou: IT
jpegPhoto: < file:///opt/ directory/photos/BJensen.jpg
uid: BJensen
mail: Bjensen@LdapAbc.org
```

The Delete Function

The changeType "delete" indicates that the entry with the DN has to be deleted from the directory.

Syntax —

```
dn: <Distinguished Name>
changetype: delete
```

Example —

```
dn: uid=CMiller, ou=IT,o=LdapAbc.org
changetype: delete
```

The modifyDN Function

The modifyDN function can:

- Change only the RDN
- Move the entry in the directory information tree
- Both of the above

Note that in LDAP (v2), the moving of entries in the DIT is not allowed. You have to delete the old entry and create a new one instead of moving it.

Syntax —

```
dn: <Distinguished Name>
changetype: moddn
[newsuperior: <Distinguished Name of new superior>]
[deleteoldrdn:] (0 | 1)
[newrdn: <new RDN>]
```

Examples — Let us assume that Barbara Jensen moves from IT to Marketing. This calls for a change of the DN, a new superior entry, and removal of the old entry. The resultant changes in the LDIF file are as follows:

```
dn: uid=BJensen, ou=IT,o=LdapAbc.org
changetype: moddn
newrdn: uid=Bjensen
newsuperior: ou=Marketing, o=LdapAbc.org
deleteoldrdn: 1
```

The new DN of Barbara Jensen is now: uid = Bjensen, ou = Marketing, o = LdapAbc.org

Now let us see an example where the RDN changes. For example, we have a new person that would have a uid in conflict with an existing one. Let us assume there will be a new person — Joseph Smith, uid = JSmith — and that there is already a uid "JSmith" from a person "James Smith." Let us further assume that the IT department will avoid future conflicts by naming the new JSmith as JSmith1 and the original as JSmith0. To make the change in the directory, we would say:

```
dn: JSmith, ou=Marketing, o=LdapAbc.org
changetype: moddn
deleteoldrdn: 1
```

```
newrdn: JSmith1
```

One word about renaming an entry that has children. This action would require renaming an entire subtree. If you would like to do this via ldapmodify, you have to do this in three steps:

1. Create a new entry with the new DN
2. Change the RDN of all children
3. Delete the old DN

Again, an example makes this clear. Let us assume that Human Resources is to be changed to HR (perhaps to avoid typos).

```
dn: ou=HR, o=LdapAbc.org
changetype: add
objectclass: top
objectclass: organizationalUnit
ou: HR

dn: PSmith, ou=Human Resources, o=LdapAbc.org
changetype: modrdn
newrdn: PSmith
deleteoldrdn: 1
newsuperior: ou=HR, o=LdapAbc.org

dn: ou=Human Resources, o=LdapAbc.org
changetype: delete
```

The second step you have to do for all children. If the children have further children, you have to create down the hierarchy all entries having children, rename the children, and delete the old entries. If you have an extensive subtree, this can become painful. The alternative is to export the whole directory, rename all "ou = Human Resources" into "ou = HR," physically delete the old directory files, and import the new directory. We will see more about this in Chapter 7, "LDAP Directory Server Administration."

The Modify Function

The modify function changes the attributes of an entry in the directory. Thus, there are three different types of modification:

1. Add an attribute
2. Delete an attribute
3. Replace an attribute

Syntax —

```
dn: <Distinguished Name>
changetype: modify
```

```
<modify type> <attribute>
[<attribute name> <attribute value> ? ]
```

Examples — The following example shows the addition of a mobile attribute to the entry with distinguished name JSmith1, ou = Marketing, o = LdapAbc.org.

```
dn: JSmith1, ou=Marketing, o=LdapAbc.org
changetype: modify
add: mobile
mobile: 0170 64738 8374 377
```

The following would change the new assigned number:

```
dn: JSmith1, ou=Marketing, o=LdapAbc.org
changetype: modify
replace: mobile
mobile: 0170 64738 8374 477
```

The following would delete the number again:

```
dn: JSmith1, ou=Marketing, o=LdapAbc.org
changetype: modify
delete: mobile
```

LDIF: Conclusion, an Example in Perl

One common task is synchronizing the directory with a database or some other data source. The data source provides a listing of all entries, and this list can be used to update the directory so that the LDAP database reflects the new data.

The first approach is to look up every entry to see if it exists and verify that the values are still the same. This entails sending all the data over the network to the directory so that the values can be compared with those held in the directory. If the number of employees in your enterprise is not too high (several hundred), this could be a reasonable solution. However, it can be problematic if there are any restrictions on the queries you can make against the directory.

Another alternative is to obtain a dump of the entries in a plain file, e.g., database.txt. When the sync request arrives, you rename the old file database.old.txt and produce, via the diff system call or a customized utility, an instruction list that updates the directory. This instruction list can then be printed out in the LDIF format. In order to do this you need three functions:

1. *deleteEntry*: Deletes an entry from the directory
2. *addEntry*: Adds a new entry to the directory
3. *modEntry*: Modifies an entry in the database

Exhibit 24. Perl Function that Produces LDIF Output to Add an Entry into the Directory

```perl
sub addEntry {
      my ($EntryPtr) = $_ ;
      my %Entry = %{EntryPtr} ;
      my @objectClasses =
("top,""organizationalPerson","inetOrgPerson");

      printf("dn: uid = %s, ou=%s, o=%s\n",$Entry{uid},
$Entry{ou}, $Entry{o}) ;
      printf("changetype: add\n");
      foreach $class (@objectClasses) {
          printf("objectClass: %s\n",$class);
      }
      printf("sn: %s\n",$Entry{sn});
      printf("cn: %s %s\n",$Entry{givenName},$Entry{sn});
      printf("givenName: %s\n", $Entry{givenName});
      printf("ou: %s\n",$Entry{ou});
      printf("telephoneNumber: %s\n", $Entry{phone});
      printf("mail: %s\n",$Entry{mail});
      printf("uid: %s\n",$Entry{uid});
      printf("\n\n");
}
```

The Perl functions shown in Exhibit 24 generate an LDIF file that reflects these changes in the directory. The first function that we need is the addEntry function, which takes an associative array as a parameter. The array contains the attribute names as keys.

The second function that we need is the delEntry function. The simplest of the three, it is as follows:

```perl
sub delEntry {
        my ($EntryPtr) = $_ ;

        %Entry = %{$EntryPtr} ;
    printf("dn: uid = %s, ou=%s, o=%s\n",$Entry{uid}, $Entry{ou},
$Entry{o}) ;
        printf("changetype: delete\n"):
}
```

The third function, modEntry, is something different. To handle all possible situations while keeping the code simple, it first deletes the entry and then adds the entry with the new values:

```perl
sub modEntry {
        my ($EntryPtr) = $_ ;
        delEntry($EntryPtr);
        addEntry($EntryPtr);
  }
```

What is missing is a program uniting all of these operations: First, we define the values needed for all three functions, in this case only the name of the enterprise. The program then loads the ASCII file of the directory data in an associative array. Then we execute a function that looks to see whether the values of the attributes in the entries and the database are the same. For each "yes," it deletes the corresponding row in the associative array. If there is a discrepancy, it calls the function "modEntry" to resolve the discrepancy and then deletes the row in the associative array. If there is no line corresponding to the entry, it calls the function "addEntry." After processing all entries, the program looks to see whether there are any rows remaining in the associative array. If there are, then this indicates that some of the entries have been deleted in the data source. To deal with these lines, the program then calls the "delEntry" function. Exhibit 25 shows the code to perform all of these functions.

The functions still missing are getDirectoryEntries and its counterpart putDirectoryEntries. These could be functions that simply write down and read the entries in the form "key: value." The key is then used for the lookup. Another function that is missing is the one that produces the NewEntries hash or associative array, which should have the same syntax as the two previously mentioned functions. It could also be interesting to use objects instead of these hashes. In this case, the addEntry, delEntry, and modEntry functions could be implemented as methods.

The program logic also works if we simply install all entries new from scratch. In this case, the hash DirectoryEntries is empty, so the statement:

```
if (! $DirectoryEntries{$dn}
```

is always true and the entry is added.

Exhibit 25. Main Perl Function to Produce LDIF Output

```
%DirectoryEntries = getDirectoryEntries();
%NewEntries = getNewEntries();

foreach $dn (keys %NewEntries)) {
        if (! $DirectoryEntries{$dn}) {
            addEntry($DirectoryEntries{$dn}) ;
        } else {
            if ( $DirectoryEntries{$dn} == $NewEntries{$dn}) {
                delete($DirectoryEntries{$dn}) ;
            } else {
                modEntry($DirectoryEntries{$dn}) ;
                delete($DirectoryEntries{$dn}) ;
            }
        }
}
foreach $dn (keys % DirectoryEntries) {
        delEntry($NewEntries($dn)) ;
}
putDirectoryEntries(%NewEntries);
```

The program produces a file in the LDIF format that can be used to update the directory with the command "ldapmodify."

Just for completeness, the Net::LDAP package has an object called Net::LDAP::LDIF that reads and writes a complete LDIF file in a single step. Have a look at the Web site dedicated to the perl package or consult the documentation delivered with the software distribution. Software and documention are available at the Net::LDAP project site: http://perl-ldap.sourceforge.net.

LDAP URLs

As promised in Chapter 2, we now take a closer look at LDAP URLs, which are used to search in a directory. LDAP URLs are a handy tool to use in a browser because they allow us to query a directory using any number of widely available clients (Netscape, Opera, Internet Explorer, or others). The Konquerer Web browser — available for Linux (e.g., with the SuSE Linux distribution from version 7 and up) — is a favorite of the author. This browser allows you to browse inside a directory as you would a file system.

Note that LDAP URLs are not limited to use in Web browsers. They could also be used by programs (Perl, Java, C, etc.), by preprocessors in Web servers (such as PHP), and CGI (common gateway interface) scripts. For more information about LDAP URLs, see RFC 2255, "The LDAP URL Format."

Let us have a look at the syntax of an LDAP URL:

```
"ldap://"[hostname [":" portNumber] ] "/" baseDN [ query ]
```

where the query is:

```
["?" attributeList ["?" scope "?" filter ["?" extensions ] ] ]
```

- *hostname*: IP number or host name of the directory server
- *portNumber*: Port that the directory server is listening on
- *baseDN*: Distinguished name needed to start the query
- *attributeList*: Attributes to be returned by the query
- *scope*: Scope of the query, which can be one of the values: base, one, sub (see the "Search Revisited" section at the beginning of this chapter for more information about the scope)
- *filterString*: Query filter (see the discussion of filters in the "Search Revisited" section)

The square brackets indicate that the data inside them is optional. The rest — such as the quotation marks, colons, the slashes, and the LDAP text — have to be typed in.

You have to pay particular attention to the characters allowed in URLs. Indeed, a number of characters have special meaning and have to be "escaped" using the "%" prefix as describe in RFC 1738, "Uniform Resource Locators (URL)." The classic example is the space sign escaped with %20. For example, the URL o = University of Michigan, c = US would give:

```
ldap://www.openldap.org/o=University%20of%20Michigan,%20c=US?sn,
cn?sub?sn=Zeilenga
```

Exhibit 26 lists the prohibited characters in LDAP URLs and their associated escape sequences.

Differences between LDAP (v2) and LDAP (v3)

This section identifies the most significant differences between LDAP (v2) and LDAP (v3). The points listed here appear throughout this book when we discuss the corresponding arguments. The following items are supported by LDAP (v3) and are absent in LDAP (v2):

- Directory server entries (DSE) provide information, including the versions of the LDAP protocol supported, a list of the controls, extended operations, and SASL (simple authentication and security layer) mechanisms supported by the server. They also define the naming contexts of the server, i.e., they specify the portion of the directory tree managed by the server.

Exhibit 26. Prohibited Characters in LDAP URLs and Their Escape Sequences

Prohibited Characters	Escape Sequence
space	%20
<	%3C
>	%3E
"	%22
#	%23
%	%25
{	%7B
}	%7D
|	%7C
[	%5B
\	%5C
]	%5D
^	%5E
`	%60
~	%7E

- The DSEs also allow publishing of the directory information tree (DIT), making it possible for the client to see the directory tree and adapt its behavior to the information contained in the tree.
- The modifyDN function can move an entry inside the DIT.
- The user can specify controls (both on the server and on the client) that extend the functionality of an LDAP operation.
- The user can request the server to perform extended operations (beyond the standard LDAP operations).
- Attribute values and distinguished names have been internationalized through the use of the ISO 10,646-character set.
- Most protocol data elements can be encoded as ordinary strings (e.g., distinguished names).
- SASL mechanisms can be used with LDAP to provide associated security services.

Conclusion: Work in Progress

At the time of this writing, the standardization process for LDAP remains a work in progress, with work is still under way in several different areas. In this section, we review the projects that are under way and describe each briefly. These projects are in the draft status, and you will find them on the IETF Web site (http://www.ietf.org) under "drafts." It is very probable that by the time you read this book many of the drafts will not exist any more because, of course, drafts expire. Every draft has an expiration time when it becomes obsolete. Once it is obsolete, work on it may continue or it may become RFC (entirely or in part combined with other drafts.)

You can find more information at the site of IETF at http://www.ietf.org, where you can search for "working groups."

LDAP Duplication/Replication/Update Protocols (LDUP)

There is a workgroup addressing the following problems associated with replication:

- The overall architecture describing the key components of replication and its interaction
- The replication information model responsible for maintaining the schema and data held by different LDAP (v3) servers. This contains the following points:
  Replication agreements
  Consistency models
  Replication models
  Managing deleted objects and their states
  Administration and management
- Extended protocol specifications to allow replication of data

■ Protocol specifications to allow administration of replication agreements

■ Procedures for detection and resolution of replication conflicts

■ Profiles

■ Client update that enables the client to synchronize with the LDAP server

A list of available drafts can be found in Appendix B of this volume.

LDAP Extensions (LDAPext)

This working group is extending the LDAP protocol with a number of useful features:

■ Server-side sorting of search results. Until now, sorting was the job of the client. This should enable the client to specify the sort order and retrieve a limited result list.

■ Language tags, which will allow the full range of international characters to be represented

■ Dynamic directories, which will allow refresh operations for frequently changing data

■ Referral and knowledge maintenance. Until now, only referrals that are returned to the client have been standardized. The new standard will specify how referrals are to be held in the directory.

■ LDAP server discovery, which should help the client to detect a suitable LDAP server

■ LDAP APIs. Until now, the only API specification was for the C language. The API specified in RFC 1823 will be updated to include the latest features of LDAP (v3) and to accommodate a Java API.

■ Signed directory information. The directory information provided by the directory server should be validated before delivery to the client. A standard is being developed with a mechanism to ensure the integrity of the information delivered.

For a list of available drafts, go to Appendix B. Work on this group has been closed recently because of a lack of consensus on remaining issues. However, the discussion list is still open and the proposed extensions are now handled as individual submissions.

LDAP (v3) Revision (LDAPbis)

This workgroup will deliver working standards from a series of drafts defined as RFCs 2251–2256 and 2829–2831. It will deliver an "applicability statement" defining LDAP (v3). For a list of available drafts, go to Appendix B.

Chapter 5

Distributed Architectures

Until now, we have seen only simple directory architectures. We had a single directory server holding the whole directory and serving a number of clients. However, life is rarely so simple, and you probably have a somewhat more difficult implementation in place.

A single directory server is not always sufficient to meet your requirements. Sometimes it is necessary to keep a copy of the same data at different locations to optimize access speed. There are many good reasons to do so, and we will discuss them later in greater detail. For now, let us review a few without further comment. For example, one reason could be to bring the server closer to the clients. This is helpful in the case of a wide-area network (WAN) with slow network connections between the different local-area networks (LANs) that make up the network. Another reason could be load balancing, where an overloaded directory server is distributed over two or more machines to increase throughput. Whatever the reason for distributing the directory over several physical servers, the pieces should form a single logical directory server.

The LDAP protocol running over TCP/IP is well suited for running in a distributed architecture. You can even design your LDAP architecture to cross enterprise boundaries. In this chapter, we will learn how.

Let us begin with a familiar example, the Web browser. The HTTP protocol running also over TCP/IP is indeed a very well known example of such a distributed architecture. Consider the myriad of Web servers holding a wealth of data; it is clear that not all the data can be held on a single server. Furthermore, it happens that the same data may be available from different places. This redundancy allows the user to choose the nearest location. It furthermore allows the user to contact another server should the first server become unavailable.

You can design the architecture so that the search for the available server becomes automatic (round-robin architecture or proxy). You can also cross enterprise boundaries, with your links pointing to Web servers outside your enterprise boundary, if the configuration of the firewall allows this. The underlying concepts are the same for LDAP.

Data distribution is closely coupled with the protocol nature of LDAP. Indeed, directory services is one piece of the distributed computing environment (DCE), which was developed by the Open Systems Foundation (OSF) that converged in the Open Group. DCE version 1.0 was released in 1992 and contained the following major services:

- Distributed time services
- Distributed file services
- Remote procedure call (RPC)
- Directory services

The distributed computing environment has the goal of coordinating resources and applications in large heterogeneous networks. A heterogeneous network is made up of computers on different hardware platforms running different operating systems. The TCP/IP and OSI protocol suites provide the basis of the communication between these computers.

The administration of such a DCE requires standards for making a number of services available over the whole network. One such service is the time service. Timing is very important when a large number of computers are linked together. Another very important service is our directory service. As we have seen in previous chapters, directory services are used to hold very different information. Naming services (e.g., domain name services [DNS]), network information services (NIS), and the distribution of configuration data (for example, alias maps for sendmail) are examples of information that should be administered at one point only but made available all over the network. To distribute directory services effectively, reliably, and efficiently, you must have the tools of replication and partitioning.

It frequently happens that a company's intranet has a number of different data repositories on different platforms. The reason is mostly historical and derives from the way applications were born. It is quite common for each application to uses its own repository. It is also common for these applications to store the same or similar data. These applications normally have grown up separately from each other and have a life of their own. In this way, a number of information islands are created in the enterprise, each of them using different hardware and software. It happens, therefore, that almost the same data is held on different systems in a different way. This not only keeps administration efforts high; it also makes it difficult to obtain a unique and consistent view of the data. The installation of a directory could potentially solve this problem, but it is not always possible to migrate all application to use a directory for data storage.

If you have such a distributed system — for whatever reason — you will need to optimize the management of and access to the data. What you have to do is to find a way of consolidating the data. This chapter addresses the issue of how to "hold together" such distributed systems. It consists of two parts, corresponding to the two reasons for why systems are distributed:

1. To divide (partition) the same architecture for a gain in performance or availability or both. The division is planned and optimized for a given situation.
2. To have the same data on different architectures (replication) for application needs. The division has historical reasons, slows down performance, and increases administration efforts. Sometimes you have to live with this situation, even if it is not optimized. However, we will see that there are strategies for improving this situation too.

Introduction to Replication and Partitioning

There are two concepts supporting the distribution of directory data over multiple directory servers: replication and partitioning.

Partitioning distributes a database over two or more LDAP servers. As mentioned previously, you cannot hold an infinite amount of data on the same server. For one thing, the amount of disk space is limited. Despite the ever-increasing capacity of hard disks, it is not possible to continue adding more disks or substituting the existing disks with larger ones. Very large databases become cumbersome for the backup procedures. The time it takes to make a backup increases with the amount of data you have to back up. Furthermore, the larger the database is, the slower will be search and access operations. Add, update, and modify operations are all affected by the size of the database. Remember that LDAP repositories are optimized for access speed, not for update speed. Therefore, with the growth of database volume, the time required for update processes increases much more than the time required for search processes.

The more data your directory holds, the more often clients will contact it. This means increased network traffic, which will slow down the response time of your server. There is also an upper limit of parallel requests supported by a directory server. If you reach this limit, you will have to think about distributing the directory over more servers.

Data ownership is another reason for holding the data on different servers. Assume that two departments need to have a directory administration of their own. Furthermore, it may be that the requirements of these two departments to the directory service are quite different.

Therefore, the configuration of their servers would be different. In this case, it is convenient to install and maintain the directory on two different servers.

Replication puts the same data onto two or more other directory servers. There are several good reasons to do so. Having more servers that offer directory services, you can distribute the client requests among these servers. This increases the performance on execution of the requests. More requests can be elaborated in parallel. Thus performance increases. If your directory server installation has reached the limit of parallel requests that it can handle, it could be a good idea to put two directory servers in place, each a replication of the other.

You can also configure your clients to use the directory server nearest to them. If this server does not respond, the client can then contact an alternative server. This strategy keeps network traffic low and results in a huge performance boost.

If the servers are located on different LANs, the clients on each LAN will continue to work even if the connection between the LANs is down. This means a gain in availability of directory services on your network in case of network failure. In the event of a server crash, clients still have the option of switching to another directory server so that they can continue to work. This is a gain in availability in case of server failure. Thus replication can protect your enterprise from both server and network failures.

Many sites also use replication for backup procedures. Imagine that you have a master LDAP server and a slave LDAP server. (We will discuss the master and slave server further in the following section.) As a backup procedure, you take the slave offline and make an offline backup. Use the master for the LDAP traffic. It will, therefore, answer the queries and accept updates of the directory. The updates cannot be transferred to the slave until the slave is down, but as soon as the backup procedure finishes and you put the slave online again, the master server will push all modifications made in the meantime onto the slave server.

In the next two sections we will cover both partitioning and replication. First we will look at how we can partition a directory and which type of partitioning is allowed. When a directory server receives a request that it cannot answer because it lacks the requisite data, it responds by telling the client that it cannot answer to its request. However, this answer is connected with a hint telling the client who it should contact to get the information it needs. It is then up to the client to decide whether to follow the suggestion of the directory server or give up and inform the user of the failure. We will see that a referral is a special object type that informs the client that it has to contact another server. It is then up to the client to follow the referral or not. There is also an alternative possibility to the referral, called "chaining."

In this case, the server does not transfer the request it received from a client to another server. Instead, it acts upon the client's request and contacts the server it thinks should handle the request. Once it gets the result back, it sends it on to the client as if it had answered the request. The client, however, has no idea at all what really happened. It sees only that its request was answered. If the server contacted by the LDAP server does not hold the information, it could contact yet another server.

Once we have done with this interesting concept, we will see the different replication scenarios. The easiest form of replication is the master-slave replication. At configurable intervals, a replication process copies the data that has been modified from the master to the slave. The multimaster replication is somewhat more complicated because you have several servers that accept update operations from clients. You have to configure a policy that allows resolving potential conflicts.

Now a word about standards: The only concept supported by standards at the time of this writing is the referral. There is also the alias, which we saw in Chapter 3. However, nearly every directory implementation supports replication. Most support chaining as well. Still, there is not yet a standard definition, which is the reason why two different implementations of a directory server cannot replicate between each other. Work is under way to define standards regarding replication. At this time, the working group called LDUP (LDAP duplication/replication/update protocols) is finishing its efforts to define a minimal standard for replication. You can learn more about what is going on at the Web site of the Internet Engineering Task Force (IETF), following the link "working groups" (http://www.ietf.org). There are several working groups for issues other than replication. Choose the ones beginning with LDAP.

Data Distribution between LDAP and Non-LDAP Systems

In the last section of this chapter, you will see that there are a number of possibilities to integrate different data sources. The most flexible of these possibilities is a broker between the different data sources and the LDAP server. This broker, however, has to be written and maintained.

The most frequent repositories you will find in an enterprise are databases of users and groups defined to access system resources. The same users, however, are defined only in the enterprise directory. We will see briefly a couple of examples of how these user databases can be integrated into the directory.

The last method to integrate different repositories into the company directory is to use the metadirectory technology. A metadirectory can integrate different information sources produced by different applications to provide one consistent view of all the available data. Nearly all suppliers of directory servers offer metadirectory solutions.

All of these issues are works in progress, because nearly all suppliers continue to provide diverse solutions to meet the requirements of the market. Because work on LDAP is far from being completed, the work on integrating directories with other important repositories required in every enterprise also has to continue.

Partitioning

Partitioning is the action of dividing one large directory into two or more smaller and therefore more easily manageable pieces that combine to form a complete, logical unit. Once divided, the clients can continue accessing the directories as if they were on the same directory server. The ability to access the directories as one logical directory can be achieved through the use of referrals or by chaining.

We will see what partitioning is and learn how to partition a directory. In the introduction we learned about the benefits of partitioning. We will learn more about this in Chapter 9, which addresses the topics of planning and design of directory services. In this chapter, we will concentrate on the technical aspects of partitioning.

Once we have an understanding of partitioning, we will look at referrals. We will learn how to create a referral and understand what happens when the directory server sends back a referral. We will also see the different kinds of referrals.

We then move on to have a look at chaining and discuss the differences between referrals and chaining. Note, however, that chaining is not yet standardized, and therefore not all directory servers support chaining.

What Is Partitioning?

Let us consider a very basic situation, as shown in Exhibit 1. Our enterprise Ldap_abc.de has grown up and now it is ldap_abc.org. The org extension indicates a change in the organization's status, but that is not the point. The point for us is that the organization now spans more than one country, with each of these countries having a directory server of its own.

For the moment, let us assume that besides the server in Germany, we now have a server in the United Kingdom, too. Exhibit 1 shows that we hold the German part of the directory on the German server, while the U.K. directory points to the U.K. server, managed completely

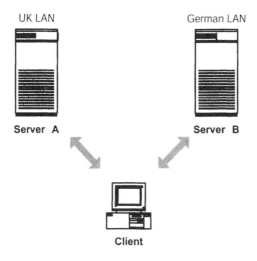

UK LAN   German LAN

Server A   Server B

Client

Exhibit 1. Partitioning of a Directory

in the United Kingdom. The main server is still in Germany and holds also the referral to the U.K. server. If a client asks for ou = UK, ldap_abc.de, it refers to the United Kingdom. I presume that users are more likely to use their own data, i.e., users in the United Kingdom are more likely to need the data held on the U.K. directory server, while users in Germany are more likely to use data held on the German directory server. But if a German user needs data from the U.K. directory server, she can access the data, if she is authorized to do so.

Partitioning also refers to a situation where a piece of the directory tree is removed and put on a different directory server. Exhibit 2 illustrates this more complicated example. This architecture has a number of advantages. Users on the LAN in the United Kingdom do not need to use the network link between the United Kingdom and Germany. This means better performance and greater availability. Should the network link between Germany and the United Kingdom be down, both sites still have access to their local data. On the other hand, if users on the U.K. LAN need access to the German data, they

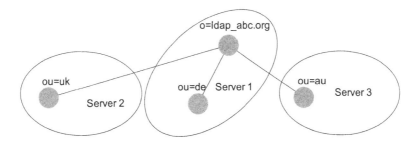

o=ldap_abc.org

ou=uk   ou=de Server 1   ou=au   Server 3

Server 2

Exhibit 2. Directory Divided into Three Partitions

can still do so using the network link if the link is up and running. However, the clients in the United Kingdom have to be configured to use the U.K. server, and the clients in Germany to use the German server. Both directory servers will send a referral to the other server if they are unable to provide the requested information. The client then decides whether to follow the referral and try to contact the server holding the desired information. We previously said that the two directories build a complete logical unit, but this is not exactly the whole truth. Using referrals, clients notice very well that a piece of the directory is on another directory server. Thus it is more accurate to say that clients can navigate seamlessly in the directory spanned by the two directory servers.

In the next example, we add a new organizational unit on a new server. Let us assume that we decide to locate all organizational units outside of the main server, which now has a simple dispatch function only. Exhibit 3 depicts this scenario. Using this setup, we can divide a large directory into a number of smaller partitions. Note, however, that each partition has to be a real directory tree. Exhibit 4 shows an invalid partition, where the two organizational units of the partition on server 2 do not have a common ancestor lying inside the partition. The directory on server 2 does not build a tree, and therefore the partition lying on server 2 is not a legal subtree of the root partition on server 0.

Exhibit 5 shows another example of an invalid partition. The partition on server 0 is illegal because the partition contains a hole. For example, there is no element between the object type "inetOrg-Person" with RDN uid = JParker and the organization "o = ldap_abc.org." To make the partition legal, we could move the organizational unit in the partition on Server 0 or move the person with RDN uid = JParker into the partition on server 1.

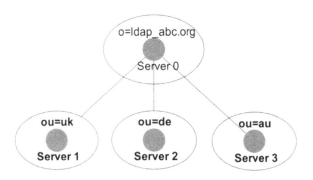

Exhibit 3. A Main Server with Three Organizational Units on Different Partitions

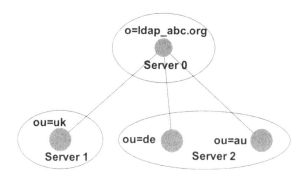

Exhibit 4. Example of an Illegal Partition

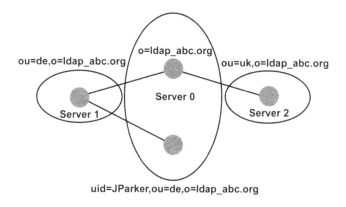

Exhibit 5. Example of Illegal Partition, Ancestor Missing

Gluing the Directories Together

Now assume we have partitioned our directory servers and want to get them up and running. However, there is still one point missing. Look again at Exhibit 3. How does directory server 0 know that the subtree "ou = de" is located on directory server 2? And how, in turn, does directory server 1 know that its ancestor is located on directory server 0?

These details are held in the "knowledge information." The "superior knowledge information" points to the directory server containing the ancestor of the current directory root. The "subordinate knowledge information" points from the ancestor to its child. Most directory server implementations hold this information in the root DSE (DSA specific entry). Recall that DSA is the name used in the X.500 protocol for the directory server (directory server agent).

Note that there is still no standardization. Work is under way, but you can learn more about the knowledge information and other questions about referrals in a draft report available from IETF (draft-ietf-asid-ldapv3-referral-xx.txt).

Referrals

This is the only concept in LDAP (v3) now defined as a standard by an RFC. If a client asks a directory server for an entry it does not contain, the server sends the referral information back. Its function is to tell the client that the desired entry is not available on this server and suggest where to find the desired information. The referral has the following structure:

- The host name of the directory server
- The port number of the directory server
- The base DN of the new target. If omitted, the client tries the same DN it searched on this server.

There are two types of referrals: The smart referral implements the "subordinate knowledge information," and the "superior knowledge information" is implemented by the global referral. The referral that implements the subordinate information is sometimes identified in the literature as a "smart referral," and the global referral is simply called a "referral." In any case, the global referral refers to another directory server if the server you are querying does not have the requested information. In the case of a superior knowledge information, the referenced server does have this information and delivers it to the client. In this way, the directory server could be thought of as a kind of proxy server. All requests it is not able to resolve are forwarded to another directory server that may contain smart referrals to the directory server containing this information. The client has to express explicitly that it wishes to follow the referral. The analogy to the proxy server is, however, not to be considered strict. A proxy server works more as a chaining server than as a referral. The client using a proxy server has no idea that the one that actually holds the data and elaborates the query is not the proxy itself but another server.

Examples

Until now, the discussion may have been interesting, but an example will explain much more than an entire chapter of theory. So let us change our example slightly to see data distribution at work. This time, let us assume that we have a brand-new directory server installed in the United States. This directory server will be used to administer all information regarding the United States. Clients located in the United States will use this directory server, while clients located in Germany will use the German one. Exhibit 6 shows this scenario. In our example, one directory server is running on the standard port, and the other directory server is running on Port 700. This example is not presented

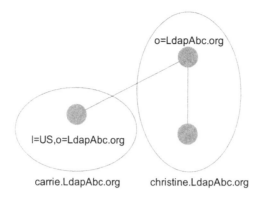

o=LdapAbc.org

l=US,o=LdapAbc.org

carrie.LdapAbc.org   christine.LdapAbc.org

Exhibit 6. New Location in United States Will Need a New Directory Server

to show that it is easy to listen at a nonstandard port. No, the objective is to allow you to try out this example even if you own only one server for test purposes.

The machine called christine.LdapAbc.org is running the directory server with directory root:

```
"o=LdapAbc.org"
```

On this directory server, we will find the entire directory information tree except the subtree:

```
"l=US, o=LdapAbc.org."
```

On the server called "carrie.LdapAbc.org," we find the directory server containing information regarding the U.S. location. This directory server has the directory root entry:

```
"l=US, o=LdapAbc.org"
```

Once the two directory servers are configured and running, everything seems to work quite nicely. If we query Christine, it will report any data located on its directory server. If we query Carrie, its directory server will do the same. If we want to have information from Carrie regarding the search base:

```
"ou=IT, l=US, o=LdapAbc.org"
```

we will get a "no such object" message. If we ask Christine about entries not contained in the l = US subtree, the server cannot answer us.

First we will explain to the LDAP server mounted on Carrie how to retrieve the information in the l = US subtree. This we can achieve

via the referral object. The next line shows our first attempt to find a
Mister Seidl, working in the United States, on our directory server.

```
ldapsearch -b "o=LdapAbc.org" -h christine.LdapAbc.org
"(&(l=US)(sn=Seidl))"
```

The server will not report any result. Then we add the referral that
explains how to arrive at the subtree where Mister Seidl is located.

The distinct name of the referral is just the mount point between
the two servers. The object class is "referral," which inherits from
"extensibleObject." The last attribute in the referral entry is the LDAP
URL where you can find the subtree. Now the search should work
fine. But, as you note, we do not get the information. We get instead
from the server a hint to look at the directory server

```
ldap://christine.LdapAbc.org/l=US, o=LdapAbc.org
```

using the distinct name:

```
l=US, o=LdapAbc.org
```

If we want to get all of the information in one step, we have to tell
the client to follow automatically all referrals. With the command line
we are using, it is enough to specify the -c flag.

So one part of our job is done. The client asking the central server
for information on the U.S. site gets a referral or gets the data directly.
If a person in the United States connects with the directory on her
site now, she still gets "no such object." You have to tell the server
Christine to contact the server Carrie if it does not contain the requested
information, by setting up a global referral to the server Carrie. The
specific command depends on the implementation of the directory
server. In the OpenLDAP configuration file, all you have to do is to
add this line:

```
referral ldap://Carrie.LdapAbc.org
```

to set up a global referral to the server Carrie.

And Now ... from the Client Point of View

Concluding the discussion about referrals, it is worthwhile to have a
look at the previous example from the client point of view. We will
use the example mentioned above.

The LDAP Server A with the root DN "o = LdapAbc.org" has the
organizational unit ou = US. This entry in reality does not live on
server A, but is a referral pointing to Server B with root DN "ou = US,
o = LdapAbc.org." Since not everybody has two machines to test out

the example, this exercise uses two LDAP servers listening on two different ports: one on the standard port and one on port 700. For this experiment, you should create a configuration file equal to server A, but with root DN ou = US, o = LdapAbc.org, and start it on port 700. Look at the documentation shipped with your directory server software to learn how to do that.

Furthermore, you should create some entries. I suggest creating the same entries as in server A, only with different root DN and different surnames/given names to test out queries on both servers. You have to configure two things:

■ The subordinate knowledge information on server A:

```
ref: ldap://127.0.0.1:700/ou=US,o=LdapAbc.org
```

■ The superior knowledge information on server B:

```
referral ldap://127.0.0.1
```

After configuring and restarting the server, we can try it out using the LDAP command-line tools as well as a Java program to test our implementation.

Let us first search an entry on the first server using the command-line tool. The entry with sn = Voglmaier resides on server A. The command shown in Exhibit 7 does the job. The response to our request gives the hint that there could be further information available using the reported URL. It is now the job of the client software to decide if it should follow the LDAP URL

```
ldapsearch -LLL -b "o=LdapAbc.org" -h localhost -p 700
"(sn=Voglmaier)"
```

Exhibit 7. Search Command to Find Entry on Server A: Its Output

```
ldapsearch -LLL -b "o=LdapAbc.org" -h localhost -p 389
"(sn=Voglmaier)"

dn: uid=RVoglmaier,ou=IT,o=LdapAbc.org
objectClass: top
objectClass: person
objectClass: organizationalPerson
objectClass: inetOrgPerson
cn: Reinhard Erich Voglmaier
sn: Voglmaier
givenName: Reinhard Erich
ou: IT
uid: RVoglmaier
mail: RVoglmaier@LdapAbc.org

# refldap://127.0.0.1:700/ou=US,o=LdapAbc.org??sub
```

or instead deliver the following result:

```
Referral (10)
Referral: ldap://127.0.0.1/o=LdapAbc.org??sub
```

Again, we see the hint to have a look at the localhost that could contain further information.

The query:

```
ldapsearch -LLL -b "ou=US, o=LdapAbc.org" -h localhost -p
700"(sn=King)"
```

results in the output shown in Exhibit 8, which shows as the entry of Stephen King. Here the directory server knows that only itself has information about the base ou = US.

```
ldapsearch -LLL -b "ou=US, o=LdapAbc.org" -h localhost -p
700"(sn=Voglmaier)"
```

The search for Voglmaier, which does not exist in ou = US, does not deliver anything because Voglmaier resides in Italy. Leave out "ou=US" and you should get back the referral.

Exhibit 9 shows a brief program in Java that does the same thing.

Chaining

Exhibit 10 shows the concept of chaining in action. The concept is nearly the same as for referrals. The objective of chaining is to keep the directories together in a logical unit.

If a client in the United Kingdom wishes information located in Germany, it will first ask the directory server in the United Kingdom. The directory server checks to see if it contains the requested data. If it does not, it will search to identify the server that contains the information required. In the case of a referral, the directory server would send this information back to the client, which then decides whether to follow the referral or not. In the case of chaining, however,

---

Exhibit 8. Output from Search Command against Host B

```
dn: uid=SKing,ou=Marketing,ou=US,o=LdapAbc.org
objectClass: top
objectClass: person
objectClass: organizationalPerson
objectClass: inetOrgPerson
cn: Stephen King
sn: King
givenName: Stephen
ou: Marketing
uid: SKing
mail: SKing@LdapAbc.org
```

Exhibit 9. Java Program following Referrals

```
 1 import netscape.ldap.* ;
 2 import java.util.* ;
 3
 4 /**
 5  * Simple example of referral usage
 6  */
 7
 8 public class Referral1 {
 9
10   public static void main(String args[]) {
11
12     String name      = args[0] ;
13     String baseDN     = args[1] ;
14     String host       = args[2] ;
15     int port          = Integer.parseInt( args[3]);
16
17     int searchScope=LDAPConnection.SCOPE_SUB;
18     String searchFilter = "(sn=" + name + ")";
19     String getAttrs[] = {"cn," "mail," "uid"};
20
21     LDAPConnection ld = new LDAPConnection();
22
23     try {
24            ld.connect(host,port);
25            ld.getSearchConstraints().setReferrals( true );
26            LDAPSearchResults res = ld.search( baseDN,
27                                               searchScope,
28                                               searchFilter,
29                                               getAttrs,
30                                               false );
31            while ( res.hasMoreElements() ) {
32              LDAPEntry Entry = null ;
33              Entry         = (LDAPEntry) res.next();
34              System.out.println("DN: " + Entry.getDN()) ;
35            }
36            ld.disconnect();
37     } catch ( LDAPReferralException e) {
38         LDAPUrl refUrls[] = e.getURLs();
39         for ( int i=0 ; i < refUrls.length; i++ ) {
40            System.out.println(refUrls[i].getUrl() );
41         }
42     } catch ( LDAPException e ) {
43         System.out.println( e.toString() );
44     }
45
46   }
47 }
```

the server does not report anything to the client. Instead, it contacts the server it thinks contains the information on the behalf of the client. Once it has the information, the server sends it back to the client. In the meantime, the client waits.

In this case, too, the knowledge information is stored in the server. There is not yet a standard defining the chaining process, so check your vendor's documentation for guidance.

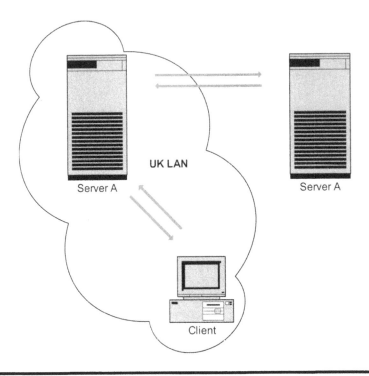

Exhibit 10. Chaining Client Requests

Security Aspects Using Chaining

Look again at Exhibit 10. The client contacts server A. Server A does not hold the information required by the client and therefore asks Server B, which does hold the information. Server B then sends the information to server A, and server A relays it back to the client. This is okay if the information exchanged is public. However, if the information can only be accessed upon previous authentication, things get slightly more complicated. In this case, when server A asks for the information from server B on behalf of the client, server A must also pass the user credentials to Server B.

Such an authentication scheme may be good enough for an intranet environment. In an insecure environment like the Internet, things get even more complicated. In this environment, the client must have assurance that server A really is server A and not an impostor running an LDAP server. This impostor could then steal the user's credentials and use them to gain access to the system. Thus when communicating over the Internet, it is absolutely necessary to use certificates to ensure that communicating parties really are who they claim to be.

Difference between Chaining and Referrals

Chaining and referrals are both used to contact another server if one server cannot provide an answer. However, referrals and chaining are two very different concepts as seen from the client's and the server's points of view. Using the referral strategy, the server simply sends a referral back to the client if it cannot execute the operation requested by the client. With the referral, the server also sends back a message identifying the server where the requested information resides. Thus the server acts nearly as it would upon receiving a request for data that it actually holds. The server does its job by informing the client, and then it is the client's job to handle the situation from there. In this case, the client has to do the work of interpreting the answer it got from the original server and then constructing the new address and distinguished name so that it can request the information from the new server identified in the referral. The client also has to decide whether to follow the request automatically or allow the user to decide what to do. In the case of a referral, the burden of work lies on the client and, consequently, on the client programmer.

In the case of chaining, the client knows nothing about these server transactions. Now the server has to do the work, and the vendor implementing the LDAP server has to invest much more work in the programming of the server software. In a chaining scheme, the originally contacted server handles all of the traffic from the final server holding the requested information as well as the directory client that made the request. Because a single request can result in more than one response, the original server may have to collect multiple responses and send them to the client. The client programmer has no direct control of the information flow between client, which is speaking with a kind of broker and not with the server itself.

A last difference between chaining and referrals lies in network performance. Obviously, performance is affected by the number of requests arriving at a server. If the server does not hold the requested information and thus must redirect the requests to other servers, the effect on performance is even greater. Because the client knows nothing about the chained transactions among the servers, it continues to send subsequent information to the original server, generating even more server-to-server transactions. Depending on the number of requests traveling this way and on the network architecture, this could have a negative effect on network performance. If the client is configured to recognize that the original server cannot execute the desired operation, it may be possible to switch its focus to the relevant server that can execute the requests directly. However, this feature is not available in all applications.

Replication

You may decide to duplicate a part of the directory or the whole directory on two or more other directory servers. This action of duplicating the directory is called "replication." The LDAP literature uses the terms "consumer" and "supplier." These expressions come in handy when describing the data flow. The server that sends the data is called the supplier. The server that receives the data from the supplier is called the consumer. These roles are not exclusive. The consumer server can be a supplier server for other servers, as we will see in the next section, "replication scenarios."

Furthermore, there are master servers and slave servers. The slave server runs in a read-only mode, getting its data from a master. The clients, therefore, cannot update the data on a slave server. Only the master server can modify data on the slave server, whose only function is to serve clients for search operations. Of course, the master server can also modify the data in the directory it contains. A directory application can have more than one master. However, the so-called multimaster replication is more difficult to implement. In this first section we will speak about master–slave replication only. In the section on multimaster replication, we will have a look at what is different in a configuration with more than one master directory server.

Replication has a number of advantages. It can improve:

- *Availability*: Upon the failure of one server, another can continue to provide information to the clients.
- *Performance*: Distribution of the workload among multiple servers increases efficiency by dividing the type of work each one performs. For example, you could have one server dedicated to data updates and another for data retrieval.
- *Bandwidth*: Efficient configuration increases bandwidth. Most enterprises have a large geographical extension and thus a geographically extended WAN. In this situation, it may be convenient to bring the directory closer to the clients by putting a directory server on every LAN and keeping these directory servers synchronized. The main advantage is a gain in bandwidth that you can use for other applications.
- *Maintenance*: Organizations that span multiple time zones must always have an active server. If each time zone has its own directory server, directory servers that are not being used can be safely taken offline. If you offer 24/7 service, you can take a server offline for maintenance as long as there are enough servers to respond to client requests. As mentioned before, a master–slave pair can also be used for offline backup. While the offline backup of the slave is active, the master continues its work. Once the backup is finished, you can put the slave online again.

Note, however, that there are no formal standards for replication or for a replication protocol at the time of this writing. Work is under way, and the workgroup is now releasing an important milestone of its work, but it will still take some time to create a standard. You can monitor the state of the art at the Web site of IETF (http://www.ietf.org). We will discuss this in greater detail in the section called "Work in Progress." The lack of a standard combined with vendors' desire to meet the needs of the market has led to the current situation where every LDAP implementation has it own replication solution.

Let us see how OpenLDAP is implementing replication. In Appendix D you will find a detailed discussion of the configuration of OpenLDAP for replication. You have to configure one server as master and one server as slave. The master server maintains a replication log. This log describes the changes to the directory the master server has applied. The slave server has to be configured to accept modifications of the master server. OpenLDAP delivers a replication server that does nothing else but communicate to the slave server the changes in the directory the master server has applied. Replication server and master server are two different programs. If I want to be precise, I should have stated the following: the slave server has to be configured to accept modifications from the replication server. That's enough, however, for the sake of this example. More in Appendix D.

Previously I said that ever vendor has its own solution for replication, and these single solutions, unfortunately, are not compatible with each other, so you cannot set up a replication between directory servers of different suppliers.

You can replicate the whole directory or one part of the directory, and you can replicate one server to more servers. There are a number of possibilities for implementing replication, and you can also combine these implementations. You can even combine replication with partitioning. We will address these subjects in Chapter 9, where we consider design questions.

However, bear in mind that not all implementations support all of the features that we have mentioned. It is best to check the documentation of the various LDAP implementations while you are still in the planning phase. Of course, most users are not in the fortunate position of choosing their LDAP software based on its replication options. In most cases, replication does not become an issue until the directory services system is successfully deployed and the workload increases. At this point you have to live with the options that your implementation offers. The reason for underestimating the workload is simple. When the directory services are up and running, more and more application programmers will use them. The real use of directory services is typically far greater than expected. We will address this issue later. For now, we will have a look at the different replication scenarios.

Replication Scenarios

In this section, we will briefly look at a few of the possible replication scenarios. We will return to this topic in Chapter 9, when we examine the design of directory services.

Exhibit 11 depicts the most basic scenario: a simple master–slave replication. The master server A replicates to the slave server B. The replication in this case has the goal of increasing the availability of directory services. If server A is down, then the clients can use still directory services through server B.

Exhibit 12 shows a different scenario. We still have master–slave replication, but the main scope here is to make the data available in a different subnet. If the connection between the two networks is down, the clients on the location of either the slave or the master still have directory information, although the information on the slave side may be out of date. The main advantage in this configuration, however, is that the traffic on the network link caused by the directory servers is kept as low as possible. Server A sends only the data that has been modified to server B. Both sites use their own directory server. The network link is used only for replication updates. The bandwidth that otherwise would be used by the clients is now available for use by other applications. Both sites can continue to use the directory, even if one of the servers is unavailable, because in this case its replication partner takes over its workload.

Exhibit 13 shows an example of a cascading replication, where the replicated server replicates furthermore on a second slave server. Not

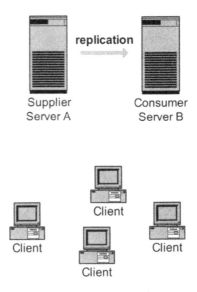

Exhibit 11. Simple Master–Slave Replication

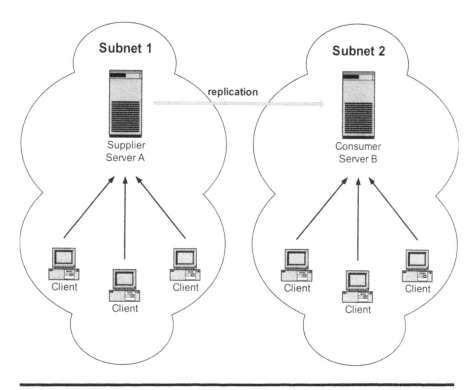

Exhibit 12. Simple Master–Slave Replication between Subnets

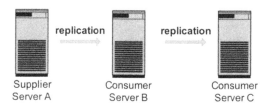

Exhibit 13. Cascading Replication

all directory server implementations support this architecture. In the case of OpenLDAP, where you have a dedicated consumer server, a cascading architecture would not be possible.

Exhibit 14 depicts a somewhat more complex configuration. The master server holds the database, and all changes (insert, modify, delete operations) are made on this server. There are four consumer servers, each serving one subnet. These four servers can be put much closer to the clients they are serving than the master server. The master replication server in this configuration has two functions. First, it speaks with the clients requesting a directory update. Then it distributes these updates to the single consumer servers.

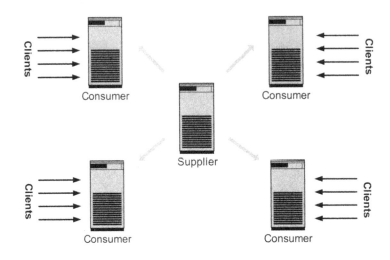

Exhibit 14. Supplier Server with Several Consumer Servers in Different Subnets

Performance can be improved even more by putting a further replicating server between the master replication server and the slaves, working practically as a hub. In this configuration, the supplier server leaves the distribution of the updates to the hub and concentrates on its job as LDAP server. It receives the messages from the clients and executes the necessary steps on the directory.

Schema Information and ACL

In LDAP (v3), schema information should be held in the form of a subschemaSubentry object. Some implementations use this mechanism to propagate changes in the schema from the supplier to the consumer. Because the exact syntax for the representation of the schema in the subschemaSubentry is not yet defined in a standard, every supplier uses its own. Thus it is best to have a common schema for both the supplier and consumer and to avoid changing the schema.

Since there is no standard defining access control lists (ACLs), some directory server implementations hold the ACL in the configuration files, and others keep it where the data is, in the directory. When the ACL is part of the directory, updates in the ACL can be propagated through replication.

Work is under way to define a standard for both mechanisms. A major goal of this effort is to allow directory servers from different suppliers to exchange information. Once these standards are defined, it will still take some time until the first suppliers implement the standards.

Single Master versus Multimaster

Until now we have seen only configurations featuring a single master server. Updates of the directory are made on the master server, which replicates them on the slaves or slave. In all these cases, the access is to slave servers running in read-only mode, which means that they cannot modify any entry. The only one who can do this is the master server. However, this does not mean that a client connected to the slave server cannot modify an entry. Indeed, the client can ask the slave server to update or delete an entry, and the request is handled like a referral. Upon the request to the slave server, the client receives from the slave server the location of the master server and its IP number. With this information, the client submits its request to update information to the master server. Normally, the client software handles this automatically, and the transaction is hidden from the user. Alternatively, the update request could also be handled using chaining. The client asks the slave server to update an entry. The slave server asks the master server to make the update. After the master server sends the return code in the form of a message object, the slave server informs the client.

There are also situations where you may wish to have more than one master server. In this case of multimaster replication, more than one directory server has write access to the directory. This obviously complicates the situation. Clients in such an architecture can submit update requests to any of these master servers. If in a master–slave solution the master is no longer available, you can read the directory, but you cannot update it anymore. Whether this is acceptable depends on the particular application. If you have two masters, though, you continue to work both in read and update, even if one of the masters is not available. As soon as the disabled master becomes available again, it will be updated.

This solution has its advantages, but it also introduces a big problem. If more than one server accepts updates from the clients, the same entry can be updated on two different servers. An entry might be updated with one value on server A and another value on server B. Exhibit 15 depicts such a situation. The server software has to have some sort of policy to resolve such conflicts. The servers could use the time stamp of the update action to decide which update to keep and which one to discard. Using Exhibit 15, imagine that a client in the United States updates the room number to 512 at 4:01 p.m. and one minute later a client in the United Kingdom updates the room number to 528. Most directory servers keep the most recent update and discard the previous one. This obviously requires that the time between the servers is perfectly synchronized. Note, however, that there is no correct way to handle this situation because, for the directory server, no client's update is better or worse than the other.

Again, how these details are handled depends on the implementation because there is no standard yet. Check the documentation shipped with your software. Given the lack of a standard, it is clear that replication cannot be implemented between software from different suppliers. It is not only the multimaster replication that does not work between products of different suppliers. It is the replication protocol between the directory servers that has not yet been standardized.

Exhibit 15 shows a very interesting scenario of replication. This architecture is particularly interesting because it is a thing between multimaster and single-master replication. Two directory servers (server A and server B) share a common directory. The goal is that if server A is unavailable, server B can continue its work. Because both directory servers use a common directory, you need not replicate it to keep both servers aligned. If the client wants to connect with the directory server, it gets the IP number from the DNS and then connects with the directory server. If server A should answer, the DNS gives the address of server A. If server B should answer, the DNS gives the address of server B. The switch from server A to server B is therefore achieved by the DNS server that resolves the names. Let me make the example clearer. The client asks the address ldap.abc.de from the DNS server. If we want server A to respond, the DNS says to the client: "Look, the address of ldap.abc.de is 245.94.37.2." If we want server B to respond, we tell to the client: "The address of ldap.abc.de is 245.94.37.7."

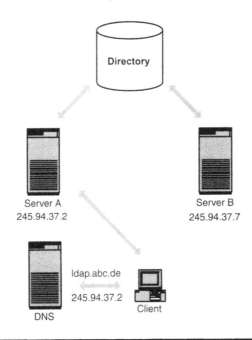

Exhibit 15. Two Servers Sharing One Directory

Replication Agreements

Once the architecture is established, replication still has to be set up to work properly. You set up replication by defining a handful of agreements between supplier and consumer servers. These are the arguments the server has to agree upon:

- Supplier- or consumer-initiated replication
- Frequency of replication
- Unit of replication
- Incremental or total replication
- Replication account

We will have a brief look at each of these points. Please keep in mind, however, that each directory server handles replication in a different manner, so some points may be just configured and you cannot change them. Refer to the documentation delivered with your directory server.

Supplier- or Consumer-Initiated Replication

This describes which of the partners initiates the replication. In a supplier-initiated replication the supplier contacts the consumer and pushes all the data changed since the last replication to the consumer. In a consumer-initiated replication, the consumer contacts the supplier and pulls down all data changed since the last replication. The end result for both replication types is the same. The choice of which to use depends on the particular architecture. The supplier-initiated replication can push an update to the consumer as soon as the data in the supplier changes, thus minimizing the delay between the update of supplier and consumer. Using this strategy, the consistency between supplier and consumer is strong. The consumer-initiated replication is used when the connection to the consumer is not very stable, for example in a dial-up connection. When the consumer connects to the LAN, it can request the supplier to begin the replication.

Frequency of Replication

The frequency of replication depends on the degree of consistency required between consumer and supplier. As the divergence between consumer and supplier becomes more critical, replication should occur more frequently. However, the more frequently the server is busy with replication, the greater is the loss of performance against connections to the clients.

Unit of Replication

You can also decide which part of the DIT you will replicate. Some implementations only allow you to replicate the whole directory.

Incremental or Total Replication

This defines whether you replicate the whole directory or just the part that has actually changed. Total replication is used when you set up replication for the first time or if you reload the entire directory on the supplier. For normal operation, you will normally use incremental replication between supplier and consumer.

Replication Account

You must define an account that the supplier and the consumer can use for the replication process. The replication account must have sufficient rights to achieve the operation on the partner server.

Load Sharing

Replication has different objectives, one of which is load sharing. We have already seen two possible methods of load sharing. The first possibility is to use two or more directory servers and distribute accesses to these directory servers via DNS. The client asks for the directory server "directory.Ldap_Abc.org." The DNS server gives an IP number, and the client then contacts the directory server with this IP number. When the next request arrives at the DNS, it delivers another IP number. Thus, the requests are distributed among all directory servers. Exhibit 16 shows this architecture. The disadvantage of this architecture is that the DNS does not speak LDAP and therefore does not understand if one of the LDAP servers does not answer. Furthermore, the distribution among the directory servers is not guided by the nature of the requests.

Another possibility is to use a gateway, as noted in the previous section on "replication scenarios." Every directory server in this schema is specialized on a particular activity. Exhibit 17 shows the architecture. One or more supplier servers accept all the data maintenance operations. Remember that data maintenance operations are more resource consuming than read operations. The supplier pushes the changes onto the gateway, which distributes the data to the consumer servers. The consumer servers, in turn, handle the read operations for the clients.

A last possibility is to use an LDAP proxy server, as shown in Exhibit 18. Because the proxy server speaks LDAP, it understands the requests made by the clients. Therefore, the LDAP proxy can decide on a

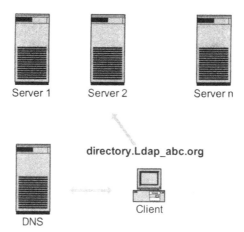

directory.Ldap_abc.org

Exhibit 16. LDAP Load Balancing Using DNS

Exhibit 17. LDAP Gateway

configurable and "intelligent" way to distribute the requests. It can furthermore decide to hide certain attributes from the client or to put together two data sources and make them appear as a unique data source to the client. Most of the commercial vendors also offer an LDAP proxy server. However, this is a very expensive solution. Fortunately, the OpenLDAP implementation can be compiled to work as a proxy server. We previously mentioned the need to compile OpenLDAP in a particular way to get it work as a proxy. Chapter 7, "LDAP Directory Server Administration," provides more information about the installation of LDAP, and Appendix D tells you how to compile and configure the OpenLDAP proxy server.

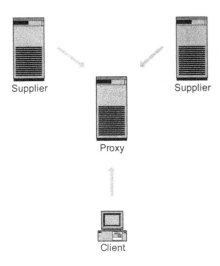

Exhibit 18. LDAP Proxy

Security Aspects

The security considerations for the conversation between a consumer and supplier server are the same as for a conversation between a client and server. Most server implementations offer a variety of options to secure this conversation. Your choice of method depends on your particular requirements.

In an insecure environment like the Internet, it is very important that both the supplier and the consumer servers are sure about the identity of the partner. However, even in an intranet environment, security issues should be a concern. Many intranet administrators assume that the "bad guys" are outside the network. Unfortunately, experience has shown that "bad guys" could also be inside the system.

As mentioned before, directory servers can exchange schema information and ACLs. In a so-called man-in-the-middle attack, this information can be forged if transmitted in the clear without encryption. Thus such information should be encrypted before transmission. The same holds true for user data. User data stored in the directory contains the users' passwords. When this information is transmitted between consumer and supplier servers, anyone listening on the network can capture it.

The available security options depend on the implementation you are using. Refer to the documentation delivered with your software to understand which options are appropriate for your application. Again, there is no standard, and every software vendor has a solution of its own. A number of suppliers offer an LDAP proxy. For example, Sun has one in its Sun One server suite that also includes an LDAP proxy server.

Work in Progress

The replication process, like much of LDAP, is a work in progress. A working group called LDUP (LDAP Duplication/Replication/Update Protocol) is in the process of standardizing master–slave (also called single-master) and multimaster replication. You can learn more about their work from the IETF Web site at http://www.ietf.org/html.charters/ldup-charter.html.

The following lists reflect the latest information drawn from the workgroup's Web site at the time of this writing. Given the time lag in publishing, you would be wise to refer to the Web site for recent updates. The LDUP working group has divided its activities into seven areas, each of which is documented by one or more papers:

1. *LDAP (v3) replication architecture*: Describes the overall architecture of the LDUP protocol, i.e., the LDUP components and how these components work together.
2. *LDAP (v3) replication information model*: Defines the schema information necessary for replication to work. It includes replication agreements, consistency models, replication topologies, management of deleted objects, and administration. This information has to be maintained by the replicating servers.
3. *LDAP (v3) replication information transport protocol*: Defines extended operations that allow LDAP itself to propagate the information to be replicated
4. *LDAP (v3) mandatory replica management*: Management protocol to administer replication.
5. *LDAP (v3) update reconciliation procedures*: Procedures for the detection and resolution of replication conflicts. Replication may try to update the same element from different information sources. These procedures should resolve conflicts.
6. *LDAP (v3) profiles*: LDAP (v3) replication architecture, information model, protocol extensions, and update reconciliation procedures
7. *LDAP (v3) client update*: Enables the client to synchronize with update in the LDAP server and receive notification about modifications in the database.

At the time of this writing, the work of the LDAP group has produced the following documentation:

- RFC 3384, "LDAPv3 Replication Requirements"
- "General Usage Profile for LDAPv3 Replication," draft available from http://www.ietf.org/internet-drafts/draft-ietf-ldup-usage-profile-03.txt
- "LDAP Client Update Protocol," draft available from http://www.ietf.org/internet-drafts/draft-ietf-ldup-lcup-03.txt

Data Distribution between LDAP and Non-LDAP Systems

What should you do if part of the data resides in non-LDAP systems, like relational databases, applications, or flat files? The first thing to consider is moving all of the data into one common LDAP repository. However, it is not always possible to migrate existing applications to another architecture. Nor is it always a good idea to convert everything into LDAP. There are many different factors that might hamper your efforts to move disparate data to a common repository. For example, an application might not be available in an LDAP-enabled version. Other reasons could be of a political nature. For example, a data "owner" might want to continue to maintain his repository using his familiar software without having to go through the enterprise directory to maintain the data. There are also cases where it is simply impossible for one reason or another to migrate the database to LDAP.

The most flexible way to create a common platform for all data sources is to design a broker that can put all the systems in contact, allowing you to maintain and query the data in a consistent way. Exhibit 19 shows an example of such a mixed-up environment.

Broker

Before we look at commercial implementations, let us first have a brief look at the requirements for a broker connecting different repositories. These requirements depend very much on the particular implementation. As mentioned previously, the directory can be interconnected with a number of different repositories. Thus, the first thing to do is to understand the different repositories holding the data and the types of data they hold.

For each of the repositories (LDAP, RDBMS, application, flat file, etc.), you need to build a connector to regulate the data flow. This

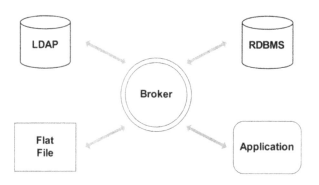

Exhibit 19. Connecting Different Repositories

connector is specialized to keep a connection between the data source and the directory. As such, it has to know the direction of the data flow, i.e., it has to know which of the two partners is the master and which is the slave.

If both of the partners accept modifications, there must be a strategy module to decide which of the modifications should be kept in the event that both sources receive an update. The strategy module also has other jobs to do. A data source that accepts modifications is called a "data producer." There is usually more than one data producer. The strategy module therefore has to decide on a sequence for the different data producers so that they are synchronized with the directory. If two or more data producers can update the same data, there is a possibility of generating conflicting data. The strategy module has to be configured to resolve such conflicts. (The conflicts are the same as those that can occur with multimaster replication of LDAP servers.)

Conflicts are mostly a sign that there are problems in the data flow. A conflict indicates that there is more than one source responsible for the maintenance of the same data. In most cases, it is good to review the business logic that requires this redundant maintenance and find a solution of a master–slave relationship. We will discuss this further in Chapter 9 when we learn more about LDAP server design.

Security is another important consideration. You have to determine what types of user credentials should be used to pass information between different systems. You may also need to set up the exchange of certificates to allow conversing partners to verify each other's authenticity.

The broker centrally controls all of these connections and the data flow between the different repositories. The frequency of the update between the repositories is yet another important consideration. You need to define how much time it should take for the different repositories to become aligned. It is also important to decide which of the repositories should be considered as the authoritative data source.

It is not overly difficult to set up an environment connecting different repositories so that they can communicate with each other. However, as the saying goes, the devil is in the details. This means that the framework needs to be carefully designed and implemented. Needless to say, a home-grown implementation has the advantage of exactly meeting your particular application and security requirements. However, you will need the skills of people who can design, develop, and maintain the software. Most of the commercial directory servers offer a solution that sits on top of their directory server, a metadirectory. We will learn more about metadirectories in the next section.

Metadirectory

If you do not want to develop your own solution for data distribution, you can adopt a ready-to-use product called a "metadirectory." The function of a metadirectory is to synchronize a central directory with the different repositories on different systems. The way a commercial product performs this task is similar to the theoretical approach described in the previous section. One central strategy module (that can also be called a broker) looks around at the various repositories and tries to keep the central directory in sync with the repositories. The central strategy module can be configured to describe the locations of the various repositories, the update frequencies, the interrogation sequence for the different data sources, and the authoritative data source.

The number of vendors of metadirectory solutions is constantly growing. The major names are Siemens with its DirX 6.0 product, Sun One metadirectory, Microsoft metadirectory, and many others. Metadirectories are a relatively new area, and vendor brochures have created high customer expectations.

As previously noted, behind the problems a companywide metadirectory should solve, there are mostly organizational or design problems. The tool will not solve these problems. However, the tool may be helpful in uncovering these problems and may lead to a change in the business logic, thereby avoiding data inconsistencies.

DSML

One interesting means of exchanging directory information is the DSML standard. The directory services markup language DSML is a dialect of extended markup language (XML). DSML takes advantage of the XML syntax, enabling applications to share data using a simple human-readable format.

A thorough explanation of XML is beyond the scope of this book. For our purposes, it is enough to say that XML is a standard of representing Web content in ASCII format. As opposed to HTML, it allows the user to define her own tags and thus extend the language. As such, XML can be put on any Web server and transferred like any other Web document.

DSML was created initially by Bowstreet Inc. in July 1999. It is intended as an open standard and is maintained on the Web site of OASIS http://www.oasis-open.org/committees/dsml. OASIS is sponsored by Netscape, Sun Microsystems, Oracle, Novell, Microsoft, IBM, and other enterprises. At the time of this writing, DSML is in version 2. DSML (v1) provides a means of representing directory content in XML. DSML (v2) extends the functionality to allow a client to formulate queries, delete, insert, and modify actions as XML documents. Perhaps obviously, the results of these operations are sent back in XML format.

The big advantage of DSML is that it is an ASCII format markup language and therefore the directory content can be made available via a Web server. This means that you can distribute directory content across enterprise boundaries, for example in your extranet, or even make it available to customers over the Internet. Since it is ASCII, you can export your directory content in DSML and import it into a completely different repository, for example a directory server from a different supplier. This means that even a client unable to speak LDAP can access a directory. This could, for example, be an application developed using XML tools and then be integrated in a directory-driven environment.

At this point, a few examples are very helpful to get a basic understanding of how all this works. These examples are drawn from the DSML draft available from OASIS. First, Exhibit 20 shows you how to formulate a search using DSML. As you may notice, the request is included in the <searchRequest> and </searchRequest> tags. Meanwhile, the filter is defined in <filter> and </filter> tags. Exhibit 21 instead shows the result. As you can imagine, using a style sheet you can easily format this XML code into a pretty good-looking HTML page.

Finally, Exhibit 22 and Exhibit 23 show an example of adding an entry to a directory. Exhibit 22 shows the request the client has to produce, and Exhibit 23 the response the client gets. Exhibits 20 and 21 and Exhibits 22 and 23 are taken from the DSML draft document.

DSML Tools

There is a handy tool set written in Java that helps to export directory content to DSML and import it into an LDAP database. The tools are named LDAPtoDSML and DSMLtoLDAP. The software has been developed by Gervase Markham and is available at http://www.dsml-tools.org.

These tools make it easy to export and reimport LDAP data. The following line exports data from our LDAP repository:

```
LDAPtoDSML
```

To import data into an LDAP repository, use the following line:

```
DSMLtoLDAP
```

Exhibit 20. Example of Search Request in DSML

```
<searchRequest dn="ou=Marketing,dc=Microsoft,dc=com"
        scope="singleLevel"
        derefAliases="neverDerefAliases"
        sizeLimit="1000">
    <filter>
        <substrings name="sn"><final>john</final></substrings>
    </filter>
</searchRequest>
```

Exhibit 21. Example of Search Result in DSML

```
<searchResponse>
<searchResultEntry dn="OU=Development,DC=Example,DC=COM">
<attr name="allowedAttributeEffective">
<value>description</value>
<value>ntSecurityDescriptor</value>
<value>wwwHomepage</value>
</attr>
</searchResultEntry>
<searchResultEntry dn="CN=David,OU=HR,DC=Example,DC=COM">
<attr name="objectclass"><value>person</value></attr>
<attr name="sn"><value>Johnson</value></attr>
<attr name="givenName"><value>David</value></attr>
<attr name="title"><value>Program Manager</value></attr>
</searchResultEntry>
<searchResultEntry dn="CN=JSmith, OU=Finance,DC=Exam-
ple,DC=COM">
<attr name="objectclass"><value>top</value></attr>
<attr name="objectclass"><value>person</value></attr>
<attr name="objectclass"><value>organizationalPer-
son</value></attr>
<attr name="sn"><value>Smith</value></attr>
</searchResultEntry>
<searchResultDone>
<control type="1.2.840.113556.1.4.621" criticality="false">
<controlValue xsi:type="xsd:base64Binary">
U2VhcmNoIFJlcXVlc3QgRXhhbXBsZQ==
</controlValue>
</control>
<resultCode code="0"/>
</searchResultDone>
</searchResponse>
```

Castor

As we close the DSML section, we should briefly mention the Castor framework, which provides data binding. Castor is developed by Exolab, an organization working in the development of open-source software based on Java and XML.

Data binding facilitates the transfer of one data model into another. For example, Castor can map an XML data model into Java classes by

---

Exhibit 22. Example of Adding an Entry in DSML: Request

```
<addRequest dn="CN=Alice,OU=HR,DC=Example,DC=COM">
    <attr name="objectclass"><value>top</value></attr>
    <attr name="objectclass"><value>person</value></attr>
    <attr
name="objectclass"><value>organizationalPerson</value></attr>
    <attr name="sn"><value>Johnson</value></attr>
    <attr name="givenName"><value>Alice</value></attr>
    <attr name="title"><value>Software Design Engineer</value></attr>
</addRequest>
```

Exhibit 23. Example of Adding an Entry in DSML: Response

```
<addResponse>
    <resultCode code="0"/>
    <errorMessage>completed</errorMessage>
</addResponse>
```

---

generating Java classes from an XML document. It can also use instances of these classes to store data in XML form. Castor is also capable of binding data from Java classes to tables, rows, and columns of a RDBMS. One of the functionalities being investigated at the time of this writing is the development of mapping from LDAP to Java and finally to XML.

Castor DSML remains (at the time of this writing) a work in progress. You can learn more about the Castor project at the Castor home page: http://castor.exolab.org.

Conclusion

In this chapter, we have seen a number of interesting distributed architectures for data maintenance. The previous chapters assumed that there is only one directory holding all the data in our enterprise. However, life is rarely so simple. There are many situations where it makes sense to divide the directory over more than one server, assigning each of these directory servers the responsibility for one part of the directory information tree. The user, however, should be able to get the whole picture, retrieving information held on the different directory servers as if the data was held on a single server.

We furthermore have seen how to replicate data from the directory on other directory servers. There are many reasons to replicate a directory, including availability, performance, and administrative issues.

We also learned how to integrate data from different sources into a directory server to form one unique architecture using metadirectories.

The last part of this chapter showed how to use the markup language XML and the directory standard LDAP, thus allowing access to your directory via XML. The advantage of this technique is that applications developed in XML have the ability to use the enterprise directory without the need of an LDAP-enabled client.

Chapter 6

LDAP APIs

Until now, we have seen many LDAP examples using command-line tools, which are not a very user-friendly way of communicating with the LDAP server. In this chapter, we will first revisit the command-line tools to see whether they can be used in a more ergonomic way. Then we will see some examples of languages offering LDAP support, some of them just native support and some of them extensions in the form of libraries.

For the remainder of the chapter, we turn our attention to the most frequently used programming languages. The discussion focuses on languages available over a broad spectrum of platforms; languages available on only a single platform are not mentioned. As you will see, however, the manner of using an LDAP API is always the same, regardless of the programming language. Thus, if you have seen some examples in the C language, you will have no difficulty in recycling your knowledge when you are using Java instead.

LDAP Command-Line Tools

The command-line tools seem to be the most spartan API available to access an LDAP directory. They have been part of the standard distribution ever since the very first LDAP implementation written at the University of Michigan. Nevertheless, the command-line tools are available in nearly all distributions, and they all work in the same way. Furthermore, there are situations where these simple tools can come in handy. For example, an administrator might need to quickly control a certain entry in the directory or change an attribute of an entry. In such cases, an "on-the-fly" command-line filter can be a powerful tool. The command-line tools enable such quick tests without having to write an application (for example in Perl) to do the job.

177

The command-line tools can be helpful in other situations too. Because they behave like all of the other commands available in your shell, they can be used to write shell scripts. This is an interesting option in an existing system-administrating environment where the system administrator already has a library of scripts and wishes to integrate the LDAP administration jobs also. In this chapter, we will see some examples of using the command-line tools in collaboration with other tools available in the standard shell. The shell and their commands are available as standards in the UNIX environment only. However, they have also been ported to other systems that lack similar tools, for example, the Win32 environment.

The following sections show the command-line tools. The examples are based on the OpenLDAP implementation on UNIX. It is quite probable that your implementation will use a slightly different syntax, but the underlying logic will be the same. Have a look at the documentation shipped with your implementation or the online documentation (manual pages in UNIX, "help" in the MS World).

Selected Commands

On the OpenLDAP implementation, you will find the following tools in the script directory:

- `ldapadd`: Add an entry
- `ldapdelete`: Delete an entry
- `ldapmodrdn`: Modify the relative distinguished name (RDN) of an entry
- `ldapsearch`: Search for an entry
- `ldapcompare`: Verify the presence of an entry
- `ldapmodify`: Modify an entry

Depending on your specific implementation, you may see more tools or less. The most important tools, however, are available in all implementations:

`ldapsearch and ldapmodify`

With these two tools, you can do everything the other tools can do. The functions "ldapadd," "ldapdelete," and "ldapmodrdn" can be seen as convenience functions because ldapmodify can do exactly the same things, as we will see in the next paragraph.

ldapmodify

You can use ldapmodify in two ways:

- 1. Type in all data interactively
- 2. Use a file in LDIF format for the data input

The syntax is exactly the same, so the choice is a matter of personal preference. I recommend the second method. It helps you to avoid typos, and you can keep track of what you did and can undo the actions very easily in case of errors. A further reason why you might prefer the second method is that it may be possible for you to generate automatically the input file, which is very handy if you insert more than one similar entry. At the end of this paragraph, you will see a sample shell script that generates the LDIF file automatically. But first let have us a look at the syntax. Exhibit 1 shows the ldapmodify call with the most important parameters. It is possible that your implementation offers more parameters or switches. The OpenLDAP implementation does. The following is a brief description of the most frequently available parameters. For a complete description, consult your documentation.

- `host`: Hostname the directory server is running on
- `port`: Port number the directory server is listening
- `bindDN`: Distinguished name you will be authenticated as
- `password`: Corresponding password
- `InputFileName`: Name of the LDIF file from which the command gets its input

The "-a" switch is a shortcut to indicate that you want to add entries. Using this, you can omit the "changetype: add line" command. On most implementations, there is an "ldapadd" function as a synonym for "`ldapmodify -a`."

If you omit "-f <InputFileName>," ldapmodify will wait for you to enter line by line the LDIF instructions.

The "-W" switch indicates that you do not wish to type the password as clear text. You simply omit the -w "password" and ldapmodify will prompt you for the password, protecting it with "*" characters when you are typing it in.

Some implementations also have an "-n" switch, analogous to the "make" utility, which shows what it would do but does not actually execute the command.

Exhibit 1. Syntax of ldapmodify with Frequently Used Parameters

```
ldapmodify [-a] -h <host> -p <port>
   -D "<bindDN>"
   -w "<password>"
   -W
   -f <InputFileName>
```

Some Examples of ldapmodify

Let us now see a few examples of the use of ldapmodify. Exhibit 2 shows how to add an entry to the directory. Exhibit 3 shows how to delete an entry from the directory. Examining Exhibits 2 and 3, you see that the command lines are identical (the file names are different, of course). Thus, if you still have the file from the first example, you can recycle it as a handcrafted undo mechanism, guaranteeing the DNs are identical. The syntax of the LDIF files was described in Chapter 4 when we spoke about LDIF. See Chapter 4 for more details.

To conclude the discussion about the usage of ldapmodify, we will examine a little shell script that generates a file in the LDIF format suitable for the ldapmodify command (Exhibit 4). The script gets its input from a csv (comma-separated values) file, such as the format exported from Excel files.

The script reads the file "InputFile." The heart of the script is the AWK utility. AWK got its name from its creators Aho, Weinberger, and Kernighan. It reads the input line by line and splits the lines up in records. The single records are available inside the script using the

---

Exhibit 2. Example of ldapmodify: Add an Entry

```
ldapmodify -D "cn=admin,o=LdapAbc.org" -w password1 -f
add1.ldif

the file add1.ldif contains:

dn: uid=RHaller,ou=IT,o=LdapAbc.org
changetype: add
objectClass: top
objectClass: person
objectClass: organizationalPerson
objectClass: inetOrgPerson
sn: Haller
cn: Rudy Haller
givenName: Rudy
uid: RHaller
mail: RHaller@LdapAbc.org
```

Exhibit 3. Example of ldapmodify: Delete an Entry

```
ldapmodify -D "cn=admin,o=LdapAbc.org" -w password1 -f
delete1.ldif

the file delete1.ldif contains:

dn: uid=RHaller,ou=IT,o=LdapAbc.org
changetype: delete
```

Exhibit 4. Example of Script Preparing the Input File for ldapmodify

```
01 #!/bin/sh
02 ##########################################################
03 #
04 # Name:        GenerateLDIF.sh
05 # Version:     1.0
06 # Date:        10.08.2002
07 # Author:      Reinhard E. Voglmaier
08 # Description: Generates LDIF File from CSV File
09 #
10 ##########################################################
11
12 InputFile=EmployeesMarketing.csv
13 cat $InputFile | awk ' BEGIN {
14    # Input File Separator:
15       FS = "," ;
16    # Parameters:
17       Organization="LdapAbc.org";
18       OC[1] = "top" ;
19       OC[2] = "person" ;
20       OC[3] = "organizationalPerson" ;
21       OC[4] = "inetOrgPerson" ;
22    }
23
24    {
25    # From input:
26       GivenName = $1 ;
27       sn              = $2 ;
28       Department  = $3;
29
30    # Construct Composite Variable
31       uid       = sprintf("%s%s", subbstr(GivenName,1,1),sn);
32
33    # Output Section:
34       printf("dn: uid=%s, ou=%s, o=%s\n", uid,Depart-
ment,Organization);
35
36       for (i=1;i<5;i++)
37          printf("objectClass: %s\n",OC[i]);
38       printf("sn: %s\n",sn);
39       printf("cn: %s %s\n",GivenName,sn);
40       printf("givenName: %s\n",GivenName);
41       printf("uid: %s\n",uid);
42       printf("mail:%s@%s\n\n", uid,Organization);
43    } '
```

built-in variables $1, $2, ..., $n. The default record separator is one or more space characters, although you can use other characters as well. For example, we set the record separator to comma (FS = ",") in line 15 of the script. The BEGIN section is used to set up the parameters for this script.

In this example we have an input file that consists only of three words per line: surname, givenName, and Department. AWK reads the input line by line and splits every line into records. The records are denominated $1, $2, and so on. In lines 26 to 28 are assigned more human-friendly variable names. You can easily adapt this script for more variables. After these lines, all data that has been read in from the csv file can be printed out in the desired form in the lines 34 to 42.

AWK is available on all UNIX systems (Win32 versions are also available from Cygnus). AWK is easy to read and understand, and because it is a scripting language, you do not have to compile it. It is very handy for little scripts such as this one. In the next section, we will expand it a little to show you how to work with ldapmodify and ldapsearch using such tools as AWK and the stream editor (sed), a further handy tool available in the UNIX environment and ported to other operating systems.

ldapsearch

Like the ldapmodify function, ldapsearch is also part of every (or nearly every) LDAP server distribution. Initially it was intended as an example of how to write an LDAP client. If you are curious about its implementation, you can download the source code of the OpenLDAP distribution. If you are interested in better understanding what is going on behind the scenes, it should be instructive to look over the source code of ldapsearch and the other utilities shipped with the OpenLDAP distribution. Also instructive is the test suite used to test all the utilities of OpenLDAP after the compilation.

Now let us have a brief look at the syntax of ldapsearch. As in the previous example, we will consider only the parameters and switches that should reasonably exist on all LDAP implementations. Exhibit 5 shows the syntax plus the parameters and their explanation.

Exhibit 5. Syntax of "ldapsearch" Function

```
ldapsearch -h <host> -p <port>
 -D "<bindDN>"
 -w "<password>"
 -b "<searchbase>"
 <filter> <result-attributes>
```

- `host:` the hostname the directory server is running on
- `port:` the port number the directory server is listening on
- `bindDN:` the distinguished name you will be authenticated as
- `password:` the corresponding password
- `filter:` query filter for the search
- `result-attributes:` attributes of the result entries to be returned

Some Examples of ldapsearch

The simplest form of a search delivers the entry knowing the sn attribute:

```
ldapsearch –h ldap.LdapAbc.org –p 389 –b "o=LdapAbc.org"
"(sn=Parker)"
```

If the search runs on the same machine as the directory server, you can leave out the "-h" attribute. We will assume that it does, and furthermore we will use for these examples an installation using the standard port (389), so we can also omit the "-p 389" parameter.

If we wished to have only the sn, cn, uid, and mail attribute to be returned from the search, we would say:

```
ldapsearch "o=LdapAbc.org" "(sn=Parker)" sn,cn,uid,mail
```

As shown in Chapter 2, when we made our very first experiments with the LDAP command-line tools, we can also express more-complicated queries, for example:

```
ldapsearch "o=LdapAbc.org" objectclass=inetOrgPerson
 (&(&(sn=Parker)(givenName=J*))(mail=*))
```

This query would deliver all entries with object class "inetOrgPerson" that has sn Parker AND the given name beginning with J (e.g., James, Joseph) AND that has the mail attribute (used here as a so-called presence filter). To learn more about the search function, see the discussion in Chapter 4 about the filter attribute.

Now you will learn how the command-line tools can be used together with the shell and the tools sed and AWK. The first script extends the previous script for ldapmodify. It not only prepares a file suitable for the insertion of new users from a csv file, but it queries the directory to see if the uids already exist. If they do, the script tries to create unique uids. The first 29 lines of both scripts are identical. Line 31 in the original script, which builds up the uid from sn and givenName, is replaced by the following line:

```
uid = GenUid(givenName,sn);
```

"GenUid" is a user-defined function that searches the database to see if the distinguished name exists. If it does, it recreates the uid in a different manner. In the first trial, it takes the first letter of the given name and attaches it to the surname. If this uid also exists in the directory, the function starts a second trial, taking the first two letters of the given name and attaching these to the surname. Again it tests to see if the distinguished name exists, and so on. The function also maintains a hash, where it stores the userIDs assigned during the run of the script, since the data will be inserted only in a second run. Exhibit 6 shows the additional functions.

Line 11 constructs the search base as:

```
<SearchBase> = "uid=<UserId>, ou=<Department>,o=<Organization>"
```

Line 13 constructs the search as:

```
Ldapsearch -b <base> | grep sn
```

For example, for James Parker in the IT department of o = LdapAbc.org, the search would read:

```
Ldapsearch -b "uid=JParker, ou=IT, o=LdapAbc.org | grep Parker
```

The system call reports the exit status of the command, bringing the grep command into play. The exit status of the search command always

---

Exhibit 6. Example Shell that Looks Up in the Directory and Generates Unique Distinguished Names

```
01 function GenUid (givenName,sn) {
02
03 # Construct Composite Variable
04    Status = 0 ;
05    L     = 1 ;
06
07 # Lookup in the database if the name exists
08   while (Status == 0) {
09     uid         = sprintf("%s%s",
10     substr(givenName,1,L++),sn) ;
11     Base = sprintf(" \"uid=%s, ou=%s, o=%s\" ",
12                        uid,Department,Organization);
13    Cmd = sprintf("ldapsearch -b %s | grep %s > /dev/null",
14                      Base,sn);
15     Status = system(Cmd);
16     }
17
18   # Lookup in the array of assigned uids
19   if (UidList[uid]) {
20        Status = 0;
21    } else {
22      UidList[uid] = "1";
23    }
24
25    while (Status == 0) {
26      uid         = sprintf("%s%s",
27      substr(GivenName,1,L++),sn) ;
28      if (!UidList[uid]) {
29          UidList[uid] = "1";
30            Status = 1 ;
31       }
32    }
33    return(uid);
34 }
```

reports no error, whether the item was found or not, because it is not the command that failed. The grep command, on the other hand, exits with status OK if the sn is contained in the results set, or it exits with status ERROR if sn is not contained in the results set.

In the following example, we want to list the members of the various organizational units: IT department, the marketing division, etc. We do not want to look up every entry, since this could be time consuming. What we can do instead is to create a special object for every organizational unit, the object "groupOfUniqueNames." For the IT department, for example, this would be:

```
dn: cn=IT, o=LdapAbc.org
objectClass: top
objectClass: groupOfUniqueNames
cn: IT
ou: IT
uniquemember: uid=JParker, ou=IT, o=LdapAbc.org
...
```

The script has to perform the following steps:

- Search for all organizational units and generate a list (in a temporary file)
- Generate for each organizational unit:
    The groupOfUniqueNames list
    All "uniquemember:" entries

You might expect a complicated program with a lot of "if," "else," and "while" constructs. Instead, look at how simple the shell script is. The following discussion breaks the script down into its logical units.

Exhibit 7 shows the first part of the script, the search functionality. The ldapsearch command lists all organizational units. The "grep dn" prints only the lines of the ldapsearch output we are interested in, and the expression

```
sed 's/dn://'
```

Exhibit 7. Group Generation Script: Part One, Searching

```
01  #!/bin/sh
02
03  DepartmentList="DepartmentList"
04
05  ldapsearch -b "o=LdapAbc.org" objectclass=organizationalUnit dn | \
06                      grep dn: | sed 's/dn: //' > DepartmentList
07
```

substitutes "dn:" with an empty string. Thus, we get a temporary file containing only the distinguished names of the various organizational units.

Exhibit 8 shows how we proceed further with the temporary file. In the next step, we generate the LDIF file. The record separator is the "," (ou = Marketing, o = LdapAbc.org). Line 18 calls the function that prints out the header of the groupOfUniqueNames list, and line 19 calls the function that prints out all of the group members.

The function PrintGroup in Exhibit 9 simply prints out the required fields. Line 22 strips the "ou =" prefix from the organizationalUnit attribute.

The last function listed in Exhibit 10 is more interesting because it executes a query in the directory and prints the output into the temp file. The ldapsearch command is constructed in line 33. It searches using the base organizational unit and the filter "objectclass = inetOrg-Person." It further specifies to return only the distinguished name (split into cmd2 and cmd to keep the length of the line shorter). It applies two filters on the output produced by the ldapsearch call. The first

---

Exhibit 8. Group Generation Script: Part Two, Creating Groups

```
08 cat DepartmentList |                          \
09    awk ' BEGIN { # Input Record Separator
10                      FS="," ;
11                      OutputFile="OUT";
12                  }
13                  {
14                      #Gather information from the two fields:
15                      OU = $1 ;
16                      Base = $2 ;
17                      PrintGroup(OU,Base);
18                      PrintUserList(OU,Base);
19                  }
```

Exhibit 9. Group Generation Script: Part Two, PrintGroup Function

```
21 function PrintGroup(Dep,Base) {
22    sub("ou= ","",Dep) ;
23    printf("dn: cn=%s, %s\n",Dep,Base) >> Out ;
24    printf("objectClass: top\n") >> Out ;
25    printf("objectClass: groupofUniqueNames\n") >> Out ;
26    printf("cn: %s\n",Dep) >> Out ;
27    printf("ou: %s\n",Dep) >> Out ;
28 }
29
```

Exhibit 10. Group Generation Script: Part Two, PrintUserList Function

```
30  function PrintUserList (OU,Base) {
31     Post1 = | grep dn: " ;
32     Post2 = " | sed 's/dn:/uniquemember:/i' " ;
33     Cmd2  = "objectclass=inetOrgPerson dn ";
33     Cmd   = sprintf("ldapsearch -b \"%s, %s\" %s %s>> %s",
34                        OU,Base,Cmd2,Post1,Post2,Out);
35     system(Cmd);
36     printf("\n") >> Out ;
37     }'
```

---

one filters out only the lines containing the distinguished name (grep dn:). And the second one substitutes the "dn:" with "uniquemember:" that is needed for use later on in the object class "groupOfUnique-Names."

All we need to do now is to execute ldapmodify:

```
ldapmodify -D "cn=admin, o=LdapAbc.org" -w password1 -f Out
```

At the end, we could clean up the temporary files.

Command-Line Tools: Conclusion

We have seen only two command-line tools in this section, but these two alone are enough to manipulate the directory and extract whatever information you need. To use the command-line tools effectively, you need to understand the LDIF format and know how to construct search filters. Both concepts were covered in Chapter 4. If you download a C software development kit (SDK) and the OpenLDAP distribution, you can use the source code written in C to build command-line tools that exactly fit your needs.

We have also seen examples of shell scripts demonstrating how to integrate the command-line tools. These scripts only hint at what is possible. For example, they do not distinguish between lowercase and uppercase text, which can be an issue. Nor are they very robust in the event of failures of a single commands.

In the next few sections, we will learn how to access the directory in more sophisticated ways.

LDAP and Programming Language Support

The command-line tools may come in handy if you just want to type an on-the-fly test or an update. They are also useful additions to the system administrator's toolbox. Still, if you typically execute complicated scripts or even a whole application, you will rarely use them.

Instead, you have a large assortment of programming languages offering support for LDAP.

The scope of this book prevents a description of all of the available languages. Instead, we focus on a handful of languages — C, Java, Perl, and PHP — that are available on more than one platform and are popular in the networking environment. The classic C language was the first API and has an RFC of its own. The ubiquitous Java language offers such interesting possibilities as the use of applets to run in a browser, servlets to be executed on the server side, and the handy JavaBeans that allow the user to combine bits of prefabricated code without knowing anything about its inner workings. Perl and PHP, sometimes called scripting languages, are both used frequently in Internet/intranet environments, a field where LDAP unleashes its full strength.

Exhibit 11 is a pseudocode representation of a typical LDAP program flow. As stated previously, the schema underlying all of the APIs is always the same; it derives directly from the functional model as described in Chapter 3. The parameters are omitted in this pseudocode representation. Before you can actually bind to the LDAP server, you have to establish a connection to the LDAP server. In the connect-request you specify the server name and the port the server is listening on. If the port number is omitted, the standard port number is assumed. If you do not specify the host name, a connection to "localhost" is requested. Once you have established the connection, you authenticate yourself to gain the correct access rights. If you omit the userID and password, an anonymous logon is arranged, giving you the access right of an anonymous user, as defined in the server configuration files. Indeed, the server configuration may not allow anonymous access at all. If you are authenticated with userID and password, the server looks up the access rights defined for this particular UserID.

Exhibit 12 shows a typical query program flow in pseudocode. It reflects the object-oriented philosophy of LDAP, which most program-

---

Exhibit 11. Typical LDAP Program Flow

```
// establish connection to the LDAP server
connect(Server,Port);
// logon anonymous or with user/password
bind();
// do some work, search, update, delete …..
while (some-condition) {

  do some stuff …
  }
// logoff and close the connection
unbind();
```

Exhibit 12. Typical Query Program Flow

```
QueryResultObject = query (BaseDN,Filter) ;
while (Entry = QueryResultObject->getNextEntry()) {
  print Entry->getDistinctName ;
  while (Attribute = Entry->getNextAttribute()) {
    print Attribute->getValues ;
  }
}
```

---

ming languages follow very closely. You get a result object from the query, and this result object allows you to handle exceptions. Remember that the LDAP server delivers not only the result but also an error code. With this result object, you can get the number of hits your query produced. From the result object, you further can iterate along the entries matching your query. The entry object allows you to iterate inside the corresponding attributes, giving you the number of attributes together with the distinguished name. Note that the distinguished name has a particular importance and is not handled like the other attributes. The DN is the index that allows the directory server to access the entry. If an ordinary attribute is changed, the hierarchical position in the directory tree does not change. However, modifying the distinguished name could change the hierarchical position, or the requested change might even be impossible. This is why the distinguished name is handled differently. There are particular methods (or functions) available for access to the distinguished name. Once you are connected and authenticated, you can execute any commands to which you have access rights. After that, you unbind to close the connection and release the resources the directory server had allocated for you.

This chapter is not intended to serve as a manual for the APIs presented here. It should give you only an understanding of the philosophy underlying each API. As such, it provides a few working examples for each of the programming language treated here. You have just to try them out. As always, play around with them, extend the code, and see what happens. This is the best way to gain confidence with the programming language API.

The chapter focuses on languages that are available for a wide variety of platforms. Thus, we will see SDKs for the C language, Java, Perl, and PHP. Every API is available from more than one supplier. Most of them are available for free, and some are even open source. For security reasons, many companies and government agencies require open-source software to be installed in their systems. So my choice is to use open-source software whenever possible.

Note that the section covering LDAP and PHP is very extensive. We use PHP as a paradigm to illustrate how LDAP works together with a programming language. Because PHP is an easy-to-use language, you can concentrate fully on the new topic at hand, the

LDAP API. The paradigm presented in the following section applies to all of the other programming languages.

LDAP and PHP

PHP is a multipurpose scripting language that is well suited for use in Web development because it can be easily embedded in HTML documents. PHP stands for PHP hypertext preprocessor (originally, PHP was an abbreviation for personal home page). The language was originally written for use in hypertext documents, and that remained its main purpose until version 4.2.0. Since the introduction of version 4.2.0, PHP has included a new API, in PHP parlance called SAPI (server application programming interface), i.e., a command-line interface. This interface made it possible to execute PHP scripts from the command line and extend the use of PHP to other, nonhypertext-oriented applications too. The LDAP software development kit is easily available, and it is free. In the PHP v4.2.0 release, this feature is still experimental. The upcoming version (at the time of this writing) is available at http://snaps.php.net for both UNIX and Win32 platforms.

The big advantage of PHP is that it is very easy to use; one can begin writing scripts after half an hour of study to learn the language, which is well documented. PHP has a syntax that draws from C, Java, and Perl. Later, if you need more-sophisticated features, you will discover a vast choice of libraries, for example SQL, Mail, HTTP, PDF, TCP/IP, and of course LDAP. Furthermore, PHP has object-oriented features, so the programmer has the option of working at the cutting edge of technology. Finally, PHP is available on a vide variety of platforms, including UNIX, Win32, MacOS, NetWare, and even OS/2.

This chapter is not a PHP tutorial. If you need more information about this language, please refer to the online documentation available at the official PHP Web site, http://www.php.net. As stated in the introduction to this chapter, we dedicate much more space to this language because of its simplicity, which enables the programmer to concentrate on the LDAP part of the work.

We have just a few more words before getting down to the business of reviewing the LDAP library of PHP. As mentioned before, you can use PHP from the command line or embedded in HTML pages. The only difference is that PHP code embedded in HTML has to use HTML elements for formatting purposes of the output. For example, in the command-line mode you will use "\n" for the new-line character, but in HTML you will use <BR>. In both cases, however, you have to tell the PHP parser that it has to interpret the code as PHP. The code shown in Exhibit 13 does the job. Everything outside the brackets will just to be echoed. Other than that, you can proceed as with other scripting languages. For the Win32 platform, you have to declare that

---

Exhibit 13. Example of php Script

```
<?php

// php code . . .

?>
```

Exhibit 14. Call of LDAP Interpreter Inside a php Script on UNIX

```
#!/usr/local/bin/php
<?php

    // php code . . .

?>
```

---

files with "php" extensions are LDAP code. In the UNIX world, you can precede the PHP code with a call to the PHP interpreter. For example, if your interpreter resides at "/usr/local/bin/php," the PHP frame will look like the code shown in Exhibit 14.

First Steps with PHP-LDAP

As with all the LDAP libraries, we have to use the well-known paradigm of

- Connecting to the server that LDAP is running on
- Binding to the LDAP server
- Executing the requested operations
- Unbinding from the LDAP server

Let us now look at some examples showing the use of PHP. The first example in Exhibit 15 shows a connection for an anonymous user who executes a query. (We assume that the anonymous user has the right to do so in our example installation.) The relevant commands are:

- `ldap_connect`: Establishes the connection
- `ldap_bind`: Binds to the LDAP server after the work is done
- `ldap_unbind`: Unbinds the LDAP server and close the connection

The commands will be explained in more detail in the next few paragraphs. This chapter is structured much like Chapter 3, where you find the functional model of LDAP.

Exhibit 15. Simple Example of Connect, Bind, Search, and Unbind

```php
<?php
// Example1: Connect to the LDAP server, bind, execute a query
and unbind

$LDAP_Server    = "ldap.ldap_abc.de" ;
$BaseDN         = "o=ldap_abc.de" ;
$Filter         = "(sn=c*)";

printf("Connecting . . . \n");
$ConnectionID = ldap_connect($LDAP_Server) ;

if ($ConnectionID) {
   printf("Connected to %s\n",$LDAP_Server);
   printf("Binding as anonymous \n");

   $BindRes = @ldap_bind($ConnectionID) ;
   if ($BindRes) {
     printf("Bound to LDAP server \n");
     $Result = @ldap_search($ConnectionID, $BaseDN, $Filter);
     if (! $Result) {
        printf("LDAP Error (%d)\n Description: %s\n",
           ldap_errno($ConnectionID),
           ldap_error($ConnectionID));
     } else {
        $entries = ldap_get_entries($ConnectionID,$Result);
        for ($i=0 ; $i < $entries["count"] ; $i++) {
           printf("DN: %s\n",$entries[$i]["dn"]);
        }
     }
   } else {
     printf("Could not bind to LDAP Server \n");
   }
}else {
   printf("Unable to connect to %s\n",$LDAP_Server);
}
ldap_unbind($ConnectionID);
?>
```

Authentication and Control Operations

ldap_connect

Before binding to the LDAP server, you need to establish a connection. You do this using the `ldap_connect` command:

```
resource ldap_connect(string hostname, [int port])
```

The parameters are the hostname you wish to connect to and an optional port number. If you do not specify the port number, the standard port 389 is assumed. If the connection request has been successful, a resource identifier is returned; otherwise you get FALSE.

ldap_bind

Before you can ask the LDAP server to execute commands on your behalf, you to have to authenticate yourself against the LDAP server. The **ldap_bind** command does this. Here is the syntax:

```
bool ldap_bind (resource link_identifier [, string bind_dn [, string
bind_password]])
```

The first parameter is the resource identifier you got from your connection to the server. By the way, you could also open two connections and handle them independently from each other. The optional parameters are the distinguished name and the password. If you do not specify DN and password, an anonymous connection is assumed. Otherwise, you have the access rights defined for the DN you logged in with. Exhibit 16 is a code fragment illustrating a bind with userID and password.

ldap_unbind

The ldap_unbind operation releases the user-specific data structures and closes the connection. It takes only one parameter, the resource identifier of the connection. Here is the syntax:

```
bool ldap_unbind (resource link_identifier)
```

It returns TRUE for success, FALSE for failure.

ldap_close

The ldap_close function is a simple synonym for ldap_unbind. The syntax is the same. There is no abandon function available yet.

```
bool ldap_close (resource link_identifier)
```

Exhibit 16. Bind with Distinct Name and Password

```
$DistinctName = "uid=JamesParker,ou=Marketing,o=ldap_abc.de" ;
$Password = "secretPassword" ;
$BindResult = ldap_bind($ResourceID, $DistinctName, $Password) ;
if (!$BindResult) {
   printf("Could not bind to LDAP Server \n%d: %s\n",
      ldap_errno($ConnectionID),
      ldap_error($ConnectionID));
}
```

More about Authentication in a Web Environment

In many cases, you will want to control access to your Web pages or Web applications. The authentication mechanism frequently should also provide more information about the authenticated user. For example, the PHP script may need the common name and surname of the user so that it can be printed on the welcome page of the application. Exhibit 17 is a sample script for authentication. This example contains two interesting concepts not directly related to LDAP: session maintenance and transport of session data. These are achieved, respectively, with the session_start/session_end and session_register functions. Again, refer to the PHP online manual for the exact syntax. What we are interested in here is the authentication procedure. From the initial authentication form (a simple HTML form), the script gets the credentials using for the UsrId $HTTP_POST_VARS['login'] and for the password $HTTP_POST_VARS['password']. These variables are provided by the Web server contained in $HTTP_POST_VARS['variable'] where variable is the name of the field in the HTML form. The variables "login" and "password" are the names of the fields in the HTML form and will probably be different for your application.

After the bind, your application has to establish the user's level of control if the variables for the distinguished name and the password contain any values. If they do not, the application refuses to deliver the pages. You have to handle this case explicitly; otherwise, the LDAP server would assume an anonymous connection and would not report any error.

Another observation about the bind command is mainly a cosmetic consideration. Look at the line with the bind command, which is prefixed by the "at" sign ("@"). Standard output for the bind command would normally print out an ugly error message. The @ sign suppresses this message and allows you to handle eventual error messages.

You can use the following functions to handle errors:

- int `ldap_errno` (resource `link_identifier`): Returns the error number of the last command. Parameter is the resource identifier of the LDAP connection.
- string `ldap_error` (resource `link_identifier`): Returns the error text of the last executed command. Parameter is the resource identifier of the LDAP connection.
- string `ldap_err2str` (int `errno`): Converts from the error number to an error string. The parameter is the error number you got from the `ldap_errno` command.

One last observation regarding the `ldap_unbind–ldap_bind` combination. You might wish to unbind from one userID and bind with another one without shutting down the connection to the server. The new bind effectively unbinds from the old userID and releases all user-

---

Exhibit 17. Example of Authentication

```php
<?php session_start();
  // Configuration:
  $LDAP_Server = "LdapAbc.org" ;
  $LDAP_BaseDN = " ou=IT, o=LdapAbc.org" ;
  $Error_HTML = "/Error.html" ;
  $TimeOut_HTML = "/TimeOut.html" ;

  // Grabbing Parameters from Script Environment:
  $CallingScript = $HTTP_SERVER_VARS['PHP_SELF'];
  $login = $HTTP_POST_VARS['login'] ;
  $password = $HTTP_POST_VARS['password'] ;
  Location=sprintf("http://%s/%s",
    $HTTP_SERVER_VARS['HTTP_HOST'],
    dirname($HTTP_SERVER_VARS['PHP_SELF']));
  // Register the session:
  session_register('CallingScript');
  $check = !empty($login);
  if (is_array($authdata)) {
    $now = time();
    if ($now - $start 1000) {
      $Location = $Location.$TimeOut_HTML ;
      Exception($Location);
  // The session should be destroyed,
  // and will be destroyed by the error mask
    }
    $start = time();
  } elseif ($check) {
    $ds=ldap_connect($LDAP_Server);
    $r=ldap_bind($ds);
    $udn="uid=".$login.",".$LDAP_BaseDN ; $res=@ldap_bind($ds,$udn,$
        password);
    if ($res && (chop($login) != "") && (chop($password) !="")){
      session_register('authdata');
      session_register("start");
      $authdata=array("login"=$login);
      $start = time();
      // Everything's ok, so we don't do nothing at all.
    } else {
      unset($authdata);
      $Location = $Location.$Error_HTML ;
      Exception($Location);
    }
  } else {
    unset($authdata);
    $Location = $Location.$Error_HTML ;
    Exception($Location);
  }

  function Exception($Location) {
    echo "" ;
    echo "window.location.replace(\"$Location\") ; " ;
    echo "" ;
  }
?>
```

Exhibit 18. Entry for a Person

```
DN: uid=uv467_rz28, ou=Marketing, o=abc_ldap.de
objectclass: top
objectclass: person
objectclass: organizationalPerson
objectclass: inetOrgPerson
cn: Tim Parker
givenName: Tim
sn: Parker
uid=uv467_rz28
mail: Tim.Parker@abc_ldap.de
userPassword: 4d2tUdzXVlVNz
```

Exhibit 19. Code Example for Two Binds

```
$Name        = $HTTP_POST_VARS['Name'];
$SurName     = $HTTP_POST_VARS['SurName'] ;
$Password    = $HTTP_POST_VARS['Password'] ;

$Filter      = sprintf(" (& (sn=%s) (givenName=%s))" , $Name,
                  $SurName) ;
$Filter      = " (& (sn = $Name) (givenName = $SurName)) " ;

$ConnectionID = ldap_connect($LDAP_Server) ;
$BindRes       = @ldap_bind($ConnectionID) ;

$WantedAttributes   = array("uid");
$ ConnectionID      = @ldap_search($ConnectionID, $BaseDN, $Filter,
                         $WantedAttributes);
$entries            = ldap_get_entries($ConnectionID, $ConnectionID);

$DistinctName    = sprintf("uid=%s, ou=Marketing, o=abc_ldap.de",
                     $entries[0]["uid"][0]);
$BindRes         = @ldap_bind($ConnectionID, $DistinctName, $Password) ;
```

---

related data before binding with the new userID. You might wonder why this would be useful. Exhibit 18 shows an entry for a person with a computer-calculated userID. We wish to let the user log on using his name, surname, and password, thus shielding the user from the complex details of the transaction. Your application would first allow an anonymous connection to get the userID, construct the distinguished name, and then bind with the DN and the password. Exhibit 19 shows the code fragment that accomplishes this task.

Search and Associated Commands

ldap_search

We saw a few examples of the search operation earlier in this chapter, and we used a few parameters to return only certain attributes. Now we will take a closer look at the parameters for the ldap_search function.

```
resource ldap_search (resource link_identifier, string base_dn,
string filter [, array attributes [, int attrsonly [, int sizelimit
[, int timelimit [, int deref]]]]])
```

The `ldap_search` command has three required parameters and five optional parameters. The three required parameters are:

1. *resource link_identifier:* Identifier of the LDAP connection
2. *string base_dn:* Base DN where the query should start
3. *string filter:* Query filter

The five optional parameters are:

1. *array attributes:* An array of attribute names you wish the query to return. The array limits the results set of the query, thus keeping the network traffic low.
2. *attrsonly:* If the switch "attrsonly" is set to "1," only the attribute names are reported, not the values. The default is "0," which returns attribute names and values.
3. *sizelimit:* Specifies the number of entries returned by the query. If set to "0" (default), there is no limit. Note, however, that the LDAP administrator can impose a value in the server configuration that limits the number of entries returned. This value cannot be overwritten.
4. *timelimit:* Specifies the number of seconds the search is allowed to run. Once this time limit is reached, the query stops. Again, this value cannot exceed a serverwide setting configured by the administrator.
5. *deref:* Specifies how aliases should be handled during the search. The following four values are possible:

- LDAP_DEREF_NEVER (default): Aliases are never dereferenced.
- LDAP_DEREF_SEARCHING: Aliases should be dereferenced during the search but not when locating the base object of the search.
- LDAP_DEREF_FINDING: Aliases should be dereferenced when locating the base object but not during the search.
- LDAP_DEREF_ALWAYS: Aliases should be dereferenced always.

If you have read about the functional model in Chapter 3, you might wonder why the parameter indicating the scope of the search is missing. Actually, it is not missing. Note that ldap_search executes a search with the scope set to LDAP_SCOPE_SUBTREE, which means that it searches the entire subtree specified by the base DN. To limit the search further, you have to use the ldap_read function or the ldap_list function.

ldap_read

The ldap_read function takes the same parameters as the ldap_search command. It works much the same, except that it sets the scope to **LDAP_SCOPE_BASE**.

```
resource ldap_read (resource link_identifier, string base_dn, string
filter [, array attributes [, int attrsonly [, int sizelimit [,
int timelimit [, int deref]]]]])
```

ldap_list

The ldap_list function takes the same parameters as the ldap_search command. It works the same with the scope set to **LDAP_SCOPE_ONELEVEL**.

```
resource ldap_list (resource link_identifier, string base_dn, string
filter [, array attributes [, int attrsonly [, int sizelimit [,
int timelimit [, int deref]]]]])
```

ldap_compare

The ldap_compare function queries the LDAP database to see whether an entry has a certain attribute with the desired attribute value. It turns TRUE if it does and FALSE if it does not.

```
bool ldap_compare (resource link_identifier, string dn, string
attribute, string value)
```

There are four parameters:

1. *resource link_identifier*: Identifier of the LDAP connection
2. *string dn*: Distinguished name of the entry you want to check
3. *string attribute*: Attribute in the entry that you want to check
4. *string value*: Attribute value that you want to check

Exhibit 20 shows us an object "Tim Parker" (recycled from Exhibit 18). Assume that we want to know whether the attribute "mail" for "Tim Parker" has the value Tim.Parker@abc_ldap.de. Exhibit 21 shows the code snippet that carries out the required action.

Working with the Result Identifiers

The search and the read functions deliver result identifiers, but we need additional data to make use of these results. What we need are the single entries and, more importantly, the single attributes with the corresponding values. There are powerful functions to accomplish these ends. PHP recognizes operators that work like iterators. In this

---

Exhibit 20. Entry of objectclass inetOrgPerson to be Changed

```
DN: uid=uv467_rz28, ou=Marketing, o=abc_ldap.de
objectclass: top
objectclass: person
objectclass: organizationalPerson
objectclass: inetOrgPerson
cn: Tim Parker
givenName: Tim
sn: Parker
uid=uv467_rz28
mail: Tim.Parker@abc_ldap.de
userPassword: 4d2tUdzXVlVNz
```

Exhibit 21. Little Example with ldap_compare

```
$DN       = "uid=uv467_rz28, ou=Marketing, o=abc_ldap.de" ;
$attrNam  = "mail" ;
$attrVal  = "Tim.Parker@abc_ldap.de"
$result = ldap_compare ($DN, $attrNam, $attrVal) ;
if ($result) {
  echo " In $DN the attribute $attrNam has the value: $attrVal " ;
}
```

---

section, we will look at operations on entries as well as operations on the single attributes.

There are two ways of working on entries and attributes. The first way is to retrieve the whole results array; the second is to treat one entry or attribute a time. The `ldap_get_entries` and `ldap_get_attributes` functions are very similar, both returning a multidimensional array of results values. Both functions return arrays. The arrays use the conventions defined in PHP, i.e., $Array["count"] is the number of entries in the array; $Array[0] is the first element; and elements in associative arrays can be identified both by their slot number and their key.

ldap_get_entries

The syntax of the **ldap_get_entries** function is:

```
array ldap_get_entries (resource link_identifier, resource
result_identifier)
```

The two parameters for the function are:

1. *resource link_identifier*: Identifier of the LDAP connection
2. *resource result_identifier*: Resource identifier returned by the search

The results array is as follows:

```
$ResArray=ldap_get_entries (resource link_identifier, resource
result_identifier);
```

`$ResArray ["count"]:`	number of entries in the result
`$ResArray [0]:`	refers to the details of first entry
`$ResArray [i]["dn"]:`	DN of the ith entry in the result
`$ResArray [i]["count"]:`	number of attributes in ith entry
`$ResArray [i][j]:`	jth attribute in the ith entry in the result
`$ResArray [i]["attribute"]["count"]:`	number of values for attribute in ith entry
`$ResArray [i]["attribute"][j]:`	jth value of attribute in ith entry

ldap_count_entries

The **ldap_count_entries** function counts the number of entries in the results sct, much the same as the "count" field in the associative array you get from the search function.

```
int ldap_count_entries (resource link_identifier, resource
result_identifier)
```

The two parameters are:

1. *resource link_identifier:* Identifier of the LDAP connection
2. *resource result_identifier:* Resource identifier returned by the search

ldap_sort

The ldap_sort function sorts the array returned by the search function. "Sortfilter" indicates the attribute used for the sort function. Internally, a "strcmp" function is used, i.e., the attribute values are sorted in alphabetically ascending order. Note, however, that it is not the LDAP server that executes the sorting. It is your application that sorts the array in memory.

```
int ldap_count_entries (resource link, resource result, string
sortfilter)
```

The three parameters are:

1. *resource link_identifier:* Identifier of the LDAP connection
2. *resource result_identifier:* Results returned by the search
3. *string sortfilter:* Attribute to be sorted; problems arise with multi-value attributes

ldap_parse_result

The **ldap_parse_result** function is rather like a debugging utility or, more precisely, a utility used if something goes wrong with the query. It takes the resource link identifier and the result resource and provides additional information about the results set.

```
bool ldap_parse_result (resource link, resource result, int errcode,
string matcheddn, string errmsg, array referrals)
```

The six parameters are:

1. *resource link_identifier*: Identifier of the LDAP connection
2. *resource result_identifier*: Results returned by the search
3. *int errcode*: Error code produced by the search
4. *string matcheddn*: DN closest to the requested entry, in case the requested entry does not exist; this feature is available only in LDAP (v3)
5. *string errmsg*: Additional error message returned by the server
6. *array referrals*: Array of referrals returned by the server

ldap_get_attributes

The **ldap_get_attributes** function has the following syntax:

```
array ldap_get_attributes (resource link_identifier, resource
result_entry_identifier)
```

The two parameters are:

1. *resource link_identifier*: Identifier of the LDAP connection
2. *resource result_identifier*: Resource identifier returned by the search

The result array is as follows:

```
$ResArray = ldap_get_attributes (resource link_identifier, resource
result_identifier);
return_value["count"]:            number of attributes in the entry
return_value[0]:                  first attribute

return_value[n]:                  nth attribute
return_value["attribute"]["count"]: number of values for attribute
return_value["attribute"][0]:     first value of the attribute
return_value["attribute"][i]:     (i+1)th value of the attribute
```

Exhibit 22 shows an example using ldap_get_entries. Another possibility would be to iterate through the single entries or attributes. We will first look at the syntaxes for the relevant functions —

Exhibit 22. Use of Result Set After Query

```
$ResEntries = ldap_get_entries($ConnectionID,$ResultRes);

   for ($i=0 ; $i < $ResEntries["count"] ; $i++) {
     printf("DN: %s\n",$ResEntries[$i]["dn"]);
     for ($j=0 ; $j < $ResEntries[$i]["cn"]["count"] ; $j++) {
       printf("CN: %s\n",$ResEntries[$i]["cn"][$j]);
     }
   }
 ?>
```

---

ldap_first_entry, ldap_next_entry, ldap_first_attribute, ldap_next_attribute, ldap_get_dn, ldap_get_values, and ldap_get_values_len — and then see an example using all of these functions.

ldap_first_entry

The **ldap_first_entry** command gets the first entry returned from a query. Remember, the query also returns a result identifier.

resource **ldap_first_entry** (resource link_identifier, resource result_identifier)

The two parameters are:

1. *resource link_identifier:* Identifier of the LDAP connection
2. *resource result_identifier:* Resource identifier returned by the search

ldap_next_entry

The **ldap_next_entry** command get the next entry identifier from the previous one.

resource **ldap_next_entry** (resource link_identifier, resource result_entry_identifier)

The two parameters are:

1. *resource link_identifier:* Identifier of the LDAP connection
2. *resource result_entry_identifier:* Resource-entry identifier returned by the search, similar to "resource result_identifier" returned by the ldap_first_entry function

ldap_first_attribute

The **ldap_first_attribute** command gets the first attribute in a result entry.

```
string ldap_first_attribute (resource link_identifier, resource
result_entry_identifier, int ber_identifier)
```

The three parameters are:

1. *resource link_identifier:* Identifier of the LDAP connection
2. *resource result_entry_identifier:* Resource-entry identifier returned by the search
3. *int ber_identifier:* Integer variable that PHP uses internally for subsequent ldap_next_attribute calls. You need only to provide this variable. You do not have to set it, as PHP does the rest for you.

ldap_next_attribute

The **ldap_next_attribute** command gets the next attribute in a result entry.

```
string ldap_next_attribute (resource link_identifier, resource
result_entry_identifier, int ber_identifier)
```

The three parameters are:

1. *resource link_identifier:* Identifier of the LDAP connection
2. *resource result_entry_identifier:* Resource-entry identifier returned by the search
3. *int ber_identifier:* Integer variable that was set by PHP in the previous call (or first_attribute or next_attribute)

ldap_get_dn

The **ldap_get_dn** command returns the distinguished name of the entry.

```
string ldap_get_dn (resource link_identifier, resource
result_entry_identifier)
```

The two parameters are:

1. *resource link_identifier:* Identifier of the LDAP connection
2. *resource result_entry_identifier:* Resource-entry identifier returned by the search

ldap_get_values, ldap_get_values_len

These two commands get the value/values of an attribute.

```
array ldap_get_values (resource link_identifier, resource
result_entry_identifier, string attribute)
array ldap_get_values_len (resource link_identifier, resource
result_entry_identifier, string attribute)
```

The three parameters are:

1. *resource link_identifier*: Identifier of the LDAP connection
2. *resource result_entry_identifier*: Resource-entry identifier returned by the search
3. *string attribute*: Attribute value in the entry that you want to check

The function call returns a simple array containing the required value or values, if there are any. The difference between these two functions is that ldap_get_values returns ASCII values, and ldap_get_values_len returns binary values.

Conclusion: An Example

Exhibit 23 illustrates the use of these functions. Note that it presumes that you have already done a search and thus have a resource-result identifier called "$ResultRes." The variable $ConnectionID is the usual resource link identifier you get from the ldap_connect function.

Adding, Deleting, and Modifying Entries

You have seen how to search a directory and how to get single entries and attributes. In this section, you will learn how to update the directory. The update functions are:

- Adding new entries
- Deleting entries
- Modifying entries

ldap_add

We will start with the add function. The syntax is as follows:

```
bool ldap_add(resource link_identifier, string dn, array entry)
```

The three parameters are:

1. *resource link_identifier*: Identifier of the LDAP connection

Exhibit 23. Example of Iteration through the Result Set

```
$Entry = ldap_first_entry($ConnectionID,$ResultRes);
  printf("DN: %s\n",ldap_get_dn($ConnectionID,$Entry));
  while($Entry = ldap_next_entry($ConnectionID,$Entry)) {
    printf("DN: %s\n",ldap_get_dn($ConnectionID,$Entry));
    $Attribute = ldap_first_attribute($ConnectionID,
                   $Entry,$Ber);
    printf("attribute: %s\n",$Attribute);
    while ($Attribute = ldap_next_attribute($ConnectionID,
        $Entry,$Ber)) {
      printf("attribute: %s\n",$Attribute);
      $Values = ldap_get_values($ConnectionID,
                  $Entry,$Attribute);
      for ($i=0 ; $i < $Values["count"] ; $i++) {
        printf("\t\t%s\n",$Values[$i]);
      }
    }
  }
```

Exhibit 24. Example for ldap_add Function

```
$BindRes = @ldap_bind($ConnectionID,$AdminDn,$PassWord) ;
  if ($BindRes) {
    $data["cn"] = "Eddie Thomson" ;
    $data["sn"] = "Thomson" ;
    $data["givenName"] = "Eddie" ;
    $data["telephoneNumber"] = "0045 78 21 384" ;
    $data["employeeNumber"] = 03230 ;
    $data["mail"] = "EThomson@ldap_abc.de" ;
    $data["uid"] = ethomson283 ;
    $data["objectclass"][0] = "top" ;
    $data["objectclass"][1] = "person" ;
    $data["objectclass"][2] = "organizationalPerson" ;
    $data["objectclass"][3] = "inetOrgPerson" ;
   $DN = "employeeNumber=03230, ou=Marketing, o=ldap_abc.de" ;
    $Result = ldap_add($ConnectionID,$DN,$data);
    if ($Result) {
      printf("DN %s added\n",$DN);
    }
  } else {
    printf("Couldn't bind to %s\n",$LDAP_Server);
  }
```

2. *string dn*: Distinguished name of the entry to be added
3. *array entry*: Array containing all the entries plus their relative values. The array has the same structure as that returned by the get_entry function call.

The syntax is straightforward, as demonstrated by the example in Exhibit 24.

ldap_delete

The **ldap_delete** function is still easier, inasmuch as it takes only two parameters.

```
bool ldap_delete (resource link_identifier, string dn)
```

The two parameters are:

1. *resource link_identifier*: Identifier of the LDAP connection
2. *string dn*: Distinguished name of the entry to be deleted

Exhibit 25 deletes what we created in Exhibit 24.

ldap_modify

There is more than one update function, depending on what we wish to update in the entry. We could add an attribute, delete an attribute, and replace an attribute within an entry. Consequently, PHP has three operations:

1. `ldap_mod_add`: Adds a new attribute to an entry
2. `ldap_mod_del`: Deletes an attribute from an entry
3. `ldap_mod_replace`: Replaces an attribute value

And there is still one more function, called simply "ldap_modify." Just like the other functions, ldap_modify takes an array as a parameter, replaces the old attribute values with the new values, and eventually adds new ones. The ldap_modify function does not delete attributes. Here is the syntax of the functions. Note that the parameters are the same for all four functions.

```
bool ldap_mod_add(resource link_identifier, string dn, array entry)
bool ldap_mod_del(resource link_identifier, string dn, array entry)
bool ldap_mod_replace(resource link_identifier, string dn, array entry)
bool ldap_modify(resource link_identifier, string dn, array entry)
```

Exhibit 25. Example of ldap_delete Function

```
$BindRes = @ldap_bind($ConnectionID,$AdminDn,$PassWord) ;
  if ($BindRes) {
    $DN = "employeeNumber=03230, ou=Marketing, o=ldap_abc.de" ;
      $Result = ldap_delete($ConnectionID,$DN);
      if ($Result) {
         printf("DN %s deleted\n",$DN);
      }
  } else {
     printf("Couldn't bind to %s\n",$LDAP_Server);
  }
```

The three parameters are:

1. *resource link_identifier:* Identifier of the LDAP connection
2. *string dn:* Distinguished name of the entry to be modified
3. *array entry:* Array containing all the entries plus their relative values. The array has the same structure as that returned by the get_entry function call.

For the sake of illustrating the update functions, let us assume we did not delete the entry for Eddie Thomson in Exhibit 25. Exhibits 26 through 28 show examples of these update operations.

After the action in Exhibit 26, the entry corresponding to Eddie Thomson now has two phone numbers. Exhibit 27 shows how to change one of them. Recall that now you have to treat the attribute as an array because it has more that one value. Look at Exhibit 28 to see how to delete the phone number again.

Exhibit 26. Example of ldap_mod_add: Add an Attribute

```
if ($BindRes) {
      $data["telephoneNumber"] = "0045 78 21 385" ;
   $DN = "employeeNumber=03230, ou=Marketing, o=ldap_abc.de" ;
      $Result = ldap_mod_add($ConnectionID,$DN,$data);
      if ($Result) {
          printf ("DN %s added\n",$DN);
      }           ("attribute added to DN % \k", $DN);
   } else {
      printf("Couldn't bind to %s\n",$LDAP_Server);
   }
}
```

Exhibit 27. Example of ldap_mod_replace: Modify an Attribute

```
if ($BindRes) {
      $data["telephoneNumber"][0] = "0045 78 21 385" ;
      $data["telephoneNumber"][1] = "0045 78 21 387" ;
   $DN = "employeeNumber=03230, ou=Marketing, o=ldap_abc.de" ;
      $Result = ldap_mod_replace($ConnectionID,$DN,$data);
      if ($Result) {
          printf ("DN %s added\n",$DN);
      }           ("attribute modified in DN %s \k", $DN);
   } else {
      printf("Couldn't bind to %s\n",$LDAP_Server);
   }
}
```

Exhibit 28. Example of ldap_mod_del: Delete an Attribute

```
if ($BindRes) {
    $data["telephoneNumber"][1] = "0045 78 21 387" ;
    $DN = "employeeNumber=03230, ou=Marketing, o=ldap_abc.de" ;
    $Result = ldap_mod_del($ConnectionID,$DN,$data);
    if ($Result) {
       printf ("DN %s added\n",$DN);
    }           ("attribute deleted in DN %s \k", $DN);
  } else {
    printf("Couldn't bind to %s\n",$LDAP_Server);
  }
}
```

---

ldap_rename

The ldap_rename command changes the DN of an entry. This function works as described in the functional model in Chapter 3, i.e., the function not only permits changing the RDN, but also moving the entry inside the directory tree and specifying a new parent for the entry. You can specify whether you wish to leave the old entry or to remove it. Here is the syntax:

```
bool ldap_rename (resource link_identifier, string dn, string
newrdn, string newparent, bool deleteoldrdn)
```

The five parameters are:

1. *resource link_identifier*: Identifier of the LDAP connection
2. *string dn*: Distinguished name of the entry to be modified
3. *string newrdn*: New relative distinguished name (note that this is the RDN, not the DN)
4. *string newparent*: Eventually, the new parent entry
5. *bool deleteoldrdn*: Boolean value to indicate whether the old entry has to be deleted. Set to TRUE, it will be deleted; set to FALSE, it will be left.

What Remains?

There are still some functions that have not been covered. These are functions to work with references, such as ldap_parse_reference or ldap_first_reference, and functions that permit changing the format, such as `ldap_t61_to_8859` or `ldap_explode_dn`. We will not review these functions here. If you want to work with LDAP and PHP, check the PHP online manual for more information about these functions.

Perl and LDAP

The Perl language has grown in scope and popularity over the last ten years. The first Perl manual, "Programming Perl," was written by its creators Larry Wall and Randal L. Schwartz in 1991. Since then, Perl has developed object-oriented features and has advanced from version 4.0 to version 5.8. You can download it from CPAN (Comprehensive Perl Archive Network). CPAN provides an overwhelming number of libraries for this extremely powerful programming language. The invaluable advantage of Perl is its pattern-matching functions. These functions allow you to write in one line of code what would require ten lines in the C language. The language is interpreted,* and this makes it a rapid prototype development tool. Note that there is also a Perl-to-C compiler available.

As with all open-source software, Perl too has a library for LDAP. Actually, it has multiple libraries from which you can choose. If you search on the Internet it is easy to get confused, because sometimes the same software is known under different names. There are substantially three main threads:

1. Net::LDAPapi from Clayton Donley, outdated (only LDAP [v2]), but still heavily used
2. PerlLDAP available from http://www.mozilla.org/directory/perldap.html
3. Net::LDAP bundle from Graham Barr, also available from Source-ForgeNet with the name "perl-ldap," at http://perl-ldap.source-forge.net

In this section, we will use the third option, Net::LDAP. The first two options rely on C, but Net::LDAP is completely native Perl code, so you need only Perl to make it work. However, the differences between the different libraries are not so great, so if you have some idea of the Perl language you should be able to use a different Perl library. Actually, the term "library" is not technically correct because most of these "libraries" use the object-oriented aspects of Perl. The term we should use for all the examples in this section on Perl is "package." If we use these terms interchangeably in this chapter, bear in mind that "package" is the correct term.

There are some interesting libraries worth checking out if you are interested in LDAP programming with Perl. One is the Tie-LDAP library from Taisuke Yamada, which allows you to treat an LDAP directory just as an associative array. The other is the DBD-LDAP

---

* An "interpreted" language as opposed to a "compiled" language is a language that does not need to be compiled in order to be executed. Because compilation takes time, the development of programs in interpreted language is faster. Execution, however, is slightly slower.

library from Jim Turner. This library allows you to access a directory as if it were a database by using the DBI (database interface) and speaking SQL (structured query language).

Like every other API, the Perl API follows also the afore-mentioned procedure, i.e.:

■ Connecting to the LDAP server
■ Binding to the server
■ Doing some work
■ Unbinding to release the resources

Our First Perl LDAP Program

As with the other APIs, let us first look at a real-life program, this time written in Perl. Exhibit 29 shows a short Perl program using the Net::LDAP module. If you have read the previous section covering PHP and LDAP, you will see the same concepts presented here.

First you create an LDAP object specifying the host you will connect to. This allocates a structure in memory for you. With this LDAP object, you bind to the LDAP server. In this case, we bind anonymously. The search method delivers a result object. In the case of errors (the code () method has a return value not equal to 0) methods unequal 0), the method "error()" describes what went wrong. You can use a number of methods on the result object: "count()" delivers the number of entries satisfying the search, and "all_entries" delivers the whole array of entries. The "dump" method applied on a single entry dumps out all its attributes, including the distinguished name. In the rest of this section, we will review the most important objects in the Perl API and its methods.

Perl Objects

There are six objects you will use in a Perl program. These objects are:

1. `ldap`: The base object that executes nearly all operations on the directory. You will find all the methods described in the functional model in Chapter 3. This object also provides access to the directory schema and the `root_dse`.
2. `search`: The search method on behalf the LDAP object returns a search object. This object is a container object for the search result. It offers methods such as the count on the total number of found entries and fetch methods to get single entries from the results set.
3. `entry`: This object lets you access the single attributes of an entry. An entry object can be created in two ways: first as the result of

Exhibit 29. Our First Perl LDAP Program

```
01  #!/usr/local/bin/perl -w
02  use Net::LDAP ;
03
04  $User = $ARGV[0] ;
05  print "Searching: $User \n" ;
06
07  local $Base = "ldap_abc.de" ;
08  local $Filter = "uid=$User" ;
09  local $Host = "localhost" ;
10
11  $ldap = Net::LDAP->new($Host) or die "$@" ;
12  $ldap->bind || die "Could not bind to $Host" ;
13  $result = $ldap->search (base => $Base, filter => $Filter);
14  $result->code && die $result->error ;
15  if ($result->count == 0) {
16     print "NO ROW FOUND \n" ;
17  }
18  foreach $entry ($result->all_entries) {
19     $entry->dump;
20  }
21  $ldap->unbind ;
```

an explicit creation via the new operator, second via one of the fetch methods using the search object

4. message: The message objects lets you analyze errors reported by LDAP operations. It holds the error number and the error message in a human-friendly format. It also has the sync method that allows you to run asynchronous requests on the server.

5. reference: The reference object has only one method, "references," that displays a list of references returned by the directory server.

6. schema: The schema object allows you to explore the schema.

The LDAP Object

First of all, we have to create an LDAP object, and this happens via the new constructor. (Most object-oriented languages use a special method to construct a new object. This method is called "construction.") The constructor must specify the host you wish to connect to. You can furthermore specify a number of options.

```
$ldap = new Net::LDAP(<Host>,
                      port    => <Port>,
                      timeout => <TimeOut>,
                      async   => (0,1),
                      version => (2,3)
                     );
```

Host, port, and timeout are straightforward, and the default value for timeout is 120 s. "Async 1" means that all the actions have to be executed asynchronously. With "version," you can specify whether you wish to use LDAP (v2), the default value, or LDAP (v3). There are still more parameters. For more information, refer to the manual pages of the Net::LDAP package.

The LDAP object recognizes the methods identified in the functional model plus some special ones.

Authentication/Control Methods

Authentication/control are achieved by the bind, unbind, and abandon methods. The bind can be anonymous or authenticated via the user's distinguished name and password.

```
$Message = $ldap->bind([DN],
                   password   => <password>,
                   control    => <Control>,
                   callback   => <Callback>,
                   sasl       => <Sasl>
              );
```

We have already seen an anonymous bind, so let us see in Exhibit 30 an example of authentication using a distinguished name and password. The bind method has further arguments, which can be found in the manual pages of the Net::LDAP package. Some additional authentication types include:

- *no authentication*: Indicates an anonymous connection, in which case you do not have to supply the DN
- *password*: User supplies DN and the password
- *sasl*: User binds using the SASL mechanism. You can obtain the argument via the Authen::SASL object. (See the Perl documentation for more details.)

The unbind() method takes no argument at all. The abandon operation takes the messageID of a long-running command. This must be an asynchronous command because synchronous commands do not return a result until the command has been completed. The following example shows a typical abandon in action.

```
$message = $ldap->search(@SearchArgs);
$ldap->abandon($message);
```

You could also write this abandon as a method acting upon the message object:

```
$message = $ldap->search(@SearchArgs);
$message->abandon();
```

Exhibit 30. Example of Authentication Using DN and Password

```
$host     = "ldap.AbcLdap.org" ;
$port     = 389 ;
$DN       = "cn=admin, o=LdapAbc.org" ;
$pasword  = "password1" ;

$ldap = new Net::LDAP($host,port => $port);

$ldap->bind($DN,
                password => $password,
                version  => 3,
            ) || die "Could not bind to server";
   . . .
$ldap->unbind();
```

Interrogation Methods

Here we have the usual search and compare methods. "Search" takes as arguments the search base, the scope, and the filter parameters. You can also specify the attributes to be returned.

```
$Message = $ldap->search (base      => <base>,
                          scope     => <scope>,
                          sizelimit => <sizelimit>,
                          timelimit => <timelimit>,
                          typesonly => (true|false),
                          filter    => <filter>,
                          attrs     => <attrs>,
                          control   => <control>,
                          callback  => <callback>,
                          );
```

The relevant arguments are:

- `base`: Search base
- `scope`: (base, one, and sub)
- `filter`: Search filter
- `timelimit`: Limit in seconds; 0 means no time limit
- `sizelimit`: Limit in entries to be returned; 0 means no limit

For the other parameters, see the online documentation.

Exhibit 31 shows an example of the search method. The other interrogation method is "compare()." It reports "true" if the entry identified with DN has the specified attribute with the specified value. Here is an example:

```
$DN = "uid=JParker, ou=IT, o=LdapAbc.org" ;

if ($ldap->compare($DN,
                   attr=>givenName,
                   value=>"James") {
    printf("Found correct Person\n");
}
```

Exhibit 31. Example of Search Method

```
$base = "ou=IT, o=LdapAbc.org" ;
$filter = "(sn=Parker)" ;
$attributes = ["sn","cn","uid","mail"] ;
$Message = $ldap->search (base => $base,
                          filter => $filter,
                          attrs  => $attributes,
                          );
$Message->code() && die "$Message->error()" ;
foreach $entry ($mesg->all_entries) {
  $entry->dump;
}
```

Exhibit 32. New Entry Creating a New Entry Object

```
use Net::LDAP::Entry ;
$entry = new Net::LDAP::Entry();
. . . (see entry object later)
$ldap->add($entry);
```

Update Methods

The update methods are add(), delete(), modify(), and moddn().

Add an Entry — There are two ways to add an entry:

1. Using the Net::LDAP::Entry object, as depicted in Exhibit 32.
2. Specifying the attributes in the add() method, as seen in Exhibit 33.

Delete an Entry — The delete method is straightforward. You need only the DN. See Exhibit 34 for an example.

Modify an Entry — Exhibit 35 is an example showing how to modify an entry in a directory. Some comments on the code:

- The add and replace key needs a pointer to an associative array.
- The delete key needs a pointer to an associative array if you wish to delete only an attribute with a specified value. This is used mostly for multivalue attributes. For example, the e-mail address could have multiple values. Here we delete the value at ldapabc.de.

If the whole update refers to one distinguished name, you can use the shortcut "changes" as shown in Exhibit 36.

Exhibit 33. New Entry Using the Add Method

```
$Msg = $ldap->add($DN,
            attrs => [
                    objectClass => ["top",
                                    "person",
                                    "organizationalPerson",
                                    "inetOrgPerson",
                                    ],
                    sn          => "Voglmaier",
                    givenName   => "Reinhard",
                    cn          => "Reinhard E. Voglmaier",
                    uid         => "RVoglmaier",
                    mail        => Rvoglmaier@LdapAbc.org",
                    ],
            );
$Msg->code() && die "$Msg->error()" ;
```

Exhibit 34. Delete an Entry

```
$DN = "uid=JParker, ou=Marketing, o=LdapAbc.org" ;
$Msg = $ldap->delete($DN);
$Msg->code() && die "$Msg->error()" ;
```

Exhibit 35. Example Modifying Entries

```
$host    = "ldap.AbcLdap.org" ;
$port    = 389 ;
$BindDN  = "cn=admin, o=LdapAbc.org" ;
$BindPW  = "password1" ;

$ldap = new Net::LDAP($host,port => $port);

$ldap->bind($BindDN,
                password => $BindPW,
                version  => 3,
            ) || die "Could not bind to server";
$dn = "uid=JKahn,ou=Marketing,o=LdapABc.org" ;
$ldap->modify($dn,
                add => [ telephonenumber => '428' ],
            ) ;
$Msg->code() && die "$Msg->error()" ;
$ldap->modify($dn,
                delete => [mail => 'JKahn\@ldapabc.de'],
            );
$Msg->code() && die "$Msg->error()" ;
$ldap->modify($dn,
                delete => [telexnumber],
            );
$Msg->code() && die "$Msg->error()" ;
$ldap->modify($dn,
                replace =>[ fax => '827' ],
            );
$Msg->code() && die "$Msg->error()" ;
        $ldap->unbind();
```

Exhibit 36. Further Possibility to Modify an Entry

```
$Msg = ldap->modify($dn,
                changes => [
                    add => [ telephonenumber => '428' ],
                    delete => [mail => 'JKahn\@ldapabc.de'],
                    delete => [telexnumber],
                    replace =>[ fax => '827' ],
                ],
            );
$ldap->unbind();
```

Exhibit 37. Modify the Distinguished Name

```
$dn = "uid=JKahn,ou=Marketing,o=LdapABc.org" ;
$Msg = $ldap->moddn($dn,
                newrdn => "uid=JKahn",
                deleteoldrn => true,
                newsuperior => "ou=HR,o=LdapAbc.org",
            );
```

Modify Distinguished Name — To modify the distinguished name, you can use the moddn() method. As discussed in Chapter 3 when we discussed the functional model and in Chapter 4 when we saw the LDIF format, there are a number of possibilities for changing the distinguished name. You can change the distinguished name while keeping the old distinguished name. Otherwise, you have to specify "deleteoldrn." In LDAP (v3) you can move the entry in the directory by specifying "newsuperior." In our new example in Exhibit 37, Mr. Kahn moves from Marketing to Human Resources.

Schema Exploring (LDAP [v3])

One of the new properties of LDAP (v3) is that it stores information about itself in the directory. That permits the client to obtain useful information about the directory and to adapt its actions on the directory structure it discovered. For example, can the client find out which version of LDAP the server uses (v2 or v3). The Net::LDAP object gives you two methods of retrieving information about the directory: the schema() method and the root_dse() method.

root_dse() — You get the root DSE simply by calling the root_dse() method. As a search method, you can supply a reference to the list of attributes to be returned.

```
$ListPtr = ["subschemaSubentry","supportedExtension"] ;
$root_dse = $ldap->root_dse(attrs => $ListPtr);
```

The attrs with the pointer is optional

```
$root_dse = $ldap->root_dse();
```

If you omit the attrs option, the method gives you information about following variables:

```
subschemaSubentry
namingContexts
altServer
supportedExtension
supportedControl
supportedSASLMechanisms
supportedLDAPVersion
```

Schema() — The schema() methods returns the schema object. You will learn more about the schema object in the corresponding paragraph later in this chapter. Exhibit 38 shows how to explore the schema using Perl LDAP objects.

Callback

Most of the methods accept a callback option. The value for the callback option should be a reference to a subroutine. Exhibit 39 shows an example of code registering the callback; Exhibit 40 shows the definition of the callback itself.

Remember that LDAP is a message-oriented protocol. The client sends a request to the server and gets one or more responses to its request. The subroutine referenced with callback will be called each time one of these responses arrives at the client. When the subroutine is called, it gets a message object as its first argument. If the method was a search, the second argument is a search object. If the server instead sends back a reference, the second argument is a reference object.

Exhibit 38. Exploring the Schema

```
$schema = $ldap->schema();
# print out all objectClasses:
foreach $OC ($schema->objectclasses()) {
    printf("%s \n",$OC);
}
# print out all attributes:
foreach $AT ( $schema->attributes()) {
    printf("%s \n",$AT);
}
```

Exhibit 39. Using Callbacks

```
$base = "ou=IT, o=LdapAbc.org" ;
$filter = "(sn=Parker)" ;
$attributes = ["sn","cn","uid","mail"] ;
$Message = $ldap->search (base      => $base,
                          filter    => $filter,
                          attrs     => $attributes,
                          callback  => \$SearchCB(),
                         );
```

Exhibit 40. Callback for Exhibit 39

```
sub SearchCB {
  my $mesg = shift;
  my $obj = shift;
  if (!$obj) {
    # Search complete
    #
  }
  elsif ($obj->isa('Net::LDAP::Reference')) {
    my $ref;

    foreach $ref ($obj->references) {
      # process ref
    }
  }
  else {
    # Process Net::LDAP::Entry
  }
}
```

The Search Object

The search object is a container object that simply holds the result list of a query. There are several methods to access the entries satisfying the query, such as:

- `entries()`: Returns an array of entries returned by the search
- `entry(INDEX)`: Returns entry with index number INDEX
- `shift_entry/pop_entry`: Shifts/pops an entry from the internal result list
- `sorted([attribute list])`: Returns the entries sorted by the attribute list

An interesting method is count(), which returns the number of entries found and references the reference objects returned by the directory server. Most of these methods will be seen in the next section.

The Entry Object

The entry object has two functions:

1. Construct a new entry
2. Access the individual attributes on an existing entry

Let us create an entry and add it to the directory. Exhibit 41 shows you the Perl code that does the job.

Next, we modify some existing entries found via the search object mentioned in the previous section. However, we print out only the values we retrieve via the "get method" call, as shown in Exhibit 42.

As seen in the example, you can access the individual attributes via the get_value() method. You also can set the attributes via the

---

Exhibit 41. Example Using the Entry Object

```perl
#!/usr/bin/perl -w
use Net::LDAP ;
use Net::LDAP::Entry ;

#Define some values:
local $host    = "127.0.0.1" ;
local $port    = 389 ;
local $DN      = "cn=admin, o=LdapAbc.org" ;
local $pass    = "password1" ;

$ldap = Net::LDAP->new($host, port => $port) or die "$@" ;
printf("Server %s contacted, connection OK\n",$host);

$ldap->bind($DN,
            password => $pass,
            version  => 3) || die "Could not bind" ;

$ObjectClasses = ["top",
                  "person",
                  "organizationalPerson",
                  "inetOrgPerson"] ;

$entry = new Net::LDAP::Entry();
$entry->dn("uid=SPalmer, ou=Marketing, o=LdapAbc.org");
$entry->add(objectClass => $ObjectClasses ,
            sn          => "Palmer" ,
            givenName   => "Stephen",
            cn          => "Stephen Palmer",
            uid         => "SPalmer",
            mail        => "SPalmer\@LdapAbc.org",
        );

$mesg = $entry->update($ldap);
$mesg->code && die $mesg->error ;

$ldap->unbind();
```

Exhibit 42. Example Using the Entry Object and the Get Method

```
# as the previous example:
printf("Server %s contacted, connection OK\n",$host);

$mesg = $ldap->search(base => "o=LdapAbc.org",
                      filter => "(sn=P*)",
                     );
my $max = $mesg->count();
printf("Found %d entries\n",$max);

for($i = 0 ; $i < $max ; $i++) {
   my $entry = $mesg->entry($i);
   printf("Distinct Name: %s\n",$entry->dn());
   foreach my $attr ($entry->attributes) {
       printf("%s: %s\n",$attr,
                         $entry->get_value($attr));
   }
}
```

---

set_value() method. The access to the distinguished name is different; you get and set it via the dn() method. You set the distinguished name if you give it as parameter to the dn() method. See Exhibit 41.

The entry object also offers all the methods required to update entries, i.e., delete, add, or modify attributes. Again, refer to the documentation of your installation.

The Message Object

The most important methods of the message object are: the code() method that is set to "1" if an error occurs and the error() method that gives you the error message. We have seen these methods in action in the previous examples.

The message object has two methods of controlling asynchronous requests:

1. sync(), to wait for the execution of the request
2. done(), to ask if the request has been completed

The Reference Object

We have nothing new to add to the previous discussion of the reference object. The reference object is a container object to hold the references returned by the directory server.

The Schema Object

The schema object is interesting, inasmuch as it allows you to explore the schema. Exhibit 43 shows how to use the schema object. As you see from Exhibit 43, the schema object contains the complete schema

Exhibit 43. Schema Exploring

```perl
#!/usr/bin/perl -w
use Net::LDAP ;
use Net::LDAP::Entry ;

#Define some values:
local $host    = "127.0.0.1" ;
local $port    = 389 ;

$ldap = Net::LDAP->new($host, port => $port) or die "$@" ;
$schema = $ldap->schema();
# print out all objectClasses:
printf("ObjectClasses:\n");
foreach $OC ($schema->objectclasses()) {
    printf("%s oid: %s\n",$OC, name2oid($OC)) ;
}
printf("Attributes:\n");
foreach $AT ($schema->attributes()) {
    printf("%s oid: %s\n",$AT, name2oid($AT)) ;
}
printf("Matching Rules:\n");
foreach $MR ($schema->matchingrules()) {
    printf("%s oid: %s\n",$MR, name2oid($MR)) ;
}
printf("Matching Rules:\n");
foreach $MRU ($schema->matchingruleuse()) {
    printf("%s oid: %s\n",$MRU, name2oid($MRU)) ;
}
printf("Syntaxes:\n");
foreach $SY ($schema->syntaxes()) {
   printf("%s oid: %s\n",$SY,name2oid($SY));
}
```

information. In the example, we get a list of all object classes, attributes, matching rules, matching rules use, and syntaxes.

There are also functions to test whether a given element (object class, attribute, etc.) is part of the given schema. The methods is_objectclass, is_attribute, is_syntax, and is_matchingrule report "true" if the element is part of the schema and "false" if it is not.

In Exhibit 43, the method "name2oid" was used. This method prints out the oid of the given element. If you want all information available in the schema, you can simply dump it out using the dump() method, as shown in Exhibit 44.

You can also explore single entries to understand which attributes are required (the must() method) and which are optional (the may() method). Look at the lines in Exhibit 45 that do this for the entry inetOrgPerson. Note, however, that the "may" and "must" methods do not print out attributes inherited from the parent. You can get the name of the parent with the method "superclass" and, in this way, construct a program that really does dump out all attributes.

Exhibit 44. Dump Method

```perl
#!/usr/bin/perl -w
use Net::LDAP ;
use Net::LDAP::Entry ;

#Define some values:
local $host    = "127.0.0.1" ;
local $port    = 389 ;

$ldap = Net::LDAP->new($host, port => $port) or die "$@" ;
$schema = $ldap->schema();
$schema->dump();
```

Exhibit 45. Dumping a Single Entry

```perl
#!/usr/bin/perl -w
use Net::LDAP ;
use Net::LDAP::Entry ;

#Define some values:
local $host    = "127.0.0.1" ;
local $port    = 389 ;


$ldap = Net::LDAP->new($host, port => $port) or die "$@" ;
$schema = $ldap->schema();
for $attribute ($schema->must("inetOrgPerson")) {
      $MustList .= $attribute ;
}
for $attribute ($schema->may("inetOrgPerson")) {
      $MaytList .= $attribute ;
}

printf("Must: %s\n", $MustList);
printf("May:  %s\n", $MayList);
printf("Parent: %s\n", $schema->superior());
```

Conclusion

In this section, we have seen the Perl library and learned that it provides a very comfortable interface to directory servers. Perl is often used in common gateway interface (CGI) scripts, which makes it easy to write gateways to access directory services via the HTTP protocol. Moreover, Perl is available on a wide variety of platforms, and many third-party tools offer Perl libraries, allowing you to connect directory services over a broad range of platforms and applications. Perl also has libraries to access RDBMS (Oracle, Informix, ODBC, DBM, and many others), so you can write connectors between your database applications and your directory server.

Like the LDAP protocol, the LDAP Perl interface has to be considered a work in progress. We could not include all methods available, as this would be beyond the scope of this book.

A last word of advice before closing this section: When you are developing LDAP software using the Perl libraries, it is a good idea to have a look at the CPAN Web site. There, under Net::LDAP, you can find a number of useful scripts that may be helpful in resolving problems you may encounter. The following section lists some examples. By the time you read this book, there may be many more, as the CPAN site is continuously evolving.

Scripts

- jpegDisplay.pl

   A script to display a jpeg picture from the jpegPhoto attribute of an LDAP directory entry
   Author: Clif Harden <charden@pobox.com>

- jpegLoad.pl

   A script to load a jpeg picture into the jpegPhoto attribute of a directory entry
   Author: Clif Harden <charden@pobox.com>

- ldifdiff.pl

   Generates LDIF "change diff" between two sorted LDIF files
   Author: Kartik Subbarao <subbarao@computer.org>

- ldifsort.pl

   Sorts an LDIF file by the specified key attribute. The sorted version is written to standard output.
   Author: Kartik Subbarao <subbarao@computer.org>

- ldifuniq.pl

   Culls unique entries from a reference file with respect to a comparison file
   Author: Kartik Subbarao <subbarao@computer.org>

The C LDAP API

The C-language API is the only one (at the time of the writing) being documented in the collection of RFCs. You will find it as RFC 1823, "The LDAP Application Program Interface." This RFC describes the API for LDAP (v2). The API for LDAP (v3) is still in draft form (draft-ietf-ldapext-ldap-c-api-05.txt) and is available from the Internet Engineering Task Force (IETF) Web site (http://www.ietf.org).

You can get an SDK from various vendors, some even for free, for example from the Web sites of Netscape, Novell, or Microsoft. With the OpenLDAP distribution, you also get the C libraries, which we will use for the examples in this chapter.

Nearly all function calls exist in two versions: synchronous and asynchronous. The synchronous function calls are postfixed with _s, as seen in the following example for the search functions:

- `ldap_search` is the asynchronous function
- `ldap_search_s` is the synchronous counterpart

Because synchronous and asynchronous function calls act differently, they do not deliver the same result codes. The synchronous functions return a result code indicating success or failure. The asynchronous functions, however, cannot report success or failure because they report immediately, without knowing whether the function succeeded. Instead, the asynchronous functions return the message ID of the operation that has been initiated. This message ID can be used later, for example to give the user the option of interrupting the function if it should take too much time (possibly a search function reporting too many results).

When compiling the code, remember to include the correct files and link them to the correct libraries of LDAP functions before compiling. Which libraries and files you have to include depends heavily on the platform you are working on and the particular SDK you are using. On UNIX systems, be sure that your compiler can find the dynamic libraries. On Solaris, you include the path the compiler needs to search using the LD_LIBRARY_PATH environment variable. Hewlett Packard uses SHLIB_PATH instead. The LDAP libraries need the nsl and socket libraries (-lnsl, -lsocket).* If you get an error message complaining about a symbol named "inet_aton," you will have to compile in the "resolv" library (-lresolv), too. This depends on the platform you are working on.

If you have any problems, look at the documentation shipped with the SDK you are using. Exhibit 46 shows the makefile on a Sun Solaris box. The makefile saves typing if you have to debug and recompile your programs. It is also useful as future documentation in case you ever need to know exactly what it was that you did when you compiled this piece of code successfully.

---

*The nls library provides national language support; the socket library is the interface.

Exhibit 46. Example Makefile Using LDAP and C

```
# Example Makefile to compile LDAP programs

EXTRALDFLAGS=-lsocket -lnsl -lresolv
LDAPLIB=-lldap -llber
INCDIR=/usr/local/include
LIBDIR=/usr/local/lib

LIBS=-L$(LIBDIR) $(LDAPLIB) $(EXTRALDFLAGS)
CFALGS=-I$(INCDIR)

CC=gcc

PROGS=Example1

all:       $(PROGS)
Example1:  Example1.o
           $(CC) -o Example1 Example1.o $(LIBS)
clean:     /bin/rm -f $(PROGS) *.o a.out core
```

LDAP SDK v2 versus v3

As mentioned previously, the LDAP C API is standard (informal RFC) for LDAP (v2). Briefly, here are the differences between LDAP (v2) and LDAP (v3):

- LDAP (v3) clients can follow referrals and references. They will automatically follow them unless, via the ldap_set_option, the standard value is not overwritten.
- Character encoding of the distinguished name and string values are encoded using UTF-8 encoding in v3. In v2, SDK US-ASCII or T.61 encoding is used
- With LDAP (v3), you have to enable v3 with the ldap_set_option call. For compatibility reasons, the default value is v2.

Our First LDAP Program in C

Let us have a look at a simple LDAP example borrowed from RFC 1823 with some modification. The program retrieves the attributes of a number of entries. The only thing that you have to do is to adapt it to your needs. If you are still using the examples from Chapter 1, you can use the program in Exhibit 47 without any modification. As you see, there is nothing special about the program. You will recognize the main steps as described in the introduction:

Exhibit 47. Our First LDAP Program in C

```c
#include <stdio.h>
#include <ldap.h>

/* Specify the parameters here. */
#define HOSTNAME "localhost"
#define PORTNUMBER 389
#define BASEDN "o=ldap_abc.de"
#define SCOPE LDAP_SCOPE_SUBTREE
#define FILTER "(sn=Parker)"

main() {

        LDAP            *ld;
        LDAPMessage     *res, *e;
        int             i;
        char            *a, *dn;
        void            *ptr;
        char            **vals;

        /* open a connection */
        if ((ld = ldap_open(HOSTNAME, LDAP_PORT)) == NULL)
            printf("Error connecting to %s\n",HOSTNAME);
            exit(1);

        /* authenticate as nobody */
    if (ldap_simple_bind_s(ld, NULL, NULL) != LDAP_SUCCESS) {
                    ldap_perror(ld, "ldap_simple_bind_s");
                    exit(1);
        }

        /* search for entries using FILTER and BASEDN */
        if (ldap_search_s(ld, BASEDN, LDAP_SCOPE_SUBTREE,
                    FILTER, NULL, 0, &res)!= LDAP_SUCCESS) {
            ldap_perror(ld, "ldap_search_s");
            exit(1);
        }

        /* step through each entry returned */
        for (e = ldap_first_entry(ld, res); e != NULL;
            e = ldap_next_entry(ld, e)) {
            /* print its name */
            dn = ldap_get_dn(ld, e);
            printf("dn: %s0, dn);
            free(dn);

            /* print each attribute */
            for (a = ldap_first_attribute(ld, e, &ptr);
                a != NULL;
                a = ldap_next_attribute(ld, e, ptr)) {
                    printf("attribute: %s0, a);
            /* print each value */
            vals = ldap_get_values(ld, e, a);
            for (i = 0; vals[i] != NULL; i++) {
                printf("value: %s0, vals[i]);
            }
            ldap_value_free(vals);
                    }
            }
            /* free the search results */
            ldap_msgfree(res);

            /* close and free connection resources */
            ldap_unbind(ld);
    }
```

- `ldap_open(HOSTNAME, LDAP_PORT):` Opens the connection to the server
- `ldap_simple_bind_s(ld, NULL, NULL):` Authenticates, in this case as "anonymous"
- `ldap_unbind(ld):` Ends the session

Note the iteration through the results set, accomplished here with a "for" loop.

Now let us have a closer look at the API, beginning with the structures used and then moving on to review some of the available functions. Note that we will not cover all of the available functions here. For more information, have a look at the standards definition in RFC 1823 or in the draft for LDAP (v3). A look at the documentation shipped with the software you are using is also helpful.

Structures

The SDK uses several structures to put in results and error messages. SDKs for both v2 and v3 of LDAP recognize the following structures:

- *LDAP structure*: A structure returned by the ldap_open call
- *LDAP message structure*: Used to return entry, reference, result, and error information
- *BerElement structure*: Used to hold data and state information about encoded data
- *BerValue structure*: Used to represent arbitrary binary data and its fields
- *Timeval structure*: Used to represent an interval of time and its fields

For more information, have a look at the standards definition in RFC 1823 or in the draft for LDAP (v3). A look at the documentation shipped with the software you are using is also helpful.

Overview of LDAP Functions

The API offers a number of different functions that could be grouped as follows:

- Authentication and control operations, such as bind, unbind, abandon
- Interrogation operations, such as search and compare
- Iteration commands through results sets
- Update operations, such as add, delete, modify DN, modify

Let us have a look at each group.

Authentication and Control Operations

In Exhibit 47, we saw an example of one of these types of operations, the bind function. Now let us complete the picture. Like any LDAP API, we first have to establish a connection to the server LDAP is running on. In Exhibit 47, the connection is opened by the following line:

```
if ((ld = ldap_open(HOSTNAME, LDAP_PORT)) == NULL)
```

This not only opens a connection to the server, but also allocates resources needed for subsequent actions. In the case of the C language, the "open" call returns an LDAP structure if it is successful or reports NULL if it is not. The LDAP structure returned by the ldap_open call, also called "connection handle," identifies this connection and must be used in subsequent calls on behalf of this connection.

The next step is to authenticate against the LDAP server. This is done using the ldap_bind function. Again, let us look at the example in Exhibit 47:

```
if (ldap_simple_bind_s(ld, NULL, NULL) != LDAP_SUCCESS)
```

In this example, we connect to the LDAP server as an anonymous user. It is also possible to connect with a userID and password. Regarding authentication, LDAP (v2) and LDAP (v3) are different. Both LDAP (v2) and LDAP (v3) C APIs offer simple authentication, i.e., the user authenticates with userID and password. LDAP (v2) APIs should furthermore offer SSL and Kerberos authentication. LDAP (v3) APIs (in draft status at the time of this writing) instead use SASL and consider Kerberos as deprecated. Look at the documentation of your LDAP SDK for further details.

The syntax for a simple asynchronous bind is:

```
int ldap_simple_bind(
        LDAP            *ld,
        const char      *dn,
        const char      *passwd
);
```

For a synchronous bind, the syntax is:

```
int ldap_simple_bind_s(
        LDAP            *ld,
        const char      *dn,
        const char      *passwd
);
```

Both approaches express the type of authentication (simple) in the function name. It is also possible to specify the type of authentication as a parameter in the bind call:

```
int ldap_bind(LDAP *ld, char *dn, char *cred, int method);
```

In LDAP (v2), the available methods are:

- LDAP_AUTH_SIMPLE
- LDAP_AUTH_KRBV41.
- LDAP_AUTH_KRBV42

In LDAP (v3), we have:

- LDAP_SASL_SIMPLE (i.e. NULL)
- text string identifying the SASL method

After the successful bind call, you can ask the LDAP server to perform actions upon the directory. When you have finished, you close the connection using ldap_unbind():

```
ldap_unbind(ld);
```

In the previous example, for both anonymous connections and authenticated ones, the unbind call takes only the connection handle as a parameter.

The control function "ldap_abandon()" abandons a particular request. The syntax is:

```
int ldap_abandon(LDAP *ld, int msgid);
```

where "msgid" is the identifier of the abandon operation.

Interrogation Operations

As specified by the functional model (see Chapter 3), the C LDAP API recognizes two interrogation operations:

1. `ldap_search`: Searches for an entry and returns a message structure. This message structure is used in subsequent function calls to iterate through the results set, to get particular entries, or to operate one of the modify functions on it.
2. `ldap_compare`: Searches in the directory to determine whether, within a particular distinguished name, an attribute has the required value.

First, we see an example of the ldap_search function call. From the example in Exhibit 48, we learn the usage of the ldap_search function and discover a framework for writing a customized LDAP search tool. The command-line tools differ from implementation to implementation.

Exhibit 48. LDAP Search Tool in C: Get the Switches

```c
#include <stdio.h>
#include <stdlib.h>
#include <string.h>
#include <time.h>
#include <getopt.h>

#include "ldap.h"

static char      *base = NULL;
static char      *binddn = NULL;
static char      *ldaphost = NULL;
static int        ldapport = 0;
static struct berval passwd = { 0, NULL };
static char      *progname = NULL ;

main (int argc, char **argv) {

   LDAP    *ld ;
   int     scope, rc, parse_rc = 0;
   int     version=-1;
   int     i ;
   char    **attrs=0;
   char    *param, *filtpattern ;
   char    *pwd ;

   progname = strdup(argv[0]);

   /* First we read the options of the program call:
    */
   while ((i = getopt(argc, argv, "b:D:h:p:s:w:")) != EOF) {
     switch(i) {
        case 'b': /* search base */
           base = strdup(optarg);
           break;
        case 'D': /* base dn */
           binddn = strdup(optarg);
           break;
        case 'h': /* host */
           ldaphost = strdup(optarg);
           break;
        case 'p': /* port */
           ldapport = atoi(optarg);
           break;
}
        case 's': /* scope */
           if (strcasecmp(optarg, "base") == 0) {
             scope = LDAP_SCOPE_BASE;
           } else if (strncasecmp(optarg, "one", sizeof("one")-
1) == 0) {
             scope = LDAP_SCOPE_ONELEVEL;
           } else if (strncasecmp(optarg, "sub", sizeof("sub")-
1) == 0) {
             scope = LDAP_SCOPE_SUBTREE;
           } else {
```

-- continued

Exhibit 48. LDAP Search Tool in C: Get the Switches (continued)

```
        fprintf(stderr, "scope should be base, one, or sub\n");
        }
    case 'w':
        passwd.bv_val = strdup(optarg);
        {
            char* p;
            for(p = optarg; *p != '\0'; p++) {
                *p = '\0';
            }
        }
        passwd.bv_len = strlen(passwd.bv_val);
            break;
        default:
    fprintf(stderr, "%s: unrecognized option -%c\n", PROG, optopt);
    }
}
```

As noted previously, if you are not happy with the command-line tools of your implementation, you can always create your own.

To minimize the amount of code, the example in Exhibit 48 does not contain all possible switches. However, the example does allow you to specify the search filter and the attributes that the search should return. The allowed switches include the host, the port-number, the user credentials (dn + uid), and the scope.

The example in Exhibit 48 has two parts: the framework reading the parameters and the real search function implemented in C. Of course, the example does not include all of the control mechanisms that you will need in real life, but it is not difficult to add these mechanisms once you understand the program logic.

The first part of Exhibit 48 parses the switches that the user typed in the command line when the program was executed. This portion of the program gets the options from the program invocation. Regarding LDAP, there is nothing remarkable to say about it. The heart of the program is the "getopt" function call. Have a look at the documentation if you are not fluent in its usage. The password uses a structure called "berval". This structure contains both the length of the password and the password itself (see Exhibit 48).

In Exhibit 49 we construct the filter. The program interprets the string following the options (if any) as a filter. If the user did not supply a filter, the program sets a reasonable value (objectclass = *), i.e., any object class.

Now, finally, we get to the LDAP (see Exhibit 50). We open the connection to the server that the directory is running on. If the user does not specify anything, then localhost and port 389 are assumed. The set_option function sets the default version to 3. You can easily implement a new switch -v to allow the user to set the version. At the end, we authenticate against the directory server using simple bind.

Exhibit 49. LDAP Search Tool in C: Get the Filter

```
/* Here we get the filter, if the user did not
 * specify nothing we suppose she want to see
 * all objectclasses, i.e. objectclass=*
 */

  if ((argc - optind < 1) ||
     (*argv[optind] != '(' /*')'*/ &&
     (strchr(argv[optind], '=') == NULL))) {
     filtpattern = "(objectclass=*)";
  } else {
     filtpattern = strdup(argv[optind++]);
  }

if (argv[optind] != NULL) {
  attrs = &argv[optind];
}
```

Exhibit 50. LDAP Search Tool in C: Binding to the Server

```
if ((ld = ldap_init(ldaphost, ldapport)) == NULL) {
  perror("ldap_init");
}
if (version == -1) {
  version = LDAP_VERSION3;
}

if (ldap_set_option(ld, LDAP_OPT_PROTOCOL_VERSION, &version) !=
    LDAP_OPT_SUCCESS) {
 printf("Could not set LDAP_OPT_PROTOCOL_VERSION %d\n",version);
  exit(1);
}

printf("Binding with: %s and %s\n",binddn, passwd.bv_val);
if (ldap_simple_bind_s(ld, binddn, passwd.bv_val) != LDAP_SUCCESS) {
  ldap_perror(ld, "ldap_bind");
  exit(1);
}
```

We could also have written the bind command in a different format, as shown in Exhibit 51.

Now we can execute the search. Exhibit 52 shows the function call that does the job. In the next section, when we learn how to use the result structure, we will extend this search utility to print out the results found in the directory.

Iteration Commands through Results Sets

Let us continue with the command-line search tool we began using in the previous section. Until now, we have been getting an error

---

Exhibit 51. LDAP Search Tool in C: Alternate Bind Function Call

```
authmethod = LDAP_AUTH_SIMPLE ;
if (ldap_bind_s(ld, binddn, passwd.bv_val, authmethod)
                                != LDAP_SUCCESS) {
```

Exhibit 52. LDAP Search Tool in C: Executing the Search

```
rc = ldap_search_s(ld, base, scope, filtpattern, attrs, attrsonly,
     res);
  if (rc != LDAP_SUCCESS) {
   fprintf(stderr, "ldap_search_s: %s\n",ldap_err2string(rc));
   return(rc);
  }
```

message when the search is not successful, a discouraging result when using a search command-line tool. The search function delivers a structure that lets us access the entries matching the search filter. The structure is the second of the two structures mentioned in the introduction: the message structure. The message structure delivers the error code and converts the error code into a human-readable message, thus allowing the user to analyze eventual errors. Moreover, it also allows us to iterate through the results set, to count the entries contained in the results set, to sort the entries, and to fetch the single entries.

The first thing we will do is to iterate through the results set, printing out each distinguished name of the entries found. Exhibit 53 shows the code you must attach after the search. It is fairly simple. Now let us produce professional output using the code shown in Exhibit 54. We simply attach this piece of code at the line printing the distinguished name, and we get the same output we received from the command-line tool from our software distribution. The only difference is that now we can conveniently adapt it to our personal preferences.

Exhibit 53. LDAP-C Iterating through the Result Set

```
printf("Found %d entries matching the search\n",
       ldap_count_entries(ld,res)) ;
for (e= ldap_first_entry(ld,res) ;
     e != NULL ;
     e = ldap_next_entry(ld,e)) {
  printf("DN: %s\n",ldap_get_dn(ld,e));
}
```

Exhibit 54. LDAP-C Iterating through the Result Set - Version2

```
for (attr = ldap_first_attribute(ld, entry, &ber) ;
       attr != NULL ;
       attr = ldap_next_attribute(ld, entry, ber)) {
   if ((vals = ldap_get_values(ld, entry, attr)) != NULL) {
         for (i=0; vals[i] != NULL ; i++) {
               printf("\t%s: %s\n",attr,vals[i]);
   }
         /* release memory allocated for the vals array */
         ldap_value_free(vals);
   }
         /* release memory allocated for the single attribute */
         ldap_memfree(attr);
}
/* release memory allocated for the ber structure */
if (ber != NULL) {
   ber_free(ber,0);
}
```

Update Operations: Add, Delete, Modify DN, Modify

Let us begin with the easiest case of all, deleting an entry. The only thing we need is the distinguished name of the entry to be deleted:

```
dn = strdup(argv[optind++]);
rc = ldap_delete_s(ld,dn);
```

We get the DN from the argument in the program invocation. The modifydn call is also not very complicated.

The add and modify functions both use the structure "ldapmod." Let us have a brief look at the structure:

```
typedef   struct ldapmod {
        int                 mod_op;
        char                *mod_type;
        union  mod_vals_u {
               char             **modv_strvals;
               struct berval    **modv_bvals;
        } mod_vals;
} LDAPMod;
#define mod_values          mod_vals.modv_strvals
```

The structure holds three pieces of information:

1. The type of modification to be applied
2. The attribute affected
3. The values that should be assigned to the attribute (this could be a pointer to an array of strings or a pointer to an array of binary data)

The syntax of the add function is:

```
int ldap_add_s(
     LDAP              *ld,
     const char        *dn,
     LDAPMod           **attrs
);
```

The syntax of the modify function is:

```
int ldap_modify_s(
     LDAP              *ld,
     const char        *dn,
     LDAPMod           **mods
);
```

In both function calls, ld is the connection handle and DN is the distinguished name. The third parameter is an array of LDAPMod structures.

Following are two examples: The first adds an entry to the directory, and the second executes some modification to an existing entry. In both cases, we have to populate the array of LDAPMod structures. In real life, you would read the data in from a file. However, because we are concentrating on the LDAP code, we fill the example array by hand to show you what it looks like.

For every attribute, we have to construct the structure like this:

```
/* 9 attributes + NULL as last value:
LDAPMod            *attributes[10] ;
/* the single attributes:
LDAPMod            attribute1, attribute2, ....

/* array for the first attribute values, NULL terminated.
char * objectclass_vals = { "top",
                            "person",
                            "organizationalPerson",
                            "inetOrgPerson",
                            NULL } ;
char * cn_vals = {"James T. Kirk"} ;
/* here we repeat for every attribute . . .

attribute1.mod_op = LDAP_MOD_ADD ;
attribute1.mod_type = "objectclass" ;
attribute1.mod_values =  objectclass_vals ;

attribute2.mod_op = LDAP_MOD_ADD ;
/* here we repeat for every attribute . . .

attributes[0] = &attribute1 ;
attributes[1] = &attribute2 ;
. . .
attributes[9] = NULL ;
```

The above array is for the ldap_add operation. The array for ldap_modify operations is similar. The only difference is that the mod_op variable would be changed to either "replace" or "delete." The function call is straightforward. For "add," the function call is:

```
rc = ldap_add_s (ld, DN, attributes) ;
```

For "modify," the function call is:

```
rc = ldap_modify_s (ld,DN, attributes) ;
```

The modify distinguished name (or, more precisely, modify relative distinguished name) operation does not require such a complex structure. However, the syntax depends on which LDAP version you are using. Note that LDAP (v2) does not offer the possibility of moving the entry inside the directory information tree. Here is the syntax for LDAP (v2) for a synchronous function call:

```
int ldap_modrdn_s(ld, dn, newrdn)
LDAP *ld;
char *dn, *newrdn;

int ldap_modrdn2_s(ld, dn, newrdn, deleteoldrdn)
LDAP *ld;
char *dn, *newrdn;
int deleteoldrdn;
```

For asynchronous calls, simply delete the trailing "_s" from the LDAP commands. The second function deletes the old entry.

The situation is somewhat different in LDAP (v3). For synchronous calls, the syntax is:

```
int ldap_rename_s(
    LDAP            *ld,
    const char      *dn,
    const char      *newrdn,
    const char      *newparent,
    int             deleteoldrdn,
    LDAPControl     **serverctrls,
    LDAPControl     **clientctrls
);
```

For asynchronous calls, the syntax is:

```
int ldap_rename(
    LDAP            *ld,
    const char      *dn,
    const char      *newrdn,
    const char      *newparent,
    int             deleteoldrdn,
    LDAPControl     **serverctrls,
    LDAPControl     **clientctrls,
    int              *msgidp
);
```

Conclusion

In this section we have seen the LDAP C API. This API offers a vast set of functions, and it is not possible to list all the possibilities. At the time of this writing, only LDAP (v2) is covered by an official standard. The LDAP (v3) C API is still in draft form, although it may well be a valid RFC by the time you read this book. If you want to see some good working examples of the C API, take the OpenLDAP distribution and look at its implementation of the command-line tools. You will really learn a lot. Furthermore, these examples will enable you to customize and implement your own command-line tools.

The Java LDAP API

Unlike the C API, the Java API still has no RFC standard. However, work is under way, and there is a draft standard to define the Java API. The draft (draft-ietf-ldapext-ldap-java-api-18.txt, "The Java LDAP Application Program Interface") is available from the IETF Web site.

There are several sources of Java libraries for LDAP. In the following examples, we will be using the Java SDK from Netscape. Other vendors such as Novell also provide SDKs.

Like the previously discussed languages, Java provides an SDK, but it also offers several interesting ancillary technologies. A discussion of all the possibilities of Java is a subject worthy of its own book. Unfortunately, we have to limit the discussion to the Java SDK. Nevertheless, we will briefly review some interesting Java technologies at the end of this section.

As in the preceding sections for the other languages, we first view some simple applications to get an idea of what a class looks like when using the LDAP API. Then we take a look at the classes Java offers. A few further examples show how to implement the most important functionalities, such as search, update, and delete entries and how to display the results set of a search.

As with all the LDAP libraries, we have to use the well-known paradigm of

- Connecting to the server that LDAP is running on
- Binding to the LDAP server
- Executing the requested operations
- Unbinding from the LDAP server

Like the other languages, Java can send requests synchronously and asynchronously.

Our First Java Class

At this point, we have some experience with LDAP and programming language support. So we can skip the basics and begin this chapter with a complete program showing how to use the LDAP support offered by Java. Exhibit 55 shows a complete Java program that connects to an LDAP server and executes a simple search operation. The syntax to make the program work is:

```
search1.java <Host> <Port> <SearchBase> <Filter>
```

Note that the program as presented in Exhibit 55 does no error checking for missing arguments. In a real-world application, you would obviously insert error checking to avoid strange error messages from the Java interpreter, messages that could confuse the end user. We bypassed the issue of error checking to maintain our focus on LDAP.

The "try" part of the program (line 20) tries to open a connection to the LDAP server using the connect method. (We will see the connect method later in more detail.) Once the connection is opened, a search is executed using the search method, which delivers an object of type `LDAPSearchResults`. This object has the method `hasMoreElements`, which checks whether all elements in the results set have been visited (line 28), and the method "next," which delivers the next element in the results set (line 30). The "next" method delivers the single entry as an object. The getDN method (line 31) delivers the distinguished name of the entry, and the `getAttributeSet` (line 33) delivers the object `attributeSet`, which has "get" and "set" methods to access the single attributes.

We will take a closer look at single objects and methods in the following sections. This section, however, is not intended to be an exhaustive tutorial on Java-LDAP programming. Refer instead to the documentation shipped with the Java development for LDAP. Most of them include tutorials and numerous examples.

Authentication and Control Operations

Connect and Bind

First of all, we have to create an LDAPConnection object. This object is used later on to enable all operations such as authentication, searching of entries, modification of entries, and deletion of entries.

```
LDAPConnection ld = new LDAPConnection();
```

Then we connect to the server that LDAP is running on:

```
ld.connect(host,port);
```

Once connected, we bind to the LDAP server:

```
ld.authenticate(BaseDN,password);
```

Exhibit 55. Your First LDAP Program in Java

```
01  import netscape.ldap.* ;
02  import java.io.* ;
03  import java.util.* ;
04
05  public class search1 {
06
07     public static void main(String[] args) {
08
09        /* Get variables from command line */
10        String host      = args[0] ;
11        int port         = Integer.parseInt(args[1]);
12        String base       = args[2] ;
13        String filter     = args[3] ;
14
15        int scope         = LDAPConnection.SCOPE_SUB ;
16        int version       = 3 ;
17
18        LDAPConnection ld = null ;
19
20        try {
21           ld = new LDAPConnection();
22
23           ld.connect(version,host,port,null,null);
24
25           LDAPSearchResults res =
26              ld.search(base,scope,filter,null,false);
27
28           while (res.hasMoreElements()) {
29              LDAPEntry findEntry = null ;
30              findEntry = (LDAPEntry) res.next();
31              System.out.println("DN: " + findEntry.getDN()) ;
32              LDAPAttributeSet attributeSet =
33                 findEntry.getAttributeSet();
34
35              for (int i=0; i<attributeSet.size(); i++) {
36                 LDAPAttribute attribute =
37                    (LDAPAttribute) attributeSet.elementAt(i);
38                 String attrName = attribute.getName() ;
39                 Enumeration enumVals =
40                    attribute.getStringValues();
41                 if (enumVals != null) {
42                    while (enumVals.hasMoreElements()) {
43                       String nextValue =
44                          (String) enumVals.nextElement();
45                       System.out.println(nextValue) ;
46                    }
47                 }
48              }
49           }
50
51           if (ld!= null) {
52              ld.disconnect();
53           }
54        }
55
56        catch(LDAPException e) {
57           System.out.println(e.toString());
58        }
59
60     }
61  }
```

There are two ways to bind (authenticate):

1. Bind anonymously, where BaseDN and password are null:

```
ld.authenticate(null,null);
ld.authenticate ("", "");
```

2. Bind with a user DN and password:

```
ld.authenticate("uid=JKirk,ou=IT,o=LdapAbc.org",
                password1);
```

As shown in the example, you can combine the two steps of connecting and binding into a single step:

```
ld.connect(host,port,BaseDN,password);
```

As explained previously, there are servers running LDAP (v2) and servers running LDAP (v3). The SDK assumes LDAP (v2) as the default. In the example, we explicitly specified to use LDAP (v3). You can ask the directory server which version it supports and set the version to take advantage of the extended functionality of version 3:

```
ld.connect(version,host,port,BaseDN,password);
```

Unbind

There is not much to say about the unbind operation. The unbind works on the LDAPConnection object, releasing the resources allocated for the connection.

```
ld.disconnect();
```

Clone

The Java API helps to keep network traffic low when you need more than one connection to the LDAP server in one application. Instead of creating a brand-new connection, you can share the existing one by using the clone() method. Exhibit 56 shows a code snippet that clones a connection. The clone() method creates a logical new connection independent of the existing one using the same network resources. However, this can be done only if you use the same host, the same port, and the same user credentials.

Search and Compare Operations

Search

The syntax for the search operation is as follows:

Exhibit 56. Cloning a Connection

```
LDAPConnection ld = new LDAPConnection();
ld.connect(host,port);
ld.authenticate(BaseDN,password);

LDAPConnection ld2 = ld.clone();
```

```
public LDAPSearchResults search(String base,
                                int scope,
                                String filter,
                                String[] attrs,
                                boolean typesOnly)
throws LDAPException
```

The search operation needs the following five parameters:

1. **base:** Base distinguished name the query is starting from
2. **scope:** Search scope of the query. Values can be:
   LDAPConnection.SCOPE_SUB
   LDAPConnection.SCOPE_BASE
   LDAPConnection.SCOPE_ONE
3. **Filter:** Query filter
4. **Attributes:** Attributes to be returned by the query
5. **Typesonly:** Set to "true," the query returns only the attribute names, not the values.

Exhibit 57 shows a code snippet executing a search. This example shows a search that returns four attributes. The typesOnly parameter is set to false because we are only interested in the values of the attributes.

Compare

The compare method searches the directory to see if the entry distinguished name (DN) has the attribute with the specified value. The

---

Exhibit 57. Search Method

```
String base = "ou=IT, o=LdapAbc.org";
String host = 389 ;
String host = www.ldapabc.org;
String attrs = {"sn", "cn","commonName", "mail","uid"};
ld = new LDAPConnection();

ld.connect(version,host,port,null,null);

LDAPSearchResults res =  ld.search(base,scope,filter,attrs,
                                   false);
```

---

method returns a value of "true" if it does and "false" if it does not. The syntax is as follows:

```
public boolean compare(String dn,
                       LDAPAttribute    attr)
throws LDAPException
```

The example in Exhibit 58 verifies whether the entry with the distinguished name:

```
"uid=TMorris, ou=Marketing, o=LdapAbc.org" ;
```

has the e-mail:

```
TMorris@yahoo.com
```

Working with Search Results

If the search method gets a hit, it generates an object class "LDAPSearchResults." This object makes it possible to retrieve single entries, search referrals, find the number of entries returned, sort the entries in the results sets, etc. The "LDAPSearchResults" object also creates yet another object class "LDAPEntry" that is useful in evaluating the search. The "LDAPEntry" object, in turn, creates a third object class "LDAPAttributeSet" via the method "getAttributeSet." The example in Exhibit 59 shows how these three objects interact to give you the complete results. Of course, the user must have the requisite access rights to obtain the requested information.

Working with Search Constraints

In the search method, you can limit the attributes returned in the results set by giving as a parameter an array containing the attributes

---

Exhibit 58. Compare Method

```
String dn        = "uid=TMorris, ou=Marketing, o=LdapAbc.org" ;
String attrname  = "mail";
String attrval   = "TMorris@yahoo.com" ;

ld = new LDAPConnection();
ld.connect(version,host,port,null,null);

LDAPAttribute attr = new LDAPAttribute(attrname, attrval);

if (ld.compare(dn,attr)) {
      System.out.println("DN: "+ dn + " contains \n") ;
      System.out.println(attr1 + ": " + attrval);
}
```

Exhibit 59. Playing Around with the Result Set

```
LDAPSearchResults res = ld.search(MY_SEARCHBASE,
                                   ld.SCOPE_ONE,
                                   MY_FILTER,
                                   null,
                                   false);

/* Loop on results until finished */
while (res.hasMore()) {
  /* Next directory entry */
  LDAPEntry findEntry = res.next ();
  System.out.println(findEntry.getDN());
  /* Get the attributes of the entry */
  LDAPAttributeSet findAttrs = findEntry.getAttributeSet();
  Iterator enumAttrs = findAttrs.iterator();
  System.out.println("Attributes: ");
  /* Loop on attributes */
  while (enumAttrs.hasNext()) {
    LDAPAttribute anAttr = (LDAPAttribute)enumAttrs.next();
    String attrName = anAttr.getName();
    System.out.println(" " + attrName);

    Enumeration enumVals = anAttr.getStringValues();
    while (enumVals.hasMoreElements()) {
      String aVal = (String)enumVals.nextElement();
      System.out.println(" " + aVal);
    }
  }
}
```

---

you need. You also can specify further constraints on the search. Every object of the type "LDAPConnection" has an associated object of the type "LDAPConstraints." This object specifies the maximal number of results, the maximum time allowed for the search process, whether the server should dereference aliases, whether the server should automatically follow referrals, and other parameters. The code snippet in Exhibit 60 shows how to set up a number of constraints.

With this example, we conclude our discussion of the search and compare methods. There are many more methods included in the software development kit. To explore them all you can use the Internet draft provided by IETF and study the documentation shipped with the SDK you are using. The Netscape development kit we have used in our examples ships with a complete reference manual, well-documented examples, and an instructive programmers guide.

Update Operations

The last group of methods required by the functional model are the update functions. These include:

Exhibit 60. Using Constraints with the LDAP Java SDK

```
ld = new LDAPConnection();
ld.connect(version,host,port,null,null);

String attributes = {"sn", "cn","commonName", "mail","uid"};
int timelimit = 30 ;
int maxresults = 10 ;
LDAPSearchConstraints constraints = ld.getSearchConstraints();
Constraints. setServerTimeLimit(timelimit);
Constraints. setMaxResults(maxresults);

LDAPSearchResults res = ld.search(MY_SEARCHBASE,
                                  ld.SCOPE_ONE,
                                  filter,
                                  attributes,
                                  false,
                                  Constraints);
```

- `add:` Add a new entry into the directory.
- `delete:` Delete an entry from the directory.
- `modify:` Modify an entry in the directory. Here we could:
    Add an attribute
    Modify an attribute
    Delete an attribute
- `modifyDN:` Modify the distinguished name of an entry. Again LDAP (v2) and LDAP (v3) are different in this aspect. LDAP (v3) allows you to move the entry inside the DIT and lets you specify the new parent entry.

Add

The add method takes one argument only, the entry to be added in the form of an LDAPEntry object. You build the entry with the constructor using the distinguished name of the new entry and the attribute set the new entry should contain. The example in Exhibit 61 shows the process. The example is self-explanatory, but let us review the steps necessary to add a new entry to the directory. Once we have an LDAPConnection object and we are connected with the directory server, we have to:

- Construct the individual attributes.
- Bundle the attributes into an attribute set.
- Combine the attribute set with the distinguished name and construct the entry.
- Add the entry to the directory.

Exhibit 61. Adding an Entry to the Directory with Java

```java
try {
    // construct an LDAPConnection object and bind to
    // the directory server
    ld = new LDAPConnection();
    ld.connect(version,host,port,bindDn,pass);

    // The distinguished name:
    String dn = "uid=TMorris, ou=Marketing, o=LdapAbc.org" ;

    // Construct the single Attributes
    String objectclasses[] = {"top",
                              "person",
                              "organizationalPerson",
                              "inetOrgPerson" };
    LDAPAttribute attr0 = new LDAPAttribute("objectclass",
                                                objectclasses);
    LDAPAttribute attr1 = new LDAPAttribute("sn","Morris");
    LDAPAttribute attr2 = new LDAPAttribute("givenName","Thomas");
    LDAPAttribute attr3 = new LDAPAttribute("cn","Thomas Morris");
    LDAPAttribute attr4 = new LDAPAttribute("uid","TMorris");
    LDAPAttribute attr5 = new LDAPAttribute("mail",
                                        "TMorris@LdapAbc.org");

    // construct the LDAPAttribute set
    LDAPAttributeSet attrSet = new LDAPAttributeSet();

    // populate the LDAPAttribute set
    attrSet.add(attr0);
    attrSet.add(attr1);
    attrSet.add(attr2);
    attrSet.add(attr3);
    attrSet.add(attr4);
    attrSet.add(attr5);

    // create the new Entry
    LDAPEntry newEntry = new LDAPEntry(dn, attrSet);
    // add finally the new entry into the directory
    ld.add(newEntry);

    if (ld!= null) {
        // we are done, let us release the server resources . . .
        ld.disconnect(·);
    }
}

    catch(LDAPException e) {
        System.out.println(e.toString());
    }
```

Delete

The delete method is much easier than the add method. It takes one argument only, the distinguished name to be deleted. Exhibit 62 shows a code snippet demonstrating how the delete method is used. Again, in this example we assume that we are just connected to the directory server and therefore have the LDAPConnection object on which to

---

Exhibit 62. Deleting an Entry to the Directory with Java

```
try {
   ld = new LDAPConnection();

   ld.connect(version,host,port,bindDn,pass);

   String dn = "uid=TMorris, ou=Marketing, o=LdapAbc.org" ;
   ld.delete(dn);

   if (ld!= null) {
      ld.disconnect();
   }
}
```

---

operate the delete method. Note that the delete method delivers a result of type "void." If there is some problem in deleting the entry, the method throws an exception that we have to catch and handle.

Modify

The modify method can do three operations: it can add a new attribute; it can delete an attribute; and it can modify an attribute. The "modify method" call takes two arguments: (1) the distinguished name you want to operate on and (2) a modification set containing the operations you wish to be executed upon the specified entry. The modification set is an object implementing the class LDAPModificationSet. The example in Exhibit 63 shows all three actions. There is no "deeper logic" in the actions executed, however. Exhibit 63 only shows the underlying syntax. Again, the example is self-explanatory. Regarding the delete action, in this example the telephonenumber is deleted, regardless of it value (or values). If we wanted to delete only a particular telephonenumber, we would have to write it as:

```
LDAPAttribute attr1 = new LDAPAttribute("telephonenumber",
                                "0049-89-1729 9329");
//set delete action
modSet.add(LDAPModification.DELETE,attr1);
```

Should the attribute to be deleted not have the value specified in the attribute constructor, the modify method throws an exception at the moment of execution.

Rename

The rename method changes the distinguished (or relative distinguished) name of an entry. If you change only the relative distinguished name (both LDAP [v2]/LDAP [v3]), three parameters are passed to the method. If you change the distinguished name (LDAP [v3] only) moving

---

Exhibit 63. Modifying Entries in the Directory with Java

```
try {
    // distinguished name of the entry we operate on:
    String dn = "uid=TMorris, ou=Marketing, o=LdapAbc.org" ;

    // instantiate the LDAPModificationSet class:
    LDAPModificationSet modSet = new LDAPModificationSet();

    // construct attribute + value
    LDAPAttribute attr0 = new LDAPAttribute("mail",
                                     "TMorris@hotmail.com");
    // set modify action
    modSet.add(LDAPModification.REPLACE,attr0);

    // construct attribute + value
    LDAPAttribute attr1 = new LDAPAttribute("telephonenumber",
                                     "0049-89-1729 9329");
    // set add action
    modSet.add(LDAPModification.ADD,attr1);

    // construct attribute
    LDAPAttribute attr2 = new LDAPAttribute("telephonenumber");
    // set delete action
    modSet.add(LDAPModification.DELETE,attr1);

    ld.modify(dn,modSet);

}
```

---

the entry inside the directory information tree, four parameters are passed. Let us see an example where we change the RDN only. Let us suppose we inserted another entry for a person named Theodore Morris, and now we wish to change the uid for TMorris. In this case, TMorris should now become T1Morris. Exhibit 64 shows how to rename an entry leaving it in the same hierarchical position. The last parameter (Boolean) determines whether the old entry should be deleted. "True" stands for yes, and "false" retains the old entry. The code snippet in Exhibit 65 moves Morris into the Human Resources division, thereby changing the entry's DN and its ancestor.

LDAP URLs

The LDAP URL format is defined in RFC 2255, "The LDAP URL Format." In this section, we will see only a few example of its use with the Java programming language. Chapter 4 provides additional details.

Java has a class for LDAP URLs, the LDAPUrl class. The class has an overloaded constructor, and you have the choice of specifying as parameter the LDAP URL or giving the single components that form the LDAP URL. The examples in Exhibits 66 and 67 demonstrate the use of the LDAPUrl class. Both examples assume that you already have an active connection object named "ld." Exhibit 66 shows the con-

---

Exhibit 64. Renaming an Entry Leaving Its Ancestor Unvaried

```
try {
  // distinguished name of the entry we operate on:
  String dn = "uid=TMorris, ou=Marketing, o=LdapAbc.org" ;

  // new distinguished name
  String newdn = "uid=T1Morris, ou=Marketing, o=LdapAbc.org" ;

  ld.rename(dn, newdn, true) ;
}
```

Exhibit 65. Renaming an Entry Moving It in the Hierarchy

```
try {
  // distinguished name of the entry we operate on:
  String dn = "uid=TMorris, ou=Marketing, o=LdapAbc.org" ;

  // new distinguished name
  String newdn = "uid=T1Morris, ou=Marketing, o=LdapAbc.org" ;
  // The new parent is now HR
  String newparent = "ou=Human Resources, o=LdapAbc.org" ;

  ld.rename(dn, newdn, newparent, true) ;
}
```

---

structor using the LDAP URL. Exhibit 67 shows the other possibility, where you indicate the single components of the LDAP URL. Note that the LDAP URL can be used only to make a search and not to update the database. Thus, LDAP URLs cannot be used for adding, deleting, or modifying entries.

The LDAPUrl class has a number of other methods to extract the single components and to achieve encoding and decoding. Encoding is necessary if you have to use special characters not allowed in URLs. If you need more information about the exact URL format, have a look at Chapter 4 and RFC 1738, "Uniform Resource Locators (URLs)." For more details about LDAP URLs, such as the exact syntax of the methods, refer to the documentation delivered with the Java software development kit you are using.

JNDI — Java Naming and Directory Interfaces

The Java naming and directory interfaces (JNDI) are an alternative to the Java SDK to access a directory using Java. JNDI has been developed by Sun Microsystems in collaboration with Netscape, Novell, IBM, and others. JNDI is a generic interface to access different naming services. A naming service maps names to objects. This allows the user to access

---

Exhibit 66. Java, LDAPUrl Constructor Using URL

```
try {
  LDAPUrl url = new LDAPUrl (
  "ldap://www.LdapAbc.org:389/ou=IT, o=Ldap
Abc.org?cn,mail?(sn=S*)") ;
} catch (java.net.MalformedURLException) {
  System.out.println (e.toString());
}

try {
  LDAPSearchResults res = ld.search(url) ;
} catch (LDAPException e) {
  System.out.println (e.toString());
}
```

Exhibit 67. Java, LDAPUrl Constructor Using Single URL Components

```
String[] attrs = { "cn", "mail" } ;
String host = "www.LdapAbc.org" ;
int port = 389 ;
String baseDN = "ou=IT, o=LdapAbc.org" ;
String scope = LDAPConnection.SCOPE_SUB ;
String filter = "(sn=S*)" ;

// Now we construct the LDAPUrl object:
try {
  LDAPUrl = new LDAPUrl (host, port, baseDN, attrs, scope,
filter) ;
  } catch (java.net.MalformedURLException) {
    System.out.println (e.toString());
}
```

---

an object by its user-friendly name instead of using the name provided by the computer.

The domain name system (DNS), widely used on the Internet, is an example of a naming service. Human beings find it is far easier to remember "www.apache.org" than the IP name "63.251.56.142." A further example is the file system. The computer uses numbers to identify files (called "inodes" in UNIX), but humans prefer recognizable names. A naming system lets human users access a file by its name instead of its inode. In this sense, directory services is a special case of a naming service. Directory services associates a name (the distinguished name) with an object (the entry), thus making it available to the user.

JNDI uses one interface to access a number of different naming and directory services. It does this via so-called service providers. Exhibit 68 shows the architecture of JNDI. The whole API consists of two interfaces: (1) the JNDI interface that gives the name to the API, and (2) the SPI (service provider interface). The application developer

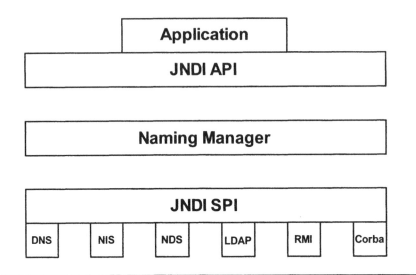

Exhibit 68. JNDI Architecture

uses the JNDI interface, and the service providers use the SPI. The naming manager bridges the two interfaces.

The API plus some of the service providers in the schema are included from the Java 2 SDK version 1.3. The following service providers are contained in this Java SDK:

- LDAP
- Common object request broker architecture (CORBA) common object services (COS) name service
- Java remote method invocation (RMI) registry

You can obtain other service providers from a software vendor, for example, NDS from Novell. If you are planning to write a service provider, you can download the instructions from the JNDI site at http://java.sun.com.

We will have a little closer look at JNDI, but first let us see a working example in Exhibit 69. First, we create a hash table to hold the parameters we will need later on. The hash table holds information such as the name of the service provider, the LDAP URL of the directory, etc. We fill the hash table using the "put" method.

The next object to be created is the context. Recall that a service associates names with objects. The association between a name and an object is called "binding." A set of bindings is called a "context." The context is represented using the javax.naming.Context interface. The context is then used to get further information from the directory. In our example, we got the attributes from the entry object.

Exhibit 69. First JNDI Program

```
import java.util.Hashtable;

import javax.naming.Context;
import javax.naming.directory.InitialDirContext;
import javax.naming.directory.DirContext;
import javax.naming.directory.Attributes;
import javax.naming.NamingException;

class PrintEntry {
  public static void main(String[] args) {
    Hashtable hashT = new Hashtable(11);
    // configure the service provider
    hashT.put(Context.INITIAL_CONTEXT_FACTORY,
            "com.sun.jndi.ldap.LdapCtxFactory");
    // the Ldap Server + BaseDn in Url format
    hashT.put(Context.PROVIDER_URL,
            "ldap://localhost:389/o=LdapAbc.org");

    try {
      // Create the directory context:
      DirContext DirContext = new InitialDirContext(hashT);
      // Get the attributes:
      char DN = "uid=TParker, ou=IT, o=LdapAbc.org" ;
      Attributes attrs = DirContext.getAttributes(DN);
    for (NamingEnumeration ae = attrs.getAll(); ae.hasMore();)
{
      Attribute attr = (Attribute)ae.next();
      System.out.println("attribute: " + attr.getID());
      // Print each value
      for (NamingEnumeration e = attr.getAll();
        e.hasMore();
        System.out.println("value: " + e.next())
      ) ;
    }
  DirContext.close();
} catch (NamingException e) {
  System.err.println("Error: "  + e);
}
```

Once you have the context object, you can get an attribute set using the getAttributes method with the distinguished name as a parameter. From the parameter set, you can choose the single parameters with the "get" method.

The JNDI API offers much more functionality, including the ability to register callbacks to an event-processing system. This allows you to program the software to take some action if a determined event succeeds. For example, you could launch a procedure if the data in a certain entry changes.

For more information about JNDI, see the documentation shipped with the software. Software, reference manuals, tutorials, and examples are available from http://java.sun.com.

Enterprise JavaBeans

Enterprise JavaBeans — a set of rules to write Java programs — is an interesting and useful technology. Nevertheless, this topic is so large that it is covered in several books, articles, and tutorials available online from Sun Microsystems at their Web site — http://java.sun.com.

So what, exactly, are JavaBeans? They are simply normal Java objects that obey certain rules. These objects behave like other Java objects. There is really nothing special about them. Beans allow other programs to understand the methods and variables they offer. The capacity to understand the structure of an object is called "reflection." Reflection allows Java programs to inspect Java objects at run time. From the application programmer's view, this means that she can use a JavaBean without knowing about its inner structure. At run time, the application can look to see which methods the Bean offers to access the single components. So the application programmer does not even rely on the documentation delivered with the Bean because she can get all information from the class itself.

A JavaBean is nothing but a layer of standardization. This allows you to use graphical tools to work with JavaBeans and to put together more JavaBeans to build an application without writing a single line of code. The standardization layer is called a "design pattern." We will not delve into the details of JavaBeans, but let us see an example of a design pattern for properties.

To inspect the properties of a JavaBean, you need the following methods:

- Method for getting the current value of the property
- Method for setting the value of the property

Let us see an example. If you wanted to write a bean for a connection to the LDAP server, you would need the following methods to get and set the distinguished name:

```
public char getDN() ;
public void setDN();
```

For a more complex task, you would need the following methods to get and set an entire entry:

```
public LDAPEntry getUser(UsrId) ;
public void setUser(UsrId) ;
```

Using this syntax, a program can automatically inspect the bean and act accordingly.

A further advantage of JavaBeans is their ability to serialize objects. This means that you can save entire objects, including all of their actual variables. Later on, you can restore this object, allowing it to spring to life and continue behaving as if no interruption had ever occurred.

As noted previously, Beans allow you to put together a number of components (i.e., Beans) with graphical tools. Sun delivers the Bean development kit available for free from the site where you get all Java software (http://java.sun.com). There are entire Java development environments that support JavaBeans, including Sun's Forte for Java, Borland/Oracle's JBuilder, IBM's Visual Age, and many others.

Conclusion

Java offers a rich choice of APIs and entire development environments to help you in programming applications that access directories. In this section, we have seen the "standard" Java SDK, the JNDI API, and JavaBeans. Unfortunately, the scope of this book prevents us from discussing these subjects at greater length. Our objective is to show you what you can achieve with this technology and direct you to Web sites where you can obtain the software, documentation, tutorials, and other useful information.

This section is far from being complete because it has not yet mentioned other possibilities that could be appealing for applications that deal with directories. Server-side Java or application servers using Java server pages and many other technologies are available to power application development. If you want to keep up with the latest news, you should consult the following sites:

- *http://java.sun.com*: A source for all Java APIs and software development kits. The site not only contains the software, but also excellent reference manuals, tutorials, and examples. Nearly all of the software and the documentation is available for free.
- *http://www.apache.org*: Contains a lot of application servers written in Java plus a Java module that integrates the Java application server with the Apache Web server
- *http://www.openldap.org*: The open-source implementation of the LDAP (v3) standard LDAP server. Many of the people involved in the OpenLDAP project are also authors of the standards proposed in the RFCs.
- *http://www.netscape.com*: The commercial counterpart of the OpenLDAP project
- *http://developer.novell.com/ndk/*: A source for the alternative Java development kit. Like the Netscape browser, this is also available for free.
- *http://www.ietf.org*: The site that contains the standards

These are not the only sites offering good documentation about Java and LDAP-related software, but they are good starting points.

What Is Missing

We are at the end of the longest chapter in the book, and we still have not covered all of the relevant technologies. Most programming languages offer LDAP APIs, but there are too many to cover within the scope of this book. We can only briefly mention a few. If you want more information, check the Web sites provided later in this chapter.

Active Directory and ADSI

Active Directory is Microsoft's version of LDAP. First made available in Windows 2000, it runs only on Microsoft platforms, which is why we did not dedicate more space to it. This is not meant to imply that the Microsoft solution is not important. Indeed, Active Directory is more than just a directory server. It replaces Windows NT domains, similar to Novell's NDS. Active Directory organizes the domains in trees, which implies a hierarchical structure. You can inherit security configuration down the tree, greatly simplifying the organization and administration of the domain. Active Directory also allows replication and access control lists, and it holds a database of the installed software. Clearly, Microsoft has made LDAP an important part of the operating system.

ADSI (active directory service interface) is an API that one could consider as Microsoft's version of JNDI from Sun Microsystems. ADSI, based on Microsoft's COM (component object model) model, is a Microsoft standard defining how applications should talk to each other. COM can be implemented using a wide range of programming languages, including the well-known Visual Basic. But even Perl knows about COM, and portings of Perl libraries for UNIX are also available.

If you need more information about ADSI and Active Directory, check out Microsoft's Web site, where you will find good documentation and working examples.

Other Languages

There are yet other languages we have not discussed. In this final section, we mention a few other languages that can serve as an LDAP API. The list is not complete. Note that by the time you read this book, there may well be new APIs or even new programming languages. In addition, because Internet URLs frequently change, the URLs presented here may no longer be valid.

- *Ruby*: The object-oriented scripting language Ruby was created by Yukihiro Matsumoto. Ruby is available for UNIX, DOS, Windows

95/98/NT, Mac, BeOS, OS/2, and other platforms. The language itself can be downloaded from http://www.ruby-lang.org/en/index.html. The Ruby LDAP library is available at http://kt-www.jaist.ac.jp/~ttate/ruby/ruby-ldap.html.

- *TCL*: The tool command language (TCL), with its graphical extension TK, has been available for a long time. The language was developed by John Ousterhout at the University of California, Berkeley. The latest iteration is version 8.4, and you can get it from http://www.tcl.tk. The LDAP library is available at http://www.sensus.org/.

- *Eiffel*: The Eiffel language also allows you to access LDAP. The software can be obtained from the Free Software Foundation. The LDAP extension is available at http://bleu.west.spy.net/~dustin/eiffel/docs/ldap.html.

- *Python*: The object-oriented Python is available for use on a wide variety of platforms from UNIX to Win32 to Macintosh. Developed by Guido van Rossum, it is available now as version 2.2.1 at http://www.python.org. The LDAP-client API for Python can be found at http://python-ldap.sourceforge.net/.

If you prefer to use a certain language and need the LDAP API for it, have a look at the home page of the language. If it does not have a home page, try using a search engine on the Internet.

Chapter 7

LDAP Directory-Server Administration

Open-Source Software

There is no thing such as the "right choice" for LDAP server software. Many vendors offer LDAP server applications. Which one to choose? The choice depends on:

- The environment you are working in: The hardware platform and operating system (or systems) you are using may limit your options in choosing an implementation.
- The experience and the professional background of the technicians setting up directory services: Whether you use in-house talent or hire a consultant, the person in charge of the implementation will have a bias based on past experience. A consultant with experience using a particular implementation will work more efficiently when using a familiar product. The same thing holds for the operating systems. An administrator who is familiar with UNIX may not be able to work in NT.

This chapter is not intended to recommend a particular product, nor do I think a textbook is the right place to advocate for one solution over another. Moreover, computer technology changes so quickly that, by the time you read this book, the product landscape may be very different. If you need guidance in choosing the right software, you should look for an LDAP mailing list and send an e-mail to the group. In this section we will briefly review the reasons why you should at least consider using an open-source solution.

The open-source solution available at the time of this writing is OpenLDAP, available from the Web site www.openldap.org. OpenLDAP is a mature and very flexible product. In its current version, it is stable and can thus be used in a production environment. OpenLDAP has been developed and is maintained by a group of people that includes the authors of the LDAP standard. OpenLDAP is considered to be a reference implementation of LDAP, and it implements the LDAP (v3) protocol. It allows replication, but not multimaster replication. OpenLDAP is designed in a very flexible way that allows you to compile and configure it to meet your exact needs. The access to the actual data repository is done by a back-end. In the compilation phase, you can choose from a number of back-ends, including lightweight database management (LDBM), Berkeley database (BDB), relational database management system (RDBMS), Perl, or Shell repository. OpenLDAP also allows you to let the LDAP server act as a proxy. The proxy feature, called "meta back-end," offers a powerful rewrite engine configurable via regular expressions. OpenLDAP supports all security features necessary for sensitive data and can be used together with open-source software implementing security layers, such as OpenSSL (Secure Sockets Layer protocol), Cyrus SASL (simple authentication and security layer), or Kerberos.

Another good reason to choose open-source software is the possibility of code inspection. If you have the experience and the need to ensure that the software does not include unwanted "side effects," an open-source product is the correct choice. Governmental agencies are increasingly requiring the use of open-source software. Implementations that are subject to software validation could also require the use of a software product that can be verified by inspecting its code.

OpenLDAP is well documented and offers, via a large number of mailing lists, the opportunity to get help quickly and even for free. There are many consultants familiar with OpenLDAP, so you also have the option of commercial support.

Finally, LDAP is free, and you do not have to pay license fees. In a project with a small budget, this can be an important issue. Also, if you intend to distribute your software with an LDAP repository, it is a big advantage to use an open-source implementation. The open-source solution also frees you from administrative issues regarding licenses.

That is enough advocacy for open-source software. Now we will address the administration issues of LDAP.

Getting the Directory Server Up and Running

The first thing you have to do is install the directory-server software. A description of the installation instructions for all of the major software distributions would be beyond the scope of this book. So we will first review some general instructions that are valid for all installations. Then we will see two example installations. The first example is the open-source directory-server OpenLDAP. The second is a commercial product, the Sun One iPlanet directory server, formerly known as Netscape Directory Server and available from Netscape. In August 2002, iPlanet became a division of Sun Microsystems, and the iPlanet server became integrated in the Sun Open Net Environment (Sun One). These two servers were selected because both are available on Win32 and UNIX platforms. We will see both a commercial and an open-source solution available on both platforms. Now let us begin with the instructions for a general installation.

Software Installation

It normally takes some time between the moment you unpack the server software until the magic moment when the directory server is ready to be released for public access. By the time you unpack your software, the phase of analysis, planning, and design should be concluded. You should also be familiar with the details of the proposed configuration, including knowledge about the distribution of the directory among other directory servers, replication, and connections to other data sources (metadirectory, applications, synchronization, etc.).

The first recommended step is to verify that your system meets the requirements of the software you want to install. This applies not just to simple space requirements, but also to the available memory, swap space, and base system configuration. Read the delivered documentation carefully to find out whether there are any operating-system parameters that need to be modified for better performance. This is often necessary for UNIX operating systems, where you can change a number of system parameters to fit the special purpose of your UNIX server. However, under normal circumstances with a normal system load, this should not necessary.

Next, you have to gather information about your network connection. This includes verifying that your host is accessible to possible clients. Once you are sure that your clients can reach the computer where your directory server is running, make it clear that they can also access its service. Perhaps you will be providing a directory service for customers accessing the directory from the Internet, but your directory server is in your intranet behind a firewall. In this case, you should discuss with your networking team the location of the directory server. It may be that your customers will never even know that they are using your directory server, because they will use applications running on your Internet Web server, and only that application has to access the directory server. Once the location of the directory server is determined, verify that the service is visible to your client. It is quite probable that your directory server will run behind a firewall. In this case, you must be sure that the firewall will allow the LDAP protocol to pass through and that it will accept connections to the port that the directory server actually is running on.

Furthermore, you need information about the host name and the IP number of the machine your directory server is running on. It may be that you have more than one network card. If so, you must understand the requirements of your installation. It may be that the directory server has to accept requests coming from one subnet only. Check the documentation of your directory-server software to see if it is possible to listen on more than one IP address. It is possible that you will need additional IP numbers. If you have a directory server with one administration server and one directory server, you might decide to run each server on a network card of its own. With this setup, you can shut down the administration server and boot it only when you really need it. This boosts performance while increasing system security.

The last step is to clear up some base configuration questions. Some products ship with a separate administration server. If you do not have two different network cards, you could install the administration server on a separate port. To set this up, you need the name and password of the administrator of the server. Some implementations also configure an operator of the directory server. The second piece of information you need is the root of the directory information tree (DIT). Now you can begin the installation procedure.

Commercial products will include an installation guide, release notices, a "readme-first" document, a "readme before readme-first document," and so on. It is good practice, at a minimum, to look at these documents before beginning the installation. The exact installation procedure should be documented in the installation guide. If a consultant is installing the directory server for you, it is a good idea to try to understand what the consultant is doing and why. After the consultant leaves, the person administering the system will likely encounter situations where the directory server is in need of first aid or where a change in the configuration is required.

OpenLDAP Installation

OpenLDAP is available on both UNIX and Win32 platforms. It is an open-source implementation, and the most recent version, with LDAP (v3) functionality, is available at the OpenLDAP Web site, http://www.openldap.org. The site also holds a lot of documentation, including installation instructions, the administration guide, FAQs, and an archive of the OpenLDAP newsgroups. The project leader, Kurt Zeilenga, has written many of the LDAP RFCs.

At the time of this writing, the OpenLDAP version 2.1.x is the latest one available for download from the Web site, although by the time you read this book, a new version may be available. The first step is to download the software, which is available in the form of a compressed archive file. Once downloaded, you should create a new directory that will be your workbench for the next steps. Move the compressed archive into this directory and decompress the file. The commands for decompressing the file are different, depending on the operating system. Using one of the UNIX operating systems, the command would be:

```
gzip -cd openldap-2.1.8.tgz | tar xvf -
```

On a Win32 platform, you would use Winzip or a similar utility. Double-click on the file's icon and Winzip will tell you that the compressed file is an archive. It proposes to uncompress this file to a temporary file and open the archive. Click "okay" and extract the files as usual.

In both cases, you will have a directory containing the entire source code and documentation, including the installation instructions. Carefully review the "readme" file. It contains the system requirements needed to successfully install the software on your system. The following software packages are needed:

- *Standard ANSI-compliant C compiler:* If you do not have one, the best choice would be the open-source GCC compiler available from the Free Software Foundation (FSF) at http://www.fsf.org.
- *C development system:* This is available on most UNIX systems. The FSF on the C development system holds all the components on its site (http://www.fsf.org). On other operating systems, you will get the components together with the compiler.
- *Posix regex libraries:* These libraries are normally included in every standard UNIX distribution. They facilitate the implementation of regular expressions in the C language.
- *Suitable back-end to hold the repository:* The back end is the data store that finally holds the data that you put into the directory. See Chapter 1 for additional details about the underlying concepts. If you use BDB, you need to install the open-source Berkeley DB distribution available from Sleepycat (http://www.sleepycat.com). If you use LDBM, you can choose between the Berkeley DB distribution and GDBM (Gnu database manager), available from FSF. There are other back-end options available, ranging from a shell back end to a RDBMS (e.g., Oracle). See the installation instructions contained in the distribution.
- *Replication:* If you install ldap servers replicating between each other, the master series will need threading support. You will need the necessary thread libraries to be installed.

■ *TLS*: If you wish to use TLS (Transport Layer Security protocol), you need the TLS layer, e.g., the OpenSSL distribution available from http://www.openssl.org. (Also see the section "Securing Your LDAP Server" later in this chapter.)

■ *SASL*: If you would like to use strong authentication via SASL, you need the SASL libraries, e.g., the SASL distribution from the Cyrus project. You can get the software and find out more about Cyrus SASL at the Web site http://asg.web.cmu.edu/sasl/. (Also see the section "Securing Your LDAP Server" later in this chapter.)

Once you have installed the required software, you can begin compiling your LDAP application.

UNIX

In the UNIX operating system, you simply launch "configure." The configure tool tries to find out details about your operating system and about the software packages available on your machine. However, the configure tool does not always find the details it needs to know. In such cases, you may have to manually provide the necessary information. It may also be that you wish to configure the LDAP software in a different way. "Configure" can be launched using a number of parameters that are documented in the "install" file. You can find the parameters by launching "configure" with the -h switch. Exhibit 1 shows you a dump of all switches available with the "configure-h" command (available electronically as configure-h.doc).

Once the system is configured, launch "make depend" to resolve dependencies followed by "make." If the program compiles successfully, you can test the OpenLDAP program by typing "make test." If all tests are executed successfully, a process that can take several minutes, install the server with "make install." This will install the server software, the utilities, the command-line tools, the manual pages, and the configuration files. If you have problems in the compilation phase, go to the OpenLDAP home page at http://www.openldap.org.

WIN32

The software requirements are the same as before. There are a number of C/C++ compilers available for Win32 platforms. However, it is a good idea to use Microsoft's Visual C++ when installing OpenLDAP on a Win32 platform. Most of the hints regarding the OpenLDAP software installation on Win32 refer to this environment. From a technical point of view, however, other development tools should work as well.

Exhibit 1. Example of OpenLDAP Configure Script:

```
#!/bin/sh
#
#Name:   ConfigureLdap.sh
#Author: Reinhard e. Voglmaier
#Version: 1.0
#Date:   15.08.2003
#Description: Script to configure the compilation of the
#            OpenLDAP software

CC=gcc                                              \
CPPFLAGS="-I/usr/local/BerkeleyDB.4.1/include"      \
LDFLAGS="=I/usr/local/BerkeleyDB.4.1/lib"           \
./configure    --prefix=/usr/local                  \
               --enable-bdb
```

Note:
It is a good idea to fix the configuration of the compilation phase in a script. This documents the installation procedure for later use.
The line CC=gcc tells the configure utility to use the GNU compiler, the CPPFLAGS variable describes where to search additional include files not located at the standard location, the LDFLAGS environment variable where to find additional libraries not located in the standard location. Here we use the Sleepycat distribution for the Berkeley DB.

We strongly advise that you take a look at the Web site of FiveSight Technologies Inc. They have successfully installed OpenLDAP on the Win32 platform. The URL is http://www.fivesight.com/downloads/openldap.asp. From this site, you can also get a ready-to-work version of OpenLDAP for the Win32 platform.

Sun One Installation

The installation of Sun One is much more user friendly because it limits the user activity to answering a number of questions during the program setup. The answers to these questions anticipate some of the configuration you have to do later.

The first step is to get the software, which can be ordered from Sun Microsystems. If you are in a hurry, you can download an evaluation copy via the Internet from http://wwws.sun.com/software/download. If you download the software from the Internet, you should first create a working directory and download the file into this directory. Note that this is only a temporary directory and not the location where the software will be installed.

The method used to decompress the file depends on the operating system you are working in. In UNIX, you have to use the command:

```
gzip -cd directory-5[1].1sp1-us.sparc-sun-solaris2.8.tar.gz | tar
xvf -
```

In Win32/Win2000, you can use the Winzip program or a similar utility. It is enough to double click the file you downloaded. Winzip, or whatever decompression software you are using, will ask you to name a location where it should store the files contained in the compressed archive. Again, it is convenient to use a temporary directory holding only the installation files. Note that this is not the final location where the software will installed.

After decompressing the software, you will execute the installation utility "setup" for UNIX operating systems and "setup.exe" in the Microsoft environment. If you have the official software distribution on CD, you simply insert the CD and launch the installation tool from the CD. The installation procedure is nearly identical in UNIX and in the MS world, so we will only show it once.

Once you have started the installation procedure, you will see a welcome message as shown in Exhibit 2. Click on "View Readme" if you need further information about the product, or click on "Next" to proceed with the software installation.

The next screen shows you the license agreement, which you should read carefully. If you agree, answer with "yes." In the UNIX version you have to type in "yes" by hand; in the Win32 version you only click on the button "yes." Exhibit 3 shows the screen shot.

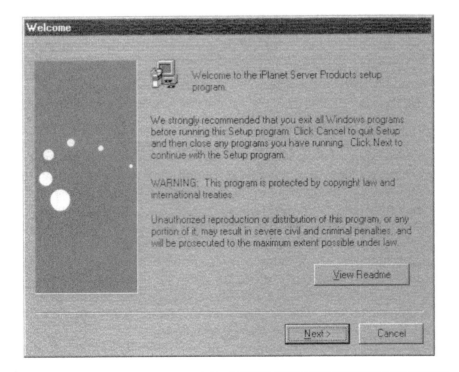

Exhibit 2. Welcome Mask to SUN ONE

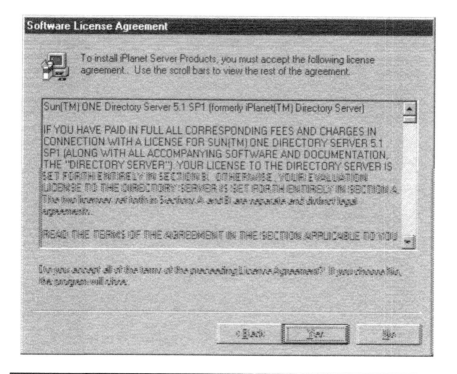

Exhibit 3. License Agreement for SUN ONE Directory Server

You then have to choose what you want to install. Because this is the first installation, choose iPlanet servers and install everything you are interested in. Exhibit 4 shows the screen shot. You could also install just the administration utility, called "iPlanet console," which provides only the administration utilities for running a remote installation. You do this if you install the directory on another machine.

Once you choose the installation type, you should decide the location where the software will be installed. The standard installation procedure suggests a location, but you are free to change it to suit your requirements. Exhibit 5 shows the screen shot.

Next, you have to choose which software you wish to install. Exhibit 6 shows the screen shot. The first three components are needed for the directory server itself. If you have more than one instance of the directory server on the same machine you could get by without one of them. Carefully read the installation instructions delivered with the software to understand which software components you will need. There are two more interesting software components to choose from. One of these is Perl, the most comfortable language for pattern matching and fast development you will ever meet. The second is the Perl library for LDAP. Both of them are maintained and provided by Sun, so you can consider this software to be stable.

If you already have installed an instance of the Sun One directory server, you might wish to administer both servers from the same

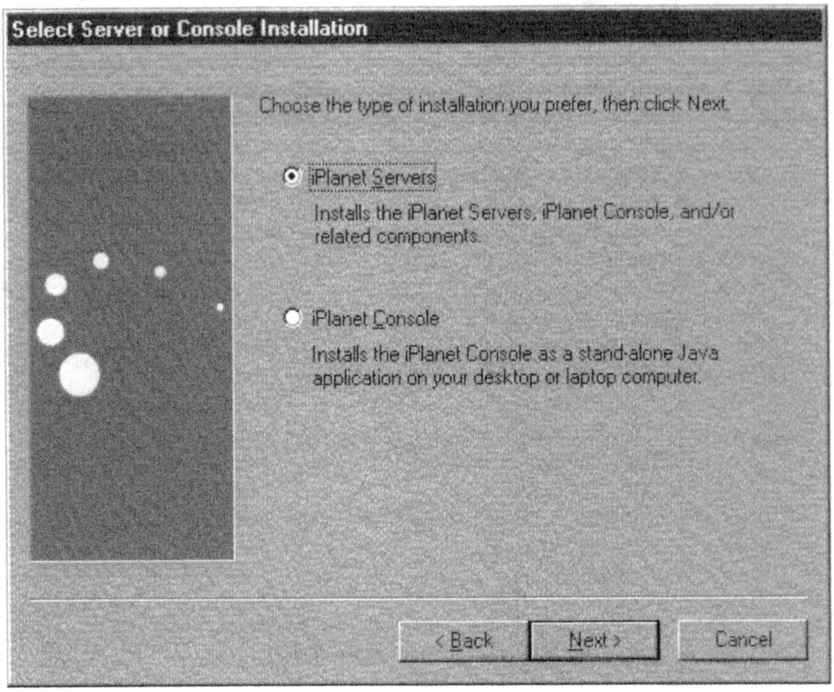

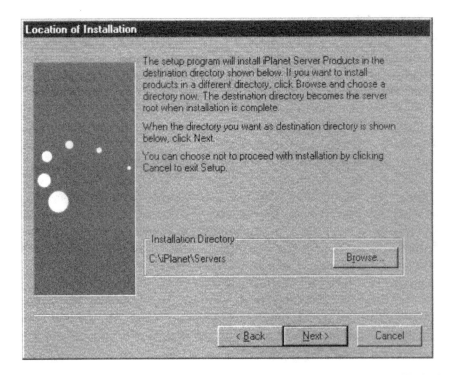

Exhibit 4. Choosing the Type of Installation

Exhibit 5. Choosing the Software Location

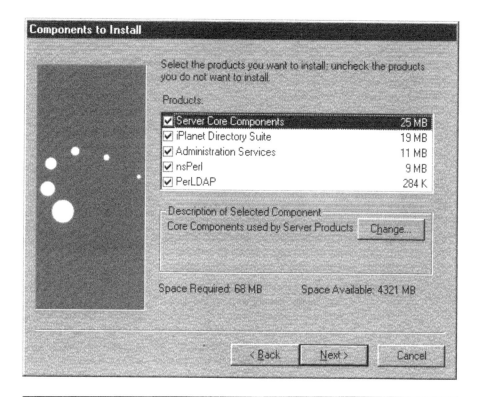

Exhibit 6. Choosing the Software to Install

console. The next mask, shown in Exhibit 7, asks whether you want to make a fresh installation or use a previously installed directory server that you could then use for administration purposes. If you already have a configuration server, fill out the answers to the questions about the port the server is listening to and the distinguished name (DN) of the administrator of this service.

The next step is to give some information about the configuration of the directory server, including the server name, the port at which the server is listening, and the suffix of the directory server. The suffix of the directory server is also known as the root of the directory tree. Exhibit 8 shows what we put in for the example application used throughout this book.

At this point, you should configure the userID and password of the person responsible for the directory, called the "directory manager." You have to insert the password twice to confirm that you have typed it in correctly. Exhibit 9 shows a screenshot of this dialog.

Next, we configure the administration server. Like all servers from the Sun/Netscape alliance, such as the proxy server and the Web server, the directory server also has an administration server, reachable via the Internet, that allows the administration. In this step, we configure the port on which this administration server can be reached. Exhibit 10 shows the form that allows you to choose the port. The choice

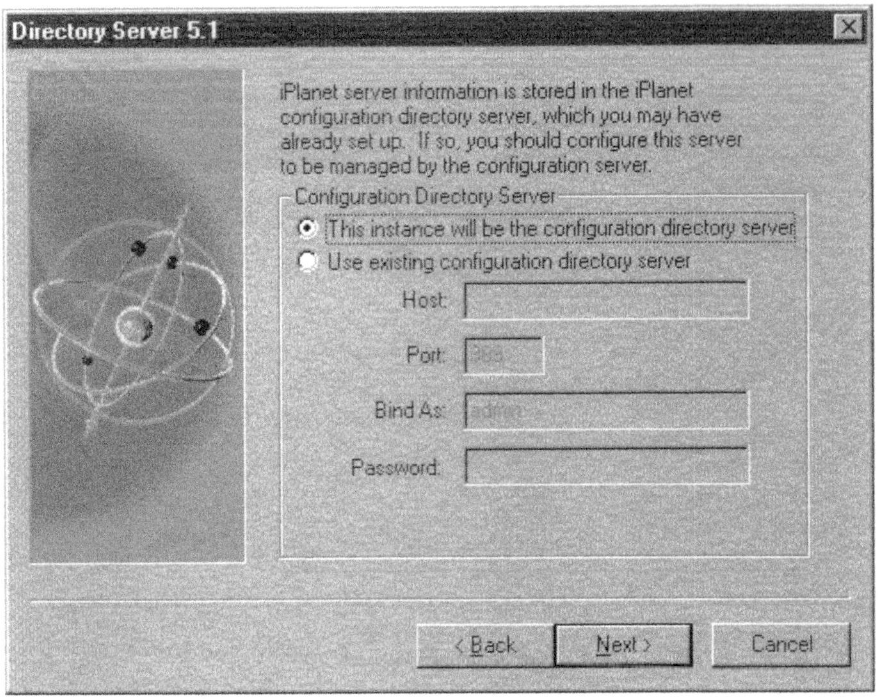

Exhibit 7. Choosing the Configuration Server

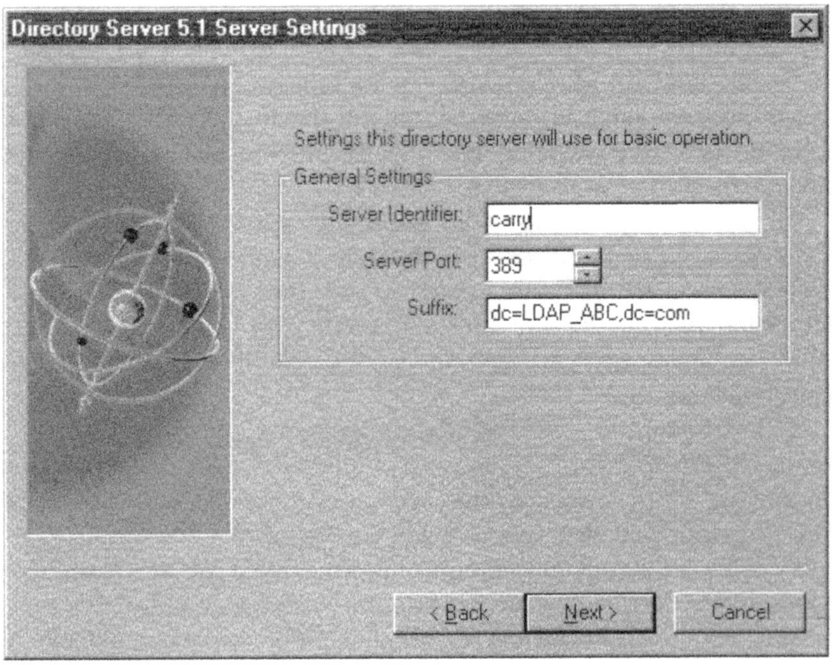

Exhibit 8. Directory Server Settings

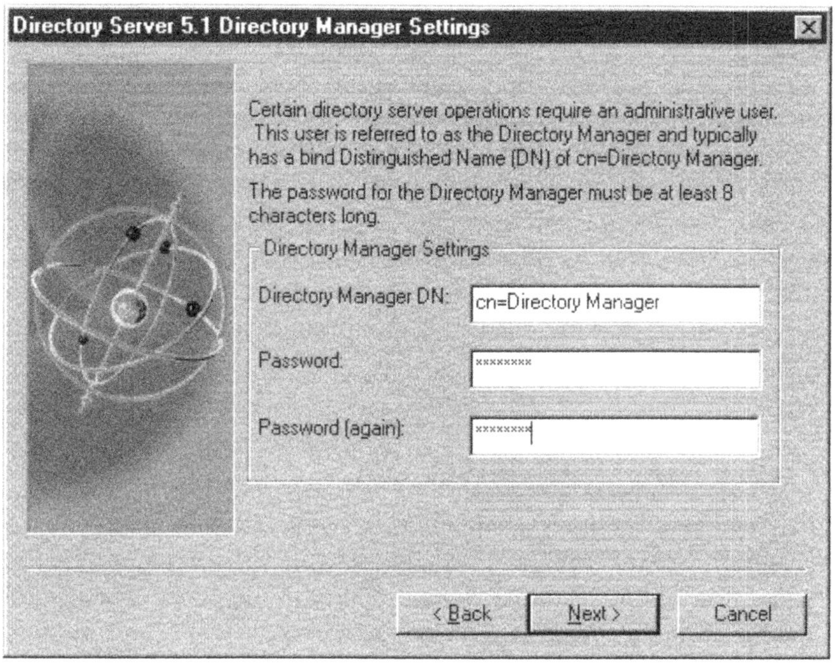

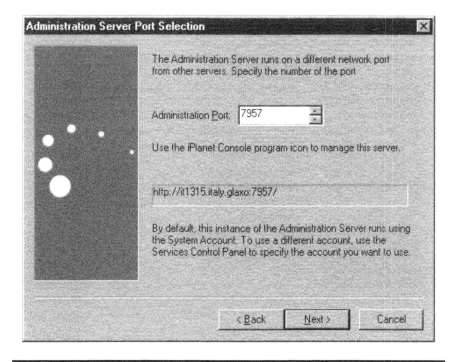

Exhibit 9. UserId and Password of the "Directory Manager"

Exhibit 10. Choose the Administration Port

you make here is not definitive because another port number can be chosen later by changing one of the configuration files.

The last step is to confirm that all of the software components have been installed. The last mask shows the list of software that is ready to be installed. You can scroll through the list, and when you are satisfied you simply click on the install button to start the installation. After that, the administration server and the directory server will be started with the data to put in during the installation procedure. The configuration has already been done during the installation procedure. Exhibit 11 shows you the last form to confirm before installation takes place.

Securing Your LDAP Server

The previously described installations provide a server speaking with its clients "in clear." This is acceptable if your server is handling data intended for public use. However, you will need to add security protection if the server is handling sensitive data that is not intended to become available for everyone who connects to the server. As mentioned previously, the LDAP protocol knows two ways of securing the conversation between the partners. The term "partners" is used

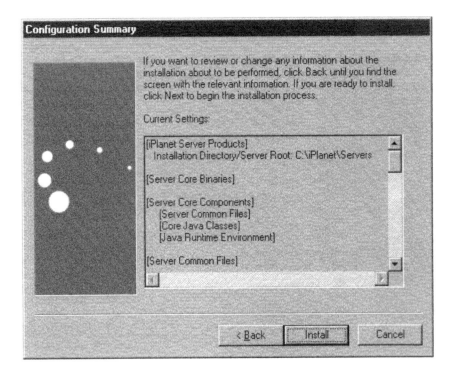

Exhibit 11. Last Confirmation before Software Installation

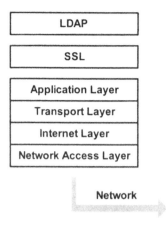

Exhibit 12. SSL/TLS Layer between the TCP/IP Stack and the Application Layer

because you need to secure not only the conversation between client and server, but also between server and server, for example, in the case of replication or chaining.

In this section, we will see two brief examples featuring the OpenLDAP and the Sun One servers. Exhibit 12 shows the underlying architecture for a security solution. SSL or TLS is a layer placed on top of the TCP/IP protocol to provide privacy and security that the underlying layers do not offer.

For both OpenLDAP and Sun One servers, you need the SSL/TLS libraries to get LDAP working above the secure layer. Sun delivers all you need. With the open-source software product OpenLDAP, you have to provide your own security layer. One possible solution would be to use OpenSSL. As the name suggests OpenSSL is also an open-source project. You can get the source code from http://www.openssl.org.

Another security option is to use SASL to secure your server. LDAP (v3)-compliant servers *should* implement SASL as an extended operation. SASL allows the partners to negotiate the security mechanism used for communication. During the communication, both partners can change their agreements about the security level used, either raising or lowering it. The LDAP server should also provide the client with information about the SASL security mechanisms that it supports.

One of the mechanisms that SASL supports is Kerberos. The Kerberos architecture is a very robust framework that offers to the communicating partners a third authority (security server) that grants tickets to the partners, allowing them to authenticate themselves. In this way, both partners are sure that the other partner really is who it claims to be. To use the Kerberos framework, you have to install Kerberos at your site. You can get the Kerberos software and documentation from http://web.mit.edu/kerberos/www. However, there are restrictions about the use of the software, depending on your physical location and the version of Kerberos you wish to use. At the time of this writing, the most recent version (Kerberos version 5) is available from MIT for residents in Canada or the United States only. The previous version (Kerberos version 4) is available from a number of universities. If you reside outside Canada or the United States and need to run Kerberos version 5 on your network, you can get a distribution from one of the following two locations:

http://www.crypto-publish.org/mit-kerberos5/index.html
http://www.pdc.kth.se/heimdal

Both of these distributions declare that they are not limited by the export conditions of the United States. Both sites also provide you with the legal background I would recommend that you read carefully.

Setting Up Security in Sun One

This section is not intended to be a substitute for the documentation shipped with the Sun One directory server, so we will not get into the specific details of setting up the security mechanisms for the Sun One server. However, this section will give you an idea of how security has to be configured in a commercial software product.

At the time of this writing, the Sun One server is available as version 5.1, which supports only SSL and certificates. SASL can be used if you install a plug-in. Kerberos functionality is not yet available. Version 5.2, which is expected to accommodate both SASL and Kerberos, may be available by the time you read this book. Have a look at the site of Sun Microsystems if you are interested.

Setting up the Sun One directory server to use SSL is very easy because everything you need is shipped with the software. You simply go into the configuration menu of the administration interface and click on the "enable SSL" radio button. You then have to restart the LDAP server. Check the port number for the encrypted directory server. The typical port number for the encrypted LDAP server is 636, but you can change it to whatever you want. However, it is a good idea to keep the standard to avoid the possibility of confusing the clients connecting to the server.

You may also wish to use a certificate on the server to prove to your clients that you really are who you claim to be. The Sun One software has a "certificate wizard" that enables you to make a request to the certificate authority of your choice. The wizard creates an encrypted certificate request that you can either send to the certificate authority (CA) you chose or paste into the online form of a CA. Once you get your certificate, you reopen the administration tool and install the certificate into the server.

The whole process is described in detail in the administrator's guide, also available via the Web from Sun Microsystems. Other commercial software products have similar utilities to install and configure security layers. We used the Sun One software as an example because it was easy to download a trial version. The choice of the Sun One product is not, in any way, intended to imply that this software is better than any other commercial LDAP product.

Setting Up Security in OpenLDAP

Setting up security mechanisms in OpenLDAP is not easy because the OpenLDAP server software is not delivered with the necessary libraries. You have a choice of which libraries you want to use. Because the libraries have to be compiled into the OpenLDAP directory-server software, you will have to recompile your directory server if you later decide to use security mechanisms.

The first step in setting up security in OpenLDAP is to get the security software. You can get the various products at the following Web sites:

- *SSL/TLS*: http://www.openssl.org
- *SASL*: http://asg.web.cmu.edu/sasl
- *Kerberos*: http://web.mit.edu/kerberos/www

Each of these software packages ships with "readme" and "install" files, and you should actually read these files before beginning the installation. Like the OpenLDAP software package, all these open-source packages have the same installation steps.

- *Configure*: In this step, the configure procedure tries to detect the hardware and software architecture, the system, and the language libraries installed. It then writes the makefiles. You can give hints and constraints to the configure procedure, for example, the data-base libraries to use, which compiler to use (the compiler distributed by the vendor of the operating system or the GNU compiler) and other system-dependent information. Do not confuse the configure procedure with the compilation of the software configuration that you will do once the software is installed.
- *Make*: Some software requires a "make depend" first to resolve dependencies for the makefiles. Then you launch the make that actually compiles the software for your particular software and hardware configuration.
- *Test*: Most software also has a test suite allowing you to test what you have compiled. This can be done with a "make test," also called a "make check" in some test suites.

- *Install*: Once you have compiled and tested the software, you can install it with the command "make install."

If you wish to use SASL with the Kerberos authentication method, you have to compile and install Kerberos before you configure the SASL compilation process. Once you have compiled and installed the security software you intend to use, you have to recompile OpenLDAP. To do so, you have to launch the configure process for OpenLDAP. If you are lucky, the "configure" scripts will detect the libraries and include the files of the SSL/TLS or SASL. Or, you may have to use the specific switches:

```
./configure - with-ssl for SSL/TLS
./configure - with-sasl for SASL
```

An important note: All configure procedures allow you to decide the location for the installed software. The location of the libraries and "include" files are of particular importance. Every system has a standard location where the compiler and linker search the libraries and "include" files. If you use locations not included in the compiler search path, you have to declare this fact to the configure procedure to get the correct "make" files. You will declare two environment variables to achieve this:

1. CPPFLAGS, which tells the compiler where to search for additional "include" files
2. LDFLAGS, which tells the linker where to get additional libraries to link into the executable

For example, let us assume that we have installed the SSL libraries in:

```
/usr/local/openssl/lib
```

and the SSL "include" files in:

```
/usr/local/openssl/include
```

Therefore, you should launch the configure procedure and insert the following:

```
CPPFLAGS="-I/usr/local/openssl/include"         \
LDFLAGS="-L/usr/local/openssl/lib"              \
CC=gcc                                          \
./configure - with-ssl
```

After the configuration, you have to launch "make depend" and compile the OpenLDAP software with "make." After compilation, you should test out the software using "make test." If all tests finish successfully, you can install the software with "make install."

Note that if you have some libraries in a nonstandard location, it may be that the slapd daemon does not start and the tests will not run. Some of the libraries may be linked dynamically, but only at run time. If the libraries to be linked dynamically are not in standard locations, the link loader needs to know where to find these libraries. You should therefore set the environment variable LD_LIBRARY_PATH before starting the slapd daemon. Remember to set this variable also in your start scripts. Here is an example:

```
export
LD_LIBRARY_PATH=/usr/local/openssl/lib:/usr/local/BerkeleyDB4.2/lib
./slapd
```

This brief introduction did not cover all aspects of the OpenLDAP installation with SSL/TLS and SASL. If you need more information, there is an excellent description of how to install a security layer under OpenLDAP available at http://www.bayour.com/LDAPv3-HOWTO.html. This page, created and maintained by Turbo Fredriksson, describes where you can get the software, how to install it, and how to configure your OpenLDAP server to use the relevant security mechanisms.

LDAP Server Configuration

Introduction

Configuration of the LDAP server involves several steps. The steps you need to follow depend on the software you are using. Most of the commercial software packages let you configure the server during installation. Indeed, you need configure only a few parameters to start a directory server. Appendix E describes the configuration file of OpenLDAP in more detail.

Configure the Root DN

In this step, you control whether the server knows just about the root of the DIT or the root DN. The root DN is also often called a suffix. In the installation procedure for most commercial products, you have just been asked about the root DN of the DIT. However, it may be that your directory-server installation has more than one root entry. It depends on the product you are using.

Configure Administrator and Operator

There is a special user in most LDAP implementations who has administrative rights. She can modify the schema and add/modify/delete entries. This user is called the administrator. There also may be other special users who have particular roles in the life of a directory. These roles are, however, implementation dependent.

The DN and the password for these users have to be configured.

For the open-source product OpenLDAP, you configure the document root and the DN and password of the administrator in the configuration file "slapd.conf." In the case of the Sun One directory server, the installation procedure asks you to input this information and then writes it into its configuration files. You can also directly access the configuration files if you wish.

Configure the Directory Schema/Schemas

Now you have to check the schema of your directory. You need to understand which object classes and attribute types to include in the schema. Most servers ship with a number of schema files that allow you to select the object classes and attribute types that you need. During this step, it may become apparent that you need to extend the schema.

Configure the Indexes

If you know which attributes will need indexes and you only have to insert a few thousand records, you can configure the indexes before loading the data. If you have a greater data volume, you should first load the data and then configure and build the indexes.

Conclusion

These four steps are the very basic configuration you need in order to be ready to run the LDAP server. It still has no data in it, but we will discuss this in the next section. Here are a few concluding words about the configuration of an LDAP server. The configuration of the directory server is very implementation dependent. SUN ONE, for example, holds most of the configuration data in the directory self, hosted in a special subtree. It offers a well designed GUI to administer these data. The GUI allows you to configure security features, replication, partitioning, user and group administration, and log management — just to mention the most important. A description of all these features would exceed by far the scope of this book. Furthermore, the administration tools are very different from implementation to implementation; therefore you need to read the documentation shipped with your LDAP server. The SUN ONE implementation, for example, offers a number of books delivered in PDF format. They are worthwhile to study if you want to get the most benefit from this product. The books you should read in any case are the "Administrator's Guide" and the "Configuration, Command and File Reference."

OpenLDAP has a configuration file holding the configuration data. Those of you who wish to know what you can configure in addition to the basic concepts mentioned previously should have a look at Appendix E, where I more fully describe the configuration file of OpenLDAP.

Load the Data

Once you have finished the base configuration, you could start the directory server, but it still would not do anything useful for you. You have to load the data first. Before loading the data, you need to think about schema checking. Remember that every time an entry is added, the directory server checks to see whether the entry is compliant with the schema. This costs additional time. Whether or not you need schema checking when importing data depends on the quality of the data source. For automatically generated data or data exported from a directory server, the data should be consistent, and therefore you could switch schema checking off during the import and switch it on again after the data has been imported into the directory.

There are several ways of loading the data:

- *Offline*: Most directory-server implementations allow you to load the data offline. The directory server must not be running for this operation to work; it must be offline. See the directory-server documentation for more information. The previously mentioned OpenLDAP server, for example, offers a tool called "slapadd."
- *Using command-line tools*: Since most implementations of directory servers ship with command-line tools, you can use them to put the data into the directory. Unless you will be inputting only a few entries, you will use the command-line tools together with an LDIF (LDAP data interchange format) file. The LDIF format has the enormous advantage that it can be generated automatically. You can generate this file using your preferred language, converting it from a different data source (Oracle database, flat file, or similar sources). You could also use an LDIF file to migrate data from a different directory server.
- *Using import tools from the administration server*: Commercial directory servers frequently offer a graphical user interface (GUI), mostly based on a Web browser. These GUIs offer import-export tools. It depends on the server implementation whether the directory has to be offline or online for this operation.
- *Using custom tools*: In many cases, the directory server is part of a larger project. This means that you installed the directory server for a particular application. In this case, the application may have a custom tool to import the data into the directory.

Log Files

Every server writes logs that are used for various purposes. They document the availability of the server; they show the activity on the server (accesses per minute, the types of requests, the IP numbers of the originators of the requests, and the data volume requested); and they show the server's resource consumption for individual clients.

The problem with log files is that they grow. Normally, you can configure your server to specify the level of detail for the log file. Of course, increasing the level of detail in the server log results in a larger log file. System administrators are keen on destroying log files as frequently as possible. On the other hand, you may need statistics on the server usage to show to your users and sponsors. The most frequent solution to this problem is called "log file rotation." For this purpose you:

- Stop the server
- Copy the log file to a different location and compress it
- Restart the server

This strategy has several advantages:

- The log files are much smaller (log files have a compression factor of one to ten).
- You can keep online log files for a longer period of time.
- Server performance increases when the log files are smaller.
- It is easier to access a specific piece of the log. For example, suppose you have received a request for log information for a given day. There is a huge difference between e-mailing an entire 100-MB log file or a 300-kB portion of the file. Furthermore, it is much easier to extract information from a 300-kB file than a 100-MB file.

Log rotation typically is not performed by hand but by automatic procedures. Exhibit 13 shows a typical script for log-file rotation. The frequency of rotation depends on the number of accesses and how swiftly the log files grow. It is a good idea to (1) start with a weekly log-file rotation (unless you know in advance that your logs are growing very fast) and (2) control the log-file dimension daily to see if the logs are becoming too large. If the logs are bigger than 10 MB, you should rotate more frequently.

Once you have set up the log-file rotation utility, you should also agree upon a log policy. You need to specify:

- How much time the log files should be maintained online on hard disk
- What to do with the log files when the online time has expired
- How long to keep saved log files (files saved to tape, CD, etc.)

Exhibit 13. Log-File Rotation Script for UNIX

```
#!/usr/bin/sh
#
# @(#) $Revision: 1.2 $
#
# Author:            Reinhard E. Voglmaier
#
# Log Rotation for LDAP server
#

# Set the environment:
PATH=/sbin:/usr/sbin:/usr/bin
export PATH

LOGFILE=/var/adm/ldap.log

TODAY=`date +%Y-%m-%d`
echo "Log Rotating Facility starting: $TODAY"

mv $LOGFILE $LOGFILE.$TODAY

echo "Stopping LDAP Server . . ."
/etc/init.d/slapd stop

echo "Starting LDAP Server again . . ."
/etc/init.d/slapd start

echo "Compressing logfile . . ."

gzip $LOGFILE.$TODAY
```

These questions depend heavily on your local site policy and your user requirements. There may also be legal issues that dictate what you have to do with these log files. Indeed, the directory contains personal data, and many countries have very restrictive legal requirements protecting such data.

Starting and Stopping the Server

You do not have to start your directory server by hand every time the system is rebooted. Commercial products provide you with tools and instructions on how to start the directory server upon system boot and how to stop it when the system is being shut down. On Microsoft servers, you configure this under "services." In the UNIX world, you have to copy start/stop scripts into the location of the "init" scripts. The exact location of these scripts depends on the UNIX dialect you are using. The architecture, however, is always the same:

The following is a script that starts and stops the server, depending on the parameter it gets:

```
slapd start : to start the server
slapd stop: to stop the server
```

Exhibit 14 shows an example of a start/stop script for LDAP. Exhibit 15 shows the configuration file that controls whether the LDAP server is to be started or stopped during system startup or shutdown.

Exhibit 14. Example of a Start/Stop Script for UNIX

```
#!/usr/bin/sh
#
# @(#) $Revision: 1.2 $
#
# Author:             Reinhard E. Voglmaier
#
# Description: Start/Stop of LDAP server
#

# Set the environment:
PATH=/sbin:/usr/sbin:/usr/bin
export PATH

LdapServerDir = /opt/ldap
LdapConfigDir=$LdapServerDir/conf
LdapCurrentJobs=$LdapServerDir/jobs

rval=0
case $1 in
start_msg)
   echo "Start LDAP servers"
   ;;
stop_msg)
   echo "Stop LDAP servers"
   ;;
'start')
   if [ -f /etc/rc.config.d/ldap ]
   then
     Servers = `. /etc/rc.config.d/ldap`
   else
     echo "LDAP Configuration File not found"
     exit 1
   fi

   for i in $Servers
   do
     Cmd=$LdapServerDir/$i/slapd
     ConfigFile=$LdapConfigDir/$i/slapd.conf
     $Cmd -f $ConfigFile
     if [ $? -eq 0 ]
     then
       echo "Ldap Server $i started"
     else
       echo "Could not start Ldap Server $i"
     fi
   done
   ;;
'stop')
   if [ -f /etc/rc.config.d/ldap ]
   then
     Servers = `. /etc/rc.config.d/ldap`
```

-- continued

Exhibit 14. Example of a Start/Stop Script for UNIX (continued)

```
else
    echo "LDAP Configuration File not found"
    exit 1
  fi
for i in $Servers
  do
    if [ -f  $LdapCurrentJobs/$i/pid ]
    then
        PID=`cat $LdapCurrentJobs/$i/pid`
        kill -TERM ${PID}
        if [ retval -ne 0 ]
        then
          echo " Could not stop LDAP Server $i"
        else
          rm $LdapCurrentJobs/$i/pid
          echo "LDAP Server $i stopped"
        fi
    else
        echo "LDAP server $i not running"
    fi
  done
  ;;
esac

exit $rval
```

Exhibit 15. Configuration File for Start/Stop Script

```
#!/usr/bin/sh
#
# @(#) $Revision: 1.2 $
#
# Author:           Reinhard E. Voglmaier
#                   GlaxoSmithKline
# Description: Configuration file for Start/Stop of LDAP server
#
# set to 1 if you want to start the server at system boot
# set to 0           otherwise

# Main LDAP Server
main_ldap=1
# LDAP Administration Server
admin_ldap=1
# LDAP Server TestApplication
test01_ldap=0
# Print Server Names to be started
for i in main_ldap admin_ldap test01_ldap
do
   echo ${i}
done
```

Backup and Recovery

Things do not always go smoothly, and this is especially true for system administration. Experience shows that the data in the directory will soon become very important throughout the whole enterprise. Applications increasingly begin to use the directory for authentication or information management, and sooner or later this data becomes of vital importance for the everyday life of the whole company.

There are several possible types of failures of directory services:

- *Hardware failure*: A hardware component fails. This could be a hard disk, a network card, the motherboard, or any other hardware component compromising the functionality of the directory server.
- *Operating-system failure*: The operating system, like any other program, is not error proof. It can crash and destroy data.
- *Software errors in application programs*: Because there will be applications updating the directory, there is a possibility that an error in one of these programs could alter the data in the directory.
- *Operator errors*: Human error in the administration and maintenance of the directory could result in accidental erasure of files or directories.

This mean that we, as system administrators, face two different categories of failure:

1. *System failures*: Resources at the file-system level become unavailable or corrupt
2. *Application failures*: Resources at the application level become unavailable or corrupt.

The first category is the responsibility of the system administrator, who provides tools to save the data at regular intervals on tape or other media and reinstalls it as needed. The system administrator also provides a maintenance contract to replace defective hardware or reinstall system software.

The second category falls under the job of the administrator of the directory server. To recover from this type of failure, the administrator needs a copy of the directory in a consistent state. It is a good idea to define a policy of regularly exporting and backing up data from the directory server.

Service-Level Agreement

The service-level agreement (SLA) is a cornerstone of backup and disaster recovery. The service-level agreement defines how much time a service can be unavailable in the case of a disaster (including both hardware and software failures). In doing so, the service-level agreement helps to define the practical requirements to maintain a guaranteed level of service.

At the level of system administration, the SLA defines the maintenance contract with the service provider. For example, the system administrator decides whether it is enough to have assistance in less than four hours or in less than two hours. She also defines the needs for redundant hardware, for example, disk mirroring or a backup server to start if the original one is unavailable.

The same holds true for the administrator of the directory server, who relies on the availability of the system and the system backups from the system administrator. However, it is the responsibility of the administrator of the directory server to maintain the availability of the directory service and the consistency of the data in the directory.

It depends on the organization of the enterprise who exactly in the IT department sets up the service-level agreement and who is the counterpart. However, the existence of such an agreement is important because it determines the decision of how to proceed to guarantee the service level of the directory.

The last but not least point of the SLA is the budget. The higher the availability of your directory services, the higher your costs. To improve availability of the directory server you may think about implementing redundancy. If your management asks you for an SLA of 99 percent, you will have to spend much more money than if you were only offering 90 percent. You have, therefore, a good basis for treating the directory service budget with your management.

Backup Methods

Once you have established the SLA, you can choose a backup method. There are several methods available, and the choice depends on your particular requirements.

Classical Backup

The most simple and effective backup method is the classical backup. In this case, you simply save the files containing the database on tape. Because copying data on tape is a time-consuming process, you should copy the file first to a new location and then execute the backup. In theory, you do not have to close the database during the copy process. However, if you do not close the database, you have no guarantee of data consistency. If files are updated in the database while it is being copied, you will not know exactly which data has been updated and which has not. Because copying the database file on disk should take much less time than copying on tape, it is better to close the directory server during the copy process.

This is the backup method offered by the system administrator (or, better, by the operators). This backup strategy is very effective because it is based on proven methods. You may copy not only the data files, but also administrative information such as configuration files. Normally, every enterprise has such an optimized backup strategy in place to guarantee that there will be no data loss after hardware or software failures. In the event of a hardware failure, it is clear that it takes some time to replace the damaged devices, to reboot the system, and to install the backup data if necessary. Depending on the type of maintenance contract and the type of hardware failure, the service may be unavailable for a couple of days.

If this is not acceptable, you can install redundant hardware. For example, you could use disk mirroring to continue the service in the event of a disk crash.

Logical Backup of the Directory

You can also back up the directory and its configuration files at regular intervals so that it can be reinstalled on the same or a different server after a disaster. There are two ways to do this. You can execute a search and save the result on tape or other device, or you can simply export the whole directory. This type of backup is helpful if your directory has been destroyed because of an error in an application program. However, it may not be enough simply to dump out only the directory. You will also need the schema and several configuration files to reconstruct completely. Look at the documentation that ships with the directory server to understand what, exactly, you need to save.

Backup via Replication

Replication is another backup possibility. If you have your directory server replicated, you still have one server running should one of the two servers be down. If you have a master–slave replication environment, it depends on which of the servers is down. If the slave server is down, you simply wait until it is available again and then replicate the whole server again. If the master server is down, you cannot update the directory for the time the server is not working. If you have a master–master or multimaster environment, it does not matter which of the servers are down because you have more than one master.

Replication can also be combined with the other backup methods. The slave server can be used for offline backup as described in the section about replication in Chapter 5. Once the backup has finished, take the slave server online again and the replication process will align the slave server in case of updates of the directory during the backup.

You have, however, a consistent backup even if during the backup updates occurred on the directory.

System Monitoring

Why Monitoring

Server administrators normally want to know how their servers are performing and what they are doing. As more and more clients and applications begin to use the directory server, the availability of the directory server becomes crucial to many other services within the enterprise. Thus, it becomes increasingly important to maintain the service level of the directory server. With the help of monitoring tools, you can detect service interruptions as soon as they occur. With timely notice of a service interruption, you may even be able to solve the problem before any user or application experiences a failure of the directory service.

It is quite probable that you have a monitoring tool installed in your intranet environment. Not only large and medium intranets, but even smaller environments, have a great number of servers and services installed, and their numbers keep growing. For this reason, even smaller enterprises need a monitoring tool. Most of the commercial system-monitoring tools allow you to expand them to monitor nearly every process you need to manage. When certain events occur (for example, the process is not responding anymore, the process not running at all, or similar events), the tool reacts with an alert on a system console, an e-mail, or whatever other communication method you have configured. Most commercially available directory servers can easily be integrated into an existing monitoring tool.

SNMP

Monitoring tools frequently use SNMP (Simple Network Management Protocol) to manage or monitor services. SNMP was first implemented in 1988, but it quickly became a de facto standard. The first implementations, however, did not include security issues. These were integrated with version 3.

SNMP is based upon three concepts: managers, agents, and the so-called MIB, the management information base. The MIB is local to the managed service and contains information about it. The agent is installed on the managed service and provides access to the MIB. The agent responds to requests from the manager to get resource values from the MIB or to set them. For example, the agent could request to send to the manager the number of search requests the directory server had to handle. Finally, the manager runs the management software.

SNMP (v3) is defined in a set of RFCs. The application of SNMP tailored specifically for directory services is defined in the RFC 2605, "Directory Server Monitoring MIB." This RFC substitutes and obsoletes RFC 1567, "X.500 Directory Monitoring MIB." If you are interested in the underlying technology, see the following RFCs.

- RFC 2271, "An Architecture for Describing SNMP Management Frameworks"
- RFC 2272, "Message Processing and Dispatching for the Simple Network Management Protocol (SNMP)"
- RFC 2273, "SNMPv3 Applications"
- RFC 2274, "User-Based Security Model for SNMPv3"
- RFC 2275, "View-Based Access Control Model (VACM) for SNMP"

As mentioned previously, you can find commercial software implementing SNMP. Because SNMP is a standard protocol such as LDAP, it is not hard to get it to work with software from different vendors. You could use a Sun One LDAP server that supports SNMP and install as SNMP manager OpenView from HP, NetView from IBM, or Tivoli, just to mention some names. Or you could develop your own homegrown implementation of SNMP.

Home-Grown Solutions

If you prefer to develop an in-house solution, you have some advantages over a commercial solution, but it comes at the cost of development maintenance for a proprietary solution. The advantages are:

- Greater flexibility
- Exact fit with your requirements

Once you have decided to develop your own solution, you can choose one of two different approaches:

- You can use SNMP
- You can use the LDAP protocol itself

Use of SNMP

If you use SNMP, you should first take your favorite search engine and have a look at the Internet. You are not the only one facing the problem of monitoring an LDAP server, and you will find that there are many tools available. Again, you will find commercial solutions, but also open-source solutions, some of them produced by vendors such as Sun Microsystems.

You can get a robust Java framework from Sun Microsystems from the following Web site: http://java.sun.com/products.

A very interesting Java framework, ModularSNMP (SNMPv3 toolkit), is available from the University of Quebec (l'Université du Québec à Montréal, Canada).

If you prefer Perl, there is a Perl module available from CPAN. An excellent example is MRTG, developed by Tobias Oetiker <oetiker@ee.ethz.ch>. The multirouter traffic grapher (MRTG) creates HTML-containing images that monitor the actual situation of SNMP-agent-controlled components. You can learn more about it at http://www.stat.ee.ethz.ch/mrtg.

Another interesting approach is SMB_SNMP, which permits you to monitor SNMP agents, treating them as shared Windows resources. You can download it from a number of universities, for example, the TU Wien (university at Vienna, Austria) using the URL http://gd.tuwien.ac.at/opsys/linux/ibiblio/system/network/management.

Other languages that offer libraries include TK/TCL, Python, and many others. Again, just browse the Internet to see what is available.

Use the LDAP Protocol

If you do not want to learn another protocol, you could use the LDAP protocol itself to understand the actual situation of your directory server. This is a simple approach that is easy to implement. Furthermore, you will see the LDAP server exactly the way your clients see it.

Log-File Analysis

Another tool for system monitoring is to analyze the log files the directory server is writing. However, it is important to understand exactly what kind of information a log file can provide. The log file informs you about the actions the directory server has undertaken in response to user requests. This includes the type of request, the time spent upon the request, the details of the request (for example, the query filter in a search), and the traffic load on the directory server. If you need to monitor problems arising from the network, the log file will not help you. In this case, you should use an SNMP tool or write a custom tool that continues to access the directory at regular intervals. You can write it in your favorite language using one of the libraries available. This tool can test several functions that the directory provides.

Again, you have the choice of using a commercial product or developing your own solution. Commercial directory servers offer built-in tools, and there are also commercial tools that elaborate the log files of your directory server. Should you choose to develop your own solution, you can use the ubiquitous Perl (developed by Larry Wall), an ingeniously flexible language. Perl offers a powerful toolbox of pattern-matching utilities that allow you to read the log files and load the activities of your directory server in data structures. Perl also allows you to quickly and easily generate graphs of this data and send an e-mail alert if there is a problem. Perl is available on a myriad of platforms.

Exhibit 16 shows an example of output from the OpenLDAP directory server. Other directory servers will produce analogous output. Most products allow you to configure the log format and the degree

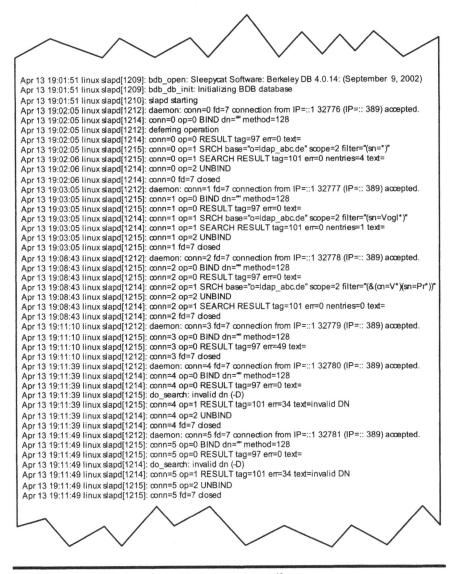

```
Apr 13 19:01:51 linux slapd[1209]: bdb_open: Sleepycat Software: Berkeley DB 4.0.14: (September 9, 2002)
Apr 13 19:01:51 linux slapd[1209]: bdb_db_init: Initializing BDB database
Apr 13 19:01:51 linux slapd[1210]: slapd starting
Apr 13 19:02:05 linux slapd[1212]: daemon: conn=0 fd=7 connection from IP=::1 32776 (IP=:: 389) accepted.
Apr 13 19:02:05 linux slapd[1214]: conn=0 op=0 BIND dn="" method=128
Apr 13 19:02:05 linux slapd[1212]: deferring operation
Apr 13 19:02:05 linux slapd[1214]: conn=0 op=0 RESULT tag=97 err=0 text=
Apr 13 19:02:05 linux slapd[1215]: conn=0 op=1 SRCH base="o=ldap_abc.de" scope=2 filter="(sn=*)"
Apr 13 19:02:06 linux slapd[1215]: conn=0 op=1 SEARCH RESULT tag=101 err=0 nentries=4 text=
Apr 13 19:02:06 linux slapd[1214]: conn=0 op=2 UNBIND
Apr 13 19:02:06 linux slapd[1214]: conn=0 fd=7 closed
Apr 13 19:03:05 linux slapd[1212]: daemon: conn=1 fd=7 connection from IP=::1 32777 (IP=:: 389) accepted.
Apr 13 19:03:05 linux slapd[1215]: conn=1 op=0 BIND dn="" method=128
Apr 13 19:03:05 linux slapd[1215]: conn=1 op=0 RESULT tag=97 err=0 text=
Apr 13 19:03:05 linux slapd[1214]: conn=1 op=1 SRCH base="o=ldap_abc.de" scope=2 filter="(sn=Vogl*)"
Apr 13 19:03:05 linux slapd[1214]: conn=1 op=1 SEARCH RESULT tag=101 err=0 nentries=1 text=
Apr 13 19:03:05 linux slapd[1215]: conn=1 op=2 UNBIND
Apr 13 19:03:05 linux slapd[1215]: conn=1 fd=7 closed
Apr 13 19:08:43 linux slapd[1212]: daemon: conn=2 fd=7 connection from IP=::1 32778 (IP=:: 389) accepted.
Apr 13 19:08:43 linux slapd[1215]: conn=2 op=0 BIND dn="" method=128
Apr 13 19:08:43 linux slapd[1215]: conn=2 op=0 RESULT tag=97 err=0 text=
Apr 13 19:08:43 linux slapd[1214]: conn=2 op=1 SRCH base="o=ldap_abc.de" scope=2 filter="(&(cn=V*)(sn=Pr*))"
Apr 13 19:08:43 linux slapd[1215]: conn=2 op=2 UNBIND
Apr 13 19:08:43 linux slapd[1214]: conn=2 op=1 SEARCH RESULT tag=101 err=0 nentries=0 text=
Apr 13 19:08:43 linux slapd[1214]: conn=2 fd=7 closed
Apr 13 19:11:10 linux slapd[1212]: daemon: conn=3 fd=7 connection from IP=::1 32779 (IP=:: 389) accepted.
Apr 13 19:11:10 linux slapd[1215]: conn=3 op=0 BIND dn="" method=128
Apr 13 19:11:10 linux slapd[1215]: conn=3 op=0 RESULT tag=97 err=49 text=
Apr 13 19:11:10 linux slapd[1212]: conn=3 fd=7 closed
Apr 13 19:11:39 linux slapd[1212]: daemon: conn=4 fd=7 connection from IP=::1 32780 (IP=:: 389) accepted.
Apr 13 19:11:39 linux slapd[1214]: conn=4 op=0 BIND dn="" method=128
Apr 13 19:11:39 linux slapd[1214]: conn=4 op=0 RESULT tag=97 err=0 text=
Apr 13 19:11:39 linux slapd[1215]: do_search: invalid dn (-D)
Apr 13 19:11:39 linux slapd[1215]: conn=4 op=1 RESULT tag=101 err=34 text=invalid DN
Apr 13 19:11:39 linux slapd[1214]: conn=4 op=2 UNBIND
Apr 13 19:11:39 linux slapd[1214]: conn=4 fd=7 closed
Apr 13 19:11:49 linux slapd[1212]: daemon: conn=5 fd=7 connection from IP=::1 32781 (IP=:: 389) accepted.
Apr 13 19:11:49 linux slapd[1215]: conn=5 op=0 BIND dn="" method=128
Apr 13 19:11:49 linux slapd[1215]: conn=5 op=0 RESULT tag=97 err=0 text=
Apr 13 19:11:49 linux slapd[1214]: do_search: invalid dn (-D)
Apr 13 19:11:49 linux slapd[1214]: conn=5 op=1 RESULT tag=101 err=34 text=invalid DN
Apr 13 19:11:49 linux slapd[1215]: conn=5 op=2 UNBIND
Apr 13 19:11:49 linux slapd[1215]: conn=5 fd=7 closed
```

Exhibit 16. Example of LDAP Server Log File

of informational detail you wish to obtain. All commercial products have a utility to monitor activity on your directory server. However, it is not difficult to write your own. Exhibit 17 shows the skeleton of a script written in Perl that parses a log file from the OpenLDAP server and produces statistics. The statistics this script produces are not very sophisticated, but the example should be enough to point you in the right direction for producing your own useful statistics.

Let us review what this script is actually doing. First, it parses the log file. Recall that the format of the log file is:

```
Month Day Hour:Minute:Second ServerName Process: Action
```

Exhibit 17. Example Perl Script of Log File Analysis

```
01 #!/usr/bin/perl -w
02
03 $LogFile = "Ldap.log" ;
04
05 # Contains connections per hour
06 my %ConnectionsPerHour ;
07   # Initialize ConnectionsPerHour:
08    for ($Hour=0 ; $Hour < 24 ; $Hour++) {
09         $ConnectionsPerHour{$Hour} = 0 ;
10    }
11
12 open(LOG,"<$LogFile") || die "Could not open LDAP Logfile :`
$LogFile" ;
13
14 # Format of the Log File is:
15 # Month Day Hour:Minute:Second ServerName Process: Action
16
17 while(<LOG>) {
18    s/(\w+)\s+(\w+)\s+(\d+):(\d+):(\d+)\s+([^\s]+)\s[^:]+:// ;
19
20    if (! registerEvent(Month       => $1,
21                        Day         => $2,
22                        Hour        => $3,
23                        Minute      => $4,
24                        Second      => $5,
25                        Machine     => $6,
26                        Process     => $7,
27                        Event       => $_)) {
28        printf("Error registering Event at %s %s %s:%s:%s\n",
29                  $2,$1,$3,$4,$5);
30    }

31 }
32 close(LOG) ;
33
34 # Once registered the Events we can produce the statistics:
35
36 if (!produceStatistics()) {
37    printf("Failed in building access statistics\n");
38     exit(-1);
39 }
```

In Perl, this is:

```
(\w+)\s+(\w+)\s+(\d+):(\d+):(\d+)\s+([^\s]+)\s[^:]+:
```

where

- \w+ means one or more alphanumeric characters
- \d+ means one or more digits
- \s+ means one or more space characters

Putting brackets around \w+ or \d+ makes characters they match available in the parameters $1 for the first bracket, $2 for the second, and so on. Have a look at the Perl manual pages or the Perl manual for more information.

Line 18 in the "while" loop parses the entire file and calls a procedure that registers the action, thus preparing the statistics. Exhibit 18 shows a straightforward example that simply adds a connection if one occurs. It assumes that a connection has occurred when it encounters the "accepted" keyword in the "action" field. It puts the connection in an associative array that holds the number of accesses for each hour. The function produceStatistics then produces the statistics. In our case, it simply prints out the connections per hour. Alternatively, you could also produce a graph here or print the data out as an Excel file.

As stated previously, this is a simplistic example, but it does clearly demonstrate how you can start producing your own statistics. If you have some idea of programming, you will have no problem in extending it.

Exhibit 18. Examples of Function to Prepare and Produce Statistics

```
01  sub registerEvent {
02    my (%Fields) = @_ ;
03    # Here in fields now we have all the data sent from
04    # the parse process before, therefore we can make
05    # all statistics we whatever want to make.
06    if ($Fields{'Event'} =~ m/accepted/) {
07      printf("Connection opened at : %s:%s\n",
08          $Fields{'Hour'},
09          $Fields{'Minute'});
10      $ConnectionsPerHour{$Fields{'Hour'}}++ ;
11    }
12    return(1);
13  }
14
15  sub produceStatistics {
16
17    for ($Hour=0 ; $Hour < 24 ; $Hour++) {
18      printf("%2d : %4d\n",$Hour,$ConnectionsPerHour{$Hour});
19    }
20    return(1);
21  }
```

User Administration

A directory stores many different types of information. It can be used as a domain name system (DNS); it can store easily retrieved information about technical devices on a network, such as plotters and printers; and it can store information about persons, commonly known as "white pages" and "yellow pages." When storing data about persons, details such as a personal identifier and password can also be stored. The personal identifier in LDAP is called a "distinguished name." In UNIX and other operating systems, it is often called "userID." Neither of these terms is precise. It should be called "user name," i.e., the string you use when you log in. The userID, instead, is the tiny number that UNIX, for example, uses to identify the user. In any case, when using LDAP, you call the personal identifier the "distinguished name."

The nature of user administration depends heavily on the product you are using. Some implementations know about user groups, roles, access control lists, and proprietary extensions. Consult the documentation that ships with the product you are using. Most commercial products offer tools for the administration of user accounts. With these tools, your users can maintain their own data, such as their phone or fax numbers.

User accounts can furthermore be used for authentication purposes. For example, a Web application could use the directory server to authenticate the user. Most UNIX operating systems offer the possibility of authenticating their users against an LDAP database. Another software system using LDAP is Samba. Samba allows you to mount file systems on UNIX systems as if they were "shares" on an NT server. It is possible to configure Samba to use the LDAP server for authentication instead of the NT primary domain controller.

Note that the LDAP protocol does not dictate a particular concept of user data. All of the data needed for user administration is stored in the LDAP directory using standard objects.

The next section shows an example of user administration using the Perl language plus the Net::LDAP modules presented in Chapter 6. The user data is stored in the object class inetOrgPerson, which makes user authentication possible. The information about groups is stored in the object class groupOfUniqueNames.

LDAP Users, Groups, and UNIX

Once you have a directory in place authenticating users, you may want to use it for user authentication on UNIX too. And, indeed, there is a standard Posix account object holding all information required for an account on the UNIX operating system. The standard is defined in RFC 2307, "An Approach for Using LDAP as a Network Information

Service." As the title implies, LDAP gives you much more than user information. LDAP can also substitute for the whole NIS/NIS+ or DNS framework. In this section, however, we will concentrate on user accounts.

Most vendors of UNIX operating systems only offer the option of using an LDAP server as a repository for user and group information. Let us review what the LDAP server should provide to the UNIX system if the server is to be used for user and group management. Exhibit 19 shows how a standard UNIX system holds user and group information. This illustration is obviously simplified, but it will help us focus on the basic concept. The user management system uses three files for user and group management. The "passwd" file holds information about the user; the "shadow" file holds the user password; and the "groups" file holds information about the groups a user belongs to. Between the user management procedure and the three system files, there is a layer that manages access to these configuration files. If we wish to use an LDAP server for authentication, all we need to do is teach this layer to consult the LDAP server instead of the system files.

As stated previously, most UNIX system vendors offer this layer of software. Let us briefly review how it works. Exhibit 19 shows the situation. What we want to achieve is what we called, in an abstract way, "user management" via system calls connected to a service. In Exhibit 20, this service is called PAM (pluggable authentication modules), which contacts an LDAP server over TCP/IP. This LDAP server provides authentication.

Now we know nearly all of the pieces depicted in Exhibit 19. The only unknown is the PAM layer providing the switch in user authentication. This PAM layer is a standard layer documented by the Open-Group. If you are interested in the original documentation, you can have a look at http://www.opengroup.org/tech/rfc/rfc86.0.html. PAM has been developed by Sun Microsystems, and the PAM layer later became a standard.

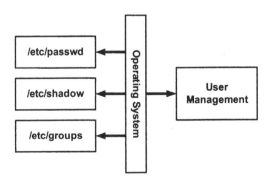

Exhibit 19. User Management in a Standard UNIX Operating System

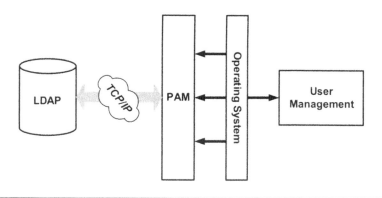

Exhibit 20. User Management Using LDAP

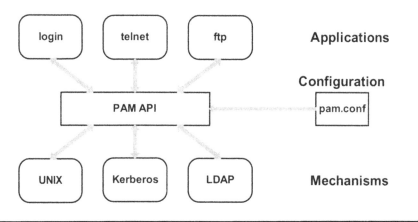

Exhibit 21. Pluggable Authentication Module

The PAM layer allows you to configure different authentication mechanisms for individual services, as seen in Exhibit 21. Each of the services contacts the generic PAM layer directly instead of contacting a dedicated authentication mechanism. From its configuration file, PAM learns which service has to use which authentication type.

This type of authentication framework has an enormous advantage. If you need a new authentication type, you simply develop an appropriate authentication mechanism, plug it into the PAM framework, and configure which services should use this authentication mechanism. As you can see from Exhibit 20, one of the authentication mechanisms available is the LDAP module.

As mentioned previously, most UNIX operating systems have an LDAP PAM module. If your operating system does not provide one, you can get it as open-source software from PADL Software Pty Ltd. The software also runs on the following operating systems:

- FreeBSD 3.x and above
- HP-UX 11
- Linux with Linux-PAM
- Mac OS X 10.2
- Solaris 2.6 and above

You can obtain software and documentation from http://www.padl.com. (Note that the name of the enterprise is LDAP backwards, read from left to right.)

Administration Utilities

Most commercial products are shipped with administration tools. Open source products, however, are not. You have to administer the software and configure the product by hand and use command line tools such as ldapmodify. Fortunately, libraries exist with a large number of programming languages that enable you to put together the tools you need for everyday adminstration activities using your favorite programming language. However, you can also review what is already available. Following are a few products you can use:

- Commercial products for LDAP administration are the Softerra LDAP administrator and Softerra LDAP Browser: both are available at http://www.ldapadministrator.com.
- LDAP Browser/Editor written in Java by Jarek Gawor at the Illinois Institute of Technology. You can find the latest version at http://www.iit.edu/~gawojar/ldap.
- A good GUI written in Python is web2ldap. The author is Michael Stroeder. You can ge the software together with Installation and Configuration instructions from http://www.huff.ca/doc/web2ldap/web2ldap.html. At the time of this writing, this tool can be used with LDAPv2 Protocol only.
- GQ, written by Peter Stamfest, is a tool written in C, and it also needs GTK installed. GTK is the GNU toolkit for development in the X-Windows Environment. This is, without doubt, a very intersting implementation of an LDAP client. You can also download it from http://biot.com.gq. GTK can be downloaded from the GNU Web site: http://www.gnu.org/directory/GNU/gtk.html.
- Mark Wilcox developed PLUMS, a set of tools written in Java. PLUMS stands for Practical Ldap User Management System. You need the following software to run it: JDK 1.15 or better, Swing 1.0, Netscape Directory SDK 3.05. The project home page is: http://www.mjwilcox.com/plums.
- Just for completeness, I will mention another link where you can get information on using the Netscape Browser to access LDAP

directories. The URL is http://developer.netscape.com/docs/manuals/communicator/ldap45.htm.

■ One more very interesting tool is the phpLDAPadmin, written and managed by David Smith. You can download the software from: http://phpldapadmin.sourceforge.net. As the product name suggests, the software is written entirely in PHP. You need a Web server with the PHP preprocessor installed in order to use this product. You also have to make sure you have the ldap support enabled when you install the PHP preprocessor. The installation of phpLDAPadmin is straightforward. You unzip the distribution in the document root of your Web server, edit the configuration file using the example delivered with the software, and that is it. You now have a fantastic GUI to administer your directory server. The software is well documented and structured, allowing you, therefore, to adapt it to your needs and personal taste.

By the time you read this book, there may be more products available. Now and then, use your favorite search engine to search the Internet to see if there are additional tools for your site.

Chapter 8

![header rule]

LDAP and Web Services

![header rule]

Introduction

Chapter 6 suggested several ways of integrating directory services into applications. Most programming languages have libraries that allow direct communication with directory servers. This chapter focuses on the collaboration of two different protocols: the LDAP protocol and the HTTP protocol.

The user-friendly HTTP is *the* language spoken on the Internet, used almost exclusively for communicating between Web servers and Web browsers. In contrast, LDAP is not very user friendly. However, LDAP is the ideal solution for directory applications, such as the frequently cited example of the "white pages."

In Chapter 6, we saw application programming interfaces (API) as one way of shielding the user from the complexity of LDAP. Sometimes the only reason for an application is to help the user access the data hosted by a directory server. In such cases, the application serves only as an interface to the directory, allowing the users to access the data stored there. Sometimes the application itself needs access to directory services to work properly. An example could be an application making lookups for user groups when LDAP substitutes for NIS+, the Network Information System developed by Sun Microsystems.

Web services provide another easy way to access directories. This chapter focuses on Web services and LDAP. Strictly defined, Web services are nothing more than an API. A Web server is a server application listening on a certain port (normally port 80) for connections coming from a client application. The client application typically is the familiar Web browser.

Although Web services are indeed normal applications, there are a number of characteristics of Web services that require particular attention for those who develop programs in this environment. In some senses, LDAP is similar to HTTP. Both are protocols located over the

TCP/IP stack; both have similar security aspects; and both are client–server applications. However, the similarity ends there. LDAP is a connection-oriented protocol, and HTTP is not. But let us return to the argument. The development of Web services requires a particular method of programming. In the first part of this chapter, we learn how to access directories in the Web environment. In the second part of this chapter, we take what we have learned in the first part to build a sample application.

There are several techniques for using directories in the Web environment:

- *LDAP URLs*: This is the most straightforward way to use directories. Some languages have functions that produce new LDAP URLs; in other languages, you have to code the URLs by hand. We have seen LDAP URLs in the previous chapters; now we will learn how to use them.
- *Web applications*: Web applications are applications executed on behalf the Web server. Such applications are better known as CGI scripts, which use the common gateway interface (CGI) to execute an application.
- *Application servers*: You can access a directory over the HTTP protocol without a Web server. The most popular implementation is Tomcat, available from the Apache foundation.
- *Gateways*: Another way of accessing a directory via the HTTP protocol is to use a gateway. There are a number of ready-to-use gateways available, the most famous of them being web500gw. But gateways can do much more than access a directory. We will look at these possibilities later in this chapter.
- *Web-server authentication*: Web servers allow you to protect certain pages with userID and password to control access to these pages. It is possible to let the Web server authenticate users against a directory, thus reducing the number of passwords on the intranet. This involves one further step versus a single sign on.
- *Preprocessors*: Preprocessors are interpreters that read the Web pages before sending them to the user. The most popular preprocessor is PHP, but Perl can also be used to perform this function. Java server pages and active server pages are further examples where an engine executes code embedded in HTML (hypertext markup language) pages on behalf of the Web server.

We will review each of these topics in the following sections. As always, our choice of products reflects our bias for applications that are as platform independent as possible. Thus, we will not consider Macintosh- or Microsoft-specific solutions. However, all of these techniques work on most platforms supporting Internet/intranet functionality. The same philosophy underlies all of these solutions, so once you have tried one solution, you will easily become familiar with the others.

LDAP URLs

Chapter 4 introduced us to the concept of LDAP URLs. In this section, we will have a closer look at how to use them. A program written in your favorite programming languages can produce LDAP URLs, but they can also be coded by hand, and as such you can write them down just as plain HTML. In this way, the browser delivers you the HTML page, you click on a URL, and the browser promptly delivers the information required. The advantage of this solution is that it will work on all modern browsers available because LDAP URLs are defined by RFC 2255. See the "LDAP URLs" section in Chapter 4 for more details.

Now lets us have a look at the HTML page necessary to look up information from the directory. Note that the user need not have any knowledge about LDAP to use this page; all she has to do is to click on a link. To get the page in Exhibit 1, all you have to do is put this link on the HTML page:

```
<a
href="ldap://www.LdapAbc.org/o=LdapAbc.org?l,ou,telephoneNumber?
one> All Departments on one glance
</a>
```

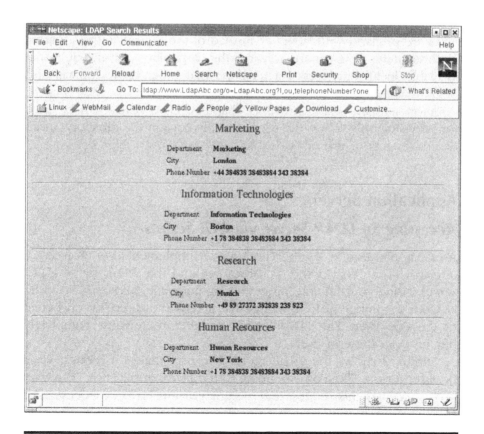

Exhibit 1. HTML Page Produced by Simple LDAP URL

That is a lot of functionality packed into a simple URL. But if you put this page in a context using frames, you can also hide the ugly-looking URL. If you want, you can even use a simple Java script to process user input.

Until now, we have dynamically produced the requests sent to the LDAP server, which then sends the answer back to the browser. What would happen if we could filter the output of the LDAP server? This could make it possible to process the output of the LDAP server and write an entire application.

How would we process the output from the LDAP server? The easiest way is via a CGI script. This is different from the approach used in the next section because you do not need any LDAP library to achieve this. You simply produce an LDAP URL and process the answer you got back from the LDAP server.

There is yet another possibility to use LDAP from the browser, but this depends on the browser you are using. As mentioned in the introduction, there are Web browsers that transparently can handle other protocols. The Conqueror Web browser available for LINUX is an example of such a smart browser. Given a URL, it allows you to browse a directory just by clicking on its objects as if it were a Web server. The end user does not notice much difference. If she carefully observes the URLs in the address bar, she will notice that these LDAP URLs are prefixed with "ldap://" instead of the typical "http://" prefix. Unfortunately, you cannot rely on this capability because it is not available in all browsers. Let us hope that other browsers will also begin to implement this feature.

As mentioned in the previous chapters, LDAP URLs can be used for browsing only. Thus, the user can only consult the directory; insert or update actions are not possible.

Application Servers

Accessing an LDAP Server via CGI Scripts

A CGI application is a good client–server implementation to access a directory. The client is the Web browser, and the server is the HTTP server. Using your favorite programming language, all you have to do is write a number of CGI scripts that access the directory on behalf of the end user. The LDAP protocol therefore remains completely hidden from the end user.

Exhibit 2 shows the architecture. The user makes a request via a browser for the URL corresponding to the LDAP application. The Web server receives this request and assigns it to an HTTPD process. The HTTPD process understands from the URL that a CGI script should service the request. It then launches the CGI script as a new process,

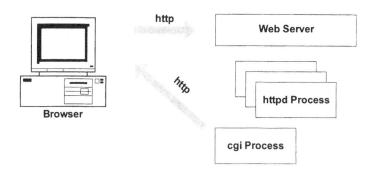

Exhibit 2. Client–Server Implementation Using CGI Scripts

delivering all the necessary parameters to this CGI script. Upon execution, the CGI script accesses the directory, formats the result in an HTTP response, and sends the output back to the Web browser.

Recall from Chapter 4 that there are a great many programming languages that offer the possibility of accessing an LDAP repository via libraries. This solution is very easy to implement because you can break down the whole application into a number of CGI scripts, each of them offering a particular functionality, for example "search.cgi," "add.cgi," "delete.cgi," and so on.

However, this solution also has disadvantages deriving from the fact that each of these CGI scripts is a different process and is therefore executed in a different context. Because the HTTP protocol is a stateless protocol, no process knows about the processes executed before. Therefore, if you wish to develop a more complicated application, you will soon face the problem of saving state information from one request to the other. There are various ways to accomplish this:

- *JavaScript*: If you put the information you wish to save from request to request in HTML fields, you can get this information back because JavaScript can access the HTML fields from the calling HTML page, i.e., the output from the previously executed CGI script.
- *Cookies*: A cookie is a number–value pair that the HTML page can store on the browser requesting this page. Thus, with the help of a cookie, you can store state information on the browser. However, many users configure their browsers to reject cookies. The browser configuration determines whether cookies are accepted or not.
- *Query parameters*: Together with an HTTP request, you can also send additional information in the so-called query parameters. This query parameter can be interrogated by the CGI script called from the HTTPD process. The CGI script then creates new query parameters that it sends along with the result HTTP that is sent back to the browser.

CGI scripts are easy to write and maintain if you are writing a limited application. The details of directory access and the LDAP protocol remain hidden from the end user.

Accessing an LDAP Server via an Application Server

You can use an application server to overcome the limits imposed by CGI scripts. The application server maintains state for you because the server site remembers who you are. The application server, like the Web server, communicates with the Web browser using HTTP, so the possibilities of maintaining state between different requests from the Web browser are the same as those for the CGI scripts. The important difference, however, is that in the case of an application server, it is the server that maintains the state for you, and you can concentrate on developing the application.

One example of a popular application server is Tomcat, a servlet container. Tomcat is developed and maintained by the Apache foundation, the same group that maintains the Apache Web server. You can download it from the Apache Web site at http://www.apachc.org (selecting "Tomcat") or directly from http://tomcat.apache.org. A servlet container also enables you to write HTML code containing particular tags with Java code. The servlet container compiles the Java code contained in these tags and runs them when the user requests this HTML page.

An application server makes it possible for a Web browser to execute programs on the server. The end user sitting before the Web browser need not know anything about the LDAP protocol to use the application. In contrast to the situation with CGI scripts, however, the programmer need not worry about maintaining state information as one request passes to the next. Furthermore, application servers provide better performance than CGI scripts because they obviate the need to continue creating new processes as requests from the browser arrive.

Gateways

Instead of developing your own application, you can check to see if there is a ready-to-use software application that does what you want. If your goal is simply to provide access to an LDAP repository using the Web browser, you can use a Web LDAP gateway.

The first servers were able to communicate using the Lightweight Directory Access Protocol instead of the original heavyweight X.500 protocol. Indeed, the very first servers were gateways speaking LDAP on the client side and X.500 on the server side. Gateways work in the

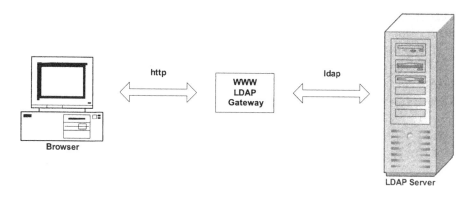

Exhibit 3. HTTP 2 LDAP Gateway

same way, connecting clients speaking HTTP with servers speaking LDAP. Exhibit 3 shows the schema for such an LDAP-HTTP gateway solution.

The gateway can consist of a Web server and an application, but it could also be a servlet container such as Tomcat or an application server speaking the HTTP protocol. An interesting solution — a gateway that runs on top of Tomcat — is available from Jon Roberts of Mentata Systems at http://www.mentata.com. As mentioned previously, Tomcat is a servlet container, i.e., a server that can process server-side Java scripts called "servlets." The application is open source and is based on standard technologies. It consists of a library of classes that are highly configurable to fit your particular needs. We will learn more about this library in the second part of this chapter when we review a sample application.

Web Server Authentication

As mentioned in the introduction to this chapter, the need to streamline authentication is often the first consideration in using LDAP. Over time, the proliferation of userIDs and passwords can become quite high in many enterprises. Indeed, it is not unusual for a single user to have ten UserID/password combinations and more. In international enterprises, the situation can be even worse because each country may have its own database of users.

Web servers did not simplify this situation. They introduced a new combination of UserID and password and, frequently, a different combination for every type of application.

The ability of LDAP to permit authentication over TCP/IP made it an ideal partner for Web servers. A Web server implies the presence of a network, so why not use this network for authentication also?

This method allows the use of one authentication method not only inside one Web server, but across all Web servers in the enterprise.

Because it is possible to synchronize NT primary domain controller (PDC) accounts with a simple Perl program with LDAP, you can use LDAP accounts for UNIX, Samba, and, finally, for Web applications. The usage in the Web server allows you to assign each user a single UserID/password combination that applies throughout the enterprise's intranet. This is obviously an ideal situation. But any strategy that can reduce the number of different accounts would be a welcome event.

This chapter is called "LDAP and Web Services" because most Web servers allow built-in LDAP authentication. The most popular Web server, the Apache Web server, has several different modules to allow built-in authentication against a directory server. Apache integrates this functionality in the form of a module.

The Web server controls the access to Web pages or applications. It achieves three objectives:

1. It executes the authentication of the user, i.e., it verifies that the user is who he or she claims to be.
2. It executes the authorization of the user, i.e., it controls whether the authenticated user is allowed to view the page or execute the application requested.
3. It delivers the userID of the authenticated/authorized user in the form of an environment variable for later use.

There are several modules available for the Apache Web server. In this chapter, we will use the auth_ldap module from Dave Carrigan, available from: http://www.rudedog.org. I use this module in my Web server implementation. The module is well documented, easy to install, and straightforward to use. This is not intended to imply that other solutions are inferior. Check the Internet to see what is out there. By the time you read this book, the software landscape may be quite different. If you are using the Apache Web server, have a look at its module registry, http://modules.apache.org. The module registry is one of the subprojects maintained by the Apache group (http://www.apache.org).

Example: The auth_ldap Module for Apache

To illustrate how the authentication in the Web server works, let us have a look at the auth_ldap module from Dave Carrigan and the Apache Web server. The installation of auth_ldap is similar to the installation of other modules available from the site of the Apache Web server. If you have problems, you can also count on the support of a user group working heavily with this module.

As mentioned previously, the Web server executes two steps before it allows the user to access the requested information:

1. The authentication phase
2. The authorization phase

The Authentication Phase

Before the LDAP module can authenticate against the directory, you first have to instruct the Web server to ask the user for a userID and password. Once these are obtained, the Web server proceeds, constructing the LDAP URL it should use for authentication. The LDAP URL is constructed following the specification described in RFC 225. Recall that the syntax of the URL is: ldap://host:port/ basedn?attribute?scope?filter. Based on this knowledge, the Web server constructs the following filter:

```
(&(filter)(attribute=username))
```

If the search succeeds and returns only one entry, the Web server tries to authenticate using the distinguished name retrieved from the search and the password supplied by the user.

The Authorization Phase

Once the user is authenticated, the Web server proceeds to see if the user is authorized to access the requested information. Based on its configuration file, the Web server controls which of the following directives return true. Valid directives are:

- *require valid-user*: Any authenticated user can access
- *require user*: Only the users with the specified userID have access
- *require dn*: Only users with the specified distinguished name have access
- *require group*: Only users of this group (groupOfUniqueNames) have access

For example:

```
AuthLDAPURL ldap://LdapAbc.org:389/ o=LdapAbc.org?uid
require valid-user
```

grants access, allowing every valid user in the directory based on the userID (uid). Similarly:

```
AuthLDAPURL ldap://LdapAbc.org:389/ o=LdapAbc.org?cn
require valid-user
```

grants access, but in this case the authentication is made using the "cn" attribute. This is not a recommended approach. You should use a unique attribute for authentication. The following code:

```
AuthLDAPURL ldap://LdapAbc.org:389/o=LdapAbd?uid
require group cn = admin, o = LdapAbc.org
```

allows access only to persons in the admin group. Finally:

```
AuthLDAPURL ldap://LdapAbc.org/o=LdapAbc.org?uid??
(|(mail=*)(uid=admin)) require valid-user
```

allows persons who have an e-mail account and who are part of the administration team.

LDAP Authentication Using CGI Scripts

The authentication in CGI scripts works like the authentication in scripts or programs. As explained in the previous section, the only difference between a program and a CGI script executed on behalf of a Web server is that the HTTP protocol does not support sessions. The concept of a session has to be simulated by the application. Most Web servers also offer session support. There are two possible strategies for maintaining a session:

1. Cookies
2. Query parameters passed from one page to the other

As we have seen in Chapter 4, there are a great many programming languages for which LDAP libraries or classes are available. It is very likely that you will be able to LDAP-enable your Web application with one of these LDAP libraries.

LDAP Authentication Using the PHP Preprocessor

PHP is a preprocessor that can be compiled into a Web server, for example the Apache Web server. For more details about the PHP preprocessor, see the "LDAP and PHP" section in Chapter 6. The software and documentation are available from the Web site of the PHP project: http://www.php.net.

The example cited in Chapter 6 shows you how authentication works. Exhibit 4 shows the PHP script again in a simplified form. The important lines are printed in bold. First, we try to get the user credentials in lines 8 and 9. Line 14 connects to the LDAP server, line 18 tries to bind with the user credentials. If the bind is successful, the page can be displayed. If there is no bind, an error page replaces the current one.

Exhibit 4. php Script for LDAP Authentication

```php
<?php session_start();

 // Configuration:
$LDAP_Server = "LdapAbc.org" ;
$LDAP_BaseDN = " ou=IT, o=LdapAbc.org" ;
$Error_HTML = "/Error.html" ;

// Grabbing Parameters from Script Environment:
  $CallingScript = $HTTP_SERVER_VARS['PHP_SELF'];
  $login = $HTTP_POST_VARS['login'] ;
  $password = $HTTP_POST_VARS['password'] ;
  Location=sprintf("http://%s/%s",
                  $HTTP_SERVER_VARS['HTTP_HOST'],
                  dirname($HTTP_SERVER_VARS['PHP_SELF']) );

  // Connect to the LDAP server:
  $ds=ldap_connect($LDAP_Server);

  // Construct the DN the User binds with
  $udn="uid=".$login.",".$LDAP_BaseDN ;

  // Bind to the directory:
  $res=@ldap_bind($ds,$udn,$password);

  if ( $res && (chop($login) != "" ) && (chop($password) !=""
) ){
  // Everything's ok, so we just do nothing,
  // that means the following HTML becomes displayed
  } else {
    $Location = $Location.$Error_HTML ;
    echo "window.location.replace(\"$Location\") ; "
  }
?>
```

The PHP script in Exhibit 4 executes every time it encounters the bind action. Furthermore, it requires the userID and password to be contained as environment variables. The user credentials are required because the HTTP protocol is a connectionless protocol, and as such, it does not maintain state information between the individual requests.

If you wish to protect an entire subsite, a better choice than a PHP script would be to use one of the built-in LDAP modules of the Web server you are using. However, it may be that you have chosen to use PHP for authentication, and if so, you have to include an authentication script in every page of the site you wish to protect. PHP lets you include a centrally maintained PHP script via the "include" clause. To avoid authentication each time an HTML page is displayed, you could use the session-tracking capabilities of the PHP language. Chapter 6 has a complete working example that includes a configurable timeout interval after which the session expires and the user has to log in again. For more information about session variables and the use of PHP inside HTML, have a look at the PHP project page.

LDAP and the Web: A Case Study

In the first part of this chapter, we discovered the possibilities of accessing an LDAP server using a Web browser, and we learned how to interconnect these two important Internet services. In this second part of the chapter, we will use these technologies in a concrete application.

Web technology has revolutionized software development over the past five years, and there are no signs that evolution of this technology is coming to an end. Because LDAP is an internetworking protocol, it is also an important part of the World Wide Web. LDAP facilitates data distribution throughout networks, not only in an enterprise's intranet but also over the Internet.

LDAP is particularly useful for the extranet because it allows you to push data out of your intranet in a defined way. The replication capacity of LDAP is of particular importance. In this section, we will see a robust framework that allows you to push data out of the enterprise to your extranet, where your customers can access this information. The LDAP protocol also allows you to receive data from your customers, data that was previously collected via your company's Web site, accessible from the Internet.

This second section of the chapter provides a case study for such an environment. It contains a number of solutions and demonstrates that LDAP can go well beyond the classic phone-book application. This does not mean to imply that the phone-book application is trivial. In most cases, a phone-book application is the first step toward "LDAP enabling" of a company.

First, we will briefly review the requirements for the application: a Web site offering a number of applications for its users. The administration and authentication of the users is made using LDAP, which is where the collaboration of Web services and LDAP comes into play. After learning the requirements, we will see the schema of the application. The proposed solution could have been simpler, but we decided to include security requirements in the case study. We then briefly review the schema of the directory, without going into much detail. After that, we will see how a Web server can use LDAP authentication and describe how to access a directory using a normal Web browser. Finally, we will learn about the design of a broker connecting different data sources.

Requirements

Note that this case study is far from complete. We tried to keep it as general as possible so that it would apply to a wide range of application requirements. That said, let us move on to the list of requirements.

Assume that we have a medium-sized company and that this company needs to install an Internet Web server. Further, assume that this Internet Web server hosts the company's entire Web site, which holds different types of content:

- Publicly available data
- Data available after subscription
- Confidential data

The Web server needs to know the identity of the user if it is to grant access to privileged content (the last two content types). The Web server may also require encrypted traffic between clients, i.e., Web browsers and Web servers.

The Web server should also run applications, e.g., discussion groups, news server, information-retrieval systems, file upload and download utilities, and similar applications. All of these Web application need to know the identity of the users trying to connect with them. Consequently, there are several categories of users:

- *Anonymous users*: Users navigating the Web and accessing publicly available data on the Web site. The user does not need to deliver any credentials.
- *Authenticated users (low level)*: Users that the system recognizes. They have access to all unrestricted information. The only purpose of authentication at this level is to deliver the user to a familiar environment, such as "my" site, with predefined user preferences (filtered news on the company server, site setup, etc.). The server requires authentication, but the conversation need not be encrypted because the data is available to everyone, including anonymous users.
- *Authenticated users (high level)*: Users that have access to restricted data. In this case, the conversation should be encrypted. The information is not confidential, so the Web server can rely on the authentication procedure to let the user access the data. An example would be a company that, for legal reasons, has to restrict access to certain information.
- *Authenticated users accessing sensitive data*: These users could be internal persons needing important data on the Internet for their daily work, e.g., employees in the sales or marketing departments. Business partners might also need to exchange sensitive information via the Internet, e.g., business-to-business (B2B) applications.

Where does the directory server get the information that restricts what the user can do and see? Some users are logged in automatically using information held in the company database. Other users can subscribe themselves. You can configure these new subscriptions to become active immediately or delay their status pending a manual or filtered review.

These are just some general restrictions, but you can further refine the restrictions to suit your needs. For example, you might want to restrict a particular user group to connect only at a certain time of the day.

LDAP Internet Environment

Now that we have an idea of what we want to achieve, we are ready to design an architecture that will meet our needs. Exhibit 5 shows the picture. The two towns represent the Internet users who connect via browser to your company Web site. However, they do not link directly to your site. Upon opening a connection to your Web site at http://www.LdapAbc.org, the user is connected to the Web server through a firewall. A discussion about the configuration of the firewall would go far beyond the scope of this book. However, it is worth mentioning that the firewall has the job of keeping out traffic that the site is not designed for. Remember, the firewall cannot keep out bad guys!

Because we only need access to the Web server, we will forbid all protocols except for the HTTP protocol. We also enable the HTTPS protocol, i.e., the secured HTTP protocol. In the same way, the LDAP directory server can use SSL/TLS as a security layer between itself and the insecure TCP/IP protocol stack. The HTTP protocol also uses this layer. We will also handle the file upload and download features via the HTTP protocol. The fewer the protocols the firewall has to negotiate, the better is its performance. You can always add a new protocol later if you really need it.

Once the request from the user's Web browser arrives at the Web server, the user gets the "welcome page." At this point, she might click on a link pointing to a location that requires authentication. As mentioned previously, we will use LDAP to authenticate the user. Of course, the Web server also has to speak the LDAP protocol. We could handle this by an application, but we will also be using static pages, and we do not want to use any scripting at all. Therefore, it is better to leave it to the server. In a later section, "LDAP Authentication and the Web Server," we will see how. For now, just assume that the server uses the LDAP protocol to communicate with the LDAP server. The Web server therefore gets an LDAP client. The Web server and the two LDAP servers are in the so-called demilitarized zone (DMZ), the zone between the firewall and the intranet. Inside the DMZ, the Web server and the LDAP server can speak LDAP. The firewall cannot pass the LDAP protocol, so the LDAP server cannot be contacted directly from the Internet.

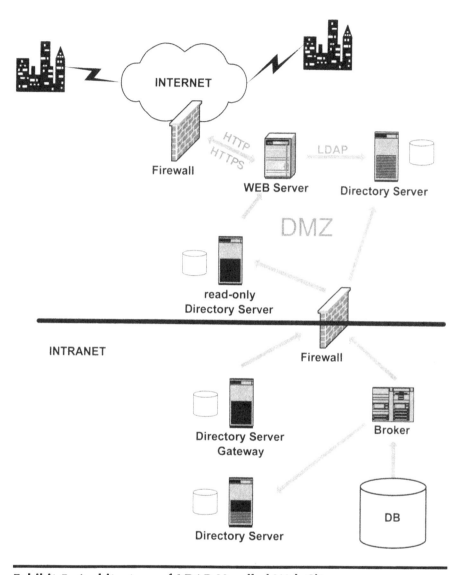

Exhibit 5. Architecture of LDAP-Handled Web Site

If the user is unknown, she can subscribe herself on the LDAP server. However, if the firewall does not forward the LDAP protocol, how can the user subscribe herself on the LDAP server? She can do so using an LDAP gateway. We will learn about a very flexible gateway later, in the section "LDAP-HTTP Gateway."

When the user subscribes to the LDAP server, nothing happens until a broker mediates the request. There is a broker in the intranet that looks from time to time to see if there is something new on the LDAP server out in the DMZ. If there is, the broker decides what to do. A number of actions are possible: subscribe the user; ask the administrator what to do; or drop the subscription. The broker gets this information from its configuration files. We will learn more about this in the section "LDAP Application Broker."

Once the broker has handled the request correctly, the new entry, if any, should go into the directory. For security reasons, we keep a copy inside the enterprise. This copy is also used to put the changes onto the LDAP gateway. The LDAP gateway pushes the updates it gets onto the read-only LDAP server in the DMZ. The HTTP server obtains authentication information from the read-only LDAP server.

The broker has yet another function. It observes changes in the directory containing the data of the employees. When something changes, it replicates this change into the LDAP directory inside the intranet. The directory holds the userIDs of the employees. It does not hold the passwords. For security reasons, the employees should not use the same password for both the Internet LDAP database and the company's intranet.

As you may have noticed, the DMZ contains two LDAP databases. One directory is read-only and is used to deliver authentication information to the Web server. The second directory is used to hold the subscription requests and the modify requests of the users. This directory is configured to allow users to insert and modify their individual entries. The broker is used to update the master directory within the intranet. The intranet directory is then used to update via replication the read-only directory in the DMZ. This somewhat complicated architecture is used for security reasons. The directory that grants access to users is reachable in the DMZ, but it is almost in a read-only state. Only one user on one machine can update this directory. In reuse, it is read-only. This directory is a replica of the directory gateway.

Now that we have an overview of the architecture, let us have a look at the details, beginning with the Web server and its LDAP module. This example uses the open-source Web server implementation from Apache. Open-source software has the big advantage of allowing programmers to look at the source code to see exactly what is going on in the program. You can tune this open-source Web server until it meets exactly your requirements. Furthermore, you can learn a lot from this implementation and can reuse this knowledge, even if you decide to use a commercial Web server.

LDAP Directory

Let us have a very brief look at how we could organize the data in the directory. We will use the standard inetOrgPerson object class because, based on our requirements, we are not interested in any attributes that this object class cannot hold.

Because we will also define groups of persons accessing a particular Web site or a particular discussion group, we will use a number of groupOfUniqueNames object classes to hold the group information.

We also want to distinguish between external persons (customers) and internal persons (employees). By assigning an organizational unit to each category, we can easily identify all customers or all employees having access to the Web server.

We have on our Web server different Web sites to protect, different discussion groups with defined access, and we want to differentiate the access of the employees. For example, we do not want a member of the sales group to gain access to the site reserved for the marketing group, and the marketing people should not have access to the sites of the sales group. It is possible to differentiate the groups into much finer categories. If you need to do so, you can simply add further complexity to the DIT. Exhibit 6 shows the DIT we will use in this example.

A big problem is always the decision of how to name the entries for the individual users. You need to make the entries unique in the directory, but you also need to assign unique user credentials to each user to guarantee that no two users have the same log-in information. The easiest way to do this is to use a unique userID. How to generate the userID is the next problem. You could let the user choose one, or you could use an automatic procedure that generates the userID, perhaps from surname and name. The decision is up to you. You could also use the e-mail address of the user, which should be unique. We will use the e-mail address because this can be handled consistently for employees and customers. However, this means that the customer must have an e-mail account. You can solve this problem by offering him an e-mail account if he does not already have one.

As you see, we have three different types of groups plus two groups that specify the province of the user:

1. Discussion groups, contained in the organizational unit labeled "lists" (ou = lists)
2. Groups to limit access to Web sites, contained in the organizational unit labeled "sites" (ou = sites)

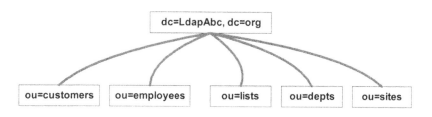

Exhibit 6. DIT of Web Site Directory

3. Groups inside your enterprise, contained in the organizational unit labeled "depts," deriving from departments (ou = depts)
4, Users from outside the enterprise (ou=customers)
5. Users from inside the enterprise (ou=employees)

With the first three group types, you can later answer such questions as "How many discussion groups are hosted by our Web server?" Also using these group types, you can develop queries that will provide useful site statistics.

LDAP Authentication and the Web Server

Recall that, for this example, we are using the open-source Web server Apache, available from http://httpd.apache.org. If we are to let the Web server authenticate the user, we also need the module that allows authentication against LDAP. This is also available as open-source software. You can find many such modules using the database on the Apache Web site. Look at http://modules.apache.org to get the list of modules available. At this link, you also will find a utility to search the module database. The module used in this example is the "auth_ldap" module written by Dave Carrigan. The software and documentation for this module are available at http://www.rudedog.org. This software works with Netscape (SUN) and OpenLDAP libraries. It also allows access to LDAP over SSL.

We used the OpenLDAP libraries to compile the mod_auth module into the Apache Web server. Because we will later also be using the HTTPS protocol, we will need to set up a secure connection using SSL. The first thing to do is to install OpenSSL, available at http://www.openssl.org. Once OpenSSL is installed, you can install Apache, adding the mod_auth module. You will need to install two Apache versions: one based upon SSL and one without SSL. Once you have successfully installed the two Apache Web servers, you can set up the authentication methods.

Before configuring the Web server to use LDAP authentication, we must first establish which types of authentication we need:

- We need to control using the userID if the user is known by the system, i.e., if the mail address corresponds to a valid user of the system.
- We need to control using the mail if the user is part of a particular group.
- We may need to give access to only a few persons, without defining for them a particular group.

The following subsections show how to configure these three log-in categories.

Control if the User Is Known by the System

Because we have two different types of users — customers and employees — we will need to distinguish between the two of them. We need to give the LDAP server three pieces of information: the base LDAP URL the entry lives in and the log-in information the user will provide.

```
AuthLDAPURL ldap://ldap1.LdapAbc.org/dc=LdapAbc,dc=org?mail
require valid-user
```

This instruction defines that every user contained in the subtree dc = LdapAbc,dc = org can gain access. The mail address is used for log-in. If you only want to log in customers, you would use:

```
AuthLDAPURL ldap://ldap1.LdapAbc.org/ou = customers, dc = LdapAbc,dc
= org?mail
require valid-user
```

Likewise, if you only want to grant access to employees, you would use:

```
AuthLDAPURL ldap://ldap1.LdapAbc.org/ou = employees, dc = LdapAbc,dc
= org?mail
require valid-user
```

Accept Only Members of Particular Groups

In this example, assume that we want to limit access to this Web page to members of the discussion group named "LDAP Fundamentals." Because we accept persons who are members of a discussion group, the organizational unit is "ou = lists":

```
AuthLDAPURL ldap://ldap1.LdapAbc.org/dc = LdapAbc,dc = org?mail
require group cn = LDAP Fundamentals, ou = lists, dc = LdapAbc,dc
= org
```

Again, we can limit access to those members who are employees with the following definition:

```
AuthLDAPURL ldap://ldap1.LdapAbc.org/ou = employees, dc = LdapAbc,dc
= org?mail
require group cn = LDAP Fundamentals, ou = lists, dc = LdapAbc,dc
= org
```

or limit access to group members who are customers:

```
AuthLDAPURL ldap://ldap1.LdapAbc.org/ou = customers, dc = LdapAbc,dc
= org?mail
require group cn = LDAP Fundamentals, ou = lists, dc = LdapAbc,dc
= org
```

Accept Only a Particular User

Here we accept only the user with the e-mail address: ReinhardVogl-maier@LdapAbc.org. Thus, the definition looks like this:

```
AuthLDAPURL ldap://ldap1.LdapAbc.org/dc = LdapAbc,dc = org?mail
require user ReinhardVoglmaier@LdapAbc.org
```

That is all you need to do to authenticate the different types of users in our environment. The credential the user provided is then further available to you using the environment variable Remote_User, which is provided by the Web server.

LDAP-HTTP Gateway

At this point in our example, we can authenticate existing users to allow them access to protected information, and we can give the Web server the information of who is making a particular request. Remember that we also wanted to allow the user to sign up and insert her name into the database for a particular group. Let us look at a detail of Exhibit 5, but view it in greater detail in Exhibit 7.

The user is connected via browser to the Web server, so the Web server and the browser are using the HTTP protocol for communication. Recall that this was the only protocol we allowed in the firewall. To subscribe to a group, the user compiles a form on the Web Server. Once compiled and submitted, the Web server launches an application that contacts the LDAP server, speaking LDAP, obviously, and asks the LDAP server to insert a new entry in the directory. The application called LDAP-enabled in Exhibit 7 can be a CGI script written in Perl, it could be a page written in PHP, or it could be a Java servlet. The whole architecture shown in Exhibit 8 is called an HTTP-LDAP gateway.

Because we want to allow the users to sign up and also to modify their own entries, we must provide a form to update the information contained in the directory. Thus, we need to configure the LDAP server to permit users to change only their own entries. If you compare the work you have to do to implement this functionality on an RDBMS with the work you need to do so using LDAP, you will see that the LDAP server comes in very handy in these activities.

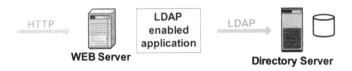

WEB Server   **Directory Server**

Exhibit 7. Web Server Speaking with an LDAP Server

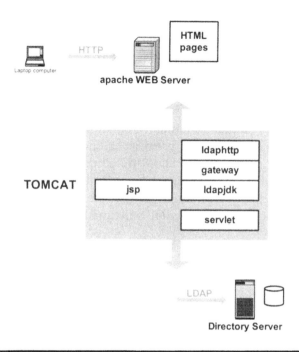

Exhibit 8. Architecture of HttpLdap Gateway (Developed by Jon Roberts, Mentata Systems.)

Once developed, the LDAP-HTTP gateway can also come in handy within the intranet. Recall that the broker brings in data from the Internet and puts it on the directory within the intranet. However, the this directory also has to be maintained. For example, there could be requests from users to reset their passwords or similar activities. To keep up with directory maintenance, you need an administration interface. You could write an application using your preferred development system and the corresponding LDAP library. But if you are using the same application logic that you used outside the intranet, you can avoid inventing the wheel again. Furthermore, you can save time later on during software maintenance if you use a similar architecture for both applications.

Instead of writing our own solution, we will use a ready-to-use framework in our example. Luckily, there is an open-source project written in Java. The framework is developed and maintained by Jon Roberts, the proprietor of Mentata Systems. It is available for download from http://www.mentata.com together with excellent documentation. The software is based on the standard servlet technology. You need a Web server that can handle servlets, e.g., Tomcat. Tomcat is part of the open-source project Java.

Exhibit 8 shows the architecture of this framework. On one end is the Web server speaking pure HTML with the browser, thus allowing the use of a standard browser. On the other end is the LDAP server speaking the LDAP protocol. The Web server holds the user interface in the form of static pages. The dynamic part is handled by Java server pages (JSP) and Java servlets that are held within Tomcat, which is also known as a "servlet container." The Web server contacts Tomcat as soon as it needs the dynamic part to be executed. For the access at the LDAP side, an LDAP software development kit (SDK) is needed. Together with the servlet container, the SDK contains the base for two packages written in Java: The gateway extends the servlet classes by adding LDAP support, and the LDAP-HTTP package offers the classes that can be used by the final application. In the application, you have nothing else to do other than overwrite the methods of the LDAP-HTTP classes to obtain the needed functionality.

LDAP Application Broker

The last piece missing in our design is the broker, which mediates transactions between the outside directory, the inside copy of the directory, and the database containing the employee data. We propose a simple design: a central broker, configured by a simple ASCII configuration file, that speaks with agents that contact the different servers. In our particular case, we have two LDAP servers — one in the DMZ where the updates are read from and one in the intranet where the updates are written to — and one RDBMS, which also receives updates. Exhibit 9 shows an overview of the architecture.

We could have avoided writing an application of our own by using a commercial metadirectory product. However, the broker architecture adds flexibility to the design that we will appreciate later when we may need to add new functionality to our LDAP sites.

To keep things simple, the design is broken down into components. Each component is called an agent, and there are local and remote agents. The remote agents are responsible for collecting the freshly modified data or writing back the data modified by another data source. The local agents keep in contact with the remote agents and interact with the broker. The broker then puts two local agents in contact, one to receive the data and one to deliver the data. The broker negotiates these transactions among the different local agents based on its configuration file.

The remote agent that updates a directory is easy to write. It only has to do the normal add, delete, and modify operations. The remote agent can interact with the RDBMS using any number of libraries that facilitate contact with an RDBMS. The remote agent that gets the modifications in the LDAP repository simply uses the log file to see whether an update in the directory has occurred. As soon as the remote agent notices an update, it contacts a local agent.

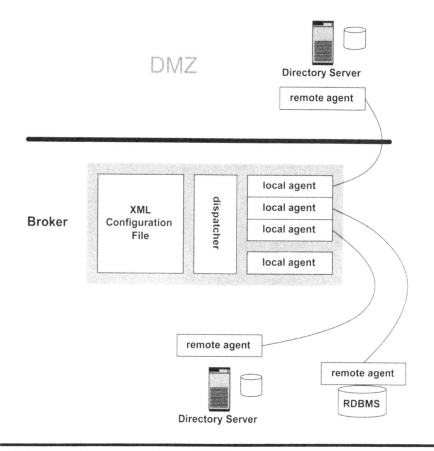

Exhibit 9. Architecture of the LDAP Application Broker

The broker uses a dispatcher that continues to create new local agents. This dispatcher uses a pool of active dispatcher processes. It always has a configurable number of dispatcher processes to contact if work has to be done.

This section has shown you how to approach the job of combining information from different data sources. As you have seen, you can achieve a lot with an easy-to-implement solution. A project to implement this broker architecture had already begun at the time of this writing. This work is also in the form of an open-source project. Sources and documentation can be downloaded from http://www.sourceforge.net.

Conclusion

In this chapter, we have seen how two of the most important Internet protocols, HTTP and LDAP, can work together to provide the user with information contained in a directory without requiring the user to know or understand LDAP. Depending on your particular implementation, the user will likely not even realize that she is contacting an LDAP repository.

In the second part of this chapter, we put together everything we had learned in the first part and saw that these technologies could be combined in an application that can be "extranet enabled" as a B2B application. We learned how to construct, from easy-to-understand and easy-to-maintain components, a robust and a reliable environment for for intranet, Internet, and extranet.

Chapter 9

The Design of Directory Services

This chapter provides a glimpse of design theory. An understanding of how to proceed in the design of directory services is useful if you have to implement directory services from scratch or if you have to redesign or upgrade existing directory services. There are entire books that address the design and implementation of directory services. If you need an in-depth understanding of the design process, you should consult one of these. On the other hand, it is clear that you cannot put your project on hold while you read 800 pages or more to become a design specialist for directory services.

The goal of this chapter is to give you a brief overview of the principles guiding the design of directory services so that you can proceed further on your own. To achieve this goal, the chapter must fulfill two objectives: First, it will give you a basic understanding of how to proceed with the planning, design, and implementation of directory services. Second, it will show you where to get more information.

The first part of this chapter presents an introduction to the design process. You will see that the design process has no clear ending point. Rather, it is a cycle. After completing the "last" step, you are likely to go back to the first step and repeat all or some of the previous steps in an effort to refine the design.

After seeing an overview of the design of directory services, we will have a closer look at the individual steps involved in the design process.

Introduction

Setting up directory services from scratch would be a clean design problem, but it is not a likely scenario. Usually, the directory services are already in place, and your job is to optimize access to the existing infrastructure. The following is a typical scenario:

You have several applications using a database for user authentication. Let us assume that you have a standard RDBMS in place, but that some applications use a proprietary database for historical reasons. Furthermore, you need authentication for your intranet; you want to enable users to access static Web pages containing sensitive data; and you need authentication for intranet applications such as CGI (common gateway interface) scripts, PHP scripts, or application servers. Most of these applications need authentication as well as additional information about the user that has been authenticated, for example, the user name, the department the user is in, and perhaps some profiling information. Obviously, you need the same information regardless of which point you connect from within the enterprise. Consequently, the first step will be to provide an authentication mechanism implemented as a directory.

Once you have the directory services in place and your authentication mechanism fine-tuned, you will begin to extend it. Any authentication process holds information about persons, for example, UserID, name, and password. LDAP can hold much more information, so why not use the LDAP server to provide additional information about these persons? Examples of information needed include:

- Phone and fax numbers of your employees
- Physical location of employees, such as town, building, floor, and room number
- Computer equipment that the employees are using
- Computer systems that the employees have access to
- Printers that the employees can use

As you begin thinking about useful information for different departments, this list will grow longer.

At this point, it is likely that you will recognize the need for a redesign. You will begin to think about questions like data replication, data distribution, and data security. And you will begin to think about what you should do with the "release zero" of your global directory services. Throw it away and design a new version from scratch? Extend your existing implementation? This chapter was written to help you decide how to resolve these and other questions about your particular situation.

Note that the design phase of directory services is the most important of phase of all because a well-designed system will prevent problems from occurring later on. It is very difficult to recover from prominent design errors, and even very grave design errors may not become apparent until late in the implementation phase.

In contrast, with a good design in hand, implementation is straightforward. It is somewhat like writing a book: Once you have written a good outline, you have completed as much as half the work. So the more time you spend on the design phase, the less effort you will need to expend during the implementation phase. Of course, your time is not unlimited, and you cannot design forever. At some point, you will have to compromise between the time spent on design and the final benefit you gain with eventual further refinement of your design. Your goal should be to make the design "good enough." This is a question of experience, but the point is: Do not stint on the time spent during the design phase.

Directory Life Cycle

When considering the life cycle of directory services, you will encounter many familiar concepts from software-development and project-management courses. We will not explain these concepts here. Instead, we will concentrate only on the specific concepts that apply to directory projects. Now let us have a closer look at the individual design phases. The steps described here are the steps that, after some experience, I have personally found useful. Unfortunately, there is no standard recipe on this subject. You will find many articles, books, and courses commenting on the steps involved in planning, designing, and implementing directory services. Exhibit 1 shows the life cycle of a directory. Note that it is not unusual to take the results of one stage and then take a step or two backward to refine a previous step.

There are many other versions of the life cycle of directory services, with some steps having additional refinements or subdivisions. The best way to proceed in your particular situation depends on your specific working environment, for example, the number of persons working on the project. Consider the following as a work list that must be completed before setting up and running directory services in your environment. Remember, furthermore, that there are no clear boundaries that clearly divide the single phases. For example, the step of "Analysis of data to be stored in your directory and data sources available in your environment" could be part of a planning stage as well as a design stage.

- Planning of directory services: Define the goal of the project, listing the objectives and producing a time plan.
- Design of directory services: Design the data the directory will hold, the schema, the tree, topology, and security measures.

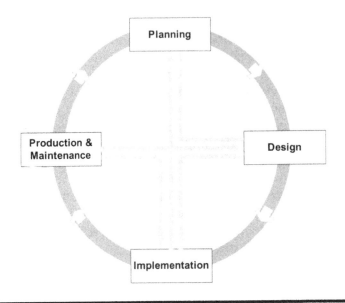

Exhibit 1. Directory Life Cycle

- Implement design of directory services: At the beginning of the project, this may only be a prototype to verify that the design meets your requirements. If it does, you proceed to the next step; if not, you jump to the point where the design needs to be improved.
- Verify production and maintenance of directory services: In this step, you finally see if your deliverable actually meets the requirements under normal workload. This is also the moment where you begin to think about improvements. And so we are back at the first step.

Now you can break down your directory project into subprojects, knowing that at the end of each subproject you will define the requirements for the next one.

Planning of Directory Services

In the planning phase, you lay the foundation for your project. As in every project, you define the overall goal and the timeline for its realization. This chapter cannot get into the details of project management, but we will discuss some aspects that are of particular relevance to the implementation of a directory. Exhibit 2 shows an overview of the steps necessary in the planning phase. As you can see, there is no strict sequence in the necessary steps. Every step will result in the output of one or more documents.

One can divide the planning phase into following activities:

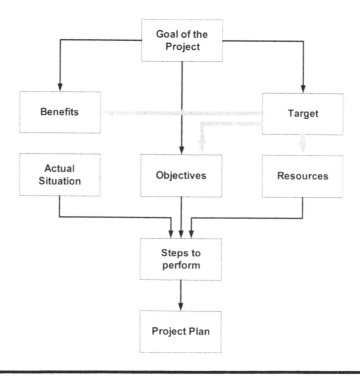

Exhibit 2. Activities in the Planning Phase

- Define the overall goal of the project
- List the benefits of the project
- Define the objectives that must be met to achieve the project's goal
- Determine the target of the project
- Analyze the actual situation
- List the steps to perform
- Identify the project plan

Goal of the Project

A directory is often a strategic project for the whole enterprise, so a proposal defining the project's goal assumes a particular importance and is typically scrutinized closely by top management. Costs aside, they want to see a clear definition of two things:

1. Goal of the directory services project
2. Metrics to determine whether the goal of the project has been achieved

An unambiguous definition of the goal helps avoid misunderstandings between the project manager and the project sponsor. Perhaps more importantly, it helps the sponsor understand the purpose of the proposed project. The proposal should also clearly define some metric for evaluating whether the goal of the project has been achieved. The sponsor surely will want to know whether the money spent for this project was a good investment. With the help of the proposal document defining these two points, both the project sponsor and the project manager should arrive at a mutually agreeable definition of the project's goal.

Benefits of the Project

Unless you are working in a pure research project, and very often even then, achieving the goal of the project will result in a benefit for your organization. This part of the planning activity explains the advantages of accomplishing the goal to management. In turn, management understands what it is buying when it agrees to invest the money required to reach the particular goal.

Objectives of the Project

To achieve the goal of the project, you need to define objectives. It is important to understand the difference between the goal and the objectives of a project. The goal is the end result achieved when the project is finished and is defined in a more general way than the objectives. Normally, a project has only one goal. To arrive at the goal, you break the project down into objectives. An objective is more specific than a goal, and a project has more than one objective. The main property of an objective is that it be measurable. The overall goal of the project is measurable in time, effort, and cost.

Because the individual objectives have to be measurable, you and the other actors involved have to agree about the appropriate metrics. This will help in avoiding misunderstandings about who has to do what and when.

The planning group will have to confer with a number of people with different roles. Again, the precise identity of those with whom you have to engage during this process depends on your environment. There are substantially three types of roles for the people involved in your project: project sponsor, management, and users. This does not mean that the sponsor and the user are different persons. On the contrary, it is very probable that the sponsor will also use the directory, and it is likely that management also assumes the role of sponsorship.

- It is a near certainty that your sponsor will want you to provide a compelling reason why she should spend money on directory services, so try to understand her perspective of what she expects your work should achieve. Note that this is not the place to address the technical aspects of the project. Indeed, the sponsor may not even understand what directory services are. Political and strategic goals should be your principal focus.

■ You will also be in contact with management. Again, you will have to understand what management wants to achieve with directory services. These goals are strategic and should define how directory services are located in your reality and set the priorities of the objectives to be achieved.

■ Finally, and most importantly, you must speak with the future users of your services. You have to understand what they expect from directory services. Here you will learn functional and technical goals. There are two types of users of directory services: technicians and end users. The technicians include the persons administering the directory server and those who are responsible for writing applications using the directory server. End users include the persons supplying data, such as human-resource people filling in new records, and the end users, who finally connect with an application to get the information they need.

Target of the Project

The target of the project describes who in the end will benefit from the project. The target can also be called the end user. You describe the target to understand the importance of the whole project. Note that it is not simply a matter of counting the number of persons who will benefit from the result of the project. You will have to measure the improvement in the performance of the target users and then calculate the benefit the enterprise will gain from this improved performance.

Note that the target is not limited to physical persons. The project also will benefit applications. Thus, part of the planning phase is to understand what applications will use your directory data. Again, you will have to see where these applications are finally located. Gaining a clear picture of where your data could be needed is not an easy task, and it is essential to maintain a very tight contact with the users. Sometimes it is up to you to discover what applications could benefit from your directory. The more potential consumers you find, the less likely it is that you will have surprises later on. And the greater the number of applications that will use your directory, the more your work will be appreciated. It is a good idea to make a list of potential application types and then check to see whether these applications are actually being used in your enterprise. Examples of candidates are mail systems, calendar systems, room booking, help-desk applications, phone books, and every type of service using authentication services.

Analysis of the Actual Situation

A further activity to be done is the analysis of the actual situation. The overall goal defines where you want to be tomorrow; this step shows where you are today. The objectives show the status of individual stations.

Because we are speaking of a project of data management, the first thing to understand is the data to be managed. That is, you need to know which repositories you actually have in place. It may be there is just one or more directories in place. Indeed, this is often the case, and then you have to understand the quality of the data in the directories. This means that you need to understand whether this data can be used in the project, including a means of controlling consistency between the individual data sources.

Analysis of the Data to Be Held in the Directory

Because directory services are handling data, an important point you need to consider is what kind of data and what kind of information your directory should hold. Do not confuse this step with the data design you will make in the next step of the project. Here, you simply need to understand whether the directory should hold the data in question or not. What you have to do is decide whether the directory is suitable for holding the data in question.

Data appropriate to be held in the directory includes the following:

- Data that is accessed from more than one application
- Data that is accessed from more than one physical location
- Data read more frequently than it is written
- Data that can be expressed in attribute form, for example, sn = Voglmaier

Data not suitable for the directory includes:

- Large, unstructured data objects like images, video, or binaries
- Frequently changing data

Other data stores can be relational databases, file systems, file servers, ftp servers, http servers, etc.

Steps to Perform

Using the objectives you have defined, your analysis of the actual situation, and your knowledge of the actors involved in the project, you will break each objective down into a series of individual steps to perform. As you can surmise from Exhibit 3, the steps to perform

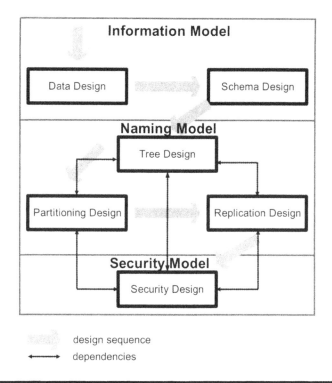

Exhibit 3. Overview of the Directory-Design Process

depend on the actual situations, the objectives, and the resources available. Feedback from the individual steps can affect nearly all activities discussed until now and can even change some of them. These steps are indeed the first confrontation with reality.

Project Plan

The last action in the planning phase is the production of a project plan. You produce the plan using all of the information you have gathered. The most important part of the project plan is the Gantt chart. The Gantt chart assigns the steps to be performed by the different teams in the project and puts the steps in a timeline specifying a date when the actions must be completed.

What your project plan will look like depends on a number of factors, including the number of people participating in the individual work groups and the budget at your disposal. It will also depend on your reality (factors such as dimensions of network, design of network, number of clients, number of servers, etc.) and the standards on your site. Furthermore, it will depend on the complexity of the directory you will develop, such as the amount of data, the type of data, how the data is connected, and similar factors. Finally, it will depend on which departments in your enterprise are involved in this project, the strategic importance of the directory, and also the dimension of your enterprise. A plan for a project involving one little department will be vastly different than a plan for a whole enterprise operating in many countries spanning different continents.

Once you have all the information at hand, you will have a very extensive document. At this point, it is worth considering whether, instead of handling a monolithic project, you should break the whole project down into a number of subprojects. Subprojects are much easier to handle and help you in a natural way to develop strategic milestones, thus keeping your timelines under control. Furthermore, it permits you to develop working prototypes quickly that you can show your sponsors to show how work is proceeding.

Design of Directory Services

Do you remember Chapter 3, where we spoke about the models standing behind LDAP? Directory services implement these models. It is the design process that breathes reality into the concepts contained in the models. Consequently, you will find the same conceptual structure that we encountered in the models presented in Chapter 3.

Exhibit 3 puts together the activities necessary for the design of a directory. The design steps are grouped together in their corresponding model context. Exhibit 3 proposes a way to proceed in the design process, as indicated by the large gray lines. Every design step is based on the result of the previous one. Note, however, that the single design activities are not independent of each other. For example, the security design — despite being based on the outcome of the tree design — itself has an impact on the tree design. The dotted lines indicate dependencies between the individual phases in the design process.

The following subsections briefly treat each of the various design steps in the directory design process illustrated in Exhibit 3.

Data Design

This is the most important step in the design process because it deals with what the directory is all about: the data. In this step, you decide which data you will put into the directory. When designing the directory data, you will analyze a set of information about the data. The following points need to be clarified:

- Who uses the data
- Who produces the data
- Who "owns" the data
- Who should have access to the data
- The type of the data

Schema Design

The schema defines the rules to obey when putting data into the directory. It defines which data can be put into the directory and the format of that data. It also defines how comparisons should be executed in the case of queries. Take, for example, the case of phone numbers. Note that 1-800-2939-2636 and 1 800 2939 2636 are the same phone numbers in two different notations. The schema defines what a phone number looks like and when two phone numbers have to be considered as equal. In this example, the schema would define that a phone number can be divided into smaller pieces and that these pieces can be limited by hyphens or white spaces. It would furthermore specify that hyphens and space shall not be considered when making comparisons between values.

Tree Design

In this step, you lay down the logical structure of your namespace. A directory tree helps in managing large amounts of data by dividing it into smaller units that can be connected to each other in a hierarchical structure. This type of structure helps in locating data in the directory and improves performance during search functions. The decisions you make in tree design will have an enormous impact on the maintenance of the directory. The next two steps, partitioning design and replication design, can benefit from a good tree design.

Partitioning Design

Directories often hold a lot of data and, consequently, may be subjected to a heavy load of user requests. You might consider dividing the directory into smaller, more manageable pieces, with each located on a server of its own. This type of design also helps bring the data closer to the consumer. For example, assume that you have two departments, one in the United States and one in Japan. Each department has its own records. Partitioning the data would allow you to put the Japanese data onto the LAN where the Japanese users are and the U.S. data onto the U.S. LAN. Both databases would be closer to the data consumer. Furthermore, this would give you the flexibility to impose different policies for data maintenance. The requirement could also allow the use of different administrative structures or different security standards for the different partitions.

Replication Design

The same considerations that might lead you to consider partitioning as a design strategy apply also to replication. Indeed replication can be an alternative to partitioning. Replication addresses the availability of the directory in much the same way as partitioning. The objective could be to get the directory closer to the data consumer, but it could also be to increase throughput in heavily loaded machines. Replication also has the added value of keeping the directory available in the event of software or hardware failures. Replication provides a redundant data design and consequently requires mechanisms to keep the duplicated data in sync.

Security Design

In this step, you will treat a lot of issues. It involves first assuring that every user can do exactly what he is supposed to do. That means that you need to know exactly which actions which user may perform on what data. The next step is to protect the conversation between client and server in the correct way. If you set up replication or chaining, i.e., architectures that require conversations between servers, you have to protect these conversations as well. You must also think about physical security of the LDAP data configuration files. Therefore, you need to know exactly who has access to the server on which you are running your installation.

Let us now look at the various design activities in a bit more detail. As you have already noticed, these design activities are by no means independent of each other. Indeed, they are strongly interconnected. We will see these dependencies in the following sections.

As explained at the beginning of this chapter, there are a number of documents that fully describe additional procedures. At the end of this chapter, you will find a list of documents where you can find more information.

Data Design

In this step, you will reap the benefit of the work you did in the planning phase. This is where you put to use the information you have painstakingly gathered.

What you have now is a list of data that you will put into your directory. The data has one or more data sources and one or more applications using the data. Because the most important job of the directory is to service applications, it is important to know which applications need what data and where the data comes from. A useful approach is to produce a matrix for each application. The matrix should hold the data name, the data type, the information source, and the data source that has to be considered authoritative. The data type is meant as a human-language description — such as password, e-mail,

Application: Phone Book Administration

Row	Data	Type	Source	Source Owner
1	SurName	String	Admin Software	HR

13	NT Password	Password	NT SysAdmin	IT Sysadmin

21	Phone Number	Phone Number	TELCO SW	Engineering

Exhibit 4. Matrix for Data-Design Process

Row	Application	App Owner
1	NT SysAdmin	IT Sysadmin
1	HP System Admin	IT Sysadmin
1	SUN System Admin	IT Sysadmin
1	Phone Admin	Engineering

Row	Application	App Owner
31	Web Pages HR	WEB TEAM
31	Phone Accounting	Engineering

Row	Application	App Owner
21	PhoneBook	WEB TEAM
21	Phone Accounting	Engineering

Exhibit 5. Mapping between Applications and Application Owner

phone number — and not a C-style type declaration such as int, char, etc. Exhibit 4 shows an example of such a matrix.

A mapping between the application and application owner as shown in Exhibit 5 is also very useful. You will then know who owns the data and who owns the application using this data. Both are partners who should be involved in the data design process.

Once you have documented all applications in this way, you can put this information together in another matrix describing what data the directory should hold. In this matrix, you will list the data name and data type along with the following information:

- Applications that put the data in
- Owner of the data, i.e., the entity that is responsible for maintaining the data

- Whether the data is publicly readable
- Whether a human user can modify personal data (e.g., password, "yes"; salary, "no")
- Who can update the data

Schema Design

Recall from Chapter 3 our discussion of the concept of a "directory schema" in the information model. The directory schema is a set of rules describing what can be stored in a directory and how information should be treated. This is achieved by the definition of attribute types and object classes. The attribute-type definitions explain how the data values are represented and how comparisons are made. The object classes are a set of attributes that frequently correspond to real-life objects. The object class further describes what attribute types are required and what attribute types are optional. It also gives a tool for retrieving a subset of an object class.

Schema design has two goals: The first is the mapping of the data defined in the previous step (data design) into attributes. The second is to put the attributes together into object classes.

One possibility is to use an existing schema. If there is no existing schema to fit your requirements, you can try to extend an existing schema. The last possibility is to create a new schema for the application at hand. If you write a new schema or extend an existing schema, you should document what you have done and eventually think about publishing the extensions you made.

You can get existing schemas from a number of sources. First of all, you will examine existing standards. You can get a standard schema from the site of IETF in the form of RFC 2256, "A Summary of the X.500(96) User Schema for Use with LDAPv3." Vendor-supplied schemas are another possible resource. Nearly every LDAP implementation is shipped with a number of standard schemas. For example, OpenLDAP gives you a number of schemas that you will find in a configuration directory called "schema." You should check to see if you can use one of these existing schemas. Your directory application also may be delivered with a schema of its own. Whatever the source, try to use a standard schema.

If your needs do not fit into an existing schema, you should consider modifying and extending one that comes close to meeting your needs. It is not recommended to modify existing object classes, because this could cause inconsistencies with your directory application and directory clients. You should instead subclass an existing class. For details about the process of subclassing, see Chapter 3, where the information model is explained.

The last possibility is to create your own schema. While the best approach is to use a standard schema or to extend an existing schema, there are situations where you really do need your own schema. However, be aware that you risk losing compatibility between your LDAP application and every other LDAP server. Your LDAP clients must also know about your proprietary schema.

Here are some considerations that you should take into account if you want to define new attribute types or new object classes:

- Use a consistent naming schema for all extensions. This helps future application programmers who may want to use your schema.
- Prefix your new object classes or attribute-type names with your project name or organization name. Because the LDAP namespace is flat, this avoids name collisions.
- Try to use meaningful names without making them too long. This avoids a lot of unnecessary typing and, even more importantly, typos.
- Get official object identifiers for your new objects. You can learn more about this at http://www.alvestrand.no.

Tree Design

In the previous step (schema design), you decided how to build object classes from attributes to project your data into the directory. In this step, you must structure your object classes to build up the directory information tree (DIT). The DIT defines the namespace where all the objects of your directory reside. The definition of the namespace helps the directory server to decide whether a client can get information from his directory or whether he should contact another directory server.

In designing the tree, you have to make the following decisions:

- Choose a suffix as a root for the DIT
- Choose a branching policy
- Choose a naming policy

We will look at each of these steps in detail, but first let us consider the importance of the namespace. The design of the DIT strongly influences the following points:

- *Data organization*: A good tree layout facilitates organization of the data, helps your users to browse the tree, and returns queries faster.
- *Replication, partitioning, and access control*: We will have to decide about replication and partitioning a bit later. However, we lay a

foundation for these future decisions when we design the directory tree. In both data replication and data partitioning, the boundaries between the single parts of the directory can only be at certain points within the namespace. The same is true for access control. It is easier to control access to a completely separated subtree than to have a tree where confidential data is mixed with public data. Furthermore, you may wish that a user or an application does not even see that there is additional private data available.

■ *Maintenance*: Changes in the tree are not infrequent. A well-organized tree will facilitate later changes.

■ *Application support*: The DIT must also support the directory applications using the directory.

Choosing a Root for the Directory Information Tree

The first step in designing the tree is to choose a root for the DIT. This root is also called a "directory suffix" or a "root distinguished name" (root DN). In most directory server implementations, it is possible to define more than one root DN in one directory server. During the installation, some implementations of directory servers configure more than one root DN. For example, the i-Planet directory server uses one root DN for the directory and one root DN for the administration of the directory server itself.

There are three different naming conventions you can use:

1. The domainComponent attribute, where you split your domain name into its individual components:

dc = bmw, dc = de

2. The domain name assigned to the enterprise:

o = bmw.de

3. The traditional X.500 naming conventions:

o = bmw, c = de

The choice of a naming convention depends on your actual situation. You may be constrained in your choice if there are already directory-enabled applications using one of these possibilities. Choosing the last one is normally a good idea because it guarantees compatibility with the X.500 standard. LDAP works with any of the three naming conventions. However, regardless of the naming convention you choose, there are things that you should bear in mind when choosing a root DN:

- The root DN has to be unique within the range of its visibility. If you are working inside the intranet of an enterprise, the name must be unique within the companywide intranet. If the directory services are meant for use over the Internet, the name must be unique throughout the worldwide Internet.
- Once chosen, the root DN should not be changed. If the root DN changes, you have to change your whole directory tree and all applications using the directory services. In a large organization, this could take months.
- The root DN should be not too long and it should be easy to remember. Your users and your application engineers will be happy, and the applications will be less error prone.

When the directory server receives a query from a client, the server decides whether it is competent to answer the query. A well-designed DIT facilitates this decision. Now all the server has to do is take the DN from the request and see whether it exists within one of the namespaces defined by the root DNs. If it is beneath one of the root DNs, then the directory server knows that it holds information useful for the query. If it does not, the directory server's response depends on its configuration. It could direct the client to another server, or it could simply answer with an error code.

Branching the Directory Tree

The question is, should you use a flat namespace or a hierarchical schema? It is a good idea to keep your tree as flat as possible, such as the completely flat schema depicted in Exhibit 17 in Chapter 3. This namespace design has several advantages. First of all, it keeps things simple. A complicated hierarchy is more difficult to understand and is consequently more difficult to use and to maintain than a flat configuration. The flatter the directory tree, the easier it is for application designers to use it. Another reason to keep the hierarchy flat is that a flat namespace reduces the probability that the tree will undergo changes later on. A flat namespace also tends to have shorter relative distinguished names (RDN). The shorter the RDNs, the easier they are to remember.

So why would anyone ever use a hierarchical schema? There are several reasons, and we will encounter some of these arguments again in the later sections of this chapter.

- *Administrative purposes*: If your enterprise is spread among several countries, then data maintenance, data backup, and statistics can be done locally. The local competence can impose branching decisions, as shown in Exhibit 18 in Chapter 3.

- *Partitioning decisions*: When the amount of data is so high that you wish to distribute your data over more machines to improve performance, you need an opportune branch point to do so.
- *Replication decisions*: You maintain your data centrally, but you want the option of replicating some of the data to local applications where the data is needed. The reason may be slow communication lines or dial-up connections.
- *Access control and security questions*: Security issues are different for different types of data. Some data is appropriate for public consumption, and some data is proprietary and should be visible only to a defined group of people. You can differentiate security among data classes by branching up your tree.

The most important consideration is to design the tree so that there will be as few changes as possible. So avoid designing a tree based upon your actual organigram, if possible. Organigrams are subject to frequent changes, and after each reorganization you will have to redesign you namespace and change all applications accessing your directory server.

Partitioning

The previous section explained how to put the entries together to build the directory tree. In the planning phase, you may only have a rough idea of how many of these entries your directory is going to hold, and this number can be considerable. If it is too high, performance will suffer. The remedy is to distribute the data on more than one directory server, and that is what this section is about.

As mentioned previously, the partitioning design is closely related to replication design. Furthermore, both partitioning and replication can modify the decisions you made in designing the directory tree. Arguments that let you decide to partition or replicate the directory are nearly the same. Another point that is related to partitioning and replication is physical design, but this is beyond the scope of this chapter.

As we have seen in Chapter 5, partitioning is the division of your directory into more parts, while replication copies a part or all of the directory onto one or more other servers. These parts can be on the same machine or on different computers on your network. Partitioning of the directory has several goals:

- *Scalability*: Directories can contain a few thousand entries or several million. The ability to distribute the entries over several servers provides a greater degree of scalability.
- *Load balancing*: Distributing the entries over several servers prevents overloads on the server as well as the network.

- *Local management:* Moving the entries to the local networks where the entries are maintained reduces network traffic and enhances performance of the local directory.

Partitioning of the directory is called for when:

- Number of entries is too high
- Network traffic to the directory is too high
- Not all of the data is equally used
- Some line segments become overloaded

Number of Entries Is Too High

If the database gets too big to be held within a single partition, you should divide it. You may wonder, "What is 'too big'?" First you have the computer, where the disk space is one limiting factor. Another limiting factor is the directory server. See the documentation delivered with your software about the upper limit of entries your server can hold. Another limitation is backup time. When it takes ten hours to back up your system and only 1 kB of data has changed, it may be worthwhile to consider partitioning the database.

Network Traffic to the Directory Is Too High

Even if both the hardware and the server can handle the amount of data, the traffic caused by the directory can penalize the part of the network where your directory server is installed. Depending on the access frequency of the individual parts, dividing the data over two subnetworks could help to increase network performance.

Not All of the Data Is Equally Used

Your directory may contain data that is used frequently by one application and infrequently by another. Partitioning of the directory may enable you to put the frequently used data on a directory server that is closer to the application that uses the data. Backup time is another consideration. Separating static data from data that is updated frequently could save you backup time, because you will reduce the frequency of backups for the nearly static data.

Some Line Segments Become Overloaded

If your company has a high-speed network distributed throughout the enterprise, overloaded line segments will not be an issue for you.

However, not everyone is so lucky. Consider the case of an international enterprise having offices in the United States, the United Kingdom, and Germany, with each office maintaining its personnel records in a central directory. Assume that the connection between two of these nodes is not a high-speed connection or, even worse, is a dial-up connection available only a few hours a day. In such cases, it may convenient to partition the directory and create a separate directory for each office.

Partitioning and Namespace

As mentioned earlier, partitioning design and tree design are not independent design phases. You can partition the directory only at branch points, which means that you can only move entire subtrees to new partitions from the main directory. See Exhibit 6 for an example of valid partitions. The accounting subtree and the human resources subtree are split up from the original partition, and two new partitions are created. Exhibit 7 instead is an example of invalid partitioning. You cannot put the accounting branch point in a separate partition because "accounting" no longer contains the subtree people and, therefore, there is a hole between people and ldap_abc.

Replication

Like partitioning, replication design can affect the design of the directory tree. So after deciding on a replication strategy, you may need to rethink some of the decisions that you made when you first designed the directory tree. You may also need to rethink some decisions you made in partitioning. However, a word of warning: Currently there is no standard regarding replication. In all of the design phases, it is recommended that you consult the documentation

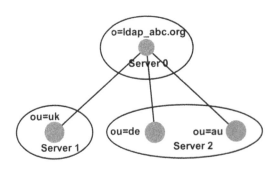

Exhibit 6. Organization of ldap_abc with Two Partitions, One for Human Resources and One for Accounting

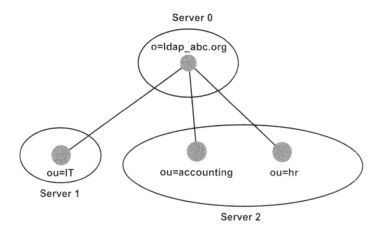

Server 0

o=ldap_abc.org

ou=IT

Server 1

ou=accounting   ou=hr

Server 2

Exhibit 7.   Example of an Invalid Partition

shipped with the product you are using. In this step, it is absolutely required. This includes verifying that the software actually supports the features you need, e.g., multimaster replication, scheduling of replications, etc.

The goals of replication are:

- *High availability*: Replication of the directory increases the availability of your directory services.
- *High performance*: Replication places directory services as close as possible to your clients, thus enhancing performance.
- *Load balancing*: Distributing the entries over multiple servers prevents overloading of the server as well as the network.
- *Local management*: Moving the entries to the local networks where the entries are maintained reduces network traffic and enhances performance of the local directory.

Replication of the directory is called for when:

- A request is made for its partitioning
- Network traffic to the directory is too high
- Some line segments become overloaded
- Network would benefit from a backup system to guarantee availability of the directory in the event of hardware/software failures

Network Traffic to the Directory Is Too High

Even if both the hardware and the server can handle the amount of data, the traffic caused by the directory can penalize the part of the network where your directory server is installed. Depending on the access frequency of the individual parts, dividing the data over two subnetworks could help to increase network performance.

Some Line Segments Become Overloaded

If your company has a high-speed network distributed throughout the enterprise, overloaded line segments will not be an issue for you. However, not everyone is so lucky. Consider the case of an international enterprise having offices in the United States, the United Kingdom, and Germany, with each office maintaining its personnel records in a central directory. Assume that the connection between two of these nodes is not a high-speed connection or, even worse, is a dial-up connection available only a few hours a day. In such cases, it may convenient to replicate the directory and create a separate directory for each office.

Replication and Namespace

Similar to partitioning, replication design and tree design are not independent design phases. Another similarity is that you can replicate the directory only at branch points. This means that you can only move entire subtrees to new replications from the main directory. See the previous section on partitioning for more details. Note that there is a lack of standards in replication, so you have to look at your server's documentation for the unit of replication. For example, the SUN ONE directory server does not allow you to replicate a subtree because the smallest unit of replication is the database.

Security Design

Security design is an important issue in an Internet environment, but it is also important in an intranet environment. At the first glance, the reason may not be obvious. However, when you store data about persons, you assume a legal responsibility to protect that data.

Attacks against your data stores are not limited to those who are outside your enterprise. They can also be initiated from the inside. Such attacks are not necessarily the work of malign hackers. Data can also be compromised by careless users who do not have much concern about security issues. Imagine an employee who, instead of making a query against the directory to get the data needed for a commodity, just prints out everything, reads the interesting data, and throws away the output. If this printed output is recycled without being shredded, you can imagine the potential security issues.

Even if the security aspects are sufficient for the intranet, at some point you may decide to make the directory available on the extranet also. If you already have a good security design in place, you will not have to change much if you decide to make the directory visible from the outside.

When designing the security aspects of the directory, you need to decide on a strategy to protect the data stored in the directory. To do this, you need to know who can access the data and how. Again, in this step you will base your work on preceding steps. You have to know who owns the data, who maintains the data, who should be authorized to update the data, and who should be authorized to consult the directory.

Security design covers three arguments:

- *Authentication*: Verifies that the user is the person she claims to be. This could range from simple authentication to complicated procedures involving the use of certificates.
- *Authorization*: Ensures that the authenticated user can access only the data she is authorized to access
- *Protection of the data*: Guarantees that data traveling on the network cannot be read or modified. The level of security depends on your particular requirements. You can let all of the traffic on your network travel in clear, or you can encrypt it.

Authentication

As mentioned previously, authentication is the activity required to control who is trying to contact you. To understand which authentication scheme to put in place, you have to understand which type of data travels on the line. Therefore, you should take the information you have produced in data design and add on the sensitivity of the data. You may produce a further matrix of data mapped against the sensitivity of the data. You could use security levels as described later in the authentication scheme for your directory server implementation. A frequent classification of levels is as follows:

- Nonsecurity — otherwise classified as data in the public domain
- Data not in the public domain that requires user credentials for access (intended as DN and password)
- Sensitive data that requires user credentials plus encrypted communication
- Highly sensitive data that requires user credentials, encrypted communication, plus use of certificates

In this design phase, the implementation of the directory server you are using again comes into play. And again it may be that in this phase, you will discover that you cannot work with only one directory server. You may need to put some of the more sensitive data in a special partition, because your directory server cannot handle different security mechanisms on the same partition. For example, the implementation you are using may not allow you to use certificates for a subtree of your directory server only. Therefore, you have to put this subtree on a partition of its own. In this phase you may also be obliged to review the tree design. Otherwise, you could end up with an illegal partition.

Authorization

This is the step where you design who can do what with which data. Again you will pull out the matrix you planned at the very first step of data design. You could create a new matrix at this point that contains the data plus the corresponding access rights. At the beginning of this design phase be as restrictive as possible. If, however, you should see that some functionality that the directory server has to offer is not possible, you can relax your security restrictions a little. Once you have documented your results, you should map your configuration onto the directory server's configuration mechanism.

Protection of the Data

Until now we have protected the conversation between client and server, we have configured who can do what, and yet the most important piece may be still unprotected. We still have to protect the physical files on repository and also the configuration files. All these files have to be protected against unauthorized access. Frequently people put in complicated security mechanisms to protect the conversation between client and server, but they forget to protect physical access both to the server and to its configuration files. In order to understand your requirements, you have to understand who besides the administrators of the directory (if anyone) has access to the server the directory is installed on. Consequently, you have to protect the data and configuration files. It is, anyway, always good practice to configure a special user as owner of the directory server including the data and configuration files. Do not give to another user or group access rights to these files if not absolutely required. And again produce documentation of this step; it helps you later to understand and remember why you made this decision.

Conclusion

In this chapter you should have learned how to proceed in setting up a new directory server implementation. We did not discuss installation and configuration questions, but we did discuss the actions that precede these steps. This chapter, obviously, is far from complete because there is only so much space in this book. However, as promised at the beginning of this chapter, I will now show you where to research and find more details about directory server design.

First, I would recommend that you look at the Internet Web sites of the major players in the directory server arena. Two of them are Sun Microsystems and Novell. Sun delivers excellent documentation with its SUN ONE directory server. Following are a few publications of the SUN ONE server:

- "Getting Started Guide"
- "Deployment Guide"
- "Installation and Tuning Guide"
- "Administration Guide"

You can find these publications by going to http://www.sun.com, clicking on documentation, software products, SUN ONE. You can download these publications at no cost. Even if you do not use the SUN ONE server, you will learn much from them.

At the Novell site (http://www.novell.com), the product page (eDirectory) offers a number of good white papers.

Another link I would recommend that you look at is: http://www. kingsmountain.com/ldapRoadmap.shtml. Here you will get a number of useful and updated links to interesting resources.

The book *Understanding and Deploying Directory Services* is dedicated nearly entirely to the design of directory services and contains a number of case studies. (Tim Howes, Mark Smith, and Gordon Good, *Understanding and Deploying Directory Services*, Macmillan Network Architecture and Development Series).

RFCs are also a very good source of information. They are, however, not easy to read for newcomers. The RFCs worth mentioning are:

- RFC1562: Naming Guidelines for the AARNet X.500 Directory Service
- RFC1617: Naming and Structuring Guidelines for X.500 Directory Pilots
- RFC1943: Building an X.500 Directory Service in the U.S.

Appendix A

Acronyms

ACI	access control instruction
ACL	access control list
ANSI	American National Standards Institute
ASCII	American standard code for information interchange
BER	basic encoding rules
BNF	Backus Naur form
CCITT	Consultative Committee in International Telephony and Telegraphy
DAP	Directory Access Protocol
DARPA	Defense Advanced Research Projects Agency
DCA	Defense Communication Agency
DCE	distributed computing environment
DIT	directory information tree
DN	distinguished name
DSA	directory server agent
DSML	directory services markup language
DSE	DSA-specific entry
ERP	enterprise resource planning
FTP	File Transfer Protocol
HTTP	Hypertext Transfer Protocol
IANA	Internet-assigned number authority
IETF	Internet Engineering Task Force
IP	Internet Protocol
ISO	International Standards Organization
JNDI	Java Naming and Directory Interfaces
LBER	lightweight basic encoding rules
LDAP	Lightweight Directory Access Protocol
LDIF	LDAP data interchange format
MIB	management information base
OSF	open systems foundation

OSI	Open Systems Interconnection
PDC	primary domain controller
PDU	protocol data unit
PHP	PHP hypertext processor
RDN	relative distinct name
RFC	request for comments
RPC	remote procedure call
SAPI	server application programming interface
SASL	simple authentication and security layer
SDK	software development kit
SLA	service level agreement
SMTP	Simple Mail Transfer Protocol
SNMP	Simple Network-Management Protocol
SSL	secure sockets layer
TLS	transport layer security
TCP	Transfer Control Protocol
TCP/IP	TCP + IP Protocol stack
UDP	User Defined Protocol
UTF-8	Unicode Transformation Format-8

Appendix B

LDAP Requests for Comments and Drafts

LDAP RFCs

This section provides a list of RFCs that describe the LDAP protocol and its extensions. All RFCs are available from the IETF Web site (http://www.ietf.org/rfc.html). You can also get an up-to-date list of all available RFCs at http://www.ietf.org/iesg/1rfc_index.txt. The Internet FAQ Consortium has a very useful Web site (http://isc.faqs.org), which offers FAQs, Internet RFCs, and Internet-Drafts (available in PDF format). This site also offers a complete and updated list of RFCs. Both sites also offer search engines to search for the RFC addressing the subject you are interested in. We will discuss the RFCs that address the LDAP protocol.

This section is divided into two parts. The first part shows you the RFCs relevant for work with LDAP, the ones defining the actual standard used. I have described these RFCs for your convenience. The second part lists all RFCs relevant for LDAP. I attached this list because it is interesting to see how the concepts have evolved over time; the list will help you to better understand what is happening behind the scenes and how the LDAP protocol got to its actual definition.

The list reflects all RFCs at the time this book was written and may not be complete because RFCs are subject to continuous update. You will need to look at the RFC site from time to time to get the updated version of the RFC list.

Comments about the Most Important LDAP RFCs

RFC3377: "Lightweight Directory Access Protocol (v3): Technical Specification": Defines the set of RFCs comprising the Directory Access Protocol v3.

RFC2251: "Lightweight Directory Access Protocol (v3)": Defines the protocol itself, particularly the specification of what really travels on the wire. This is the heart of the LDAP RFCs.

RFC2252: "Lightweight Directory Access Protocol (v3): Attribute Syntax Definitions": Describes the syntax of attribute definitions and contains a list of attributes a server should implement. It classifies the different attribute types that LDAP knows and lists the standard matching rules to use in comparisons. It also describes how the attribute values should be encoded into strings to be transmitted over the wire.

RFC2253: "Lightweight Directory Access Protocol (v3): UTF-8 String Representation of Distinguished Names": The LDAP protocol transmits messages in the form of strings; however, Distinguished Names can contain characters that have to be converted before transmission. Examples are reserved characters or language-specific characters. This RFC describes how Distinguished Names are converted into string and how strings are converted back into Distinguished Names.

RFC2254: "The String Representation of LDAP Search Filters": This RFC replaces RFC1960, extending the string filter definition. It defines the syntax of a filter expression and how to convert a filter in a string expression.

RFC2255: "The LDAP URL Format": The URL format of an LDAP search can be used in every Web browser. This URL defines the syntax of the URL format. It also defines how a client should parse and resolve the LDAP URL to a search expression.

RFC2256: "A Summary of the X.500 User Schema for Use with LDAPv3": LDAP inherits a large part of the schema of X.500. This RFC defines a set of object classes and attribute types that should be implemented in a directory server.

RFC2829: "Authentication Methods for LDAP": The first LDAP RFCs did not specify anything about authentication. This RFC specifies which authentication methods should be implemented in an LDAP server.

RFC2830: "Lightweight Directory Access Protocol (v3): Extension for Transport Layer Security": TLS is defined as a so-called extended operation in LDAP. This RFC describes how to establish a TLS session using the LDAP protocol.

List of LDAP RFCs

■ 1107 Plan for Internet Directory Services. K.R. Sollins. Jul-01-1989. (Format: TXT=51773 bytes) (Status: Informational)

■ 1202 Directory Assistance Service. M.T. Rose. Feb-01-1991. (Format: TXT=21645 bytes) (Status: Informational)

■ 1249 DIXIE Protocol Specification. T. Howes, M. Smith, B. Beecher. Aug-01-1991. (Format: TXT=20028 bytes) (Also RFC1202) (Status: Informational)

■ 1274 The COSINE and Internet X.500 Schema. P. Barker, S. Kille. November 1991. (Format: TXT=92827 bytes) (Status: Proposed Standard)

■ 1275 Replication Requirements to Provide an Internet Directory Using X.500. S.E. Hardcastle-Kille. November 1991. (Format: TXT=4616, PS=83736, PDF=62498 bytes) (Status: Informational)

■ 1276 Replication and Distributed Operations Extensions to Provide an Internet Directory Using X.500. S.E. Hardcastle-Kille. November 1991. (Format: TXT=33731, PS=217170 bytes) (Status: Proposed Standard)

■ 1279 X.500 and Domains. S.E. Hardcastle-Kille. November 1991. (Format: TXT=26669, PS=170029 bytes) (Status: Experimental)

■ 1292 A Catalog of Available X.500 Implementations. R. Lang, R. Wright. January 1992. (Format: TXT=129468 bytes) (Obsoleted by RFC1632) (Status: Informational)

■ 1308 Executive Introduction to Directory Services Using the X.500 Protocol. C. Weider, J. Reynolds. March 1992. (Format: TXT=9392 bytes) (Also FYI0013) (Status: Informational)

■ 1309 Technical Overview of Directory Services Using the X.500 Protocol. C. Weider, J. Reynolds, S. Heker. March 1992. (Format: TXT=35694 bytes) (Also FYI0014) (Status: Informational)

■ 1330 Recommendations for the Phase I Deployment of OSI Directory Services (X.500) and OSI Message Handling Services (X.400) within the ESNET Community. ESCC X.500/X.400 Task Force, ESnet Site Coordinating Committee (ESCC), Energy Sciences Network (ESnet). May 1992. (Format: TXT=192925 bytes) (Status: Informational)

■ 1430 A Strategic Plan for Deploying an Internet X.500 Directory Service. S. Hardcastle-Kille, E. Huizer, V. Cerf, R. Hobby, S. Kent. February 1993. (Format: TXT=47587 bytes) (Status: Informational)

■ 1484 Using the OSI Directory to Achieve User-Friendly Naming (OSI-DS 24 (v1.2)). S. Hardcastle-Kille. July 1993. (Format: TXT=48974 bytes) (Obsoleted by RFC1781, RFC3494) (Status: Experimental)

■ 1485 A String Representation of Distinguished Names (OSI-DS 23 (v5)). S. Hardcastle-Kille. July 1993. (Format: TXT=11158 bytes) (Obsoleted by RFC1779, RFC3494) (Status: Proposed Standard)

- 1487 X.500 Lightweight Directory Access Protocol. W. Yeong, T. Howes, S. Kille. July 1993. (Format: TXT=44947 bytes) (Obsoleted by RFC1777, RFC3494) (Status: Proposed Standard)
- 1488 The X.500 String Representation of Standard Attribute Syntaxes. T. Howes, S. Kille, W. Yeong, C. Robbins. July 1993. (Format: TXT=17182 bytes) (Obsoleted by RFC1778) (Status: Proposed Standard)
- 1558 A String Representation of LDAP Search Filters. T. Howes. December 1993. (Format: TXT=5239 bytes) (Obsoleted by RFC1960) (Status: Informational)
- 1562 Naming Guidelines for the AARNet X.500 Directory Service. G. Michaelson, M. Prior. December 1993. (Format: TXT=6884 bytes) (Status: Informational)
- 1564 DSA Metrics (OSI-DS 34 (v3)). P. Barker, R. Hedberg. January 1994. (Format: TXT=46205 bytes) (Status: Informational)
- 1567 X.500 Directory Monitoring MIB. G. Mansfield, S. Kille. January 1994. (Format: TXT=33527 bytes) (Obsoleted by RFC2605) (Status: Proposed Standard)
- 1608 Representing IP Information in the X.500 Directory. T. Johannsen, G. Mansfield, M. Kosters, S. Sataluri. March 1994. (Format: TXT=40269 bytes) (Status: Experimental)
- 1609 Charting Networks in the X.500 Directory. G. Mansfield, T. Johannsen, M. Knopper. March 1994. (Format: TXT=30044 bytes) (Status: Experimental)
- 1617 Naming and Structuring Guidelines for X.500 Directory Pilots. P. Barker, S. Kille, T. Lenggenhager. May 1994. (Format: TXT=56739 bytes) (Obsoletes RFC1384) (Status: Informational)
- 1632 A Revised Catalog of Available X.500 Implementations. A. Getchell, S. Sataluri, Eds. May 1994. (Format: TXT=124111 bytes) (Obsoletes RFC1292) (Obsoleted by RFC2116) (Status: Informational)
- 1684 Introduction to White Pages Services Based on X.500. P. Jurg. August 1994. (Format: TXT=22985 bytes) (Status: Informational)
- 1777 Lightweight Directory Access Protocol. W. Yeong, T. Howes, S. Kille. March 1995. (Format: TXT=45459 bytes) (Obsoletes RFC1487) (Obsoleted by RFC3494) (Status: Historic)
- 1778 The String Representation of Standard Attribute Syntaxes. T. Howes, S. Kille, W. Yeong, C. Robbins. March 1995. (Format: TXT=19053 bytes) (Obsoletes RFC1488) (Obsoleted by RFC3494) (Updated by RFC2559) (Status: Historic)
- 1779 A String Representation of Distinguished Names. S. Kille. March 1995. (Format: TXT=12429 bytes) (Obsoletes RFC1485) (Obsoleted by RFC2253, RFC3494) (Status: Historic)
- 1781 Using the OSI Directory to Achieve User-Friendly Naming. S. Kille. March 1995. (Format: TXT=47129 bytes) (Obsoletes RFC1484) (Obsoleted by RFC3494) (Status: Historic)

- 1798 Connection-less Lightweight X.500 Directory Access Protocol. A. Young. June 1995. (Format: TXT=18548 bytes) (Obsoleted by RFC3352) (Status: Historic)
- 1801 MHS Use of the X.500 Directory to Support MHS Routing. S. Kille. June 1995. (Format: TXT=156462 bytes) (Status: Experimental)
- 1802 Introducing Project Long Bud: Internet Pilot Project for the Deployment of X.500 Directory Information in Support of X.400 Routing. H. Alvestrand, K. Jordan, S. Langlois, J. Romaguera. June 1995. (Format: TXT=24637 bytes) (Status: Informational)
- 1803 Recommendations for an X.500 Production Directory Service. R. Wright, A. Getchell, T. Howes, S. Sataluri, P. Yee, W. Yeong. June 1995. (Format: TXT=14721 bytes) (Status: Informational)
- 1804 Schema Publishing in X.500 Directory. G. Mansfield, P. Rajeev, S. Raghavan, T. Howes. June 1995. (Format: TXT=18268 bytes) (Status: Experimental)
- 1823 The LDAP Application Program Interface. T. Howes, M. Smith. August 1995. (Format: TXT=41081 bytes) (Status: Informational)
- 1836 Representing the O/R Address Hierarchy in the X.500 Directory Information Tree. S. Kille. August 1995. (Format: TXT=20175 bytes) (Obsoleted by RFC2294) (Status: Experimental)
- 1837 Representing Tables and Subtrees in the X.500 Directory. S. Kille. August 1995. (Format: TXT=10924 bytes) (Obsoleted by RFC2293) (Status: Experimental)
- 1838 Use of the X.500 Directory to Support Mapping between X.400 and RFC 822 Addresses. S. Kille. August 1995. (Format: TXT=12216 bytes) (Obsoleted by RFC2164) (Status: Experimental)
- 1943 Building an X.500 Directory Service in the U.S. B. Jennings. May 1996. (Format: TXT=51266 bytes) (Status: Informational)
- 1959 An LDAP URL Format. T. Howes, M. Smith. June 1996. (Format: TXT=7243 bytes) (Obsoleted by RFC2255) (Status: Proposed Standard)
- 1960 A String Representation of LDAP Search Filters. T. Howes. June 1996. (Format: TXT=5288 bytes) (Obsoletes RFC1558) (Obsoleted by RFC2254) (Status: Proposed Standard)
- 2010 Operational Criteria for Root Name Servers. B. Manning, P. Vixie. October 1996. (Format: TXT=14870 bytes) (Obsoleted by RFC2870) (Status: Informational)
- 2079 Definition of an X.500 Attribute Type and an Object Class to Hold Uniform Resource Identifiers (URIs). M. Smith. January 1997. (Format: TXT=8757 bytes) (Status: Proposed Standard)
- 2120 Managing the X.500 Root Naming Context. D. Chadwick. March 1997. (Format: TXT=30773 bytes) (Status: Experimental)
- 2164 Use of an X.500/LDAP Directory to Support MIXER Address Mapping. S. Kille. January 1998. (Format: TXT=16701 bytes) (Obsoletes RFC1838) (Status: Proposed Standard)
- 2247 Using Domains in LDAP/X.500 Distinguished Names. S. Kille, M. Wahl, A. Grimstad, R. Huber, S. Sataluri. January 1998. (Format: TXT=12411 bytes) (Status: Proposed Standard)

- 2251 Lightweight Directory Access Protocol (v3). M. Wahl, T. Howes, S. Kille. December 1997. (Format: TXT=114488 bytes) (Updated by RFC3377) (Status: Proposed Standard)
- 2252 Lightweight Directory Access Protocol (v3): Attribute Syntax Definitions. M. Wahl, A. Coulbeck, T. Howes, S. Kille. December 1997. (Format: TXT=60204 bytes) (Updated by RFC3377) (Status: Proposed Standard)
- 2253 Lightweight Directory Access Protocol (v3): UTF-8 String Representation of Distinguished Names. M. Wahl, S. Kille, T. Howes. December 1997. (Format: TXT=18226 bytes) (Obsoletes RFC1779) (Updated by RFC3377) (Status: Proposed Standard)
- 2254 The String Representation of LDAP Search Filters. T. Howes. December 1997. (Format: TXT=13511 bytes) (Obsoletes RFC1960) (Updated by RFC3377) (Status: Proposed Standard)
- 2255 The LDAP URL Format. T. Howes, M. Smith. December 1997. (Format: TXT=20685 bytes) (Obsoletes RFC1959) (Updated by RFC3377) (Status: Proposed Standard)
- 2256 A Summary of the X.500(96) User Schema for Use with LDAPv3. M. Wahl. December 1997. (Format: TXT=32377 bytes) (Updated by RFC3377) (Status: Proposed Standard)
- 2293 Representing Tables and Subtrees in the X.500 Directory. S. Kille. March 1998. (Format: TXT=12539 bytes) (Obsoletes RFC1837) (Status: Proposed Standard)
- 2294 Representing the O/R Address Hierarchy in the X.500 Directory Information Tree. S. Kille. March 1998. (Format: TXT=22059 bytes) (Obsoletes RFC1836) (Status: Proposed Standard)
- 2307 An Approach for Using LDAP as a Network Information Service. L. Howard. March 1998. (Format: TXT=41396 bytes) (Status: Experimental)
- 2377 Naming Plan for Internet Directory-Enabled Applications. A. Grimstad, R. Huber, S. Sataluri, M. Wahl. September 1998. (Format: TXT=38274 bytes) (Status: Informational)
- 2425 A MIME Content-Type for Directory Information. T. Howes, M. Smith, F. Dawson. September 1998. (Format: TXT=64478 bytes) (Status: Proposed Standard)
- 2426 vCard MIME Directory Profile. F. Dawson, T. Howes. September 1998. (Format: TXT=74646 bytes) (Status: Proposed Standard)
- 2517 Building Directories from DNS: Experiences from WWW-Seeker. R. Moats, R. Huber. February 1999. (Format: TXT=14001 bytes) (Status: Informational)
- 2589 Lightweight Directory Access Protocol (v3): Extensions for Dynamic Directory Services. Y. Yaacovi, M. Wahl, T. Genovese. May 1999. (Format: TXT=26855 bytes) (Status: Proposed Standard)
- 2596 Use of Language Codes in LDAP. M. Wahl, T. Howes. May 1999. (Format: TXT=17413 bytes) (Status: Proposed Standard)
- 2605 Directory Server Monitoring MIB. G. Mansfield, S. Kille. June 1999. (Format: TXT=49166 bytes) (Obsoletes RFC1567) (Status: Proposed Standard)

- 2649 An LDAP Control and Schema for Holding Operation Signatures. B. Greenblatt, P. Richard. August 1999. (Format: TXT=20470 bytes) (Status: Experimental)
- 2657 LDAPv2 Client vs. the Index Mesh. R. Hedberg. August 1999. (Format: TXT=19251 bytes) (Status: Experimental)
- 2696 LDAP Control Extension for Simple Paged Results Manipulation. C. Weider, A. Herron, A. Anantha, T. Howes. September 1999. (Format: TXT=12809 bytes) (Status: Informational)
- 2713 Schema for Representing Java™ Objects in an LDAP Directory. V. Ryan, S. Seligman, R. Lee. October 1999. (Format: TXT=40745 bytes) (Status: Informational)
- 2798 Definition of the inetOrgPerson LDAP Object Class. M. Smith. April 2000. (Format: TXT=32929 bytes) (Status: Informational)
- 2820 Access Control Requirements for LDAP. E. Stokes, D. Byrne, B. Blakley, P. Behera. May 2000. (Format: TXT=18172 bytes) (Status: Informational)
- 2829 Authentication Methods for LDAP. M. Wahl, H. Alvestrand, J. Hodges, R. Morgan. May 2000. (Format: TXT=33471 bytes) (Updated by RFC3377) (Status: Proposed Standard)
- 2830 Lightweight Directory Access Protocol (v3): Extension for Transport Layer Security. J. Hodges, R. Morgan, M. Wahl. May 2000. (Format: TXT=24469 bytes) (Updated by RFC3377) (Status: Proposed Standard)
- 2849 The LDAP Data Interchange Format (LDIF) — Technical Specification. G. Good. June 2000. (Format: TXT=26017 bytes) (Status: Proposed Standard)
- 2891 LDAP Control Extension for Server Side Sorting of Search Results. T. Howes, M. Wahl, A. Anantha. August 2000. (Format: TXT=15833 bytes) (Status: Proposed Standard)
- 2926 Conversion of LDAP Schemas to and from SLP Templates. J. Kempf, R. Moats, P. St. Pierre. September 2000. (Format: TXT=55365 bytes) (Status: Informational)
- 2927 MIME Directory Profile for LDAP Schema. M. Wahl. September 2000. (Format: TXT=16122 bytes) (Status: Informational)
- 2967 TISDAG — Technical Infrastructure for Swedish Directory Access Gateways. L. Daigle, R. Hedberg. October 2000. (Format: TXT=209845 bytes) (Status: Informational)
- 2968 Mesh of Multiple DAG Servers — Results from TISDAG. L. Daigle, T. Eklof. October 2000. (Format: TXT=19306 bytes) (Status: Informational)
- 2969 Wide Area Directory Deployment — Experiences from TISDAG. T. Eklof, L. Daigle. October 2000. (Format: TXT=43002 bytes) (Status: Informational)
- 2970 Architecture for Integrated Directory Services — Result from TISDAG. L. Daigle, T. Eklof. October 2000. (Format: TXT=40448 bytes) (Status: Informational)

- 3045 Storing Vendor Information in the LDAP Root DSE. M. Meredith. January 2001. (Format: TXT=10518 bytes) (Status: Informational)
- 3062 LDAP Password Modify Extended Operation. K. Zeilenga. February 2001. (Format: TXT=11807 bytes) (Status: Proposed Standard)
- 3088 OpenLDAP Root Service: An Experimental LDAP Referral Service. K. Zeilenga. April 2001. (Format: TXT=19471 bytes) (Status: Experimental)
- 3112 LDAP Authentication Password Schema. K. Zeilenga. May 2001. (Format: TXT=17116 bytes) (Status: Informational)
- 3296 Named Subordinate References in Lightweight Directory Access Protocol (LDAP) Directories. K. Zeilenga. July 2002. (Format: TXT=27389 bytes) (Status: Proposed Standard)
- 3352 Connection-less Lightweight Directory Access Protocol (CLDAP) to Historic Status. K. Zeilenga. March 2003. (Format: TXT=7265 bytes) (Obsoletes RFC1798) (Status: Informational)
- 3377 Lightweight Directory Access Protocol (v3): Technical Specification. J. Hodges, R. Morgan. September 2002. (Format: TXT=9981 bytes) (Updates RFC2251–RFC2256, RFC2829, RFC2830) (Status: Proposed Standard)
- 3383 Internet Assigned Numbers Authority (IANA) Considerations for the Lightweight Directory Access Protocol (LDAP). K. Zeilenga. September 2002. (Format: TXT=45893 bytes) (Also BCP0064) (Status: Best Current Practice)
- 3384 Lightweight Directory Access Protocol (version 3) Replication Requirements. E. Stokes, R. Weiser, R. Moats, R. Huber. October 2002. (Format: TXT=66871 bytes) (Status: Informational)
- 3494 Lightweight Directory Access Protocol version 2 (LDAPv2) to Historic Status. K. Zeilenga. March 2003. (Format: TXT=9225 bytes) (Obsoletes RFC1484, RFC1485, RFC1487, RFC1777–RFC1779, RFC1781, RFC2559) (Status: Informational)

Work in Progress

In Chapter 4 of this book, I explained in detail the work on the LDAP protocol that is underway and the standardization of the LDAP protocol by various Working Groups. There are still a number of topics that are not yet standardized, e.g., the replication protocol. This section is intended mainly to complete the list of RFCs with the drafts. It contains the description of the Working Group as it appears on the Web site.

At the time of this writing, there are two Working Groups hosted on the IETF Web site (http://www.ietf.org): LDAP (v3) Revision (ldapbis) and LDAP Duplication/Replication/Update Protocols (ldup). There had been a third Working Group dealing with LDAP extensions (ldapext), but it has been closed. However, the mailing list of ldapext is still alive, and you can subscribe to it.

I will give you a short description of what each of these groups is doing; for more information, visit the IETF Web site at http://www.ietf.org/html.charters/wg-dir.html.

All Internet-Drafts are available via ftp access from the following sites:

IETF	ftp://ftp.ietf.org/internet-drafts
Africa	ftp://ftp.is.co.za/internet-drafts
Canada	ftp://ftp.normos.org/ietf/internet-drafts
Sweden	ftp://ftp.nordu.net/internet-drafts
Italy	ftp://ftp.nic.it/internet-drafts
Pacific Rim	ftp://munnari.oz.au/internet-drafts
U.S. West Coast	ftp://ftp.isi.edu/internet-drafts

LDAP (v3) Revision (ldapbis)

The work of this group is based on RFCs 2251–2256 and RFCs 2829–2831, which have been published on the IETF Web site recently. The objective is a revision of these RFCs and a publication of the revised work in the form of a Draft Standard. At the time of this writing, the Working Group has just delivered two RFCs:

1. RFC3377 "Lightweight Directory Access Protocol (v3): Technical Specification"
2. RFC3383 "Internet Assigned Numbers Authority (IANA) Considerations for the Lightweight Directory Access Protocol (LDAP)"

Following is a list of valid RFCs (at the time of this writing):

LDAP: String Representation of Distinguished Names
LDAP: The Protocol
LDAP: String Representation of Search Filters
LDAP: Authentication Methods and Connection Level
        Security Mechanism
LDAP: Uniform Resource Locator
LDAP: Schema for User Applications
LDAP: Syntaxes and Matching Rules
LDAP: Technical Specification Road Map
LDAP: Directory Information Models
LDAP: Internationalized String Preparation
IANA: Considerations for LDAP

I did not include the URLs because these drafts will be updated; for more information, go to the Working Group's Web site (http://www.ietf.org/html.charters/ldapbis-charter.html). The Working Group also maintains a mailing list, which you can subscribe to by sending an e-mail to ietf-ldapbis-request@openldap.org. Be sure to type "Subscribe" in the Subject line of the e-mail.

LDAP Duplication/Replication/Update Protocols (ldup)

The work of this team originally was to address issues on multi-master and master–slave replication, and therefore depended on the work of another Working Group exploring questions of access control. This team, however, failed to reach consensus, and therefore the objective of the Working Group changed. Due to the lack of an access control model, the Working Group decided to release an experimental rather than a standard protocol. The Working Group identified the following issues to be defined:

LDAPv3 Replication Architecture: This documents a general-purpose LDAPv3 replication architecture, defines key components of this architecture, describes how these key components functionally behave, and describes how these components interact with each other when in various modes of operation.

LDAPv3 Replication Information Model: Defines the schema and semantics of information used to operate, administer, maintain, and provision replication between LDAPv3 servers. Specifically, this document will contain common schema specifications intended to facilitate interoperable implementations with respect to:

- Replication agreements
- Consistency models
- Replication topologies
- Managing deleted objects and their states
- Administration and management

LDAPv3 Replication Information Transport Protocol: LDAPv3 extended operation and control specifications required to allow LDAPv3 to be used as the transport protocol for information being replicated.

LDAPv3 Replica Management: Specifications designed to support administration, maintenance, and provisioning of replicas and replication agreements. These specifications may take the form of definitions for LDAPv3 extended operations, controls, and new schema elements.

LDAPv3 Update Reconciliation Procedures: Procedures for detection and resolution of conflicts between the state of multiple replicas that contain information from the same unit of replication.

A General Usage Profile of the LDAPv3 Replication Architecture, Information Model, Protocol Extensions, and Update Reconciliation Procedures.

LDAPv3 Client Update: A protocol that enables an LDAP client to synchronize with the content of a directory information tree (DIT) stored by an LDAP server and to be notified about the changes to that content.

The Working Group released RFC3384 "Lightweight Directory Access Protocol (version 3) Replication Requirements," which can be found at the Working Group's Web site (http://www.ietf.org/html.charters/ldup-charter.html). There is also a mailing list, which you can subscribe to by sending an e-mail to ietf-ldup-request@imc.org; be sure to type "Subscribe" in the Subject line of the e-mail.

Appendix C

Useful Links

This section provides a number of links to sites about LDAP. Of course, new sites are always appearing, and other sites will disappear (this is particularly true in the case of personal home pages). However, the following links are a good starting point to find out more about the LDAP protocol and its application.

General

> http://www.openldap.org: Contains the LDAP source distribution and a lot of useful information.
>
> http://www.innosoft.com/ldapworld: General information about LDAP, recently the maintainer, Innosoft was aquired by Sun Microsystems.
>
> http://www.ldapman.org: List of LDAP resources.
>
> http://www.ldapguru.com: Portal for Sun™ ONE.
>
> http://www.ldapzone.com: Useful information for LDAP developers.
>
> http://www.kingsmountain.com/ldapRoadmap.shtml: An LDAP roadmap and FAQ.
>
> http://www.pinds.com/software/ldap-in-general: Introduction to LDAP.
>
> http://www.wanderlist.com/ldap: Resource listing for LDAP.
>
> http://www.labmice.net/activedirectory/AD_ldap.htm: Information and links from Microsoft's Active Directory.
>
> http:www.oblix.com/pointtofentry/poe_ldapresources.html: LDAP Resources
>
> http://www.hotldap.com: LDAP resources.

http://www.redbooks.ibm.com: Maintained by IBM; list of online books; search for LDAP or X.500.

LDAP Clients

http://www.ldapadministrator.com: Commercial LDAP administration tool.

http://phpldapadmin.sourceforge.net: LDAP administration tool in PHP.

http://www.iit.edu/~gawojar/ldap: LDAP browser written in Java.

http://www.huff.ca/doc/web2ldap/web2ldap.html: LDAP administration tool in Python.

http://biot.com/gq: LDAP administration tool written in C.

http://www.mjwilcox.com/plums: LDAP administration toolkit in Java.

http://developer.netscape.com/docs/manuals/communicator/ldap45.htm: Configuring the Netscape Communicator as LDAP client.

OIDs and Standards

http://www.iana.org: Obtain OIDs.

http://www.alvestrand.no/objectid: Site containing information about OIDs

http://ldap.akbkhome.com: LDAP Schema Viewer.

Tutorials and How-Tos

http://www.yolinux.com/TUTORIALS/LinuxTutorialLDAP-SoftwareDevelopment.html: OpenLDAP manual pages and list of LDAP resources maintained by YoLinux.

http://www.tldp.org/HOWTO/LDAP-HOWTO: LDAP tutorial maintained by TLDP (The Linux Documentation Project).

http://www.bayour.com/LDAPv3-HOWTO.html: Tutorial on the installation and configuration of OpenLDAP, including security issues.

Security

http://www.openssl.org: OpenSSL distribution.

http://www.pseudonym.org/ssl/ssl_intro.html: Introduction to SSL.

http://www.pscudonym.org/ssl/ssl_cook.html: OpenSSL Certificate Cookbook.

http://asg.web.cmu.edu/cyrus: Cyrus SASL distribution.

http://web.mit.edu/kerberos/www: Kerberos distribution from MIT (Version 5 for United States and Canada only).

http://www.crypto-publish.org/mit-kerberos5/index.html: Kerberos distribution including countries outside United States and Canada.

http://www.pdc.kth.se/heimdal: Kerberos distribution including countries outside United States and Canada.

http://www.openldap.org/pub/ksoper/OpenLDAP_TLS_howto.html: How-to for TLS questions.

SNMP

http://www.teleinfo.uqam.ca/snmp: Modular SNMP.

http://www.stat.ee.ethz.ch/mrtg: Multi Router Traffic Grapher.

http://gd.tuwien.ac.at/mrtg: SMB SNMP.

LDAP API

http://perl-ldap.sourceforge.net: Distribution Net::LDAP libraries.

http://castor.exolab.org: Castor Project home page (DSML mapping).

http://www.mentata.com/ldaphttp: LDAP HTTP gateway.

http://developer.novell.com/ndk/ldap-index.htm: LDAP classes for Java and libraries for C, maintained by Novell.

http://java.sun.com/products/jndi: JNDI (Java Naming and Directory Interface).

http://www.padl.com/: Distribution for PAM LDAP library.

http://www.codemerc.com: Software solutions and links to resources.

LDAP Server Implementations

Free Implementations

http://www.openldap.org: OpenLDAP implementation.

http://www.fivesight.com/downloads/openldap.asp:
OpenLDAP implementation for Windows 95/98/NT/2000;
source, how-to, and binary.

Commercial Implementations

http://www.hotldap.com/SLAPD: LDAP V3 implementation for
Windows 95/98/NT/2000

http://www.novell.com/products/edirectory: Novell eDirectory.

http://www.sun.com: Search for directory server (Sun™ ONE
directory server)

http://www.oracle.com: Oracle home page.

http://www-3.ibm.com/software/network/help-directory: IBM
Secure Way Directory Server.

http://www.siemens.com: Search for DirX.

http://www.cp/net/solutions/enterprise/dataDirectoryIntegra-
tion/directoryServer.jsp: Critical Path Ldap Server

http://www.microsoft.com: Search for active directory.

http://www.isode.com/products/m-vault-server.html: X.500
directory server from Isode.

http://www.hotldap.com/vendors/index.html: Comprehensive
list of LDAP software vendors.

http://www.dsmltools.org/: Querying of any LDAP directory,
with search results output as DSML.

Appendix D

Standards

This section provides an overview of the most frequently used object classes and attribute types. The notation is the one used in the RFCs and in the OpenLDAP schema definitions. Different server implementations use other syntaxes for the definition of the schema elements; you will find more about different syntaxes in Chapter 3. For more in-depth information about object classes, attribute type definitions, and syntaxes, you can use the LDAP Schema Viewer available at http://ldap.akbkhome.com. The site's excellent design (maintained by Alan Knowles) makes it an invaluable tool for anyone needing to better understand the schema elements of LDAP.

Object Classes

```
objectclass ( 2.5.6.1 NAME 'alias'
    DESC 'RFC2256: an alias'
    SUP top STRUCTURAL
    MUST aliasedObjectName )
objectclass ( 2.5.6.2 NAME 'country'
    DESC 'RFC2256: a country'
    SUP top STRUCTURAL
    MUST c
    MAY ( searchGuide $ description ) )
objectclass ( 2.5.6.3 NAME 'locality'
    DESC 'RFC2256: a locality'
    SUP top STRUCTURAL
    MAY ( street $ seeAlso $ searchGuide $ st $ l $ description ) )
```

```
objectclass ( 2.5.6.4 NAME 'organization'
   DESC 'RFC2256: an organization'
   SUP top STRUCTURAL
   MUST o
   MAY ( userPassword $ searchGuide $ seeAlso $
   businessCategory $
   x121Address $ registeredAddress $ destinationIndicator $
   preferredDeliveryMethod $ telexNumber $
   teletexTerminalIdentifier $
   telephoneNumber $ internationaliSDNNumber $
   facsimileTelephoneNumber $ street $ postOfficeBox $
   postalCode $
   postalAddress $ physicalDeliveryOfficeName $ st $ l $
   description ) )
objectclass ( 2.5.6.5 NAME 'organizationalUnit'
   DESC 'RFC2256: an organizational unit'
   SUP top STRUCTURAL
   MUST ou
   MAY ( userPassword $ searchGuide $ seeAlso $
   businessCategory $
   x121Address $ registeredAddress $ destinationIndicator $
   preferredDeliveryMethod $ telexNumber $
   teletexTerminalIdentifier $
   telephoneNumber $ internationaliSDNNumber $
   facsimileTelephoneNumber $ street $ postOfficeBox $
   postalCode $
   postalAddress $ physicalDeliveryOfficeName $ st $ l $
   description ) )
objectclass ( 2.5.6.6 NAME 'person'
   DESC 'RFC2256: a person'
   SUP top STRUCTURAL
   MUST ( sn $ cn )
   MAY ( userPassword $ telephoneNumber $ seeAlso $
   description ) )
objectclass ( 2.5.6.7 NAME 'organizationalPerson'
   DESC 'RFC2256: an organizational person'
   SUP person STRUCTURAL
   MAY ( title $ x121Address $ registeredAddress $
   destinationIndicator $
   preferredDeliveryMethod $ telexNumber $
   teletexTerminalIdentifier $
   telephoneNumber $ internationaliSDNNumber $
   facsimileTelephoneNumber $ street $ postOfficeBox $
   postalCode $
   postalAddress $ physicalDeliveryOfficeName $ ou $ st $ l ) )
```

```
objectclass ( 2.5.6.9 NAME 'groupOfNames'
    DESC 'RFC2256: a group of names (DNs)'
    SUP top STRUCTURAL
    MUST ( member $ cn )
    MAY ( businessCategory $ seeAlso $ owner $ ou $ o $
    description ) )
objectclass ( 2.5.6.10 NAME 'residentialPerson'
    DESC 'RFC2256: an residential person'
    SUP person STRUCTURAL
    MUST l
    MAY ( businessCategory $ x121Address $ registeredAddress $
    destinationIndicator $ preferredDeliveryMethod $
    telexNumber $
    teletexTerminalIdentifier $ telephoneNumber $
    internationaliSDNNumber $
    facsimileTelephoneNumber $ preferredDeliveryMethod $
    street $
    postOfficeBox $ postalCode $ postalAddress $
    physicalDeliveryOfficeName $ st $ l ) )
objectclass ( 2.5.6.13 NAME 'dSA'
    DESC 'RFC2256: a directory system agent (a server)'
    SUP applicationEntity STRUCTURAL
    MAY knowledgeInformation )
objectclass ( 2.5.6.14 NAME 'device'
    DESC 'RFC2256: a device'
    SUP top STRUCTURAL
    MUST cn
    MAY ( serialNumber $ seeAlso $ owner $ ou $ o $ l $
    description ) )
objectclass ( 2.5.6.17 NAME 'groupOfUniqueNames'
    DESC 'RFC2256: a group of unique names (DN and Unique
    Identifier)'
    SUP top STRUCTURAL
    MUST ( uniqueMember $ cn )
    MAY ( businessCategory $ seeAlso $ owner $ ou $ o $
    description ) )
objectclass ( 1.3.6.1.4.1.250.3.15 NAME 'labeledURIObject'
    DESC 'RFC2079: object that contains the URI attribute type'
    MAY ( labeledURI )
    SUP top AUXILIARY )
objectclass ( 1.3.6.1.4.1.1466.344 NAME 'dcObject'
    DESC 'RFC2247: domain component object'
    SUP top AUXILIARY MUST dc )
objectclass ( 1.3.6.1.1.3.1 NAME 'uidObject'
    DESC 'RFC2377: uid object'
    SUP top AUXILIARY MUST uid )
```

objectclass(2.16.840.1.113730.3.2.2
  NAME 'inetOrgPerson'
  DESC 'RFC2798: Internet Organizational Person'
  SUP organizationalPerson STRUCTURAL
  MAY (audio $ businessCategory $ carLicense $
  departmentNumber $
  displayName $ employeeNumber $ employeeType $
  givenName $
  homePhone $ homePostalAddress $ initials $ jpegPhoto $
  labeledURI $ mail $ manager $ mobile $ o $ pager $
  photo $ roomNumber $ secretary $ uid $ userCertificate $
  x500uniqueIdentifier $ preferredLanguage $
  userSMIMECertificate $ userPKCS12)
)

Attribute Types

attributetype (2.5.4.0 NAME 'objectClass'
  DESC 'RFC2256: objcct classes of the entity'
  EQUALITY objectIdentifierMatch
  SYNTAX 1.3.6.1.4.1.1466.115.121.1.38)
attributetype (2.5.4.1 NAME ('aliasedObjectName'
'aliasedEntryName')
  DESC 'RFC2256: name of aliased object'
  EQUALITY distinguishedNameMatch
  SYNTAX 1.3.6.1.4.1.1466.115.121.1.12 SINGLE-VALUE)
attributetype (2.5.4.2 NAME 'knowledgeInformation'
  DESC 'RFC2256: knowledge information'
  EQUALITY caseIgnoreMatch
  SYNTAX 1.3.6.1.4.1.1466.115.121.1.15{32768})
attributetype (2.5.4.3 NAME ('cn' 'commonName')
  DESC 'RFC2256: common name(s) for which the entity is known
  by'
  SUP name)
attributetype (2.5.4.4 NAME ('sn' 'surname')
  DESC 'RFC2256: last (family) name(s) for which the entity is
  known by'
  SUP name)
attributetype (2.5.4.5 NAME 'serialNumber'
  DESC 'RFC2256: serial number of the entity'
  EQUALITY caseIgnoreMatch
  SUBSTR caseIgnoreSubstringsMatch
  SYNTAX 1.3.6.1.4.1.1466.115.121.1.44{64})
attributetype (2.5.4.6 NAME ('c' 'countryName')
  DESC 'RFC2256: ISO-3166 country 2-letter code'
  SUP name SINGLE-VALUE)

attributetype (2.5.4.7 NAME ('l' 'localityName')
DESC 'RFC2256: locality which this object resides in'
SUP name)
attributetype (2.5.4.8 NAME ('st' 'stateOrProvinceName')
DESC 'RFC2256: state or province which this object resides in'
SUP name)
attributetype (2.5.4.9 NAME ('street' 'streetAddress')
DESC 'RFC2256: street address of this object'
EQUALITY caseIgnoreMatch
SUBSTR caseIgnoreSubstringsMatch
SYNTAX 1.3.6.1.4.1.1466.115.121.1.15{128})
attributetype (2.5.4.10 NAME ('o' 'organizationName')
DESC 'RFC2256: organization this object belongs to'
SUP name)
attributetype (2.5.4.11 NAME ('ou' 'organizationalUnitName')
DESC 'RFC2256: organizational unit this object belongs to'
SUP name)
attributetype (2.5.4.12 NAME 'title'
DESC 'RFC2256: title associated with the entity'
SUP name)
attributetype (2.5.4.13 NAME 'description'
DESC 'RFC2256: descriptive information'
EQUALITY caseIgnoreMatch
SUBSTR caseIgnoreSubstringsMatch
SYNTAX 1.3.6.1.4.1.1466.115.121.1.15{1024})
attributetype (2.5.4.14 NAME 'searchGuide'
DESC 'RFC2256: search guide, obsoleted by enhancedSearch-
Guide'
SYNTAX 1.3.6.1.4.1.1466.115.121.1.25)
attributetype (2.5.4.15 NAME 'businessCategory'
DESC 'RFC2256: business category'
EQUALITY caseIgnoreMatch
SUBSTR caseIgnoreSubstringsMatch
SYNTAX 1.3.6.1.4.1.1466.115.121.1.15{128})
attributetype (2.5.4.16 NAME 'postalAddress'
DESC 'RFC2256: postal address'
EQUALITY caseIgnoreListMatch
SUBSTR caseIgnoreListSubstringsMatch
SYNTAX 1.3.6.1.4.1.1466.115.121.1.41)
attributetype (2.5.4.17 NAME 'postalCode'
DESC 'RFC2256: postal code'
EQUALITY caseIgnoreMatch
SUBSTR caseIgnoreSubstringsMatch
SYNTAX 1.3.6.1.4.1.1466.115.121.1.15{40})

```
attributetype ( 2.5.4.18 NAME 'postOfficeBox'
    DESC 'RFC2256: Post Office Box'
    EQUALITY caseIgnoreMatch
    SUBSTR caseIgnoreSubstringsMatch
    SYNTAX 1.3.6.1.4.1.1466.115.121.1.15{40} )
attributetype ( 2.5.4.19 NAME 'physicalDeliveryOfficeName'
    DESC 'RFC2256: Physical Delivery Office Name'
    EQUALITY caseIgnoreMatch
    SUBSTR caseIgnoreSubstringsMatch
    SYNTAX 1.3.6.1.4.1.1466.115.121.1.15{128} )
attributetype ( 2.5.4.20 NAME 'telephoneNumber'
    DESC 'RFC2256: Telephone Number'
    EQUALITY telephoneNumberMatch
    SUBSTR telephoneNumberSubstringsMatch
    SYNTAX 1.3.6.1.4.1.1466.115.121.1.50{32} )
attributetype ( 2.5.4.21 NAME 'telexNumber'
    DESC 'RFC2256: Telex Number'
    SYNTAX 1.3.6.1.4.1.1466.115.121.1.52 )
attributetype ( 2.5.4.22 NAME 'teletexTerminalIdentifier'
    DESC 'RFC2256: Teletex Terminal Identifier'
    SYNTAX 1.3.6.1.4.1.1466.115.121.1.51 )
attributetype ( 2.5.4.23 NAME ( 'facsimileTelephoneNumber' 'fax' )
    DESC 'RFC2256: Facsimile (Fax) Telephone Number'
    SYNTAX 1.3.6.1.4.1.1466.115.121.1.22 )
attributetype ( 2.5.4.24 NAME 'x121Address'
    DESC 'RFC2256: X.121 Address'
    EQUALITY numericStringMatch
    SUBSTR numericStringSubstringsMatch
    SYNTAX 1.3.6.1.4.1.1466.115.121.1.36{15} )
attributetype ( 2.5.4.25 NAME 'internationaliSDNNumber'
    DESC 'RFC2256: international ISDN number'
    EQUALITY numericStringMatch
    SUBSTR numericStringSubstringsMatch
    SYNTAX 1.3.6.1.4.1.1466.115.121.1.36{16} )
attributetype ( 2.5.4.26 NAME 'registeredAddress'
    DESC 'RFC2256: registered postal address'
    SUP postalAddress
    SYNTAX 1.3.6.1.4.1.1466.115.121.1.41 )
attributetype ( 2.5.4.27 NAME 'destinationIndicator'
    DESC 'RFC2256: destination indicator'
    EQUALITY caseIgnoreMatch
    SUBSTR caseIgnoreSubstringsMatch
    SYNTAX 1.3.6.1.4.1.1466.115.121.1.44{128} )
attributetype ( 2.5.4.28 NAME 'preferredDeliveryMethod'
    DESC 'RFC2256: preferred delivery method'
    SYNTAX 1.3.6.1.4.1.1466.115.121.1.14
    SINGLE-VALUE )
```

```
attributetype ( 2.5.4.31 NAME 'member'
    DESC 'RFC2256: member of a group'
    SUP distinguishedName )
attributetype ( 2.5.4.32 NAME 'owner'
    DESC 'RFC2256: owner (of the object)'
    SUP distinguishedName )
attributetype ( 2.5.4.34 NAME 'seeAlso'
    DESC 'RFC2256: DN of related object'
    SUP distinguishedName )
attributetype ( 2.5.4.35 NAME 'userPassword'
    DESC 'RFC2256/2307: password of user'
    EQUALITY octetStringMatch
    SYNTAX 1.3.6.1.4.1.1466.115.121.1.40{128} )
attributetype ( 2.5.4.36 NAME 'userCertificate'
    DESC 'RFC2256: X.509 user certificate, use ;binary'
    SYNTAX 1.3.6.1.4.1.1466.115.121.1.8 )
attributetype ( 2.5.4.42 NAME ( 'givenName' 'gn' )
    DESC 'RFC2256: first name(s) for which the entity is known by'
    SUP name )
attributetype ( 2.5.4.43 NAME 'initials'
    DESC 'RFC2256: initials of some or all of names, but not the
    surname(s).'
    SUP name )
attributetype ( 2.5.4.45 NAME 'x500UniqueIdentifier'
    DESC 'RFC2256: X.500 unique identifier'
    EQUALITY bitStringMatch
    SYNTAX 1.3.6.1.4.1.1466.115.121.1.6 )
attributetype ( 2.5.4.49 NAME 'distinguishedName'
    EQUALITY distinguishedNameMatch
    SYNTAX 1.3.6.1.4.1.1466.115.121.1.12 )
attributetype ( 2.5.4.50 NAME 'uniqueMember'
    DESC 'RFC2256: unique member of a group'
    EQUALITY uniqueMemberMatch
    SYNTAX 1.3.6.1.4.1.1466.115.121.1.34 )
attributetype ( 1.3.6.1.4.1.250.1.57 NAME 'labeledURI'
    DESC 'RFC2079: Uniform Resource Identifier with optional label'
    EQUALITY caseExactMatch
    SYNTAX 1.3.6.1.4.1.1466.115.121.1.15 )
attributetype ( 0.9.2342.19200300.100.1.1
    NAME ( 'uid' 'userid' )
    DESC 'RFC1274: user identifier'
    EQUALITY caseIgnoreMatch
    SUBSTR caseIgnoreSubstringsMatch
    SYNTAX 1.3.6.1.4.1.1466.115.121.1.15{256} )
```

```
attributetype ( 0.9.2342.19200300.100.1.3
    NAME ( 'mail' 'rfc822Mailbox' )
    DESC 'RFC1274: RFC822 Mailbox'
    EQUALITY caseIgnoreIA5Match
    SUBSTR caseIgnoreIA5SubstringsMatch
    SYNTAX 1.3.6.1.4.1.1466.115.121.1.26{256} )
attributetype ( 0.9.2342.19200300.100.1.25
    NAME ( 'dc' 'domainComponent' )
    DESC 'RFC1274/2247: domain component'
    EQUALITY caseIgnoreIA5Match
    SUBSTR caseIgnoreIA5SubstringsMatch
    SYNTAX 1.3.6.1.4.1.1466.115.121.1.26 SINGLE-VALUE )
attributetype ( 2.16.840.1.113730.3.1.1
    NAME 'carLicense'
    DESC 'RFC2798: vehicle license or registration plate'
    EQUALITY caseIgnoreMatch
    SUBSTR caseIgnoreSubstringsMatch
    SYNTAX 1.3.6.1.4.1.1466.115.121.1.15 )
attributetype ( 2.16.840.1.113730.3.1.2
    NAME 'departmentNumber'
    DESC 'RFC2798: identifies a department within an organization'
    EQUALITY caseIgnoreMatch
    SUBSTR caseIgnoreSubstringsMatch
    SYNTAX 1.3.6.1.4.1.1466.115.121.1.15 )
attributetype ( 2.16.840.1.113730.3.1.241
    NAME 'displayName'
    DESC 'RFC2798: preferred name to be used when displaying
    entries'
    EQUALITY caseIgnoreMatch
    SUBSTR caseIgnoreSubstringsMatch
    SYNTAX 1.3.6.1.4.1.1466.115.121.1.15
    SINGLE-VALUE )
attributetype ( 2.16.840.1.113730.3.1.3
    NAME 'employeeNumber'
    DESC 'RFC2798: numerically identifies an employee within an
    organization'
    EQUALITY caseIgnoreMatch
    SUBSTR caseIgnoreSubstringsMatch
    SYNTAX 1.3.6.1.4.1.1466.115.121.1.15
    SINGLE-VALUE )
attributetype ( 2.16.840.1.113730.3.1.4
    NAME 'employeeType'
    DESC 'RFC2798: type of employment for a person'
    EQUALITY caseIgnoreMatch
    SUBSTR caseIgnoreSubstringsMatch
    SYNTAX 1.3.6.1.4.1.1466.115.121.1.15 )
```

attributetype (0.9.2342.19200300.100.1.60
    NAME 'jpegPhoto'
    DESC 'RFC2798: a JPEG image'
    SYNTAX 1.3.6.1.4.1.1466.115.121.1.28)
attributetype (2.16.840.1.113730.3.1.39
    NAME 'preferredLanguage'
    DESC 'RFC2798: preferred written or spoken language for a
    person'
    EQUALITY caseIgnoreMatch
    SUBSTR caseIgnoreSubstringsMatch
    SYNTAX 1.3.6.1.4.1.1466.115.121.1.15
    SINGLE-VALUE)
attributetype (2.16.840.1.113730.3.1.40
    NAME 'userSMIMECertificate'
    DESC 'RFC2798: PKCS#7 SignedData used to support S/MIME'
    SYNTAX 1.3.6.1.4.1.1466.115.121.1.5)
attributetype (2.16.840.1.113730.3.1.216
    NAME 'userPKCS12'
    DESC 'RFC2798: personal identity information, a PKCS #12 PFX'
    SYNTAX 1.3.6.1.4.1.1466.115.121.1.5)
attributetype (0.9.2342.19200300.100.1.55 NAME 'audio'
    DESC 'RFC1274: audio (u-law)'
    SYNTAX 1.3.6.1.4.1.1466.115.121.1.4{25000})
attributetype (0.9.2342.19200300.100.1.20
    DESC 'RFC1274: home telephone number'
    NAME ('homePhone' 'homeTelephoneNumber')
    EQUALITY telephoneNumberMatch
    SUBSTR telephoneNumberSubstringsMatch
    SYNTAX 1.3.6.1.4.1.1466.115.121.1.50)
attributetype (0.9.2342.19200300.100.1.39 NAME 'homePostal-
Address'
    DESC 'RFC1274: home postal address'
    EQUALITY caseIgnoreListMatch
    SUBSTR caseIgnoreListSubstringsMatch
    SYNTAX 1.3.6.1.4.1.1466.115.121.1.41)
attributetype (0.9.2342.19200300.100.1.10 NAME 'manager'
    DESC 'RFC1274: DN of manager'
    EQUALITY distinguishedNameMatch
    SYNTAX 1.3.6.1.4.1.1466.115.121.1.12)
attributetype (0.9.2342.19200300.100.1.41
    NAME ('mobile' 'mobileTelephoneNumber')
    DESC 'RFC1274: mobile telephone number'
    EQUALITY telephoneNumberMatch
    SUBSTR telephoneNumberSubstringsMatch
    SYNTAX 1.3.6.1.4.1.1466.115.121.1.50)

```
attributetype ( 0.9.2342.19200300.100.1.42
    NAME ( 'pager' 'pagerTelephoneNumber' )
    DESC 'RFC1274: pager telephone number'
    EQUALITY telephoneNumberMatch
    SUBSTR telephoneNumberSubstringsMatch
    SYNTAX 1.3.6.1.4.1.1466.115.121.1.50 )
attributetype ( 0.9.2342.19200300.100.1.7 NAME 'photo'
    DESC 'RFC1274: photo (G3 fax)'
    SYNTAX 1.3.6.1.4.1.1466.115.121.1.23{25000} )
attributetype ( 0.9.2342.19200300.100.1.21 NAME 'secretary'
    DESC 'RFC1274: DN of secretary'
    EQUALITY distinguishedNameMatch
    SYNTAX 1.3.6.1.4.1.1466.115.121.1.12 )
attributetype ( 0.9.2342.19200300.100.1.6 NAME 'roomNumber'
    DESC 'RFC1274: room number'
    EQUALITY caseIgnoreMatch
    SUBSTR caseIgnoreSubstringsMatch
    SYNTAX 1.3.6.1.4.1.1466.115.121.1.15{256} )
```

Appendix E

Configuration of OpenLDAP

In this book, I used OpenLDAP for many examples. This part of the book should give you some hints for its configuration. It assumes you have configured and tested OpenLDAP correctly, therefore I assume you have a running OpenLDAP server in your architecture. At this point you are ready to configure the OpenLDAP server to fit best your needs. This section is intended to help you with this configuration; however, it should not substitute for the excellent "Administrator's Guide," which is shipped together with the OpenLDAP source code, nor should you ignore the documentation available at the OpenLDAP Web site (http://www.openldap.org).

Nearly every LDAP-related tool installed on your computer uses the configuration file. When you install your LDAP distribution servers, command line tools, utilities, main pages, and configuration files are installed at the location you designate during compilation; if you do not specify anything else, the software defaults to the configuration file at this location.

Be sure to use the software you installed. Many operating systems (e.g., I am using Sun Solaris 2.9) contain LDAP clients, or perhaps you have a resident LDAP installation with tools such as slapcat or slapadd. A common mistake is to use them instead of the freshly compiled ones, and therefore you may use a different configuration file. In UNIX, the command "which slapcat" will tell you the path of the configuration file you are using.

Configuration Files

The default location of the configuration files is $prefix/etc/openldap. In this directory there are two configuration files (ldap.conf and slapd.conf) and the directory "schema," which contains the standard schema files delivered with the OpenLDAP distribution (to be discussed later). The ldap.conf file configures default parameters for client applications; however, every user can apply different parameters. The client tools look first in the home directory of the user launching the command if they find a file called ldaprc or .ldaprc. If such a file exists, the parameters configured in it are used; if not, the systemwide configuration file is used. What can be configured with this file you can read about in the manual page of ldap.conf (in UNIX, the command is `man ldap.conf`).

The file slapd.conf contains the configuration for the OpenLDAP server, the subject of this section.

The directory "schema" contains a number of standard schema files. If you extend the schema as described in Chapter 4 or Chapter 7, you should put your new object class and attribute type definitions in a separate file in this directory. Following is a brief look at the standard schema files OpenLDAP provides:

> *core.schema:* As the name suggests this is the core schema file, inasmuch as it provides you with the most important object classes and attribute definitions. It contains the schema elements as defined in RFCs 2252–2256 and some additional schema information from RFC 1274 (uid/dc), RFC 2079 (URI), RFC 2247 (dc/dcObject), RFC 2587 (PKI), RFC 2589 (Dynamic Directory Services), and RFC 2377 (uidObject).
>
> *cosine.schema:* LDAPv3 schema derived from X.500 cosine "pilot" schema as described in RFC 1274. This subject should be considered as "work in progress" and is documented in "draft-ietf-asid-ldapv3-attributes-03.txt".
>
> *inetorgperson.schema:* Describes the object class and its attribute definitions of the inetOrgPerson object class as defined in RFC 2798. It depends on the core and cosine schema files.
>
> *openldap.schema:* Describes object classes and attribute definitions provided by the OpenLDAP project for informational purposes only. It depends on core, cosine, and inetorgperson schema files.
>
> *nis.schema:* Describes object class and attribute definitions needed to substitute the Network Information System (defined by Sun Microsystems) with LDAP. RFC 2307 describes NIS object classes and attribute definitions.

misc.schema: Experimental description of object class and attribute definitions used for LDAP-based mail routing as described by:

- draft-lachman-laser-ldap-mail-routing-02.txt
- draft-srivastava-ldap-mail-00.txt

java.schema: Describes object class and attribute definitions needed to hold Java classes in a directory as defined by RFC 2713. The schema defines schema elements to represent Java serialized objects [Serial], Java marshalled objects [RMI], Java remote objects [RMI], and JNDI references [JNDI].

corba.schema: Describes object class and attribute definitions needed to hold CORBA references in a directory. CORBA is the Common Object Request Broker Architecture as defined by the Object Management Group (OMG).

Configuration File of the OpenLDAP Server

The configuration file of the LDAP server daemon is named by default slapd.conf. You can also use a different file. All you have to do is to start the OpenLDAP server daemon with the "-f <filename" parameter. This file is used to configure the stand-alone LDAP daemon, called "slapd," and the stand-alone LDAP update replication daemon, called "slurpd." For more information about slurpd, see Appendix F, which discusses how to configure replication with OpenLDAP. The slapd configuration file is discussed in the OpenLDAP "Administrator's Guide," which is delivered with the OpenLDAP source code distribution.

The format of the configuration file is very easy to understand:

- Blank lines are ignored.
- Lines beginning with "#" are comments.
- A white space at the beginning of a line is considered a continuation of the previous line; therefore, special characters to code line continuation such as "\" are not needed.

As explained in the "Administrator's Guide," one can break down the configuration file of the slapd daemon in various sections. Following is a schema of the OpenLDAP directory server configuration file:

```
# global configuration directives
<global config directives>
```

```
# backend and database directives

# backend definition
backend <typeA>
<backend-specific directives>

# first database definition & config directives
database <typeA>
<database-specific directives>

# second database definition & config directives
database <typeB>
<database-specific directives>

# third database definition & config directives
database <typeA>
<database-specific directives>

# subsequent backend & database definitions & config directives
```

As you can see, the configuration file contains one section with global directives that configure the whole directory server. Following this global section are sections for back-end and database definitions. We will discuss these features.

The Global Section

The configuration that appears in the global section applies to all back-end and database sections, unless they are redefined in the back-end or database section.

- Access control information
- Schema information
- Log information
- Resource limitations
- Referrals

Access Control Information

Access control information describes who can do what with which data. Following is the syntax:

```
access to <what> [ by <who> <accesslevel> <control> ]+
```

You can also define default access rights when nothing else about access modes is defined using the directive:

```
defaultaccess { none | compare | search | read | write }
```

Following is the syntax definition of an ACI list:

```
<access directive> ::= access to <what>
   [by <who> <access> <control>]+
 <what> ::= * | [ dn[.<target style>]=<regex>]
   [filter=<ldapfilter>] [attrs=<attrlist>]
 <target style> ::= regex | base | one | subtree | children
 <attrlist> ::= <attr> | <attr> , <attrlist>
 <attr> ::= <attrname> | entry | children
 <who> ::= [* | anonymous | users | self |
   dn[.<subject style>]=<regex>]
   [dnattr=<attrname> ]
   [group[/<objectclass>[/<attrname>][.<basic style>]]=<regex> ]
   [peername[.<basic style>]=<regex>]
   [sockname[.<basic style>]=<regex>]
   [domain[.<basic style>]=<regex>]
   [sockurl[.<basic style>]=<regex>]
   [set=<setspec>]
   [aci=<attrname>]
<subject style> ::= regex | exact | base | one | subtree | children
 <basic style> ::= regex | exact
 <access> ::= [self]{<level>|<priv>}
 <level> ::= none | auth | compare | search | read | write
 <priv> ::= {=|+|-}{w|r|s|c|x}+
 <control> ::= [stop | continue | break]
```

Schema Information

You can put schema information directly in the configuration file, therefore you could define it with:

```
objectclass < RFC2252 compliant Object Class definition>
attributetype < RFC2252 compliant Attribute Type definition>
```

Your directory server can use object classes and attribute types. You can also include these definitions with the **include** directive. This method is the preferred one, because it keeps the configuration file shorter and clearer. The syntax of the include directive is:

```
include <filename>
```

Log Information

The next step is to configure log information. OpenLDAP uses syslog for logging. Syslog is standard on UNIX systems; have a look at the description of the syslog utility if you need more information. You can configure the log level describing how much information the log file will contain. The syntax is:

```
loglevel <integer>
```

Following is a list of log level values and what they mean:

Level	Description
–1	Enable all debugging
0	No debugging
1	Trace function calls
2	Debug packet handling
4	Heavy trace debugging
8	Connection management
16	Print out packets sent and received
32	Search filter processing
64	Configuration file processing
128	Access control list processing
256	Stats log connections/operations/results
512	Stats log entries sent
1024	Print communication with shell backends
2048	Print entry parsing debugging

Resource Limitations

Resource limitations are used to prevent an application from monopolizing a service. There are several limits we can impose to enforce correct use of the service the directory server offers to clients.

We can configure a timeout after which an idle connection to a client is closed automatically.

```
idletimeout <number of seconds>
```

We can configure the maximal number of entries a query will return with the directive. Exceeding this size, the client will get a result code indicating that the size limit has been exceeded.

```
sizelimit <number of entries>
```

And we can define the maximal time in seconds the server can take to answer a request. After this limit, the client will get a result code indicating that the time limit has been exceeded.

```
timelimit <number of entries>
```

Referrals

Referrals have been treated in Chapter 3 section referrals. This one here is intended as superior knowledge information, i.e., it tells the client who to ask if the server itself does not answer the request. The syntax is:

```
referral <ldapurl>
```

Back-End and Database Sections

First of all let us see the difference between back end and database. In Chapter 7, when we discussed the installation of the OpenLDAP server, we had to configure which back end we would like to use. There are different back ends available:

ldbm back end: Lightweight database management system
bdb back end: High-performance database management system
shell back end: User-supplied shell scripts
sql back end: User-supplied SQL scripts
perl back end: User-supplied Perl scripts
meta back end: Back end that forwards requests to another LDAP server

We will not describe the back ends here (have a look at the documentation delivered with OpenLDAP instead). If you have the compiled file in the back end, you can use it in your directory server. The database is a collection of files that holds the data. For example, assume you have five databases: three ldbm databases and two bdb databases. Therefore, you have two different back ends (ldbm and bdb) for five different databases. In other words, the database is the physical implementation of the back end.

You can configure the back ends and the databases separately. The definitions in the back ends hold for all databases of the back-end type, if not redefined in the database section. The configuration file therefore holds three different directives:

1. Global directives valid for all back-end and database directives (if not redefined)
2. Back-end directives valid for all database directives (if not redefined)
3. Database directives

The syntax of the back-end directive is:

```
backend <backend type>
<backend directives>
```

The syntax of the database directive is:

```
database < database type>
< database directives>
```

The database and back-end directives are described in detail in the documentation relative to the single back ends. I will mention only the some of them (see the documentation delivered with OpenLDAP to learn more about it). In Appendix F we will see the directives to configure replication, and Appendix G discusses the meta back end.

System administrator access is configured using the credentials rootdn and rootpw. The syntax is:

```
rootdn <DN>
rootpw <password>
```

Note that the password should not appear in clear text. OpenLDAP delivers the utility "crypt" to encrypt the password. The system administrator is the only user not subject to the access limitations defined by the previous ACLs. In a running OpenLDAP directory server, you may comment-out these lines for security reasons and enable them if needed for administrative purposes. You could also choose to configure a separate LDAP administration server. You may also consider using SASL (Simple Authentication Security Layer); in this case the rootdn will refer to an SASL identity and the rootpw auditing becomes more difficult. See the SASL section delivered with OpenLDAP for more details.

A further important parameter is the base DN describing the root of the directory tree. The directory server can serve more directory trees. The syntax is:

```
suffix <DN>
```

You must specify which filesystem directory database lives in. The syntax is:

```
directory <directory>
```

for example:

```
directory /usr/local/var/abc_ldap_org
```

the mode directive indicates the mode in which the database files should be opened. I recommend allowing access to these files only to the owner of the ldap daemon process. The syntax is:

```
mode <mode>
```

for example:

```
mode 0600
```

The last directive I will show you is the directive to speed up access to the directory. You can define indexes to do so. The directive is:

```
index {<attrlist> | default} [pres,eq,approx,sub,none]
```

This directive instructs the back end to maintain an index for this attribute. The functionality of maintaining indexes depends on the back end. These indexes are used if comparisons are to be performed. Because you may perform different types of comparisons, you can specify for which type of comparison an index must be maintained. These types are:

> *pres:* Presence; tests only if the attribute does exist
> *eq:* Equality; tests if the attribute is equal to a given value
> *approx:* Performs an approximate comparison (language dependent)
> *sub:* Performs a substring match
> *none:* No matching for this attribute (to exclude an attribute otherwise maintained by the default clause)

With index default, you define that the LDAP server should maintain the specified indexes for all attributes. This behavior can be overwritten subsequently with a more specific one or reset with the **index <attribute> none** directive.

Following is an example of a complete configuration file matching the example of the LdapABC organization used in this book. The list of directives is not limited to those mentioned in this section; there are actually many more directives, depending on the back end you use (some of which are discussed in Appendix F and Appendix G). By the time you read this book, there may be even more because work on OpenLDAP continues.

```
01    # Example Configuration File
02    #
03    # Global Section
02    include /usr/local/etc/schema/core.schema
03    include /usr/local/etc/schema/cosine.schema
04    include /usr/local/etc/schema/inetorgperson.schema
05    include /usr/local/etc/schema/ldapabcadmin.schema
06
03    03 referral ldap://www.ldapabc.org
04    access to * by * read
05
06    # ldbm definition for dc=ldapabc,dc=org
07    database ldbm
08
09    # definition of the namespace
10    suffix dc=LdapAbc,dc=org
11
12    # System Administrator Credentials
13    rootdn cn=Administrator,dc=LdapAbc,dc=org
14    rootpw {SSHA}Dh1hgJPc+2akIahgBJyxLAvwc+UXFhg
15
16    # Database Location
17    directory /usr/local/var/LdapAbc
18
19    # Definition of Indexes
20    index uid pres,eq
21    index objectClass eq
22    index cn,sn,uid pres,eq,approx,sub
23
24    # ACI Information
25    access to attr=userPassword
26          by self write
27          by anonymous auth
28          by * none
29
30    access to *
31          by self write
32          by users read
33
```

Appendix F

Playing with Replication in OpenLDAP

In this section, we will have a brief look at implementing replication with OpenLDAP. In Chapter 5, I discussed what replication is; in this section, you will have a practical example of how it works. I will implement two LDAP servers: a master server and a slave server. Because not everyone has two computers at their disposal, I have put the master and the slave server on the same machine.

LDAP uses two server daemons to implement a master server: (1) the stand-alone LDAP server daemon called "slapd" and (2) the stand-alone replication daemon called "slurpd."

When you compile OpenLDAP, you should run the configure script using the switch -enable_slurpd, which tells the configure utility to prepare the makefiles to also produce the replication program; however, this is the default. The slapd master daemon maintains a replication log describing in LDIF format the changes applied to the master directory. The slurpd daemon reads these changes, connects to the slave daemon, and applies these changes to the slave server.

For this example, we will use a highly primitive configuration to concentrate on the concept of replication. We will use only an organization with the DN:

```
dc=LdapAbc, dc=org
```

In this organization, we will add and delete for test purposes a few organizational units.

First of all, we will configure the master server. The rootDN is dc=LdapAbc, dc=org, the DN of the administrator is DN: cn=Administrator, dc=LdapAbc, dc=org. Following is the corresponding database configuration section of the master server.

```
26      . . . .
27      # Database Section for : dc=LdapAbc, dc=org
28      database bdb
29      suffix "dc=LdapAbc, dc=org"
30
31      # Administrator Credentials:
32      rootdn "cn=Administrator, dc=LdapAbc, dc=org"
33      rootpw {SSHA}Dh1hgJPc+2akIahgBJyxLAvwc+UXFhg
34
```

Now we can start the slapd daemon with the usual command:

```
./slapd -f <configuration file>
```

Once the daemon has started we can add a few objects. Following is the `ldapmodify` dialog for adding two entries to the master directory; you can put these lines in a file and launch ldapmodify with the `-f <filename>` switch.

```
ldapmodify -D "cn=Administrator,dc=LdapAbc,dc=org" -w "password"
DN: dc=LdapAbc, dc=org
changetype: add
objectclass: top
objectclass: dcObject
objectclass: organization
o: LdapAbc
dc: LdapAbc
```

adding new entry "dc=LdapAbc, dc=org"

```
DN: ou=people, dc=LdapAbc, dc=org
changetype: add
objectclass: top
objectclass: organizationalUnit
ou: people
```

adding new entry "ou=peomple,dc=LdapAbc, dc=org

To see that the data has been successfully added, search with the filter

```
(objectclass=*).
```

Once we are done with the master server, we will configure the slave server using the same configuration file. We will have to change the lines `pidfile`, `argsfile`, and `directory` in the slave config-file. The slave server does not yet have a directory. You have two possibilities to mirror the initial directory.

1. You can copy all the DBM files from the master to the slave.

2. You can export the master repository in LDIF format using the `slapcat` command and import it into the slave location using the `slapadd` command.

When you start the slave server, you should be able to execute searches on it. You should start it on a different port than the master server with the command. I use 689, but you can use a different port provided it is not used by another program (look in /etc/services if you have doubts).

```
./slapd -f <configuration file> -h "ldap://127.0.0.1:689"
```

Now we have two directory servers, both up and running; however, we need a master server and a slave server. We will first configure the master server, but we must stop both slapd daemons if they are still running.

To configure replication, the slapd daemon needs to know where to dump out the changes applied to the directory. You provide this data to the daemon using the `replogfile <filename>` directive. Add the following line after the database section:

```
replogfile /usr/local/openldap/var/slapd.replog
```

If you want to put the replication log into another location, substitute <filename> with a file suited to your configuration.

Next, we need to configure the master slurpd daemon. To do this, we can recycle the freshly produced configuration of the slapd daemon, or better still, use the same configuration file, as we will do here. You have only to add the "replica" clause after the replogfile instruction and you are done. In the replogfile, first you specify the LDAP server the slave directory is mounted on. You do this specifying the slave server's LDAP URL, which in our example is ldap://127.0.0.1:689. Next, you configure the part of the directory tree to be replicated, which in our example is the whole tree, i.e., "dc=LdapAbc, dc=org". The rest of the parameters define the authentication of the master server at the slave server. The master connects where `binddn` is the DN, and the password is "credentials." The `bindmethod` can be either simple or sasl; we will use simple in our example. The last parameter `tls` specifies whether the master server should begin a conversation with `starttls`. In a production environment, you should use TLS; in our example, we do not to keep it simple. Following is the configuration file shared by the master server and the replication server daemon:

```
35    # Database Section for : dc=LdapAbc, dc=org
36    database bdb
37    suffix "dc=LdapAbc, dc=org"
38
39    # Administrator Credentials:
40    rootdn "cn=Administrator, dc=LdapAbc,
      dc=org"
41    rootpw
      {SSHA}Dh1hgJPc+2akIahgBJyxLAvwc+UXFhg
42
43    # Replication Agreement:
44    replogfile
      /usr/local/var/openldap/slapd.replog
45    rep      host=127.0.0.1:689
      lic
      a
46             binddn="cn=replication service,
               dc=LdapAbc, dc=org"
47             bindmethod=simple
48             credentials=password
```

Once configured, you can start the slapd daemon and test it with a couple of searches. If you update the directory, your updates will be kept in the replication log. As soon as slurpd succeeds in connecting to the slave server, it will also replicate your changes on the master server on the slave server.

Now that the master slapd daemon is up and running, we can proceed with the configuration of the slave slapd daemon. On the slave slapd daemon, you have to configure only two things: (1) the DN the replication process uses to make contacts and (2) the master LDAP server's URL to be used when clients send update requests to the slave server. Once configured, start the slave slapd daemon. Following is the configuration you must add to the slave slapd daemon:

```
37    #
38    ## Slave Server Configuration
39
40    # User updates are accepted from
41    updatedn "cn=replication service,
      dc=LdapAbc, dc=org"
42
43    ## LDAP URL of the master LDAP server
44    updateref ldap://127.0.0.1
45
```

At this point, only the replication process is missing. If you modify, add, or delete objects on the master server, you will now see them on the slave LDAP server. For this you must start the slurpd daemon.

As soon as you start the slurpd daemon, it will contact the slave server and push the updates mentioned in the replication log to the slave server.

This architecture is used for performance reasons, but can also be integrated into the backup strategy. You shut down the slave server when an offline backup has to be made. All changes in the directory are recorded in the replication log file and replicated as soon as the slave server is online again.

Appendix G

Playing with OpenLDAP Proxy Server

In this book I tried to remain as vendor independent as possible; therefore, I concentrated the discussion on the LDAP protocol and not on a particular implementation of an LDAP server. On the other hand, I repeatedly stated that it is a good idea to start with the open-source implementation of LDAP (OpenLDAP) to start your experiments and to gain a deeper understanding of the LDAP protocol. Chapter 7 demonstrated how to compile, install, and configure OpenLDAP, but there were a few things I did not mention so as not to go too far beyond the scope of the subject of system administration. Therefore, in this appendix I will discuss a few OpenLDAP-specific features that I have found very handy, using the example of a somewhat more complex installation: the back end of OpenLDAP. This also gives me the opportunity to explain how an LDAP proxy server works and how it can be configured. It will also give you a feeling of what an LDAP proxy server can be used for.

The Back End

The OpenLDAP server basically consists of a front end and a back end. The front end is what the client will see, and it runs on the LDAP protocol. The protocol has been the focus of this book, therefore we have not discussed the back end, OpenLDAP, until now; every LDAP implementation consists of the back end. I mentioned it briefly in Chapter 7 when discussing installation. During installation, you have the choice of which database to install "under the LDAP server," i.e., the back end.

In Chapter 7, I stated that you have the choice between ldbm and bdb, but this is not the only choice available for the back end.

To understand what we will achieve with this particular configuration, I will explain first the requirements. We should install a directory that contains global data used enterprisewide and local data used and maintained locally. We will assume that this configuration will be implemented in all the countries in which the enterprise is operating. Therefore, the global part of the data is maintained in a global directory, and the local copies are only replicas of the global data. The local data, however, is maintained locally and may have a different structure in different countries. In a configuration where all traffic of directory clients is directed to the LDAP proxy server, the directory server holding global data is called by the proxy if the client needs data from the global part of the directory information tree; meanwhile the local directory server is called if the proxy server understands that the client needs data held in the local tree.

I will keep the examples very simple, and assume all user-related data is global. There will be global groupings of users expressed in terms of groupOfUniqueNames objects and located on the global server. There can also be local groupings of users expressed in terms of groupOfUniqueNames objects maintained locally. For your specific implementation, check the directory information tree (DIT) of the LDAP servers.

Looking at the DIT, you may wonder why the data partitioning described in Chapter 5 was not used. First of all, you are right: the architecture can be achieved using referrals. The LDAP proxy server, however, does much more, and in this case is required. The LDAP proxy server will rewrite your requests to somewhat suit our requirements. We would like every location to have a branch called "ou=Local Groups" without the need of the client to specify which of the local groups branch it really means. I think it is enough that you contact the local LDAP server and say "local groups." It should be the job of the LDAP proxy server to be aware of the fact that local group means "de" when you are at the Munich site, "UK" when you are at the London site, or "Es" if you are at the site in Madrid (more about the rewrite abilities of the OpenLDAP proxy server later).

What We Will Need

To test the proxy capabilities of the OpenLDAP server, obviously you need a directory server that actually holds the data and the proxy server that we will play with. I do not suppose that you have two computers to experiment with; therefore, I designed the exercise to be completed with one computer only. Simply run the directory server on a different port than the LDAP proxy server. In our example, we will let the proxy server run on the standard port (389) and the directory server on a different one, e.g., 689. Furthermore, I do not want you to be bothered with DNS questions, so we will use for the local machine (the machine you are working on) the address 127.0.0.1. This special address is reserved for testing purposes on the local machine. It is also called the loopback address. So we will assume that the directory server runs on ldap://127.0.0.1:689 and the proxy server on ldap://127.0.0.1:389. I will also assume you installed and configured the directory server and you will start it up running on port 689.

Compiling the OpenLDAP Proxy

Similar to the BerkeleyDB, the OpenLDAP software also needs to be configured before compilation. The configure tools create the necessary makefiles for you, which is very helpful because there is more than one makefile. OpenLDAP offers you two proxy back ends, or one basic back end and two extensions. We will install the basic one first and have a look at the extensions later. Following is an example of a script to configure compilation of the proxy back end:

```
#!/usr/bin/sh
#
# Name        : ConfigLdapServer.sh
# Author      : Reinhard E. Voglmaier
# Date        : 27.04.2003
# Version     : 2.1
# Description : Configure OpenLDAP compilation/installation
#
# Server Name, used latger in the configure switches
Server=proxy
Main=ldap

CC=gcc                                                      \
CPPFLAGS="-I/usr/local/BerkeleyDB.4.1/include"              \
LDFLAGS="-L/usr/local/BerkeleyDB.4.1/lib"                   \
./configure                                                 \
  --bindir=/usr/local/${Server}/bin                         \
  --sbindir=/usr/local/${Server}/sbin                       \
  --libexecdir=/usr/local/${Server}/libexec                 \
  --libdir=/usr/local/${Server}/lib                         \
  --localstatedir=/usr/local/${Server}/var                  \
  --sysconfdir=/usr/local/${Server}/etc                     \
  --mandir=/usr/local/${Main}/man                           \
  --includedir=/usr/local/${Main}/include                   \
  --datadir=/usr/local/$Main}/share                         \
  --disable-bdb                                             \
  --enable-ldap
```

Notice that the proxy back end is compiled into the server with the directive:

```
--enable-ldap
```

The name suggests what the proxy is doing: it executes requests against a directory server using the LDAP protocol. I have also disabled the compilation of the bdb back end, which otherwise would have been the default behavior.

Once you have launched the configuration script, you must launch a "make depend" to allow the procedure to resolve the dependencies. After that, you are ready to launch the make, which should now succeed without errors. However, if you get errors in the compilation phase, look first at the "how to" on the OpenLDAP Web site and then examine the archives of the OpenLDAP newsgroups. If you do not find the help you need, subscribe to the newsgroup and post your problem on the board.

Notice, however, that the usual make test would result in an error because you do not have a configured database back end you can test.

Running the OpenLDAP Proxy

Now that you have successfully compiled the OpenLDAP proxy server, it is time to use it. Install and configure it at the location you previously configured. The configuration file is rather short; I forego access rights for brevity. Following is an example of a working configuration file. As always, use "dc=LdapAbc,dc=com" as root DN.

```
# Short OpenLDAP configuration file
# User administration is missing however

# Global definitions:


    pidfile         /usr/local/proxy/var/slapd.pid
    argsfile        /usr/local/proxy/var/slapd.args

# Database sections:


        database        ldap
        suffix          "dc=LdapAbc,dc=org"
        uri             "ldap://127.0.0.1:689"
```

After configuring the proxy server, you can start up the slapd daemon. If you want to see in real-time what the server is doing, start the daemon with the −d switch. Now try to run a query using the proxy server instead of the directory server. You may also compare the results with those you get if you directly use the directory server.

Further Capabilities

The proxy back end has more capabilities than just forwarding an LDAP request; however, I will mention just two of them, the map and rewrite directives.

The map directive allows you to map an attribute/objectclass from the proxy server to an attribute/objectclass on the directory server. It also allows you to filter out attributes coming from the directory server. The syntax is

```
map {attribute | objectclass} [<local name> | *] {<foreign name>
```

The star (*) has a particular meaning. As the main page states, if the local or foreign name is "*," the name is preserved; if local name is omitted, the foreign name is removed. Therefore, the three lines

```
map attribute cn *
map attribute sn *
map attribute
```

would map sn and cn on themselves, and remove any other attribute coming from the directory server.

The rewrite directive allows you to rewrite strings moving back and forth between client and directory server. The rewriting is executed according to a set of rules, which are formulated using regular expressions. The basic syntax is:

```
RewriteRule <regular expression> <substitution pattern> [ <flags> ]
```

You can read more about this module on the main page delivered with the OpenLDAP distribution.

The Meta Back End

The LDAP back end provides your OpenLDAP server with the capabilities of a proxy server, and two additional back ends deliver rewrite and masquerading abilities that complete the proxy OpenLDAP server. The meta back end is compiled with the configure instruction

```
--enable-met
```

The meta back end requires the rewrite engine code to be compiled, which is achieved with the instruction

```
--enable-rewrit
```

The meta back end extends the functionality of the LDAP (proxy) back end, and they also share pieces of source code. You must compile the LDAP back end in the OpenLDAP executable. Following is the shell script that prepares OpenLDAP for compilation:

```
#!/usr/bin/sh
#
# Name            : ConfigLdapServer.sh
# Author          : Reinhard E. Voglmaier
# Date            : 27.04.2003
# Version         : 2.1
# Description     : Configure OpenLDAP compilation/installation
#
# Server Name, used later in the configure switches
Server=proxy
Main=ldap

CC=gcc                                                           \
CPPFLAGS="-I/usr/local/BerkeleyDB.4.1/include"                   \
LDFLAGS="-L/usr/local/BerkeleyDB.4.1/lib"                        \
./configure                                                      \
  --bindir=/usr/local/${Server}/bin                             \
  --sbindir=/usr/local/${Server}/sbin                           \
  --libexecdir=/usr/local/${Server}/libexec                     \
  --libdir=/usr/local/${Server}/lib                             \
  --localstatedir=/usr/local/${Server}/var                      \
  --sysconfdir=/usr/local/${Server}/etc                         \
  --mandir=/usr/local/${Main}/man                               \
  --includedir=/usr/local/${Main}/include                       \
  --datadir=/usr/local/$Main}/share                             \
  --disable-bdb                                                 \
  --enable-rewrite                                              \
  --enable-ldap                                                 \
  --enable-meta
```

What is the difference between the proxy back end enabled with mod-ldap and the meta back end? The mod-ldap proxy back end is intended for proxying with one proxy only. The meta back end allows you to proxy to more than one LDAP server. It also helps you in masquerading the traffic between the actual LDAP servers and the clients. This means that the client has no idea which LDAP server answers its requests, nor how this LDAP server is configured. You will wonder why hiding this information can be useful. Imagine you use the proxy server on the Internet as the entry point for a directory used also for protected information. Using a proxy server that hides information from outside entry helps to protect this information. The view given to the users coming from outside disables any unauthorized request to the directory server that holds the information.

If you need more information about the meta back end, look at the manual pages of OpenLDAP distributed with the source text of the OpenLDAP distribution.

Index

L

Printed and bound by CPI Group (UK) Ltd, Croydon, CR0 4YY

17/10/2024

01775701-0002